The Names of the Python

Africa and the Diaspora: History, Politics, Culture

EDITED BY NEIL KODESH AND JAMES H. SWEET

THE NAMES OF THE PYTHON

Belonging in East Africa, 900 to 1930

David L. Schoenbrun

THE UNIVERSITY OF WISCONSIN PRESS

Why this sudden bewilderment, this confusion?
(How serious people's faces have become.)
Why are the streets and squares emptying so rapidly,
everyone going home lost in thought?

Because night has fallen and the barbarians haven't come.
And some of our men just in from the border say
there are no barbarians any longer.

Now what's going to happen to us without barbarians?
They were, those people, a kind of solution.
—C. P. Cavafy, *Waiting for the Barbarians* (1904)

Contents

Illustrations

MAPS

Acknowledgments

In a small way, this book grew out of an earlier manuscript, now abandoned, on forms of violence and their aftermaths in the western Great Lakes region. The research for that work was supported by an endowed fellowship from the National Endowment for the Humanities that allowed me to spend a year (2009–2010) at the wonderful National Humanities Center in North Carolina. I am most grateful to all who made that year as rich and challenging as it was.

When I was describing this book to people, telling them it was about ethnicity, Lynn Thomas told me it was not. Steve Feierman agreed, independently. They were correct. Carolyn Chen provided simple, freeing advice about lopping, weeding, and watering text. Dylan Penningroth cheered me on, when the going got tough. The death of my best friend, Tim Powell, drove me to finish a first draft. Karrie Stewart always welcomed me back from my writing desk.

Several paragraphs in the introduction and chapter 1 expand on issues discussed in "Early African Pasts: Sources, Interpretations, Meanings," in *The Oxford Encyclopedia of African Historiography: Methods and Sources*, Thomas Spear, editor-in-chief (Oxford: Oxford University Press, 2019), 7–44. Patty Crown, Kate de Luna, Olivier Gosselain, Jennifer Johnson, Scott Ortman, Andrew Roddick, and Ann Stahl helped me sort out chapter 1, a revised and expanded version of "Pythons Worked: Constellating Communities of Practice with Conceptual Metaphor in Northern Lake Victoria, ca. A.D. 800 to 1200," in *Knowledge in Motion: Constellations of Learning across Time and Place*, edited by Andrew P. Roddick and Ann B. Stahl (Tucson: University of Arizona Press, 2016), 216–46. Several paragraphs in chapter 3 closely follow David L. Schoenbrun, "Ethnic Formation with Other-Than-Human Beings: Island Shrine Practice in Uganda's Long Eighteenth Century," *History in Africa*

45 (2018), 397–443, especially 419–25. Chapter 4 benefited from conversations with Jehangir Malegam, during a visiting semester at Duke University (spring 2015). An important new book by Henri Médard on Buganda, the Inland Sea, and struggles over landed property came to my attention too late for its insights to be incorporated into this book. Steve Feierman, Jan Shetler, Derek Peterson, Neil Kodesh, and Rhiannon Stephens read the entire manuscript in a late form. They pointed out many ways to improve accessibility. I wish I had followed all of them. Steve Feierman has helped me in more ways than I can list. Holly Hanson's work on Buganda has inspired me for two decades. Laura Poole did the copyediting. Dennis Lloyd, the University of Wisconsin Press director, understands the mission of academic publishing. Kelsey Rydland, data services librarian, Northwestern University Libraries, drafted the maps. My thanks to each of you.

Father Dominique Arnauld welcomed me into the back rooms of the Archivio Padri Bianchi in Rome. Accommodating staffs at the Cadbury Research Library, University of Birmingham, the Weston Library, University of Oxford, the Royal Geographical Society, and the Wellcome Trust, in London, made the enjoyable tasks of archival "work" even more so. David Easterbrook, the George and Mary LeCron Foster Curator (emeritus); Esmeralda Kale, the George and Mary LeCron Foster Curator (current); Gene Kannenberg, Crystal Martin, and Florence Mugambi, all of the Melville J. Herskovits Library of African Studies, Northwestern University, provided incomparable assistance. In Rome, Dana Johnson and Mark Nelson let us stay in their amazing home near Campo Fiori. In Birmingham, Karin Barber and Paulo Farias provided exemplary hospitality, gentle education, humor, and food. In London, Michael Solinger and Juan Carlos Vasquez always took me in and shared their exciting lives. Thank you.

My broader community of constructively critical minds includes Florence Bernault, Kate de Luna, Jonathon Earle, Steve Feierman, Jon Glassman, Olivier Gosselain, Holly Hanson, Peter Hoesing, Nancy Hunt, Raevin Jimenez, Jennifer Johnson, Jim Kern, Neil Kodesh, Julie Livingston, John Lonsdale, Derek Peterson, Jan Shetler, Ann Stahl, Rhiannon Stephens, Jim Sweet, Lynn Thomas, Helen Tilley, and the wonderful cohort of African history graduate students I have the pleasure of learning from at Northwestern. They are all largely responsible for any value I have made in the book.

My broader community of laughter, love, and seriousness includes Tom Bugbee, Carolyn Hallett Bugbee, Carolyn Chen, Dylan Penningroth, Betsy Cody, Liza Doran, Eliot Ostler, Joe Pachak, Jared Farmer, Magda Maczynska, Steve Feierman, Mark Geistfeld, Janette Sadik-Khan, Dana Johnson, Julie Livingston, Bill Moseley, Annie Mohler, Sandy Strehlou, Eve Troutt Powell,

Jibreel Powell, Jon Glassman, James Kern, Sean Hanretta, Richard Schoenbrun, Zoila Schoenbrun, Tracy Sinnett, Steven Sinnett, and Mari Schoenbrun, Elissa Braunstein, R. B. Stewart, and Gaela Stewart. And Tula.

Despite everyone's best efforts to get me to weed more, I am sure I could have done better. I take solace in the thought that one person's weed is another person's flower. In this case, I trust Ugandan readers will decide which is which.

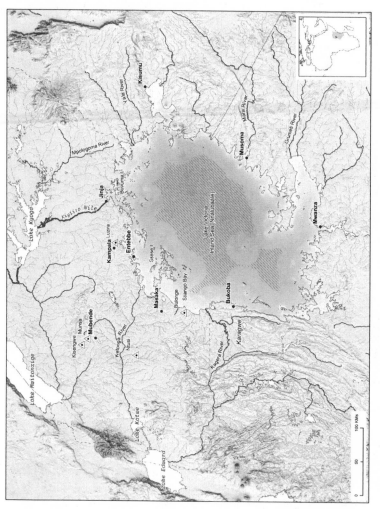

Map 1. The Inland Sea and surroundings. The clear ring around the inner rim represents the twenty-five-mile sight lines enjoyed by inshore-bound sewn canoes. Map drawn by Kelsey Rydland, Data Services Librarian, Northwestern University Libraries.

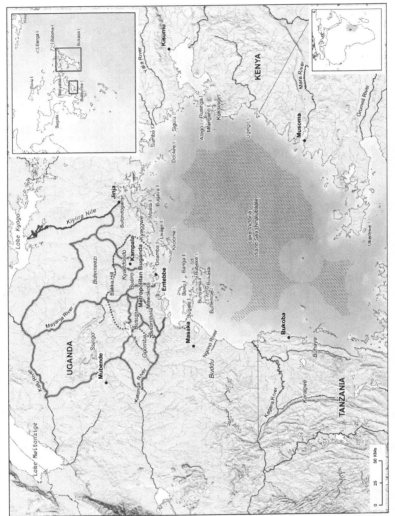

Map 2. The northern Inland Sea and islands. Map drawn by Kelsey Rydland, Data Services Librarian, Northwestern University Libraries.

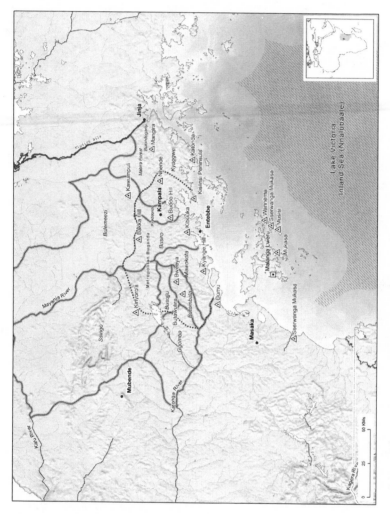

Map 3. The northwestern Inland Sea and shrines mentioned. Many more such shrines existed. Map drawn by Kelsey Rydland, Data Services Librarian, Northwestern University Libraries.

THE NAMES OF THE PYTHON

Introduction

Èmbwâ èngizzì èzaàlà ènkolya. "A good hunting dog bears one with no nose
for scent."
—Ronald Snoxall, *Luganda-English Dictionary*, 244

Kiri mu butondè bwàngè òkusekaseka. "It's in my nature to giggle."
—Ronald Snoxall, *Luganda-English Dictionary*, 34

Ggwanga, "nation, race"; *munnaggwanga,* "stranger [slur]."
Ggwanga, "vendetta, vengeance, reprisal."
—Henri Le Veux, *Premier essai de vocabulaire luganda-français,* 202

Èggwangà, "nation, tribe."
Èggwanga, "vindictiveness, rancor."
—Ronald Snoxall, *Luganda-English Dictionary*, 92

THIS BOOK EXPLORES diverse forms of groupwork over the past thousand years in one part of East Africa (map 1). It focuses on the intellectual and material dimensions of belonging. Members of any group
rely on imagination to constitute themselves as communities. The terms of
moral belonging were one thing they imagine together. Maintaining a community requires debate, reflection, and the interested labor of promoters. The
choices people made in these domains of groupwork were shaped by larger
economic circumstances and shaped the futures they tried to make together.

To frame groupwork in such broad terms relaxes ethnicity's grip on thinking about groups. Historical circumstances may prompt people to emphasize
boundaries, the cultural othering of people on the other side of those boundaries, and to construct a shared history for the group inside the boundaries.

But these sources of ethnicity neither exhaust the work of making groups nor emerge once and persist thereafter. While the book explores examples of ethnicity in earlier periods, not just in the colonial period, it mixes ethnic work with other forms of groupwork. Groupwork may be fleeting, or people may choose to make it durable. But ethnicity is not a necessary part of making social changes to belonging or navigating the risks and dangers of belonging over the long run. That is why I foreground something called "groupwork," addressing the contingent qualities of belonging and the contingent importance of exclusion to histories of making groups.

My work here discovers a series of different scales of groupwork and probes historical connections between them over the past millennium. The sequence reflects African ambitions to learn, experiment, and live morally with others. At each stage in the unfolding, people chose the futures of belonging they desired and tried to make them happen. They did not always agree. Even when they thought they agreed, the new form of groupwork they created did not always match the one they had sought.

This is a compact survey. A millennium ago, Africans converted older kinds of clans into expansive communities beyond the face-to-face. Without the tool of writing or the medium of statecraft, the promoters of this practice invited people from different places to believe they shared a future and a past with others whom they might never meet. From the thirteenth to the sixteenth centuries, the unique collections of people with different skills, knowledge, and ambition that had made clanship expansive convened multilingual, extroverted communities of people from a variety of clans, working from shrines. The wealth and knowledge attracted to those communities influenced the formation of centralized states like Buganda. Statecraft changed who belonged to the shrine communities and what they did to make shrines attractive in the sixteenth and seventeenth centuries. Leaders of groups interested in the shrines divided their knowledge in ways that gave life to a broad distinction between people of the islands and people of the mainland. At the beginning of the long eighteenth century, leaders in Buganda chose to expand their territorial reach beyond a core area. Those involved in that process adapted elements of shrine work to the legal ends of removing people from the life of the state by executing them. In the long nineteenth century, enslavement and slaveries became features of statecraft. Women of all statuses—royal, commoner, enslaved—used virtues of gendered standing and comportment to their benefit, crafting new varieties of belonging, including ethnic ones. In Uganda's Protectorate years, historically minded Catholic men debated those earlier histories of statecraft and gendered standing in idioms of noble hiding in, being hosted by, and reappearing from clans in the region. Their exchanges highlighted earlier forms of groupwork in a decades-long struggle over land. They argued that groupwork beyond descent offered a way out of their situation, but only through careful reckoning with painful pasts.

The book is titled *The Names of the Python* because words for the great snake may be associated with each sort of groupwork in the region's history. The book probes (rather than assumes) the durability of these indigenous categories of groupwork. Kinds of groupwork, like ethnicity or clanship, thus fold into histories of other sorts of groups. A quote from an article published in 1921, in *Munno* ("Your Friend"), the Luganda-language newspaper the Catholic Church had begun to publish in 1911, reflects the diversity of belonging described by scholarly terms like "ethnicity" or "groupwork."

Kifamunyanja's Rancor

I have been gone for a long time! What makes me deny myself? It is that boundary on the land which gnaws at me. Very well, in which direction are you going? Which of the canoes are sent away? What canoes? Should we not stop feeling that the Government believes Basese are reentering estate land in the Ssese Islands? I understand they read their books, like "Your Friend," but they just traffic in pointless banter. Yi, Government, Bravo! Whose notorious estate lands sustain that belief? I learned about that problem in the cotton field I prettied up, which made me proud, but then turned to famine when I had to leave in a hurry; I learned all about that food shortage! Are all the islands cut loose? Never, they're only loosed a little, just like all the others, so that a person can get something there by seizure. You know: A liar finds a believer.[1]

The author of this quote wrote in a time of reckoning with a new order. It was a particularly difficult time for those who, like the author, had ties to the islands and littoral of Lake Victoria, ravaged by a sleeping sickness epidemic only twenty years earlier. It was such a painful, dangerous time that the author used an alias, Kifamunyanja, "The Lake's Death." Because he wrote for a newspaper, we can safely assume that the author's gender was male. His bitter assessment of the day drew on three core elements in ethnic thought. He appealed to a shared past, he made statements about boundaries, and he asserted elements of cultural difference, elaborating the idea that "who we are rests on who we are not."[2]

The text also evokes other kinds of groups. One weaves lateral alliances with vertical genealogical depth. Descent ties go up and down lines of time and generation—contained in words like "estate lands" and "Basese." Some ties go out with canoes, drawing in other persons and their groups. Kifamunyanja assumes that belonging is association. Islands connect to anywhere via canoes. Connecting creates belonging with a mix of relatives and attached outsiders. Any "we" contained persons with different "origins," allowing debate about authentic and inauthentic belonging. A last dimension of belonging lies in the flow of Kifamunyanja's argument, not in the semantic content of his words. He understood that quantities in belonging emerged from holistic qualities.[3] First there is land, then there is estate land, then lines bound the land. Though not spelled out in his text, in his world a child "hatched out" of a group, rather than joining a group. The individual was not fully formed at conception or birth but was grown—"raised" as English speakers might have it. Vertical time, lateral association, and what might be called the moral duties of mitotic belonging are all much older than the world of the 1920s. Kifamunyanja understands ways to belong in addition to ethnic ways.

In the 1920s, Uganda's Protectorate government worked with the government of Buganda to allow people to return to Ssese Islands after a decade of forced removals under a policy called Sleeping Sickness Control. Famine soon followed these sudden breaks in tenure.[4] Forced removal affected many recent arrivals, who came close to Lake Victoria with chiefs who had been given title to land through the 1900 Buganda Agreement. Protectorate taxes and cotton production ensued. The creation of land markets allowed others with means to attract ambitious but poor tenants to grow those cash crops. The political geography of titled allotments sat atop more than twenty years of profound dislocation from civil war, which had followed three generations of dislocations related to enslavement. Kifamunyanja thus laments a familiar menu of imperial dispossession. He is ambivalent about print culture, as part of Protectorate boundary work, fearing its divorce from a broader public, a divorce fraught with unequal power. Kifamunyanja yearned for a time before, when he imagined none of that happened. People had lived on estate lands over the course of multiple generations. They enjoyed a vast range of lateral connections, moving among the abundant fields of political influence leveraged through land and work.

These kinds of groups long predate the world of the 1920s. This book lays out the work of imagination, assembly, and division that Africans undertook to make, sustain, and change groups over the very long run, across major transitions in the scale of social life. *The Names of the Python* thus relaxes Kifamunyanja's compressed history of woe and revises his nostalgia. Africa's past was not hyperethnic, but ethnicity is older than the nineteenth century. A great diversity of groupwork hides in plain sight in Africa today, unfriendly to (or simply uninterested in) the label of "ethnicity." The book resists ethnicity's power to dominate our attention by exploring other kinds of imagination, forms of assembly, and methods of division to understand African groupwork.

Framing Groupwork

A little more on ethnicity to put it in its place. Scholars accept that boundaries, othering, and agreeing on a shared past define ethnicity.[5] Drawing boundaries and building who you are on who you are not comes into focus by arguing over the shape of the past, provoking a round of ethnic groupwork.[6] Particular historical contexts raised questions about who might and might not belong and on what terms. These complexities of ethnicity worry intellectuals. Max Weber warned that "the concept of the "ethnic" group . . . dissolves if we define our terms exactly," making it "unsuitable for a really rigorous analysis." Ethnicity often blends into the conceptual territory of race and nation.[7] Ganda-speakers shared with Weber a modern concern about these ways of belonging. Ganda words for "vengeance" or "rancor," given in the last epigraph above, become words for "nation," "race," or "tribe," merely by changing the tone of one's voice.

Historian John Lonsdale put struggles over gender and status—or civic virtue—at the core of a moral kind of belonging.[8] In debating those constituents of civic virtue, people also debated the grounds for feeling included or excluded from belonging. People who behaved properly, by living up to the duties of their status, belonged. Those who did not do so did not belong. Such debates need not attend to boundaries between one group and another; they need not be arguments sustaining a sense that we are who we are not.[9] When the ability to debate the terms of civic virtue comes under threat, those terms lend themselves to the work of othering and drawing boundaries.[10]

As Rogers Brubaker has made clear, cognition is a core medium for all these processes.[11] People constituted themselves into all kinds of groups in part through imagination, including imagining that they shared a past. A common way to conceptualize and express that sharing lies in ideas about descent, which are susceptible to a metaphorical language that invites us to think of continuity and change crossing generations. Descent metaphors thus share deep affinities with the linear time common in historical thinking. Yet the proverbs at the beginning of this introduction express the easy cognitive dissonance we share about what descent passes along. On one hand, a fine hunting dog gives birth to one who cannot track animals. On the other hand, a person given to laughter chalks that up to her inborn personality. Clearly, Ugandans think deftly about the claims of descent to inform the terms and conditions of belonging. That is one reason *The Names of the Python* does not begin with current ethnic groups and does not chart their creation in the past. I ask broader questions about groupwork—its moral cores, the people who promote them, and the turn to politics they accommodated. It thus sets ethnic forms within larger fields of belonging, keeping ethnicity's distinctive, contingent features in sight. It punches through the colonial sound barrier identified by many scholars of ethnicity. Colonial rule needed ethnicity, but that did not mean all ethnicity in Africa emerged from colonial processes. It is the historian's task to work out when and where that was and was not so and why.

Descent implies ancestors. People made groups of the living in part by orienting them to the departed. The present book highlights the historical circumstances in which groupworkers drew boundaries between layers of ancestors, giving them a shape on the landscape that was historical. Whether they emphasized edges or centers, relations between the living and the dead always involved struggles over the past. Those struggles excluded relations to some ancestors and celebrated others. We may perceive the shapes of time and space the struggles produced and the lengths of time people made them persist. These common forms of making groups do not unfold in the same way everywhere. Today's hegemonies of ethnicity can obscure the past and present variety of groupwork. Special terms help keep that variety alive for readers.

The first term is "groupwork" itself. Groupwork claims that people make themselves into communities in part through imagination, often prompted by forms of assembly, including assembling with the departed, through possession by their spirits or making offerings to them. Throughout this book, those practices intersect, setting the terms by which people made groups persist, abandoned them, and pushed out some members, departed or present. Groupwork explores imagining communities and actualizing them at different times in the past.

In lending groupwork historical specificity and filling out the sources of friction it housed, *The Names of the Python* establishes fresh points of departure for scholars to revise categories of ethnicity, race, and nation in colonial or former colonial places. They can rethink them with histories of cognate categories deeper than those generated with European (or other) imperialisms and colonialisms. The book begins this task by exploring how various statecrafts, in different periods, invested in ethnic work. I leave it to others to explore the points of departure groupwork provides for studies of race and nation. Instead, I reveal groupwork had different life spans and different spatial qualities. My work here shows that older forms of belonging not dedicated to binding cultural othering and boundary work to a single, shared past shaped current Ugandan political cultures.

"Moral belonging" realizes the goal of "moral community." Applying a set of values to one's conduct and using these values to assess the conduct of others to improve on a present set of conditions, makes a community moral.[12] These values framed debates over the terms on which people would be included or excluded in the course of groupwork and to what ends. In the course of the debates, people could revise values in the set or put subtle differences of emphasis on them. They could break away from the community of actors and judges to pursue different combinations of values.

Moral belonging and moral community build on and clarify John Lonsdale's notion of moral ethnicity. His phrase refers to the terrain of debate on which men and women worked out the terms of internal belonging. He used it to show that such debate could exclude those who did not meet the standards under consideration but that debating those standards did not require creating and maintaining fixed boundaries or cultural othering. Lonsdale's appending of "ethnicity" to "moral" is therefore confusing.[13] Debates over community and belonging are moral when they turn to matters like gendered comportment or the responsibilities of prominent adults to help the young in pursuing a socially viable standing of their own. A moral community agrees on what constitutes the necessary inputs to adulthoods and their duties, what sorts of actions youths must undertake to renew or revise and thus carry on a given community. Members may argue over duties, who has the duties, and how they may discharge those duties.

Tensions could arise in the course of arguing over the constituents of a moral community. They could make exclusion, even violence, a domain of moral action. New historical realities could require radical revision to old behaviors, threatening those who cleaved to the past. The urgencies of a crisis like a famine or the invasion of better-armed outsiders could underwrite a radical dislocation of old adulthoods and some of their behaviors by younger ones.[14] Central Kenyans understood that the elder men and women at the head of land-holding groups had to be pushed out by a younger generation of adults. The slow accumulation of moral belonging under one generation could restrict them in responding to radical novelty. Younger adults argued that only they could find new kinds of hard work that benefited all.[15] A labor theory of value animated the land-holding group of elders. The theory explained the hard work of making home and society in central Kenya, where dense forests required collective labor on a scale that exceeded what one land-holding group could provide to convert forests into fields and pasture. That lent a moral core of hard work and discipline to modes of change. It granted to each generation particular conditions for exclusion. Elders used notions of laziness to exclude those they thought of in that register from access to land. Young adults, keen for change, used notions of breaking from the past to exclude elders from leading roles in the future's new dispensations.

Crises were not the only prompt lending exclusion the air of virtue, making it a mode of moral action. People could decline the terms of moral community, or they could fail to convince others of alternatives. They could be removed or remove themselves from belonging. In the region this book covers, someone could be ostracized from their clan. In Luganda, the verb was òkùbòòla. The prompts and techniques for "ignoring," "sidelining," or "expelling" a member of the group varied. But they shared what might be called notions of civic vice as the moral underpinnings justifying ostracism. Public judgment of a person's failures to behave consistently with prevailing moral principles rendered them vulnerable to accusations of such failures. Those accusations could lead to òkùbòòla ostracism. Accusing someone of witchcraft, of poisoning a moral community by acting selfishly and refusing to change, could send them away to a ruler's enclosure. One argued about civic virtue in a language of civic vice. *The Names of the Python* attends to such exclusions from social wholes as part of groupwork.

"Clanship," another special term, is a particular form of groupwork. It occupies a zone between the intuitive concreteness of the social action that makes kinship a domain of face-to-face interaction and the imaginary work people must undertake to form communities beyond the face-to-face. In his path-breaking book on this topic, Neil Kodesh showed clanship to be a process. It was not a static unit slotted into a middle place, between kinship and state, on a continuum of political scale. He listened to accounts of the past told at the homes of clan members. His hosts provided formal genealogies and informal discussions of the "sacred sites" where a clan's founder figures were buried. Sacred sites included landmarks, home to important spirits, "some of which included a shrine at which people engaged the area's spirit."[16] Assembling in this way embodied clanship. The rest of the time, a dispersed group of extended families, claiming descent from a single man, constituted the social universe through which clan members worked. Luganda-speakers called it the èssigà, literally, one of the three hearthstones used to support pots for cooking food and boiling water. Clan members taught Kodesh to think of their clanships as particular blends of material aspiration, the skill and knowledge to realize that aspiration, and they gave him histories of having done so. Members understood their kind of clanship to exist in the assembly of people—members of hearthstone groups and their constituent lineages. Each had different skills, with ties to distant places, whose association was oriented to the past accomplishments of common founding figures through mediumship and making offerings.

These views disrupt the uniformity promised by the English translation of "clan." Whatever clans shared when they gathered, each was a specific composition of skill and knowledge of the past put together by their members and altered by later generations and newcomers. Composition embodied the variety of groupwork herded under the term "clanship." The first three chapters of this book reveal that clan members did different kinds of groupwork. But they all shared a commitment to connection, which could nourish the formation of new clanships. Members looked outward, to opportunity, to provide the best chances for leaders and followers to thrive and realize the full benefits and duties of adulthood. Such extroversion did not mean unfettered inclusion.

"Public healing" may be understood in part as a particular forum for moral debate, extroversion, and for dealing with outcomes of inclusion or exclusion. Two dimensions of public healing have entered the literature. In one, a representative of a departed figure convened others and opened a line of social critique aimed at a contemporary issue, often the failure of people (especially rulers) to act morally. Steven Feierman focused on this idea of evanescent social criticism in elaborating his concept of public healing.[17] The other dimension of public healing also involved such representation and convening of a constituency, but formed and maintained a group, in part through social composition that ensured continuity of access to health and wealth. This dimension of public healing informed Kodesh's approach to clanship. Both relied on spirit possession. Both healed and harmed individual bodies, collectivities of people, and larger assemblages of other-than-human beings. Both could engage in social criticism. But the first was evanescent, not tied to particular places, and might focus on radically marginalized people as agents of social criticism. The second tended to temporal patterning in a particular geography. Unlike the first, it is given to historical narratives conceived of in genealogical terms. Exclusion and inclusion emerge through comparing versions. Versions formed as different moral communities debated their relationships to the past.

These distinctions are based on the work of scholars. In the region's languages, no unique lexicon separates evanescent from emplaced public healing. A healer called by the same word may behave evanescently or participate in rhythmed, emplaced public healing. Each kind of public healing only becomes clear to us in oral and written accounts of the activity. The emplaced form appears most consistently in *The Names of the Python*, in large part because it turns up in the richest ways in those accounts. Particular clanships may gain (and lose) proprietary control over parts of the socially composed whole. Control gave leverage over choosing which representatives of new clans might join a public healing group at a shrine composed of multiple clans (see chapters 2 and 3). Members used these networks of fame, obligation, and opportunity to engage the expansionist statecraft shaping the region's history from the sixteenth century.

"Sovereign knots" describes a literal arrangement of the newly centralizing power of expansionist statecraft. People required men and women with independent domains of authority to knot themselves together through marriage, descent, and ritual complementarity. The sovereign knot was also a theory, an ideology, about how statecraft worked best. By combining instrumental and creative forms of power, in various kinds of assembly, sovereigns in the knot could establish insurgent authority over fertility in a new territory, engaging residents in reciprocal obligation. It is customary to refer to such arrangements at "kingdoms." But this misrepresents the different threads of authority and knowledge people tied together into knots of power in a royal capital. The ideology of knotted interdependence made it susceptible to the kinds of social criticism forwarded in evanescent public healing and other forms of public life.[18]

Sovereign knots mean each domain of authority is independent from others but all are needed for the polity to live up to the ideals its supporters understand. Accountability through public debate embodied the ideals that rulers ruled because followers gave them what they needed to do so. People gave rulers the material wealth, the labor, and ideas that were indispensable for ruling. Rulers used all of that to balance competition among leaders for followers by expanding the possibilities for health and wealth through connection with distant places, through the projection of territorial control over some of them, and through other activities of statecraft. Those elements constituted Hanson's notion of reciprocal obligation.[19]

As Hanson and others have explained, the polity of Buganda worked in this manner, at least until the eighteenth century, largely because potential followers enjoyed a monopoly on the choice to allocate their support to whomsoever they deemed responsive to it. When territorial expansion included forms of violence and transgression that produced enslaved people, the just-sketched transactions of obligation changed. Rulers no longer needed to respond to followers' insistence on holding them accountable. Rulers with ties to enslaved people could use their labor and support to create conditions of wealth and health, putting them in the position of choosing their followers. Despite these dramatic changes in the terms and conditions of political belonging in the region, sovereign power continued to form through knots until the separate domains of land, knowledge, and history that had made up the threads in the knots had been defeated and dispersed in wars fought over the course of the nineteenth century. That defeat did not extinguish people's investments in the virtues of reciprocal obligation. In 1912, the vernacular newspaper put out by the Church Missionary Society published its first list of Buganda's rulers. Kings, their queen mothers, and the avoidance they shared through her lineage appeared in separate columns.[20] The visual form of this list took for granted the separate sources of power and standing knotted in the rule of a king, a queen mother, and others who shared a particular avoidance. Even after nineteenth-century defeats, people held onto the ideal that sovereignty worked best as a set of threads knotted together rather than as a single nub of power.

These forms of groupwork happened because interested people guided debates over their character and purpose. Clan leaders and public healers were such figures, and so were authors of dynastic or clan histories. Enslaved women who knew the ritual practices, bodily comportment, and tones of speech of their new homes worked toward belonging by promoting moral community and demoting those who could not behave in the same manner. Terms like "guide" or "promoter" lend intention to all groupwork, including ethnic forms. They remind us not to take for granted the concreteness of belonging.

Scholarly terms must not be mistaken for the historical realities of people in the past who struggled for and defended modes of belonging dear to them, their ancestors, and future generations. One could not point to a woman walking along one of Buganda's many highways early in the nineteenth century and say "there goes a public healer." One could not call a Ganda capital a sovereign knot and be understood by an eighteenth-century speaker of the Ganda language. Those phrases describe scholarly concepts. One avoids making concepts the actors in the story by focusing on actors in relation to the concepts.[21]

The Names of the Python asks broad questions about groupwork, including ethnic work. What were its moral cores? In what ways did material circumstances shape those cores? What ideas and settings did promoters of groupwork combine? In what ways, for what reasons, and how persistently did the groups in question turn to boundary work and othering? With these questions, the book sneaks up on contemporary, colonial, and earlier ethnicities. It sets them within the larger field of belonging, keeping in view ethnicity's distinctive, historically contingent features. People made groups with multiple, shifting wells of interested opportunity. Geography was an inexhaustible source.

An Inland Sea

Lake Victoria is an inland sea of some 69,000 square kilometers, about the size of Scotland.[22] Nearly 85 percent of its water comes from the sky, as rain generated by its own transpiration. The rest enters by the many short rivers—and a few longer ones—that ring the shallow basin like the cilia on a paramecium (see map 1). This relation between rain, topography, and the volume of water in the basin means the Inland Sea's level could rise and fall rapidly. Changes of three meters and more have been documented in the twentieth century and in the distant past.[23] The intimacies of its changing edges balanced the vastness.

Dwellers on the littoral developed efficient transportation of goods, people, and ideas.[24] Fish were an abundant supply of protein, whether eaten fresh or processed for storage and transport. A crenellated shore and numerous islands, often bunched in archipelagos, created diverse land–water interfaces, amplifying efficiencies of waterborne transport. The northern mainland littoral has more than 1,900 of the 3,400 kilometers of shoreline compressed in some 240 kilometers of longitude (map 1).[25] Add the littorals of the more than 125 islands in this northern tier, and it is easy to appreciate the variety of local environments. Such a long, wavering line created many opportunities for contact. To live with canoes on the littoral was to study the environment with far greater range than landlubbers.

Large chunks of territory and wealth constituted the Inland Sea. Tracts of deep forest or watercourses (often choked with papyrus) separated mainland settlements. Paths through the forest, fords, and wooden bridges crossing papyrus swamps were weak links in that network because they were narrow. Their narrowness made their controllers strong, reinforcing the granularity of settlement. The spatial reach of sewn canoes, on the other hand, created shape-shifting chunks of intercommunicating areas. The Ssese archipelago, in the northwest corner of the Inland Sea, are "hills in the expanse of water," Kifamunyanja wrote, "adorning like cowries and seed beads."[26] They were oriented to all directions of desirable trade, artisanal skill, and so on. Others in the northern tier—those of Ddamba, Kkoome, and Buvuma—had lengthy littorals. Each group lay opposite many mainland centers. Only Ssese gave access to both the northern and western littoral and only Buvuma gave access to the littorals on either side of the Kiyiira Nile (map 1).

Canoers favored inshore travel (figure 1) where they could navigate by sight and flee to safety ahead of a storm.[27] Canoes found lighter headwinds and lower waves inshore, increasing range by reducing the energy costs to paddlers. The Inland Sea was not a two-dimensional space. Islands commonly stood two hundred feet high, visible from great distances on clear days or in parts of the day prone to be free of rain, depending on the season.[28] The eastern islands of the Ssese group reach such heights, with stony, steep cliffs on their open-water sides. On a clear day, they were visible from some twenty-five miles away. The need for a canoe helmsman to stay in visual touch with land made vessels visible from dry land as well.[29] The refractive effects of water vapor and the Earth's curvature set visibility limits. Ssese's and Buvuma's many islands lie within this range of visibility, attracting canoes traveling to points east and

Figure 1. Ssese canoe on Lake Victoria Nyanza. Time and space collapsed in the thirteenth century for people living near the Inland Sea. Source: "Photograph Album 1894–1900," H. B. Lewin?; CMS/ACC 276 F2. Credit: Church Missionary Society Archives, Cadbury Research Library, University of Birmingham.

south to pass through them. Accounts of canoe travel in the later nineteenth century suggest that a determined crew with a skilled captain could cover thirty miles a day in reasonably good weather.[30] Those limits intersected with visual navigation limits to recommend particular places to stop or start journeys of different lengths. With canoes, people made Ssese and Buvuma nodes with more links to other nodes than in the other island groups.

Traders from the Indian Ocean coast called the Inland Sea Ukerewe, after the large island in its southeastern quadrant that they knew as the gateway to the wealth in ivory and slaves in lands beyond its littoral.[31] Luo-speakers, who live today mostly in its northeastern quadrant around the Winam Gulf, call it *nam*, or big water, like an ocean. In the 1860s, readers of European travel writing came to know this Inland Sea as the source of the Nile, either calling it "Lake Victoria," a name given by John Hanning Speke, or "Victoria Nyanza." Many littoral residents would call it *nyanja*, a term that may be translated as "lake," "sea," or even "large river," like the Nile. The significance of a stretch of water so named has spread widely. English word-processing software automatically capitalizes the term, giving us "Nyanja." In Luganda, a language spoken mainly in the northwestern quadrant (as well as in Los Angeles and London) today, the noun was derived from a verb, *kwànja*, or "to spread out, unfold." A nyanja is a significant expanse of water, and Lake Victoria is Africa's most expansive body of water.

Luganda-speakers could call the Inland Sea *nnàlubààle*, a name often translated as "mother of the gods," to honor the fact that important spiritual authorities in the larger region trace their roots to Ssese and Buvuma. A literal translation gives the opaque "mother of the broad rock." Travelers on these waters soon grasp the importance of prominent rocky island outcrops or cliffs for orienting themselves. Nnàlubààle, then, is the vast expanse of water out of which rose prominent rocky places, homes to spiritual figures.

The Inland Sea could be protean. Luganda-speakers have a name, *lùkwâta*, for a dangerous creature that attacked canoes. A manifestation of the Inland Sea's powers, the lùkwâta was a serpent whose head might be plumed or ringed with reeds.[32] When people launched a new canoe and fished in it for the first time without giving and acting appropriately, they might provoke Mukasa, a prominent spiritual authority. Mukasa's anger could manifest in a lùkwâta "monster," representing the uncertainty, abundance, and propriety of living with the Inland Sea.[33] Crossing its surface, people saw ports of embarkation shrink behind them and approaching destinations grow in size, revealing lùkwâta's movements. Living and moving on the Inland Sea had an unusual quality, like the feeling Europeans described when crossing the North American prairie. Paddlers called it "walking with the hands."[34] Topography offered the reassurance to know where one was at any given moment.

Fishers and sewn canoe paddlers learned the currents, the fish cultures, the weather patterns, and how to travel the winding contours of the littoral. With water as a border, people shed or added connections with ease. Littoral societies had many more "neighbors" than those who lived inland. They were stretched long and thin when the littoral was straight. Canoes zigged and zagged when the littoral snaked, snagging islands that bunched within the twenty-five-mile zone of navigation by sight on clear and calm days. That twisting circumstance described the northern tier, from Ssese to the Kaksingiri littoral (map 1). It was easy to conceptualize unbounded social wholes because so many points of contact were possible from there. African histories of inland seas are histories of feeling along edges and crossings to points of land and islands. It nourished "mixed" societies, those that embraced ancestral connections with others whose geographic distance from the isles canoe travel collapsed.[35]

The Inland Sea and a Region's History

Historians tend to study such an encompassing place as an appendage of some other theme. Common ones include the rise of trade and transport systems, or of centralized polities, the dynamics and objectives of imperial conquest, and the aims of a Protectorate to control disease, fish work, or travel. M. Semakula M. Kiwanuka, a dean of the academic study of Buganda at Makerere University, understood the importance of the Inland Sea. In a single paragraph, he underscored themes explored here: the ease of waterborne communication and mobility and the Inland Sea's abundant food.[36] Historical anthropologist Conrad P. Kottak kept the Inland Sea in his argument that banana cultivation drove the rise of a Ganda state.[37] Christopher Wrigley, Kiwanuka's contemporary, devoted a few paragraphs to the northern coast as the setting for clan alliances with eighteenth-century Ganda kings (chapter 4).[38] Henri Médard said a lot about the littoral and the islands. He located many shrines in Ssese and noted their ties with the mainland. In the nineteenth century, the scope of Ganda naval ambition influenced life on the Inland Sea. It drove the flow of commodities toward Ganda centers, created refugees from naval action, and generally directed what Andrew Roberts called a Ganda "sub-imperialism."[39]

Kodesh looked into a deeper past, attending to historical actors based on the littoral—and in the Ssese group—as exemplars of making clanship about networks of knowledge, lending public healing a political practice. He opened up many questions also explored here, enhanced by histories of fish work, making bark cloth, islands of intensive agricultures, and efficiencies of transport that outline the changing faces of public healing and groupwork.

Richard Reid's history of Buganda attended to the Inland Sea, analyzing the interplay of military, economic, and political interests in a Buganda state. He found that late in the nineteenth century, the fishers here shared habits not shared by mainlanders or by fishers who worked the rivers.[40] He noted that the state traded for salt from more than 150 miles to the east (map 1).[41] Salt trading networks had been involved in earlier, sixteenth-century experiments with expansive clanship, explored by Kodesh.[42] Reid also linked a Ganda king, Mawanda, to the use of canoes in the 1720s and 1730s to take control of lands east of Buganda. Guild historians have located in this reign the emergence of a bureaucratic layer of chiefs with ties of reciprocal obligation to a royal center.[43] Reid noticed that the eastern territory subdued in part with Mawanda's fleet, was a rich source of timber for building canoes. Involvement there provided Ganda capitals a source of lumber for building fleets independent of island sources.

Reid's focus on naval power—especially the use of canoes in raids—revealed that before the 1840s generals used sewn canoes to transport fighters, auxiliaries, and supplies or perhaps in blockades. Littoral and islander familiarity with life on the water gave them an advantage. Coupled with the first arrival at court of traders from the Indian Ocean coast, that advantage fired the sitting Ganda king, Ssuuna II, to develop naval power to direct that trade to his centers.[44] By the 1850s, naval power on the Inland Sea was indispensable to Buganda's control of commerce oriented toward the Indian Ocean world. The large canoes transported slaves and ivory east and south across the waters. Reid's interest in Ganda naval power entailed a unique degree of historical attention to the Inland Sea as a setting, providing an early nineteenth-century baseline from which to look into the deeper past.

Archeologists Ceri Ashley, Scheherazade Amin, and close collaborator Andrew Reid added that depth to an Inland Sea history. Ashley delimited a materially distinctive cultural world between 800 and 1300, with deep roots in mainland settings, oriented toward island and littoral.[45] Amin showed that "ceramic diversity in the Sesse [*sic*] Islands is much greater than observed in mainland assemblages," supporting the view of the islands as central nodes in a far-flung network.[46] Collaborating with other archeologists, notably Merrick Posnansky, Ashley and Reid rounded out the picture of a lacustrine cultural orientation. They revealed eclectic mixes of economic activity in littoral and island settings. Ever since Kiwanuka and Kottak, scholars have argued that everyone in the region relied primarily (if not exclusively) on highly productive and long-lived banana gardens for food and a flatter annual labor curve. Now we have Ddolwe Island (map 2) as a center of intensive, possibly terraced grain fields.[47] Islands in the Ssese group had very different environments, some open grassland, some densely forested, and others too rocky for any kind of farming. These archeologists reframed how people expanded social life beyond the face-to-face, putting the islands at the center of that history.

Sources

This book rests on sources familiar to historians of times and places beyond literacy. They include archeology, environmental studies, historical and comparative linguistics, ethnographic accounts, vernacular histories, vernacular newspapers published by missionary-run presses, and colonial-era documents on topics like land tenure. Each chapter relies on virtually all of these sources. As the book unfolds, the balance shifts to the latter four.

Historians know that archeologists work in a deeply empiricist register, focused on the material expressions of all kinds of human and other processes. Finding meaning and cause in a material past is as fraught for them as it is for historians. Historians know that climate science can provide detail about the shapes and timing of changes in patterns of temperature, rainfall and drought, and shifts in vegetation and other communities of life. Ethnography is always the situated practice of studying cultural difference. Anthropologists carry out ethnographic research into ways of being different from their own, in a particular time and place, affecting their interpretations. Oral accounts of the past reflect the circumstances of their performance, rendering them tricky but rich sources of information about the times before their tellers and audience lived. Historians understand that meaning is inherently multiple, the results of interested communicative practice. They know that literal or hegemonic meanings intersect with contested, partial meanings in the course of communication. So, when this book claims to know what a word used in the past meant, despite the fact that the word was not written down in the past, readers may wonder what lends credibility to that claim.[48]

Each source asks historians different things. Layers in a column of sediment drilled from a lake bed have different ratios of pollen or diatoms or biochemical properties. The causes and consequences of the ecological changes reflected in those shifting ratios are complex. Archeologists look for patterns of material culture, technological style, settlement practices, and so forth. They read in those patterns the motives of their makers and the unintended consequences of their actions. The first three chapters analyze and interpret such evidence to make historical arguments about groupwork. At many critical points, the book puts interpretive weight on claims about earlier meanings of words, practices, and traditions. In a history like this one, which debates discourses and practices of belonging by exploring them in specific historical contexts, the reader deserves to know why the present author thinks these sources can bear those burdens.

As linguists took note of Africa's languages in the nineteenth century, they applied the historical sensibilities of their time to the realities of a continent engaged with commodification, evangelism, the bankruptcies of slavery, and the dislocations and defeats of imperial conquest.[49] Establishing colonial rule created a need for knowledge of African languages that coincided with a paradigm shift in the guild study of language. The scholarly reception of Fernand de Saussure's lectures turned the emerging field of linguists away from the historical matters they had studied since the later eighteenth century. Saussure put the study of language as a system on firmer empirical ground, making language ever more susceptible to paradigmatic analysis.[50] This structuralist approach lifted language from the cacophony of speaking, hearing, and doing—in a word, communicating—that Saussure had so clearly recognized was the medium of its life.[51]

The push for a science of language left behind a theory of language change—namely, how the arbitrary relation between word and idea or thing comes to be seen as such, as "literal," through repetition and convention. Against repetition and convention new communicative practices stood out. What some people named or communicated had a particular contextual force that invited others to think and act with them.[52] Whether in a blogger's meme, a musician's phrase, or a priest's apt interpretation of a medium's utterings, admiration for well-spoken speech changed a language. Saussurean formalism could limit the study of meaning, repeatedly forcing it into paradigms aloof from the shifting social relations that meanings sustained and that in turn kept language alive in communication.

The historical classification of Great Lakes Bantu languages is one dimension of that formalism.[53] It frames the reconstructions of words and meanings. The languages spoken today in the core of the region explored here belong to a subgroup that historical linguists call North Nyanza. Studies of pronunciation, vocabulary, and grammar in the languages descended from North Nyanza has revealed more similarities than differences among them.[54] The same may be said for its neighbors to the southwest and east, Rutara and Greater Luhyia, respectively (map 4).[55] Their work gives us historically situated speech communities, labels them, and populates their linguistic repertoires with bundles of words and meanings and the grammatical processes implicated in joining word and meaning. Historians of Africa who use historical linguistics practice this method, called "words, things, and meanings."

In a book about groupwork, the reader must be warned not to assume that formalist "speech communities" automatically contained messages about boundary and difference. Groupings of languages produced by their classification do not disclose if or whether their speaking members assigned any meaning to an awareness of membership.[56] A speech community duly reconstructed as such, by the formal dictates of this method, was not an ethnolinguistic group. The historian must adduce evidence about attachments to language. Benedict Anderson revealed that feelings of belonging beyond the face-to-face were most powerfully imagined via print culture.[57] But they were promoted as such, they were not the automatic products of reading or writing. That should hold for language worlds beyond literacy.

How might one know what a word meant in the past if it wasn't written down then? One infers earlier knowledge of the world from knowing what words meant at a particular time and place and reverse-engineering possible antecedent meanings. The method holds that if a word for something—say, "beer banana"—may be reconstructed for an earlier form of a language—say, Proto–North Nyanza—then whenever and wherever people spoke Proto–North Nyanza, they knew something about beer bananas.[58] This premise obviously rests on additional assumptions.

The premise invites readers to think of language and the world existing together in the past as, indeed, experience shows them to do in the present. Yet East Central African written uses of the vernacular words in question appear

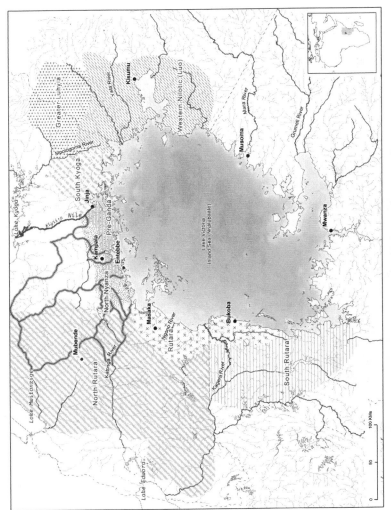

Map 4. The Inland Sea and language geography. Map drawn by Kelsey Rydland, Data Services Librarian, Northwestern University Libraries.

only after 1860. This forces historians to traditional linguistic semantics, which accepts that language and speech, competence and performance, are different orders of communication. Traditional semantic studies nonetheless focus on individual vocabulary items, building them into bundles based on shared fields of meaning. Practitioners find "an underlying signification lodged within language, by which it corresponds to an external reality."[59] They argue, in effect, that a word has a minimum representation at the core of its meaning, knowable without context. People do not create the world anew each time they converse. They create it through countless conversations over time.

Ordinary talk stretching across the generations grounds analysis of the language elicited from speakers or gleaned from documents. The meanings they attest in repeated, independent moments of expression reveal the existence in the past of this "core" meaning.[60] Once the patterns and properties of meaning have been sorted out in an ethnographic present, they may be projected into the past, deducing from them a set of possible earlier meanings. Meaning lost to all, in the past, eludes this technique. Nothing about this kind of analysis tells us who in a speech community made and used such knowledge. One guesses at that by looking at the content of the knowledge, invariably through sociological filters shaping the elicitation or textuality of the sources. Obviously, today's filters of gender, age, and status might differ from those in play in the settings in the past which the method conjures back to life. The risks of anachronism are distributed unevenly across domains of meaning because past talk implicated each domain differently.

This kind of formalism makes word-meaning reconstructions possible but limits what historians do with such hypothetical meanings. Many reconstructions are too vague to reveal anything of the social contexts of use that frame the positions speakers might take and reveal the interplay of actors and others shaping social position.[61] Scholars must establish the durability of context, inferred from the capacity to undertake and defend word-meaning reconstruction. They must also establish the changeability of context, deducible from changes in meaning.[62] To avoid the "view from nowhere"—the idea that every speaker had access to all knowledge conveyed with language—past contexts of usage must be recovered. Contexts of usage leaven semantic "rules" with a sense of action and practice.[63]

Conceptual metaphor and blending can address these issues. Metaphor can mark novelty and, if successful, become literal or taken for granted. These qualities open up the content of primordialist claims about belonging, including ethnicity. Metaphors of descent come readily to mind, but people chose additional metaphors. The proliferation of one kind of mushroom on a particular kind of termite's mound shapes concepts of belonging by associating two varieties of prolific reproduction. The behavior of mouth-brooding fish structures ideas about belonging by pointing to practices of including members of other species in a single protective group. Reconstructing such juxtapositions—and the contexts in which people found them useful—shows people choosing metaphors and making them stick. Appeals to shared descent, the uniqueness of place and distinctive cuisine, touch on intimacies of thought and action. Glassman suggested that their appeal as metaphors for belonging grows from their intimate links to everyday practices and rituals.[64] Embodied experience of the world—procreative sex, observing mushroom and termite and fish—recommends it as a source for making conceptual sense of abstract targets like belonging.[65]

Many find meaning a more elusive, contingent quality of social life than the orderly principles of conceptual metaphors imply.[66] Cultural understandings worked out in contexts of language use, not the entailments of a particular metaphor, produce meaning. But are the two mutually exclusive? Conceptual metaphors and conceptual blends work the grain of embodied experience, inventing new ways of being in the world. The structuring properties of metaphor are habits of abstract thinking; they set broad limits for the cultural work of elaboration. Details of elaborations of meaning reflect the contingencies of context. Yet the forms implicit in the structure of the juxtaposition make the metaphor shape the possibilities of meaning. Brokered or cast aside in communication, such details of meaning often elude historians of early Africa, who work without contemporaneous written documents. Conceptual metaphors and blending bridge universally embodied perceptual experience to the variety of elaborations and understanding prompted by power, scale, and culture.[67] Conceptual metaphor and conceptual blends may have both lexical and material iterations, crossing historical linguistics, oral traditions, and archeology. Chapter 1 develops the relations between pythons, spirit possession, eating, and power to get at such contexts of use a millennium ago.

Much of this book explores traditions of various sorts. From the 1860s to the 1890s, outsiders wrote up that material in French, German, and English. In the 1890s, African men began to write in and publish in English, Luganda, Lunyoro, and other languages of Uganda. They wrote on a wide range of topics, history among them.[68] Mostly they wrote to one another and to a growing Christian or Muslim readership. By the 1930s, as their generation passed, their relentless recasting of the past waned. Younger people drew on a broad set of intellectual sources, as their elders had done.[69] To use this kind of material, one must first understand why authors wrote.

The first kind of information came from oral interviews via multilingual African interpreters between European outsiders and Africans. Professional narrators produced and performed this kind of knowledge. Tale-singers accompanied themselves on the finger-harp (*ènnanga*).[70] An engraving of Speke introducing Grant to Buganda's queen-mother, Munganzirwazza, in 1862, includes a man playing an ènnanga (see chapter 5).[71] Although Europeans were interested in the exploits of kings, ènnanga players sang about a far broader range of topics.[72] The Europeans wrote down what they had learned between the 1860s and the close of the nineteenth century, in the contexts of commodified slaving and ivory hunting, imperial conquest, evangelization, and the establishment of colonial rule. The first list of kings appeared in Speke's *Journal of the Discovery of the Source of the Nile*. He named eight kings.[73] Thirteen years later, Stanley's list had grown to thirty-five names.[74] Speke assumed linear time-depth anchored claims of firstness in a politics of antiquity. The more reigns of past rulers, the weightier the antiquity of the domain they had ruled. Stanley's interlocutor lengthened the list given to Speke on realizing that unfilled zones of time meant Buganda's roots were shallower in European eyes.

Prime Minister Mayanja gave Speke the names of the last seven kings to reign, plus the ancient Kimera. Mawanda, who followed Kimera on this list, represented a new kind of rule. Speke visited a Buganda that began with Mawanda.[75] Mawanda innovated a set of chiefs to serve as local faces of the state. Mayanja took that for granted. Kateregga, credited by others with initiating Buganda's territorial expansions, was recalled to Speke as having reigned after Mawanda. In Stanley's 1875 list, Mawanda came eight reigns after Kateregga.[76] In the 1890s, Apolo Kagwa (ca. 1865–1927) revealed that Mawanda was Kateregga's great-grandson.[77] Apparently, administrative innovations loomed larger in Mayanja's mind than either the military culture that brought many of those offices into being or the descent ties among rulers.

Historians like Kagwa, writing after 1890, named the threads forming sovereign knots.[78] Their dynastic genealogy accounted for all who reigned. They tapped a gendered field of competition for the political favor of higher-ups by reciting "a long list of ancestors who had performed service to the throne."[79] In his account of each reign, Kagwa included the clan names of the holder of the titled chiefships over which royals held influence.[80] When clan traditions mention the same figures (they do not always do so), they connected to dynastic traditions. The politics of firstness and hierarchy were old, but the kind of temporality and the scope of alliance required to seize and defend position shifted often.

The meaning of such traditions emerged in the course of debate about them. Different claims about the order of reigns reflect different spheres for debate.[81] Debate raged in the later 1860s after Speke departed and Muteesa chose new burial practices, exhuming and reburying ten of his predecessors.[82] Visitors to Buganda and the ideas they brought also influenced traditions. Muslim traders came in the 1840s and Speke in the 1860s. In the 1870s, Stanley promoted Buganda as a field of imperial and evangelical enterprise. Catholic and Protestant missionaries and African catechists shaped a violent conflict between religious factions in the 1880s. Victorious Protestants used British desires for overrule to cement their hold on the chiefly positions that would make that rule indirect. In those dramas, different groups of intellectuals edited the past. The complexity of the material they left us defies the conclusion that tradition-makers made it up just to please themselves or their inquisitive visitors.

In 1862, the particular nap in the cloth of tradition that Speke, Mayanja, and Muganzirwazza worked with had been pounded into it "two generations earlier, in the reign of Kamaanya." This is the argument of Christopher Wrigley, a doyen of Buganda's history. A king Ssekamaanya appears on all of the lists of kings made between 1862 and 1894. The prefix *sse-* means "father" but its use in genealogy implies a departed ancestor. Wrigley noticed that for this name to apply to just the elder Kamaanya and not to the younger, "the Ganda tradition that speaks of Sse-kamaanya cannot have reached a fixed form before the accession of Kamaanya (the Second). But, in addition it must have crystallized before that ruler's death, for after it both Kamaanyas would have been equally entitled to the prefix Sse-." Kamaanya's sovereign knot reigned in the second decade of the nineteenth century, "a time of political consolidation after at least three generations of growth and turmoil."[83] Exhausted by conflict, players revised the past.[84] They said little about ancient sources of royal children from the clans who ran things at a place called Bakka Hill. Silence on the matter of a few clans with control over key threads in a sovereign knot advanced the fiction that the free-for-all among clans for spinning those threads, which had emerged in the eighteenth century, had always been so. The new cloth of dynastic history ennobled such alliances at the heart of territorial expansions during Kateregga's reign. Around 1800, with the consequences of enslavement for unobligated authority on full display with proliferating chiefships, tradition-makers lent antiquity to bellicosity.

Scholars have tried to put calendar dates on these lists. They have calculated that thirty years was the average length of each generation of reigning sovereign knots in Buganda's past.[85] This formula suggests that Kateregga reigned between 1640 and 1670. One multiplies by thirty the number of generations (seven) in a list of kings separating Kateregga from Muteesa. Muteesa reigned when Speke and Stanley visited, so we are certain of his calendar dates.[86] Scholars may do the same for a reign in one of the region's other dynastic lists that mentions Kateregga.[87] But calendar years are not the only way to date this material.

One may measure the proximity of its sources to the events they narrated. Some material about Ganda royals or clans were memories of events or claims about them. Others actually experienced the events, a generation or more before the teller lived. Those secondhand memories reached back as far as the 1760s. In the 1860s and 1870s, Speke and Stanley encountered the men, and a few noble women, who knew Buganda history. They had learned that history in Kamaanya's time (1812–30), from their great-grandparents, who had been youths in the 1760s. Speke's and Stanley's interlocutors, in turn, were grandparents of the people whom the African literati drew on to compose their works on popular Ganda culture and the histories of clans and royals.

Their traditions use generations to sequence transformations, telescoping the events behind them. The modularity of genealogy eases its continual revision. A teller of a tradition may simply ignore a son or daughter and their descendants or add new ones without disarticulating the skeleton of descent in a tradition. For many, this observation disqualifies such material from being used as records of the past. But the units reckoned had different relevance to the politics of revision, because some ancestral names represented a particular artisanal identity. In a word, some children must appear in the stories for audiences to recognize what the stories addressed. These included the names of founder figures of lineages and clans, the places they visited or established, and the names of particular spirits. Some names may be moved up and down a timeline and thus up and down in the rank that antiquity or profession accorded at that time.[88] Clearly, a tradition's single generation is not to be taken literally as the productive life span of a single person. It brackets a sequence of events in which its central figures were prominent actors. By putting the same sequences inside the same generations, in performances undertaken over the years, tellers and audience colluded to lend the structure of an individual life to the events in the sequence.

Out of respect for the intellectual contents of clan histories, one might ask instead about the events and processes of dispute and conflict recounted in clan histories as occasions for interested groupwork. The result is a concise vernacular chronology.[89] It defines five periods for clan "origins." Some clans were met by a culture-hero called Kintu, other clans "came with" Kintu, still others "began in Kintu's reign, some in Chwa's," and still others "came with" Kimera.[90] The residuum of clans not accounted for in the first four periods constitutes the fifth. With origins settled, clan histories explore the geography of their founder figures' most important accomplishments. Migratory itineraries draw the map. Names in a genealogy and the sequence of place names in itineraries point to the substance of clan history. A list of duties, entitlements, or conflicts relating to Ganda royals often follows.

Qualities of genealogy reveal durable social values. First is earlier, earlier is bigger. This applies to the seniority of shrine officials, the sequence of mediums, the sequence of ports and villages founded or visited by the earlier, bigger figures. Blend sequence, rank, and seniority with the semantic content of names and "oral traditions" turn into troves of information. Different orderings reveal debates about past struggles over standing. The knowledge, network, and strategic location of people and place in a tradition reveal the stakes of standing. The sequences of movement fill a stream of time. They are metonyms of local pasts being swept up into a new, larger group. Arguing over stories created vernacular chronologies for the stakes of struggle over a moral community.[91]

To recognize the ideas in traditions and understand the claims they support, the traditions themselves, like the king lists, must be deconstructed still further. The mesh of competing interests in traditions, shaped in the aftermaths of disruptive events, must be delineated.[92] Competing interests in traditions constituted exegetical communities, debaters who extracted salient meanings from the "tissue of words" that constitute a text, written or otherwise.[93] Some authors conducted research with competent speakers in the Ganda royal center.[94] Many took issue with them, applying biblical exegesis in the debate.[95] Still others carried out systematic fieldwork, finding accounts of important topics from a vantage point beyond the political center.[96] It is a sprawling archive.[97]

Transformations and Reading Traditions

Overlapping transformations in the region's social and intellectual life shaped more than the contents of tradition.[98] They should shape how we read them. The first transformation opened in the mid-eighteenth century with a pronounced increase in the volume of chiefships operating in the Ganda state. Their number had grown as a consequence of the state's expansions and the turn to enslavement it enabled, initiated two generations earlier. The florescence increased the number of locations of authority and loosened their ties to royal centers. It also brought royal centers into conflict with centers of public healing. Power dispersed in this way challenged Ganda royals and their associates to counter the centripetal effects of ordinary people's access to wealth. They did so by revising royal installation rites to co-opt and redefine the antiquity of rule associated with an authochthonous figure, Bemba (figure 2; chapter 1). Bark cloth, metals, salt, dried fish, and imports from the Indian Ocean coast moved through the proliferating chiefships. These developments prompted the revision to dynastic histories Wrigley discovered under way between 1810 and 1830, during Kamaanya II's reign.

Figure 2. Ttimbà, the serpent drum, at the kabaka's investiture. Played by a Muslim drummer, evoking the royal order of the mid-nineteenth century. Source: Albert and Katherine Cook Papers, PP/COO/K8, Wellcome Trust. Credit: The Wellcome Trust.

Proliferating centers affected clan histories, too. In the 1820s, Kamaanya moved against debilitating succession struggles by executing the sons of royal wives from particular clans. The whiplash of shifting fortunes made it wise for proscribed or weak clans to marry into or hide in other clans. That way the sons their daughters might have with a sitting *kabaka* would be recognized members of the clan their mothers had married into. That recognition provided access to the court and capital for members of their natal clan. As Rhiannon Stephens has argued, women leveraged the ambiguities of their social standing in archly patriarchal societies to play central roles in refashioning them.[99] Shifts in gendered standing shaped this material because debates about that standing were part and parcel of the changes listed here.

A second transformation opened in the mid-nineteenth century, with royal, chiefly, and others' engagement with mobile, Muslim traders.[100] It reached a turning point in 1886, when a guard of men loyal to the Ganda king Mwanga executed a number of commoner and noble converts to Christianity. The converts had been pages in the courts of important chiefs before entering Mwanga's service.[101] The aftermath of these conflicts gave a Protestant bloc the upper hand, despite being outnumbered by Catholics. In 1892, they expelled their Catholic co-religionists from Buganda's central zones. The exiles went south and west, to Buddu in particular, which had had a strong Catholic presence since 1880.[102] What had been until the middle of that decade a tolerant attitude toward these religious affiliations and practices turned to marginalizing royal women and defeating older public healing practices. Many were driven off-stage, others were reglossed with explicitly Christian meanings, and others were destroyed.[103]

The third transformation was the creation of a market in private property, following the signing of the Buganda Agreement in 1900. In 1893, three regents of Buganda, Kagwa among them, began negotiating the eventual Agreement. In the document, the British recognized the kabaka as king, the assembly of chiefs as his council, and chiefs as a landowning class.[104] It gave to the kabaka the power to select the chiefs who would rule twenty counties it constituted as Buganda's land area. Clan leaders lost ground with the creation of a system of freehold called *mailo* ("mile" in Luganda), which chiefs dominated. Clan founder figures were buried in these lands. That charged the loss of control over them with an emotional heft. Decades of political struggle over this issue ensued.[105] This rupture coincided with the spread of literacy. Historical writing, including clan histories, burgeoned.

The 1900 Agreement gave the kabaka's decision hall—the Lukiiko—the right to settle claims, decide the standing of claimants, and determine the amount of land (if any) to grant them.[106] Samwiri Lwanga Lunyiigo pointedly remarks that all the members of this political body were themselves landowners. This introduced a potential conflict of interest when parties came before them with disputes over land.[107] Their self-interest notwithstanding, Hanson showed that the council tried to redress the injustice of landless clanships.[108] The Agreement disrupted relations between living sets of clan members and the land in which their ancestors had been buried. British ideas about ownership also limited the council's success. British law had no place for land being owned by departed persons, such as the founder figures and their descendants named by clan histories. Giving land to the wrong descendants was little better. This circumstance explains the obsession with genealogy in clan histories

from Kagwa's to Michael Nsimbi's compendia, in particular clan histories, like
Buliggwanga's and those published in *Munno* from 1934.

Apolo Kagwa and his close collaborator, Canon John Roscoe, were founding researchers in this enterprise. Kagwa wrote—and his main informants
debated—in an era when the historical weight of clanship was up for grabs.[109]
Clanship had been embroiled in the destabilizing military expansions of the
eighteenth century. Late in the 1890s, Kagwa assembled a compendium of
"clan histories" under one cover. In 1905, he published a history of the Grasshopper clan, in which he claimed membership.[110] Such histories culminate by
reducing clanship to a set of responsibilities to royalty. That ending point supported the emerging consensus among royals and Europeans that the Ganda
ship of state had sailed only by subordinating clans. That view served Kagwa's
political aims to reduce to one—a king—the number of threads making up
Buganda's sovereign knot. Such brazen moves spurred others, like Eriya Buliggwanga and his team of Lungfish clan historians, or Omwami Semu Kakoma's
team of three, from another branch of that sprawling clan, to research, write,
and publish.[111] They pushed to keep the political field open.

The dispossessed crafted and deployed clan histories, advancing claims of
primacy in a particular territory. Some assumed a tight relation between estate
land, region, and clanship, a relation that had not been the norm. The politics
of this setting do not mean that specific arguments about such antiquities were
fabricated ex nihilo. There were limits to such invention. Claims of priority or
antiquity in a particular territory affected by mailo designations had to "stick."
Disputants accomplished that by arguing with categories, figures, and place
names already carrying the heft of antiquity. The doings of shrine officials and
mediums and the contributions of lineages dominated in the 1900s and 1910s
by "traditionalists" were not automatically left aside to avoid offending readers
who followed a religion of the book.[112] In the minds of the literate, nonliter-
ate, missionary, and court audiences those elements brought home the heft of
dispossession. From their appearance as vernacular interventions in a vortex of
political literacy, up to today, where scholars rely on them as potential coun-
terweights to state-centered historical and political discourse, clan histories
have been simultaneously primary and secondary sources.

A fourth change shaped sources about the Inland Sea. Between 1899 and
1905, a sleeping sickness epidemic killed some 250,000 people on the littoral.
Late in 1906 (on the mainland littoral) and early in 1908 (on the islands), Protectorate officials tried to depopulate the region.[113] Some of the dislocated,
like Kifamunyanja, publicized that history with rancor and nostalgia. The
population of the littoral and islands was reduced to tiny communities of

holdouts against the disease and confined to authorized landing spots for essential transport and trade.[114] These groups were forcibly resettled in schemes for the control of fisheries and land in which the interests of the Ganda state, the Protectorate, and early postcolonial states intersected.

Norma Lorimer, a US woman traveling in Uganda in 1908, visited Kkoome, a large island off the shores of eastern Buganda. She claimed that it had more than 10,000 people living on it, but that only some 500 people lived there when the sleeping sickness control officers arrived.[115] Ernest Lanning, a Protectorate official in Uganda since 1948, claimed that 20,000 people had lived in Ssese at some previous time. Officials forced around 11,000 people off Bugala island, as part of the draconian policy of "concentration" into sleeping sickness control camps.[116] Kifamunyanja's plea to the Ganda state and the Protectorate to reinvest in the Isles, extolled their wealth in food, fish, trade, and transport, including the rich past of the spiritual authorities in the islands.[117] In the early 1920s, the 7,000 people resettling Ssese were not all returnees.[118] The British moved from imperial conquerors to rulers of a Protectorate partly through this policy of forced removal. It lent a patina of legality to the dislocations of the so-called religious wars and the military operations imperialists called pacification.

In the 1930s, the men and women who had experienced these changes since the 1860s began to die. Their passing shifted the rhetorical focus in vernacular traditions. Jonathon Earle has shown that they debated the legacies of eighteenth-century expansions reverberating through conflicts of the later nineteenth century. Those debates framed their engagement with a high Protectorate world. Their children turned attention to the futures of such struggles, developing an array of paths ahead. Recent scholarship on East African histories of belonging, race, and nation focuses on that generation of African intellectuals.

These transformations and breaks in the continuities of social life should shape our reading of sources composed as they unfolded and closed down. The changes prompted exegetical communities to form and revise "tradition" as they defined problems and argued about how to solve them. The chapters ahead take up those issues.

The Structure of the Book

The Names of the Python is set in the littoral, islands, and mainland of the northwestern Inland Sea. It opens by tracking how and why particular kinds of people with access to large, sewn canoes capable of long-distance travel, formed an expansive clanship between the ninth and twelfth centuries. They figured out how to make durable groups whose members might never meet. They did this by revising their ideas and practices of clanship with ideas and practices of mobile spirit mediumship by developing long-distance travel and transport over the Inland Sea. The sewn canoe collapsed time and space on an order of magnitude not repeated until the 1850s, when the sail was added, or by 1900, when steam ships arrived. Expansive clanship succeeded in part by struggling over the local histories celebrating what ancestors had done to make each place worth incorporating into a larger whole. The result was the genre today called clan histories. People used pythons to reimagine the shape of clanship through offerings and choosing new emblems of belonging. They named that kind of python ènzìramìre, "the swallower of offerings and emblems."

Success paved the way for people in the thirteenth century to build a large network with a central place in one of the Inland Sea's island groups. They oriented that place to the spiritual figure of Mukasa, whose entanglements with the Inland Sea ensured success in fish work and canoe travel. With roots in one island, Mukasa's people set up their shrine on another island in the Ssese group. Shifting arrays of clans gathered and worked there from the fourteenth century. Their durable groupwork made their shrine a center without boundaries or investments in othering, until the sixteenth century, when mainland statecraft turned a possessing eye to the Inland Sea. The next two chapters explore that history.

Chapter 2 tracks the sequence of Mukasa's growth from a territorial python spirit to a more expansive spiritual authority. Gendered practices of assembly, hosted at Mukasa's shrine, made it a stable place, open to new membership from far and wide in the region. That story unfolded in a larger context of radical change in the politics of ancestors. Assembly at a central place created new resources of skills, information, and wealth. The new resources generated frictions between different actors in the networks, attracting ambitious others to join, leave, or ally with the shrine. In the sixteenth century, new mainland polities tried to draw Inland Sea resources to their centers. Shrine managers responded by arguing for the shrine's unique efficacies, drawing lines between it, other shrines, and state interests. Over the several centuries this chapter explores, the shrine's range of efficacies grew to include helping people achieve the fertility of bearing children and raising them to adulthood. With Mukasa, people could do more than succeed in fishing and travel safely over the Inland Sea.

That range of efficacies framed discourses and practices of civic virtue. It grounded the opportunities for information exchange at the shrine, in pursuit of adulthoods, in a rich moral nexus of action and responsibility. Chapter 3 explores the animating ideas and actions lending assembly with Mukasa their durable cores. Eating, gender, and sex were mutually constituted in rhythmic assemblies organized by Mukasa's officials. When visitors ate the animals offered to Mukasa, they distinguished themselves from Mukasa's mediums. When Mukasa's officials fed the Inland Sea with the blood of those animals, they activated their ties to that watery zone. They fostered safe passage and the concrete benefits of travel by water promised to those seeking socially viable adulthoods through children. Divisions of labor in refurbishing the shrine and opening it to use were gendered, with women's lateral networking displayed prominently. No one saw all that happened in refurbishing, so each task amounted to a body of knowledge and efficacy, curated by its practitioners. Segmented knowledge meant that each curator could use their special access to include some and exclude others from participation in the larger whole. Timed with lunar cycles, assembly took advantage of causality to promote reproduction, should the cycles foster fertility for the women gathered there.

On the Inland Sea littoral, senior women organized the gatherings at which children were given the names that marked their emergence from undifferentiated childhoods as members of a group. Fish from particular micro-niches on the Inland Sea were indispensable parts of that "hatching out" of children. At the same time, a sartorial revolution unfolded in which bark cloth replaced tanned hides as the preferred mode of dress. Specialists, like shrine officials, continued to dress with tanned animal skins, but ordinary people developed a stunning array of varieties, colors, and scents for their new bark cloth raiment. That fashion and skill spread around the region in part by canoe economies, lending a material dimension to the fertility on offer at Mukasa's shrine. Mukasa's people were not the only ones to work these lines of social reproduction, but they did so with the benefits of travel and networking provided by safe passage in sewn canoes.

Late in the seventeenth century, ambitious royals from Buganda allied with groups oriented to the Inland Sea in adopting a bellicose territorial expansion. Chapter 4 shifts focus to these mainland settings for statecraft. It charts the innovation of a royal legal practice that blended fertility and justice by executing prisoners marked as failed male representatives of groups. Royal and clan representatives developed this kind of execution to argue that they—not the ancestors of existing groups—had become responsible for the fertility of the region. They used a snake with a clay head and a raffia-cloth body to do so. The snake was called Mbajjwe, or "the sculpted one." They shaped boundaries with the contents of civic virtue and vice animating a moral community by removing members from within. In this case, the men stood accused of failing to win fertility, failing to win the honor and respect brought with success in such pursuit. Their failures negatively defined some parameters of belonging in an expanding eighteenth-century Ganda state.

Chapter 5 follows gendered currents in struggles over belonging. As actors and as categories, women were central to ideas about belonging and using those ideas to draw boundaries between groups. Royal and noble women, on one hand, and commoners, on the other, worked with different registers of gender. Yet they all held that the timing and location of sex lent propriety to its pleasures. Aristocrats—such as queen mothers—applied those ideas to projects of political and social distinction to police their differences from commoners. Commoner women played to an audience that often included captive women as the eighteenth century closed down. As the importance of biological motherhood took root in this milieu of dislocation, commoner women with biological fertility could defend their standing by taking up cultural practices found in Buganda, often less familiar to outsider women. In setting themselves apart from captives and other commoner women bereft of fertility, new mothers made those practices part of a Ganda ethnicity, even if they themselves were not from Buganda.

Bellicose statecraft entailed many new political shapes. Chapter 6 looks at those formed with gender, standing, and descent in a medium of print culture. It tracks debates senior men conducted about these topics between the 1910s and the 1920s, in the aftermath of the civil wars of the 1880s, the later imperial violence of the 1890s, and the struggles over private property. They fashioned a parable of misrule using historical issues from the middle of the eighteenth century and earlier. They revived the importance of historical debate to weighing the limits of belonging with descent. They zeroed in on a practice called "clan hiding," in which one branch of a clan, or an entire clan, "hid" inside another, usually after having endured "persecution" by one thread or another in a particular sovereign knot. The paradigmatic "persecutor" was a kabaka from the eighteenth century, whose misrule included unreasonable requests of followers. They wrote about clan hiding, with that eighteenth-century history in view, in a time when descendants of formerly hidden figures were reappearing to stake claims to landed position. They juxtaposed the indeterminacies of belonging with descent with the consequences of misrule for later generations. The medium of print put literati close to the core of Buganda and Protectorate power alongside the merely literate, reinventing the kind of open debate that misrule prevented. Authors invited readers into the moral failings of earlier periods, to think through gender, status, and descent in a colonial situation that threatened belonging by shrinking the routes to participation. They warned about power concentrated too tightly in the hands of the few and they worried about the endless struggles promised by relying on descent as the only way to belong. They argued that debating difficult, painful pasts could revive a moral belonging that balanced individualism with groupwork.

These chapters explore material and intellectual resources in histories of groups across the last millennium. At different moments, the group members embraced, refused, or shrugged off and thus revised the importance of boundary or othering to belonging. Their histories intertwine, mocking any attempt to herd them under a single trajectory, eventuating in ethnogenesis. Yes, statecraft hungers for organizational categories, which can figure prominently in boundary work, in othering, and in arguing over a shared past. But those three dimensions neither persist automatically nor erase other kinds of groupwork.

Historical particularity sharpens the perception of the protean qualities of belonging. Particularity pinpoints when belonging veers from community to othering. Particularity allows us to track the terms of vice and virtue animating belonging and othering as the terms shift, often in times of pronounced inequality or material constraint.[119] Bearing down on a region's history reveals groupwork that does not lead to today's ethnic imaginaries. Perhaps most surprising, the regional history told herein reveals that violence or conflict of various sorts can breathe life into virtue without producing the rigidities of ethnicity. Just as harming has been a part of healing individual bodies, collectivities, and other-than-human domains of ecology, people can choose to adopt harmful exclusions in making and remaking groups. This dimension of living comes to the surface of things in times of change. But through debate and revision, people may convert experiences of harm into sources of continuity.

This book recovers the historical contingencies shaping the region's diversity of groupwork. It might not relax the role of ethnicity in current debates over belonging in Uganda. But I show Africans imagining their futures with a rich past of belonging that exceeds ethnicity, race, or nation.

CHAPTER ONE

Python Imaginaries

Conceiving Ancient Groups beyond the Face-to-Face, 800 to 1200

Otuula bulikafo; ng'enkejje erimu minnyu.
"Settling in every home; like a salted sprat."
—Ferdinand Walser, *Luganda Proverbs*

A ROUND A MILLENNIUM AGO, the Inland Sea became a medium for expanding scales of belonging beyond the face-to-face.[1] Africans there figured out the ideas and values people could embrace in thinking and acting like members of groups whose other members they might never meet. They turned assemblies into the grounds for values of belonging that developed laterally on the Inland Sea. Archeological, historical linguistic, and oral traditions document this work in distinct ways but converge on the century or so around 1000 CE as the time of this transformative groupwork.

This groupwork raised questions for people from the different regional historical backgrounds, questions that could bring their local histories into conflict. Sometimes this meant dislodging groups and reworking their sense of an ennobling, local past. Other times, local historians successfully resisted single, overarching narratives that subsumed their ancestors' achievements. It is impossible to sort out which was which for every location so long ago. Down through generations, people curated a few cases of dramatic conflict for their rhetorical heft in making a variety of claims. Close study reveals techniques for people in larger groups to move among the local histories that sustained them by hatching out new generations.[2]

Historians tend to explore expansions of social scale in practical terms. They argue that new collective actions met specific material needs. This is often the germ explaining the creation of clans in Africa.[3] Kodesh argued explicitly that well before the sixteenth century, "dispersed clan networks ... illustrate the capacity of ritual practices to forge relationships among communities whose members did not necessarily share face-to-face interactions."[4] Kodesh developed a kind of formula for this by drawing on Feierman's notions of public healing. He showed that clanship in Buganda formed through collective action and memory work involving mediumistic contact with spirits, crafting new futures by integrating members with particular skills. Clanship reconfigured the conditions of social and political life, it framed multigenerational aspiration. This model of clanship is compelling because it is complicated. It mixes healing, harming, intellectual activity, and political culture, cutting a key for unlocking dynamics of expanded scales of social life.

Historians have spent less time thinking through the cognitive and concrete ways to expand. This chapter focuses on the techniques spirit mediums used to connect communities along the littoral of the Inland Sea around 1000 CE, to make the clans Kodesh discusses. By prompting residents to think of themselves as sharing a fate and pursuing it collectively, mediums fashioned a community's distinctive knowledge and productive skills. To tease out the intellectual contents of this project, the chapter analyzes and interprets a unique set of thousand-year-old terra-cotta figures, pots, and fishing net weights, found in the Inland Sea's northwest corner. Their significance for the emergence of political life beyond the face-to-face makes sense in the context of a climatic shift to pronounced seasonality, intensifying agricultures, the development of high-volume fish catches, and the invention of large sewn canoes.

These developments converged soon after the turn of the first millennium around the north rim of the Inland Sea. People developed concepts to blend mobility, larger scales of political activity, and the local histories celebrating places whose particular, desirable skills made them attractive in scaling up. They wove the local into the larger by using metaphors that juxtaposed eating with power and the behavior of pythons with possession by spirits. The metaphors drew boundaries between groups without othering them. With the Inland Sea, people made a living network from the new scale of belonging.

The Inland Sea, Food, and Canoes

In 1875, two grandees, Sentuma and Sentageya, responsible for minding the entrepreneurial explorer Henry Morton Stanley, called "the Alexandra Nile the 'Mother of the River at Jinja' or the Ripon Falls."[5] They meant the current that flows like a river, from the mouth of the Kagera to the falls where the Kiyiira Nile begins (see map 1). Other rivers were conceptualized as pythons.[6] Their rise and fall with the rains perhaps represented the passage of a meal through a snake's body. The anonymous author of a series of encyclopedic articles on Ugandan natural history published in the 1910s wrote about "rivers" or currents in the Inland Sea.[7] Several years ago, master boatman and fish worker Kasirye Zzibukulimbwa described currents as common dangers to fishing nets.[8] Currents and waterspouts could be the manifestations of the *lùkwâta*, the serpent monster mentioned in the introduction. People might also see the lùkwâta or the figure Luo-speakers call *atego* in the humps of islands that grow and shrink as a canoe approaches and departs.[9] The Inland Sea was not a uniform place of water, fish, wind, and rain but a world of moving parts. Its patterns took experience and skill to master and conceptual experiments to explain.

The new category of group whose members might never meet formed in a period when the timing and volume of the rains that fell in October and November grew uncertain, as reflected in the lake's paleoclimatic record. People living in the northwestern corner of the Inland Sea developed new vocabulary to signify the uncertain short rainy season.[10] Seasonality joined another shift that linked the burial of ancestors in intensively farmed banana gardens with a corresponding embrace of long-term sedentism. Itinerant mediumistic practices emerged in these contexts. Mediums extended the reach of formerly territorial spirits by dislodging them from their homes and co-opting or suppressing those in other locations.[11] At the littoral, people invested in canoe and fishery technologies, embracing mobility and range. They created the competitive networks of knowledge and skill that connected this new world of dispersed, productive communities.

In sedentary, intensive banana farming communities, people converted the spirit of an ancestor into a territorial spirit whose authority flowed from the success of its descendants in producing and reproducing in that territory. Hanson argues that burying community members in banana farms established claims to increasingly valuable land by making it part of a spiritual and economic geography.[12] Itinerant mediums from these communities converted those territorial spirits into portable ones. Their labor created the clans that Kodesh called "networks of knowledge."[13] Linking the formation of such clans with "public healing" emphasizes "the idea that groups of individuals perceive the pursuit of well-being as a collective endeavor"; they pursued well-being, in part, through critique of a status quo.[14] Permanent banana plantations celebrated the forebears whose labor and political smarts had made them productive, warranting investments in local history.

Intensive cereal farming on some islands may have also prompted the transgenerational investments of labor in land that drove the logic of public healing.[15] Contour terracing and banking protect soil from erosion but take a lot of labor to build and maintain. Like banana gardens, such fields promised long-term returns. Terraces and bunds occur on three islands about thirty kilometers apart, from Buvuma to Ddolwe, in the eastern half of the region.[16] They also occur on Bugala Island in the Ssese group, far to the west of the other three locations (map 1). On Bugala, people sharpened their hoes or bill-hooks (used to prune banana trees and harvest their fruit) in numerous long grooves in surface stone. Banana gardens (Appendix; RN 11) and permanent fields were the kind of places where past and future came together. Durable littoral communities advertised abundance. They attracted people during this period of uncertain short rains to build a network of places and relationships through assembly.

There were unintended consequences. Bananas are a poor source of protein compared with a cereal like finger millet (*Eleusine coracana*).[17] Making them a staple food created a nutritional gap in local diets that fishing easily filled.[18] The history of fish work and canoes between 1000 and 1300 reflects this dynamic. Local fishers developed gears capable of high-volume catches. They designed a new kind of canoe, fast and big enough to offer a comparative advantage in transporting dried fish and other goods to distant markets. The history of fishing and canoes has been told in some detail for the nineteenth century, but not for earlier periods.[19] Historians (this writer included) have treated fishing and fisheries as adjunct to stories of expanded commerce or agricultural intensification. But a history of fishing reveals an impetus to making groups beyond the face-to-face a millennium ago.

Today, languages in several historically related subgroups are spoken on the Inland Sea littoral (see map 4).[20] Their vocabularies are a trove of historical information about kinds of fish, the gear used to catch them, and fish process-ing.[21] Many fish names match Linnaean classifications. Their ecologies and breeding practices may be inferred from more recent studies of behavior. That can be correlated with historical linguistic evidence for steps in the develop-ment of knowledge about fish and skill in catching them.

Fishers speaking languages from speech communities with a littoral edge caught some larger and medium-sized fishes that moved between lake and river over the course of their lives. The fish were born, spawned, and died in a river. The rest of their lives they lived in the Inland Sea.[22] Some fish fed or spawned on muddy, sandy, or rocky bottoms, a fact reflected in their names.[23] Migratory fish species made rich fishing grounds out of the shallow floodplains and mouths of rivers entering the Inland Sea. Fishers could make large catches during their spawning runs when the rivers rose. March and early April on the Kagera and Ngono Rivers could be particularly productive.[24] Dry seasons on the littoral—June to August and December to January—offered casual and specialized fishers alike access to a greater diversity of environments preferred by specific fishes.

Villages on the littoral and near seasonally flooded areas enjoyed a steady supply of medium-sized fish, like catfish and lungfish. These could be taken by hand, net, basket or pot, spear or hook.[25] Fish that did not migrate were taken, too, including a kind of sardine, some catfish, and so-called elephant fish, some of which have long snouts. The common tilapia (RN 26) was not migratory. They spawned near shore multiple times between December and June. A very large net (Appendix; RN 15) could be set in the water, lined up with the spawning grounds, and secured with weights.[26] Spawning months coincided with resuming farm work along the northern littoral. Fish protein plugged food shortages and made a staple meal tasty.[27]

Local fisheries could be rich. In a study of three different swamp lakes within ten kilometers of each other, formed and altered by the entry of the Yala River (Kenya) into the Inland Sea, Peninah A. Aloo found tilapia, many different sprats, catfish, lungfish, and two other kinds of fish. Every one of the eighty rivers entering the Inland Sea repeated this diversity of fish. Changes in water level altered the distribution of particular fisheries.[28] Villagers probably preferred to build their homes near larger river mouths or the satellite lakes formed after low stands separated them from the main body of water. The fish populations in these larger, more diverse deltas weathered fluctuations in water levels more gracefully than those in smaller river mouths.[29]

Sprats, some of which move in large shoals, constituted up to 80 percent of the Inland Sea's fish biomass during these centuries.[30] Three names for them—*endagala*, *òbùmùkene*, and *ènkejje* (RN 12)—may be reconstructed to the speech communities that formed as the older ones dissolved before 1000 CE. The distributions of these names cross the boundaries of the later linguistic subgroups on the littoral. They extend into the interior, away from the Inland Sea, where sprats are not found in rivers.[31] Before 1000 CE, littoral communities used the water to move and stay in contact. But their movements were restricted to local zones of transfer, only beginning to reach into the interior along trade routes in the following few centuries.

In the North Nyanza subgroup, that development is of particular interest. When North Nyanza was spoken, between 800 and 1200 CE, it had a term for banana garden (RN 11), as well as words for fish caught in swampland, rivers, and the Inland Sea, the three main zones of fish work (RN 23–26). As the North Nyanza speech community diverged into its two subgroups, Pre-Ganda and South Kyoga (map 4), beginning in the twelfth century, fishers innovated terms for beach seine nets and fish fence (RN 15–17). Beach seines could take large numbers of sprats (and other kinds of fish) at any time.[32] Serpentine fish fences were "built along the shore, so that the fish might swim into them at the breeding season, or in places where rivers overflowed their banks during the rains, and where fish were found upon the flooded lands."[33] These technologies required skilled knowledge to build and maintain and collective labor to operate.[34]

People also developed these labor- and knowledge-intensive fishing technologies among South Rutara–speaking communities along the Inland Sea's western littoral and among Luo-speaking communities along the northeastern littoral (map 4). Each group invented different words for fishing gear capable of the same things. Thus, after the twelfth century, new centers of productive fish work exploited local populations of sprats in locations overlapping the littoral communities then investing in intensive agricultures.[35]

This included Ganda-speaking and South Kyoga–speaking communities of the thirteenth century. They no longer only took high volumes of fish at river mouths, timed with cycles of fish movement in and out of rivers, using baskets and lots of labor. The new beach seine net allowed smaller numbers of fishers to pursue high-volume catches of all sizes of fish in other parts of the littoral, such as the deeper waters near a steep-sided island or stretch of mainland littoral. The expanding scale of fish catches, reflected in the words for this new kind of net, presumably responded in part to demand for sprats. This is confirmed by another new word, òlùkanda (RN 14), shared by the same languages implicated in local, high-volume fishing for sprats. An òlùkanda tallies up to thirty skewers of sun-dried sprats sewn together into mats.[36] Each mat can be stacked for transportation as head-loads or in canoes. When dried in the sun, sprats can last several weeks before spoiling. The sprats in an òlùkanda came from the Inland Sea. The presence of this term in North Rutaran languages, whose speakers lived away from and west of the Inland Sea, attests to trade links. The few glass beads found at archeological sites there and on Ssese Islands from the twelfth century confirm that those links existed.[37] Littoral communities made protein available over a wide area. Success likely attracted others, possibly leading to local collapses in fish stocks as people learned local ecologies of food supply and fish habitat.[38] The ups and downs of specialized, intensive fishing had dawned.

Like herders and farmers, fishers developed a specialized vocabulary to structure and pass on their knowledge. They named fish at different stages of their life or size and they named different categories of fish (RN 21–25).[39] The terms reveal a fisher's attentive eye for detail, the different environmental locations for fish work, and the sorting of fish produced by different net and trap sizes. The point is that generic terms for types of fish or for stages in a fish life cycle reflected the need to experiment and learn.[40]

Great Lakes Bantu-speakers shared only a fraction of their total vocabulary for the category of fish or generic kinds of fish (RN 21–25). They shared basic terminology for taking fish by line, net, basket trap, or hand. But they shared few names for kinds of fish.[41] In several speech communities that formed and dissolved in the 2,000 years since Great Lakes Bantu broke up, people used distinctive names for fish types. Basic familiarity with fish work was ancient, but specialization was younger, regional, and focused on different kinds of fish.[42] Learning about and naming the fish ecology took time. It was a cumulative enterprise in creating and passing along new knowledge.

Many fish names, including generics, show areal distributions (RN 21). Their names are found in the vocabularies of languages belonging to different subgroups. As fishers learned the fish ecologies of the Kivu Rift and Inland Sea, the knowledge traveled easily because the larger region had a shared ecological history.[43] Fishing success—perhaps especially in large-volume catches—drew on local knowledge that could be applied elsewhere.[44]

A last piece in this puzzle of mobility and fishing eased the challenge of making groups beyond the face-to-face. It involved the invention of a new, larger kind of canoe in which people could travel swiftly and relatively safely in open water. This canoe expanded the scale of mobility by shrinking the time it took to cross great distances, enabling bulk transport of food, bark cloths, iron bloom, people, and information. The inventers of the new canoe lived in the regions creating groups beyond the face-to-face. The sewn canoe embodied their networks.

The sewn canoe (RN 13; figure 1) differed dramatically from a dugout canoe. Master carpenters bended long planks (wash strakes), sewed them together with rope, and sealed the gaps between them. The bottom strake was fixed to a massive keel, fifteen meters or more in length, fashioned from the trunk of a single tree. Thwarts doubled as seats and stabilizers. A prow stood above the heads of the paddlers, helping a captain steer. In the nineteenth century, it was "decorated with a pair of antelope horns or a bunch of red feathers made from parrots' tails, below which is sometimes a handsome kind of collar of beadwork."[45] Red clay coated the wash strakes.

Terms for this kind of canoe and its complex prows, among other distinctive parts, occur in Ganda and Soga, but not in the other two languages constituting the North Nyanza group. They have regularly corresponding sounds and tones, making them derivable from the repertoire of pronunciation in that speech community. The principal historian of that group and its leading comparative linguist, Rhiannon Stephens, has argued on a variety of grounds that the ninth to the twelfth centuries encompassed the language's life.[46] The safest inference from this evidence is that boat builders invented this sewn canoe in the thirteenth century, as the North Nyanza speech community dissolved into Ganda and South Kyoga subgroups (map 4).

Sewn canoes collapsed time and distance in an unprecedented manner for littoral residents. Pedestrians moved along paths well inland to minimize the delays and difficulties of crossing the numerous inlets, bays, and swamps crenellating its shore.[47] Littoral communities linked two different worlds of mobility. A time warp like this would affect the region again in 1903, when the first steamer service, coordinated with the railway schedule, connected Kisumu to Entebbe.[48]

The utility of canoes, the demand for fish protein, and the uneven distribution of raw materials and expertise suggest why entrepreneurial mediums translated political-spiritual entailments of settled, intensive agricultures into a larger conceptual world of political life beyond the face-to-face. Canoes and fish helped create the diverse groups brought together under the label of clanship. The wealth available through canoe mobility produced networks that clan histories describe as the itineraries attributed to founder figures.[49] Of course, networks do not automatically become groups. The shared past that enlisted a person's investment in collective action must be fostered, translating the dynamics of groupwork into the conceptual riches of story-telling.

Expansive Clanship and Its Antecedents

As we have seen, Kodesh set aside the idea that clans are kinship groups writ large to argue they are socially composed "networks of knowledge."[50] He reached this conclusion by analyzing oral traditions widely known in the Inland Sea's northwest, one of which tells that founding figures of the Pangolin clan defeated a python by cutting off its head.[51] Listening to this story at shrines on the core estates of clans in the region, Kodesh came to understand it as an account of "dislodging spiritual entities from their territorial bases" to extend "the territory for which a particular spirit and its earthly representatives might ensure collective health and prosperity."[52] The serpent, called Bemba in this story, embodied the spirit in question. By decapitating Bemba and giving the snake's head to Kintu, a well-connected spirit medium (who began to be promoted as a founder king of Buganda in the eighteenth century),[53] the Pangolin clan expanded its powers over health and wealth at Bemba's expense.

Before this victory, a leader of the Monkey clan told John Cunningham that Bemba had vanquished "levy after levy" sent against him. Piles of crushed bones told the tale of repeated failure to dislodge the knot of power embodied by the python-leader. Upon discovering the secret to renew life—to reverse the flow of time—known by Kintu's tortoise ally, Bemba could no longer laugh dismissively at Kintu. Tortoise people knew that after cutting off one's head every night, a new one appeared every morning. One would not age. After watching the tortoise people rest safely in their headless carapaces and awaken in the morning with fresh faces, Bemba asked to have his and all his followers' heads cut off, that they might again be young and strong. The deed done, the tortoise people laughed at the gullible Bemba, surrounded by the piles of bones the python had accumulated.[54] Laughter denied the respect and renown Bemba had earned.

Competitors sought to dislodge Bemba because the python embodied the historical connection between the living and the ancestors who had made the python's territory wealthy. To thrive in a place, one needed access to the forces conditioning its prosperity and fecundity.[55] Those forces were the successes of past people and their spirits. The numerous offspring, productive agricultures, abundant fishing grounds, and thriving artisans in a particular place proved that. People enjoying such abundance understood it in part as the product of ties to ancestral figures with whom they communicated by offerings and through mediums. Mediumistic activity at shrines, some of which had a resident python, bound place and history.[56]

African rock pythons love water and are common in Uganda, especially on Inland Sea islands, "swimming freely between them and the mainland."[57] They may be comfortable around people.[58] They slough their skin as they grow, have vestigial hind limbs, and hunt by stalking or lying in ambush before springing at their quarry. In this they behave like lions, leopards, and crocodiles, which people also saw as familiars for spirits a millennium ago. Unlike those predators, African rock pythons do not protect a territory, and they kill their prey by constriction. They distend their lower jaw to swallow prey whole and headfirst. Their bodies and behavior separated pythons from other kinds of snakes and other kinds of predators.

We have a detailed account from early in the twentieth century of a shrine with a resident python.[59] The shrine was a large conical house, twenty feet across and twenty-five feet high, located in a forest by a river at Bulonge, on the Inland Sea's mainland littoral west of the Ssese Islands (map 1). The python lived in one side of the house, entering and exiting through a hole cut into the wall. A female attendant lived in the other half of the house. The python drank milk mixed with kaolin from a large wooden bowl she held. The python had two names: Sselwanga and Magobwe.[60] A male medium canoed to an island in Ssese to get the cows that provided this milk. Members of a senior lineage from the Heart clan kept the house, providing an interpreter who received offerings of thanks from supplicants. The medium fed the offerings of poultry and goats to the python to ensure success in fishing and reproduction. The medium made noises while possessed. The interpreter explained the noises, telling the people whose requests had been attended what they must do to bring about their desired result.[61] Descriptions of shrines always mention beer drinking.[62] The events at Bulonge occurred on each of seven days following the sighting of a waxing moon.

These practices echo in the assemblage of terra-cotta objects discovered in 1929 by a press-gang of Africans expanding the colonial-era Luzira prison (map 1; figure 3). They found a set of figures made out of clay, weights used to set fishing nets, and ordinary and embossed clay pots.[63] The ordinary pottery, associated with the figures and fishing net weights, provided a proxy date of about 1,000 years ago for the whole assemblage.[64] This "Luzira Group" was probably not unique during its time. But nothing like it is made today or has been found nearby. One figure is a bodyless head, two others are headless bodies. The headless bodies wear wrist bangles. The bodyless head's face has bulging eyes and parted lips, evoking the experience of spirit possession. A ring of clay winds around the neck, like a constricting python.[65] The site lies within walking distance from the Inland Sea, ten kilometers from the hill where Bemba lived before being decapitated.[66] The assemblage represents a group of mediums and interpreters, associated with fish nets, oriented to a territorial spirit, such as the python figure of Bemba.

Mediums, priests, and other shrine personnel grounded well-being in territorial histories embodied in the snake and in features of the environment where people understood such spirits to reside. But making a group out of dispersed communities presented challenges of scale involving different places, ancestors, and histories. People managed the challenges by expanding the experience of spiritual embodiment. Language evidence sheds light on the process. An older practice in which a medium called a leader's ancestral ghost from its residence in these places and life forms to come and possess her was supplemented with a practice in which people understood the medium and her patron spirit as the same. The noun *mbàndwa* (RN 2) can refer to both the spirit that possesses a medium and the medium. The polysemy captures the relations between the two.

Dislodging territorial spirits and connecting communities through mobile mediumship and a new form of clanship were part of the common development of Proto–North Nyanza, after about 800 CE.[67] Before then, leaders from lineages claiming a long-standing local presence, represented in part by their ancestral spirits (RN 7), instigated encounters with embodied spirits at shrines with resident pythons, like the one at Bulonge. This provided access to a new kind of spiritual authority with a territorial reach, relevant to everyone within that ambit. A term exists today in many of the region's languages for such a territorial spirit (RN 3). Limited to Bantu languages spoken on the Inland

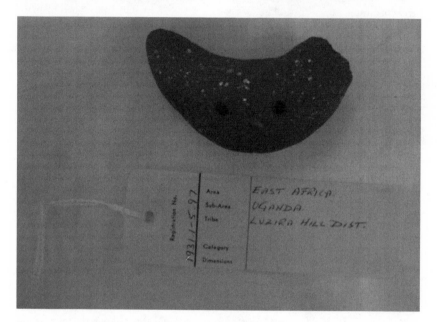

Figure 3. Luzira head, headless torso, and net weight. Nothing like this millennium-old bundle of objects has been found again. Source: head and torso © Trustees of the British Museum; net weight photo by author.

Sea's littoral, or just behind, its distribution crosses the boundaries between the established subgroups of Great Lakes Bantu shown in map 4. The noun has different prefixes in different parts of the distribution, but everywhere, it refers to ideas of spiritual authority over a territory. These features of the evidence suggest that different Bantu-speaking societies used this practice to make the Inland Sea home. They used it earlier in the first millennium, after settling at the littoral, before the ninth century, when the North Nyanza subgroup had formed. The different prefixes suggest separate events of contact or spread of speech communities in which these slightly different forms emerged as norms. Had there been a single, continuous spread, the form of the word would have been the same. As we saw already, some vocabulary related to fish work has these characteristics of variation. The differences allow us to set the inferred spreads and contact only in a broad first millennium. But they point unmistakably to movement around the rim of the Inland Sea.

That period closed when Proto–North Nyanza existed as a speech community on the northwestern littoral, from the ninth to the twelfth centuries (map 4). In North Nyanza, the word for the spirit mediumship involved in gaining access to territorial spirits grew polysemic (RN 2). Today, North Nyanza languages have the same set of polysemic meanings for the word. The sounds of the word, pronounced in each of those languages, correspond regularly. This supports the argument that the word, mbàndwa, and the configuration of polysemic meanings it carried at the turn of the twentieth century were derived by speakers of the North Nyanza proto-language. People passed them into the present across generations of talking about these ideas.

People, some of whom were called mbàndwa, began to travel between communities, very likely in sewn canoes, not later than the thirteenth century. They instigated encounters with spirits, developing conceptual resources for people to think of them as both medium and spirit. Learning to live in a world beyond the face-to-face had long been part of making the Inland Sea home. The distribution of the term for territorial spirit attests to this. But beginning as early as the ninth century, people converted the networks involved in that older process into groupwork with a different ground of stability. They linked dispersed settlements into the new scales of interaction with shifting affiliations. Kodesh called them "clans" and North Nyanza–speakers called them èbìkà (RN 4).

In the wider Great Lakes region, many Bantu languages have a word, *ngàndá (RN 1) that can be glossed in English as "clan" or "family."[68] The word appears in languages belonging to noncontiguous branches of Eastern Bantu, implying considerable antiquity for the idea and practice of composing clans. Membership was marked by combinations of shared avoidances, different ways of marking birth, unique drum rhythms, and children's names as well as vague claims of descent from a shared ancestral figure or figures of either gender.[69] While collapsing the difference between a medium and a spirit (RN 2), to promote spiritual portability, North Nyanza–speakers displaced the old ngàndá (pl.) with a new term, èbìkâ, as their word for "clans."

This shift involved new practices of initiated mediumship, described with a different verb than kubàndwa.[70] The new practices juxtaposed the same kind of experience of being seized or caught by a spirit with the condition of being an initiated medium in the state of possession. Òkùsamìra is a prepositional verb in North Nyanza languages and in smaller sets of languages in the neighboring Rutara (west) and Luhyia (east) subgroups of Great Lakes Bantu. The verb can be glossed in English as "to possess by a spirit." By adding a prepositional suffix to the verb òkùsamà, "to snatch," a speaker may say "to possess by a spirit."[71] One Catholic lexicographer at the turn of the twentieth century recorded a Ganda sentence that links this kind of possession with pythons. He translated the sentence "Omukazi oli asamira" as "She is a pythoness."[72] The noun—òmùsamìze (RN 9)—formed from this verb refers to the medium who initiates new mediums of a particular, named spirit.[73] Like sámbwa before it, the distributions of this noun and verb cross borders between subgroups of languages to form three contiguous clusters in North Rutara, North Nyanza, and Central Luyhia. All the terms are found in all the languages of only one subgroup, North Nyanza. Unlike the sámbwa example, the morphology of òmùsamìze and òkùsamìra correspond regularly. Thus, the words can be derived from the proto-language of North Nyanza and be understood as having spread later to the adjacent subgroups. The directionality of the semantic shift represented in the specialized meanings of the noun (òmùsamìze) hints at the sources for juxtaposing "being caught" with "to possess by a spirit." A medium facilitated initiands being snatched or possessed by a spirit. In understanding that work, people drew on the capacious field of òkùsamà, "to catch or snatch," which was not restricted to talking about spirit mediumship.

A hunting python lies in wait before launching itself at its prey. The python's weight knocks the intended meal off its feet. The snake then twines around the prey and begins constriction. The vocabulary for conceptualizing mediumship and possession—mbàndwa and òmùsamìze—probably grew richer in the communicative practices of North Nyanza–speakers, at shrines with a resident python. The areal spread of the second word points to the expansive reach of the kind of mediumship it signifies. The fact that òmùsamìze names a medium but not a particular spirit—as mbàndwa does—implies that it was likely used in contexts of initiation into a group of mediums. The òmùsamìze socially reproduced mobile mediums. In the practice of mobile mediumship, people emphasized the figure of the medium and her colleagues in interacting with spirits. That allowed spiritual entities to travel with their mediums, creating a social imaginary—and its histories—that exceeded the local. At Bulonge, for example, the python's medium canoed to Bubembe Island, in the Ssese group, 100 kilometers to the east, to fetch the cows whose milk the python drank.

A thousand years ago, people pursued opportunities for wealth and health in the presence of such mobile, initiated mediums. Mediums embodied the spiritual authority of newly mobile territorial spirits—*misámbwa* and *énkuní* (RN 3, 8)—to whose power people in particular territories needed access to succeed. David William Cohen first drew attention to the portability of énkuní and misámbwa spirits when he wrote, "the *nkuni* might travel with clan segments as they dispersed to secondary settlement places within Busoga [east of the Nile], but the primary *nkuni* site in Busoga was remembered as such."[74] Canoe keels were common abodes for such spirits because they were made from the trees that housed the spirits.[75] The distribution of these institutions conforms neither to linguistic subgroups nor to nineteenth- and twentieth-century ethnicities. They were institutions on the move. Working with words, things, and people, mobile mediums improvised solutions to the challenges of expanded scales of social life. Part of that process included a shift in attitudes toward the past, reflected in pottery.

Some potters on the littoral made ceramic vessels in a style with roots in the last millennium BCE. Calling them Classical Urewe wares sets them off from Transitional Urewes, the internally diverse variations on Classical ones that potters developed exclusively across the northern littoral. Transitional Urewes appeared in the eighth century CE, were widely dispersed by the ninth century, eclipsed Classical ones by the eleventh century, and disappeared in the thirteenth century. Transitional Urewe potters shifted from Classical Urewe's careful decoration and many vessel forms to fewer forms with less finely executed decoration but a greater degree of internal variation.[76] In the 1000s, some potters began to make Entebbe ware, unique in decoration and vessel type. Its large bowls implied new kinds of feasting. All known Entebbe ware sites lie less than seven kilometers from the littoral. In the Ssese Islands, these variations and more coexisted into the thirteenth century.[77]

Transitional Urewes pointed to the historical depth of Classical Urewe wares, in effect marking them as classical. At eighth- to tenth-century sites with both Classical and Transitional Urewes, but no Entebbe wares, settled farmers, fishers, and perhaps sewn canoe users made the littoral home, in part by transforming ancestral ghosts into territorial spirits. Sites with these features all occur near the littoral and in Ssese, mapping a world of territorial spirit centers in the late first millennium CE. The process involved promoting a historical depth to a leading lineage's ties to a place. Potters included ancient decorative syntaxes and vessel shapes in the Transitional Urewe oeuvre, linking it to Classical Urewes.

Sites like Luzira, where Entebbe pottery appears with the two Urewes, were not any larger than the others but they reflected a shift in orientation. Entebbe ware pots broke with the historical depth of Urewe wares, they did not evoke or repeat ancient decorative syntaxes or vessel shapes and sizes. Their decoration, shapes and sizes were new. Potters scored the interiors of the new bowls, promoting fermentation and implying their use in making beer. The bowls were huge. When full of beer, they would have been hard to move. Their large size implied a larger scale for public events, like those commonly associated with offerings and feasting at new moon ceremonies held at shrines like Bulonge.[78] The feasts at sites like these were among the first to involve mobile mediums, perhaps traveling by sewn canoe, implicating these places in early attempts to remake clans by connecting local territorial groups.

By the 1200s, sites with Entebbe pottery but no Urewe pottery of any sort began to appear only along the northern littoral. They were founded by the immediate descendants of the generations that had experienced uncertainty over the arrival of the short rains and the dramatic, intimate drops in the shoreline recorded by paleo-hydrologists and dated to two distinct periods from 1140 to 1160 and 1180 to 1200.[79] They invested in intensive cereal and banana agricultures and probably began using the large, speedy sewn canoes. They developed the technology to take large catches of sprats and migratory fish. They used the standardized unit of prepared skewers of dried sprats that could be transported as head loads or in canoes. Sites with Entebbe ware's large (but no longer new) bowls for feasting were new communities. They bring us back to the Luzira Group.

The Luzira Group was broadly contemporary with the time of Transitional Urewes, no younger than its advent, in the eighth and ninth centuries CE.[80] It was possibly as young as the disappearance of Transitional Urewes in the thirteenth century. The Classical Urewe found with it first turned up in this part of its known distribution in the sixth and seventh centuries CE. When the Luzira Group was buried, it could have been that old. Its association with Classical Urewes suggests a great depth of antiquity.[81] However, most of the pottery found with the Luzira Group is Transitional Urewe, with one shard of Entebbe ware. Thus, the Luzira Group was likely made in the ninth and tenth centuries, when Transitional Urewe was ubiquitous and when people were converting ancestral ghosts to territorial spirits here. It was likely buried during the twelfth century, when people were converting territorial spirits into portable ones and linking dispersed communities into expansive clanship. By burying the Luzira Group, people turned from the deep past to new horizons, prompted by mediumship and materialized in the new Entebbe ware.

Itinerant mediums organized the network. They oriented the aspirations of constituent communities, whose wealth and knowledge rested on deep local histories, toward this expansive project of clanship. They developed the conceptual resources to create and sustain larger networks, converting participants into members of a group with a shared past and a common future. They marked the new practices as elaborations of older ideas linking eating and power, mediumship, the experience of traveling in sewn canoes, and territorial spiritual authority. They dislodged, co-opted, or suppressed local power within expansive clanship. The Luzira Group's curatorial life, reflected in its condition at burial, suggests that a territorial spirit's authority could come to an end. This particular example was part of the invention of expansive clanship and the new social and historical orientations reflected in the advent of Entebbe wares. People stopped making the objects constituting the Luzira Group around 1200 CE, in a new world of expansive clanship that defeated or dislodged some local spiritual authorities.

History's Burdens

Expansive clanship created struggles over local histories of spiritual authority, some of which endured into the recent past. Exploring them is a precondition of using clan histories to think about how the groupwork this chapter examines involved revision. Different accounts of the iconic conflict center on the figure called Bemba and reveal struggles over making local histories into histories of larger groups. All judged Bemba's rule negatively but claimed different connections to Bemba. A Lungfish clan history composed early in the twentieth century by Eriya M. Buliggwanga (with the help of more than 100 others) claimed Bemba as a founding ancestor.[82] Kagwa's sources did not claim Bemba as a Lungfish ancestor.[83] Some authors dismissed the very existence of the Bemba figure.[84] A third Lungfish clan history made Bemba and Kintu siblings of an already established ruling figure.[85] These accounts addressed (or ignored) belonging in a time before Kintu, the founder figure claimed by sitting royals and their officials.

The two histories claiming some connection to Bemba departed from Kagwa's version. They gave Bemba and other public healing networks a richer backstory than that of playing the foil to a powerful Kintu expanding political scale. In providing clans with a deep root for their grievances against the outcomes of the 1900 Agreement, discussed in the introduction, the two teams added detail to a history of the northern littoral before Kintu arrived. In short, Kintu's people were not the first network to pursue the benefits and challenges of making spiritual efficacy portable with expansive clanship.

The two histories claiming a genealogical home for Bemba developed a history of autochthony on the northern littoral.[86] With the people of the Lungfish at its center, they rejected noble claims that Kintu had come from elsewhere.[87] They argued that clans predated royalty and that the Lungfish clan had been among the most important in those early days. Buliggwanga claimed that Lungfish estate holders saw Kintu as their "grandchild."[88] One Lungfish history appeared in print in 1950, at the height of nationalist, anti-Protectorate debate. It was actually composed in 1903, in the immediate aftermath of the 1900 Agreement.[89] Buliggwanga's book appeared in print in 1916.[90] The pressing concerns of political circumstance in the 1910s and 1950s do not explain the detail these books rain on readers.[91] The books set groupwork against a distant past of competing sovereignties. They used durable metaphors and clichés to make their points, revealing the stakes in creating expansive clanship.

Most accounts of the conflict foreground Kintu's clever allies in the Pangolin clan and the figure of Nfudu, the ageless tortoise, in defeating the network around Bemba. In Buliggwanga's text, a figure named Mukiibi prevailed over the clever tortoise by fighting and showing mercy to captives. Captured warriors escaped judgment when Mukiibi took responsibility for their actions. Buliggwanga depicted the warriors as ordinary people who relied on their canoes and strength in numbers to displace Bemba.[92] The inconclusive outcome added three other surprises to the long list of them in Buliggwanga's text. First, Bemba is never actually defeated. Second, the conflict divided the islands from the mainland. Third, struggle and coalition-building nourished the new political scale Kodesh has argued the Kintu figure fostered in the region.[93]

Opening up that larger world led to a reckoning with the ability of the past to return. Buliggwanga took that on directly. After the armed coalition defeated Bemba, the children of one coalition leader fetched a medicine from Buddo that would hinder Bemba from returning as a spirit to haunt the victors.[94] Buliggwanga mentions that other Lungfish clan nodes struggled with Bemba in the sixteenth century, marking a preeminence for them on the Inland Sea littoral before Buganda statecraft emerged.[95] The men and women in those older nodes of mediumship made up the political map, consolidated through the portable spiritual authority of the Kintu institution, with the help of Nfudu, Mukiibi, and others.

Collaboration crossed political affiliation. Buliggwanga's account of Bemba's struggle with Kintu's team introduced a figure with the title "Mukama Ppookino," a son of the Colobus Monkey clan, who married Nakku, a daughter of the Civet Cat clan.[96] Using the title "Mukama" and specifying his task as an ironsmith placed this figure among the aristocrats from the neighboring and rival polity of Bunyoro, where *Mukama* fairly translates Kabaka, the Ganda word for important, independent leaders. At the same time, Mukama is given a queen sister, and each of them is given a twin (their named umbilical cords), marking them as Ganda aristocrats. With this ruler-smith, Nakku bore Kintu and three other children, including Nambi Nantuttululu, future wife of Kintu. "Some" are said to claim that Mukama Ppookino's father's name was Kintu-kya-Mukama and that he was a son of Bukuku.

This genealogy gave autochthony a deep past. It linked Kintu with Bukuku, a famous character in traditions told away to the west about a new kind of public healing coming into existence. The practice there was called *cwezi kubándwa*. It was not associated with Buganda. In cwezi kubándwa, mediums did not need a genealogical connection to a particular spiritual patron or matron to practice their craft, a development with important parallels on the Inland Sea (discussed in the next chapter). Buliggwanga and Kakoma named Kintu's parents and their clans and put them firmly in regions outside metropolitan Buganda. They provided the lot with a genealogical connection to Bukuku, the father of Nyinamwiru, the woman who figured out how to bring Isimbwa, a nonrelative, out of Ghostland and into the land of the living, to become with Bukuku the mother of Ndahura, the first cwezi figure.

The point here concerns finding in texts like Buliggwanga's and Kakoma's some connection to the earliest history of expansive clanship, between the ninth and the thirteenth centuries. The connections appear in their rhetoric. It mixed the verisimilitude of detail with the heft of cliché. Place names, titles, and personal and object names conveyed historical and moral pith to audiences. Buliggwanga's names for men and women, spirits, and the power objects that embodied their managers' range of network and accompanied armies into battle, disclosed material and moral dimensions to early groupwork. These expansive visions of the past were not confined to ethnicities, like Ganda or Nyoro, rooted in an elite vision of statecraft. In the early 1900s, people debated the same kinds of questions in a new context.

Let us dwell a little further on some of the rhetorical hooks—the names and objects—in Buliggwanga's history. They tell of durable ideas about how to make a group beyond the face-to-face. When Bemba realized that the alliance between Nfudu and Mukiibi meant his defeat, he gave Mukiibi the five powerful medicines a skilled diviner had given him. One was called Kasiiko, or "canoe-load." It "helped Mukiibi a lot, it killed many people in the region." Another one took the form of a spitting cobra, a powerful snake like Bemba.[97] The cobra "agreed to fight, it fought a lot." These medicines were a kind of power-object called *èjjèmbê*, taken up in chapter 4. Usually made with the horn of an animal, they were filled with different materia medica and other items. The ingredients mapped the network that brought them together inside the horn. Bemba bequeathed to his adversaries the weight of knowledge and the reach of the backing that had originally drawn them.[98]

Another architect of Bemba's defeat, Ssemanobe, taught the warriors who vanquished Bemba how to fight with spears. As a titled figure, Ssemanobe played a prominent role hosting the royal installation ceremonies created in the middle of the eighteenth century and performed on Buddo Hill, at Bemba's old center.[99] Buliggwanga wrote (within living memory) of a Ssemanobe having managed the shrine on that hill, a badge of the precedence of the Lungfish clan at Buddo. Buwule, a grandson of the clever tortoise, and Walusimbi (a Civet Cat clan founder figure, discussed in chapter 6), had fourteen named siblings with different unnamed mothers. Their number embodied the prosperity won by a group of healers whose skill attracted diverse followers. It included a noble daughter, the clever tortoise's "wife," and the clever tortoise's "mother," who guarded his umbilical cord or "twin." Buwule returned late in the conflict with the tortoise's armies, still a leader despite his father having been speared in battle. In this tale, Buliggwanga's sources called him Buwule Katwe.

In the irresistible game of folk etymology, we are given one of two accounts. Either the additional name linked Buwule to a small forest whose saplings were cut to make the stretcher to remove the tortoise's wounded son from the battle, or the new moniker was to be taken literally. Buwule Katwe was a small-headed raider.[100] Whatever spin made the most sense, when people debated these events, Buwule reinvigorated the fighters they led by invoking their avoidances, the emblems of their membership in particular clans. Buwule embodied a commitment to the virtues of avoidances in maintaining clans.

That virtue came with gender anxiety. Ssemanobe may be translated as "father of runaway wives or mediums." Three verbs, each pronounced the same, can derive the name. One verb refers to the social condition of a man whose wife has run away. Another refers to raiding, particularly for cattle. A third refers to the act of hitting, beating, or throwing something to the ground with great force. That last verb can refer to a very precise meaning, still present in the twentieth century, of the second person to spear a hunted animal.[101] The moral urgency of these names—wifeless men, raiding, and hunting—echoed from the littoral's deeper past in a colonial world of struggle over private landed property where the respect and influence farmers could hope to win through service and seniority were at risk.

Mediumship, public assembly, and power objects played key roles in Bemba's defeat. Their effectiveness argued that political power turned on access to past generations of knowledge—gained and curated by groups of healers and materialized in power objects whose efficacies flowed from the expansive networks stuffed into them as ingredients. But it also turned on the strength, sweat, and skill of the living. Buliggwanga's sources invoked canoe loads, spitting cobras, wifeless men, raiding, hunting, and agentive mothers, among others. They reminded readers that the risks to social reproduction posed by political conflict and exploitation were well within the powers of clans to resolve. They argued that shrines and healers were indispensable techniques of access to—and modes of debate over—the knowledge ancestors created.

Buliggwanga retreated to the most distant figures in a genealogy to establish the temporal and spatial preeminence of the Lungfish clan and the Kintu figure. Neither firstcomers nor newcomers, Buliggwanga's team figured Buganda's culture hero and its largest clan as indigenous or autochthonous. They made Bemba a patrilineal descendant of Wanga, tying him to a first generation of portable territorial spirits (taken up in the next chapter). But he made Wanga a son of one of the Lungfish clan's founder figures, tucking the charter for Lungfish standing into the deepest recesses of cultural time. Buliggwanga's discourse on Bemba confirmed an aura of antiquity for the transition to expansive clanship. But he grounded it in a set of genealogies politically more complex than Kagwa's. The moral duties of leadership were on trial in a turbulent colonial moment. The weight of the criticism reminded listeners and readers that groupwork should flow from multiple sources of gendered social power.

Struggles over the historical standing of Bemba clearly did not drive people to abandon the figure of the python. Lungfish clan histories, as we just saw, treat Bemba as both ancestor and defeated tyrant. They keep the python category alive in the figure of Sematimba, who was made the clan's judge when an ancestor placed a copper bracelet on his wrist.[102] Sematimba means "father of the pythons."[103] Different Lungfish clan members claimed, disowned, or forgot Bemba as a founding ancestor. But they all used the figure of the python to revise their histories. Pythons connect the vernacular writing and orature of colonialism to ancient expansive clanship.

Expansive clanship involved conceptual experiments at shrines. Mobile mediums marked existing territorial spirits—like Bemba or Bulonge's python—to debate their authority or efficacy. Like Buliggwanga did with his text, mediums reconfigured a community by prompting members at a face-to-face gathering at a shrine to imagine they were connected to others neither present nor in the present. Mediums, interpreters, and other shrine personnel facilitated participation by guiding imagination beyond local practice and aligning it with other places.[104] Shrine officials and supplicants formed clans novel enough that people referred to them with a new word, èbìkâ (Appendix; RN 4).

People did all this in ways that exceed the histories of clans and the semantic fields signified by words. Belonging beyond the face-to-face did not emerge automatically by Entebbe wares eclipsing Urewe or by improving fish work and the reach of trade. It took shape by wielding metaphors and metonymies, with lexical and material iterations that juxtaposed eating, totemic avoidances, and pythons in contexts of spirit possession. That bundle connected dispersed communities, and it framed struggles over doing so. The power to steer things to a moment of larger belonging grew from local discourses of affiliation. Scaling up turned on the appeal of conceptual metaphors that made belonging beyond the face-to-face stick.

Python Work: How to Eat Local History

Conceptual metaphors helped dislodge or co-opt such local authorities, and they are indispensable historical sources for understanding that process. They provide insight into context, they reveal how innovators got their innovations noticed. They point to communication and interaction available to most historians who work with well-dated documentary records but notoriously difficult to reconstruct from the conventional kit of sources for Africa's earlier histories. Metaphor makes meaning, its locus classicus in historical linguistics and a common theme in literary studies.[105] Effective metaphors make meaning accessible.

Yet the property of metaphor that interests me most is a dimension of human experience that people use to make meaning with objects and spatial form, not only with language.[106] So many variables of social position, gender, age, power—in a word, context—shape meaning-making that one hardly knows where to start in thinking historically about the subject. Why not take things literally? Anthropologist Webb Keane tells us that literal meanings are "basic assumptions about what signs are and how they function in the world" and "what kinds of agentive subjects and acted-upon objects might be found in the world."[107] In other words, literal meanings are only obvious—that is, literal— to people sharing these assumptions. Such assumptions apply to objects, like those bundled in the Luzira Group, to other-than-human beings, like a python or a spitting cobra, and to language. Literal meaning makes interpretation a process, capable of lending coherence to or reshuffling people's social lives. Literal meaning is meaning as action. Framing it in this way, we can ask what something can mean rather than thinking only about stable fields of meaning.

Conceptual metaphors have ordering properties that assist in creating and conveying knowledge. They channel understanding in particular ways, reducing confusion. But they are layered. They are not first of all linguistic forms. Primary conceptual metaphors, as cognitive linguists call them, are image schemas or maps, drawn from embodied experience. They structure the conceptualizations that motivate linguistic or material metaphorical expressions.[108] For example, the conceptualization of an angry person as a container under pressure has a basis in the experience of one's body temperature rising with intensifying emotions. The simultaneous unfolding of those associations in embodied experience is structured. The structure guides elaborations, such as the sense of containment of the heat and emotion generated by building pressure. Containment raises questions about how the pressure builds, "what fills the container, what consequences the explosion has."[109]

People fill out such metaphor mapping in specific ways. They may form in compound words, in polysemy, and in sequences of semantic shifts. Each kind may be placed in a sequence of language change such as the formation and divergence of speech communities, and trails between them may be recognized by word borrowings.[110] Specific metaphors may appear as phrases in song, proverbs, or accounts of the past. Some appear in decoration, form, spatial organization, and in the use and curation of objects, like pots.[111] We work with these so-called cultural conceptual metaphors in our daily lives in exploring what a word, a thing, or a spatial arrangement can mean.

Using bodily experience to think about abstract targets in new ways is not the only way metaphor and concept interact productively. Conceptual blends occur when something in the target did not exist in the source until someone improvised that relationship, giving rise to new ideas.[112] A good example appears in the sentence "The fence runs all the way down to the river." The sentence blends stasis and motion, as Edwin Hutchins explains. A fence and a river's edge are blended with "a shape of motion (movement down a hill to the edge of a river) along the relevant dimension of a static object (the length of the fence)." This is a blend because the emergent entity (the way to look at the fence, as "running") is not present in the source or the target but is a combination of an element of the source (the fence's long shape) with an element of the target (the fact that one runs from point A to point B, in a line, in a temporal sequence). The "fictive motion" accorded to the fence "blends the shape of a movement through space with the spatial shape of an object to produce a temporal sequence of attention to the shape of the object."[113] Conceptual metaphors convey complex meanings.

Marking is important to innovating meaning with words and things.[114] The figures of the Luzira Group were marked because they stood out from other objects made from clay, like pots. Markedness does not make meaning, it only renders words and things available for others to evaluate. However, the circumstances of marking point directly to the actors' motives. Marking reveals the "moment" concepts emerged and reveals something about the techniques used to make the new idea stick.

For example, when North Nyanza–speakers marked *èkâ*, "homestead" or "at home" with the *èkì-* prefix, producing *èkìkâ*, "clan," they proposed a new conceptual frame for a kind of group. They suggested it be understood in part as an analog to peoples' experiences of homesteads.[115] Speakers of Luganda, one of the languages that formed as the Proto–North Nyanza speech community dissolved, used the conceptual frame of the homestead to name smaller groups making up an èkìkâ. An èssigà or an òmùtuba are often translated into English as "lineage," but each word is polysemous. An èssigà is one of the three stones—often lumps of termite earth—forming the hearth over the fire on which women prepare meals in a homestead. An òmùtuba is a kind of *Ficus* tree, whose bark is used to make cloth. Ubiquitous in homesteads, they are epiphytes in forests. Another word often given the English translation of "lineage" is òlùnyiriri. It departs from the entailments of the homestead framing because it is also a word for "line," "row," or "verse." Lines, rows, and verses are not obviously part of a homestead. The departure reveals that people were not blindly hemmed in by the conceptual framing of clanship. They inserted other ideas such as the importance of reckoning descent through a line or row of generations. But the homestead frame was also implicated in naming the clan head and the small parts of clans formed by individual extended families, usually three generations deep. An àkàsolyâ, an òluggyà, and an ènjû name these small units of a clan. The àkàsolyâ is also the roof of a house, the òluggyà is also the courtyard outside the house, and the ènjû is the structure of the house itself.

Juxtaposition can offer ideological meanings, open to debate because they were new. The new idea or object stuck by making it literal through elaboration in the social interactions that kept it alive through use. A stylized python, with a clay head and a raffia-cloth body was used in the seventeenth century to extract confessions from royal prisoners held by the Ganda state (taken up in chapter 4).[116] An important drum in eighteenth-century Buganda's royal percussion battery is called ttimbà ("python" [RN 10]). It bears a bas-relief of an undulating python (figure 2).[117] Elaborating cultural conceptual metaphors made them durable. But some metaphors, like the Luzira Head, fell out of use. They no longer generated elaborations and blends. Contests over literal meaning produced those changes.

A widespread conceptual metaphor, eating is power, has a lexical form reconstructed to the mid–first-millennium language group from which North Nyanza (among others) emerged. The verb kùlyâ may be glossed as "to eat; rule; provide prosperity" (RN 6) in the languages of that group.[118] These three meanings associated with a single verb allowed speakers to juxtapose the destruction, pleasure, waste, growth, and transformation in the experience of eating with practices of giving, redistributing, and transforming wealth into more wealth. These are core elements of the politics of feasting.[119] Recall that the scale of feasting increased between the tenth and the twelfth centuries, reflected in Entebbe ware's large bowls.[120] The shift to larger publics does not reveal a particular strategy for forming them. We cannot say definitively why people began to feast in larger groups, but we know that they did. It is easy enough to imagine participants in larger feasts drawing on new experiences of eating and drinking to elaborate ideas about other social processes. They could wonder about the capacity to put on such feasts and the opportunities for offering new ideas that feasting afforded their hosts.[121] When juxtaposed to the standing and prosperity of hosts, the experience of eating at feasts could guide guests to ponder relations between eating and leading, such as the idea that leaders were master hunter-eaters like leopards, lions, crocodiles, or pythons. The idea was signified by *miryamirye* (RN 5), a name for the African rock python that expressed its capacities for swallowing prey whole.

In the same regional language group, those predators were also familiars for territorial spirits, called mìsámbwa (RN 3). The polysemy marked the metaphorical proposition that spirits are predators. The noun *mùsámbwa* (sing.) was derived from the verb *kùsambwà*, "to be kicked," grounding spirit, its familiar, and place in the experience of possession as the experience of being physically attacked. Ordinary people's experiences of possession, as a python familiar's physical attack on a medium, marked pythons as spirits, not just predators.[122]

Mediums behaved in this manner. The medium at Bulonge "went down on his face and wiggled about upon his stomach like a snake."[123] Their actions prompted people to elaborate that distinction in another metaphor: mediums are pythons. That idea took lexical form as *èmmandwà* (RN 2), a word that signifies both "a medium" and "a spirit." Only the Ganda language, one of the two languages formed by the twelfth-century dissolution of the North Nyanza speech community, today has the glosses "python" and "bull" as well as "spirit" and "medium." Ganda-speakers could use the same word to think and talk about these objects.

When North Nyanza was still an interacting speech community, between 800 and 1100, people on the Entebbe peninsula could also think and act with the material metonymies of the Luzira figures, in which the python figured prominently.[124] The Luzira head's coiled neck ring evoked a python constricting its prey. It marked that aspect of the snake's behavior as belonging in some way to mediumship. To appreciate this conceptual blend's power over thinking and action, pythons beckon again.

Ordinary villagers a millennium ago rarely encountered pythons. But a python's love of water brought them into contact with people at springs, lakes, swamps, and watercourses. A shrine's resident python surely stood out from

the sheep, goats, cattle, guinea fowl, dogs, and chickens of the village, which
could be offerings at shrines.[125] Visitors to python shrines could wonder about
the differences between large snakes they didn't eat but which ate distinctively
and the domestic animals they ate or milked. Or they could compare pythons
and other large predators not consumed by people, noting their distinctive
eating. The resident python at Bulonge swallowed the offerings brought by
supplicants, including the things they avoided in marking belonging in a
group like a clan. Pythons were marked from other wild animals linked with
territorial spirits because they killed their prey by constriction and ate it whole
and head-first. They did not kill it and tear it with their teeth, like lions or
leopards. They did not drown prey, as crocodiles do.

The drama of possession lent mediumistic practice its social power in a
world of assumptions where spirits could possess mediums, mediums could
have access to ancestral knowledge, and participants could create a new kind
of belonging. Pythons living at shrines like Bulonge anchored these practices
and the knowledge they could produce. The terra-cotta figures from Luzira
did so as well.

These objects were broken before being buried in the ground, the place
where people understood many spirits resided.[126] In moving the broken pieces
below the surface of the Earth, did people decommission or recommission
them? Did they remove the objects from active life or provide them with pur-
chase on a new phase of activity? A clear answer is elusive. No intact, analo-
gous figures exist. We do not know which pieces were buried in each of the
pits. Still, we can say at least that at the moment of their deposition, the frag-
ments pointed to the flesh and blood people the terra-cotta figures represented. Those persons and their histories—or simply the broader categories
they embodied—hovered near the terra-cottas as they were buried.

These figures were broken in a way that echoes in the story of Bemba's
decapitation. The Luzira head is built on a coiled pot. It has been torn from
some sort of base. What were presumably heads and hands have been torn
from the torsos. Burying the head rendered a living medium unavailable to
possession by a patron spirit that manifested as a python. Burying the torsos
rendered local living interpreters—whose identity is suggested by the bangles
the torsos wear—unavailable to manage and translate the medium's messages
while possessed. By giving Bemba's head to Kintu, the Pangolin clan expanded
its powers over health and wealth at the snake's expense. Versions of the
encounter told since Kagwa and Buliggwanga wrote agree that Bemba ruled
from a hill ten kilometers from Luzira.[127] Buliggwanga's Lungfish clan history
claimed Bemba as an ancestor. The evidence suggests that creating expansive
clans, like Lungfish and Pangolin, involved contests over objects, language,

and narrative. Mediums used pythons in those contests to prompt debate over displacing or integrating local histories into histories of a new clanship, connecting the other local communities.

Archeologists assign the Luzira Group proxy dates of between the eighth and the twelfth centuries, the same period during which the North Nyanza speech community formed and began to diverge into two branches. Only the Ganda branch, centered on the northwestern littoral, had in its lexicon all these terms: òmùsambwâ, èmmandwà, ttimbà, and ènzìramìre (RN 3, 2, 10, 5). *Ènziramire* (RN 5), or "avoidance/offering swallower," expressed the conceptual metaphor of eating is power. The other three expressed the conceptual blends, spirits are pythons, mediums are pythons, and pythons are drums, respectively. The blends suggest the Luzira figures represented a medium and their interpreters who were patronized by the territorial spirit of a python. The Luzira Group's burial with net weights, Classical Urewe and Transitional Urewe—the last of which has a littoral distribution—suggests the figures were local authorities in that watery world.

Metaphors juxtaposing eating and mediumship facilitated people at one shrine imagining that they shared things with people at other shrines, whom they might never meet. Mixing experiences of mediums being possessed by a python with groupwork, such as what was enacted at shrines like Bulonge, metaphors and blends mapped meaning in particular ways. The python's compound name, ènzìramìre or *uruziramire* (RN 5) referred to the creature's capacity to swallow the offerings supplicants brought to secure their preferred outcomes. It also referred to swallowing the things that members of a group avoided, allowing new groups to form. Members created new belonging by transforming older ones. This mix was not new. If the antiquity of these terms is accurate, people had been doing this kind of groupwork for centuries before the Luzira figures were made. The group of healers who facilitated productive and reproductive success for a local community, materialized by the Luzira figures, was familiar and easily transferred across time and space because people already relied on such groups of flesh-and-blood mediums for consequential encounters with the spirits that mattered in their territories.

After 1000, individual mediums and their interpreters changed. They became what educational theorist Étienne Wenger calls "brokers," who "introduce elements of one practice into another."[128] They connected dispersed localities with valuable accumulations of skill in canoe travel and knowledge of fishing grounds through a community of healing practice that detached their spiritual authority from particular territorial bases. Eating, mediumship, and pythons marked fields of imagination. Mediums used them to align particular localities with other communities to respond to local needs by enlisting the

emerging network's nonlocal resources. By swallowing both the offerings supplicants brought to shrines and the avoidances that marked their belonging to
one group and not another, python workers formed a larger collectivity from
local ones. That larger collectivity in turn attracted the attentions of the Kintu
figure and his allies. The contested results of their "victory" over Bemba, alive
in debates over this period in the region's history that bubbled into print after
1900, turned on matters of othering—was Bemba a malign raider or a respected
autochthonous ancestor of the Lungfish clan? They also turned on the temporal boundary separating a time before royalty from all that came after.

Pythons were old symbols. As people with deep local histories on the Inland
Sea's littoral interacted beyond the face-to-face, they used pythons to craft new
histories constituting that groupwork as mobile networks called clans. The
label "clan" suggests a misleading uniformity in that groupwork. Yet each one
included people with different histories of skill. They were the shifting pieces
composing the wholes called clans, conceived of as homesteads writ large.
Mediums and interpreters used metaphors of descent, of eating as power—the
transformative potential of assembling to feast and debate the future—to organize ordinary people's creative belonging with clanship. People who belonged
in this way might never meet all the others who also did so. They might never
encounter through possession all who had come before them, whose accomplishments and skill made different places rich and safe in the present. Yet with
mobile mediums and local pythons, they could imagine the others whom they
would never meet doing as they did.

Historians have argued that this upscaling occurred in the fourteenth and
fifteenth centuries as intensive agriculture sharpened struggles over access to
and inheritance of lands best suited to bananas or grains.[129] The story told
here suggests the process was older, multifaceted, and contingent. It was tied
not just to a politics of intensive agricultures but also to opportunities for
efficient travel on the Inland Sea and the importance of the regular supplies of
protein offered to communities in need by a complex body of skill and knowledge related to fish work. Reduced to an equation, expansive clanship emerged
from converting ancestral spirits (àbàzimù) into territorial spirits (mìsambwà),
associating them with particular arrays of health and wealth in a territory and
then making the spiritual authority over that health and wealth portable in
canoe keels, python work, and mobile mediums.

Mediums, interpreters, and their followings faced a big challenge in converting the accomplishments of ancestors, evident in a territory's abundance, into
the grounds to attract others to join their larger groups.[130] They had to let some
local details slip out of new histories of an expansive clanship. Constellating

interaction between localities, mediums and locals had to integrate the historical knowledge that gave locals authority. This is a persistent challenge of group-work. Collective histories frame members' views of themselves and their aspirations as part of an unfolding story, with temporal depth and spatial reach, oriented toward a promising future. Python mediums swallowed the bonds of shared avoidances so that new groups could form. They helped details of a local past slip away as histories of multiple localities took shape.

Threats of failure imperiled access to key resources like fish protein and iron bloom. Twelfth-century changes in water levels shifted the best places to fish in unpredictable ways. Fishers had to relearn their local ecologies with the benefit of sewn canoes. Uneven local access to such wealth magnified the moral weight of superior access to material and intellectual resources on offer from the constellating groupworkers of expansive clanship aided by sewn-canoe travel. Unequal access to wealth called moral communities into question and put some people's actions under scrutiny, as causes.

Accounts of Bemba's demise imply a failure of good leadership. Bemba made people vulnerable to the competition of larger collectivities, separating the great snake from its head. The decapitation cut off those whom the snake patronized from access to their ancestral figures. Yet those figures were the true owners of the wealth and knowledge that had made Bemba's people worth attacking in the first place. This was a circumstance of political failure. The technologies of abundance and security that sustained Bemba's group did not deliver on their promise. The collective sense of worth and efficacy that made the group hum with a future faded, opening the way for blame, the settling of scores, and improvising alternative ways forward. Early in the twentieth century, Lungfish clan literati could still debate those issues. This chapter has argued that such debates have great time depth. Mobile groups of python mediums turned canoe transport and regular supplies of fish protein into solutions for the inequalities that a twelfth century of dramatic, intimate swings in rainfall visited on communities relying on a protein-poor diet of bananas and a pointillist supply of grain for staple foods.

Expansive clanship removed blockages in some of the links through which wealth flowed around and inland from the littoral. That worked by forgetting the suspicion and rancor that accompanied the failure of groups whose networks had stopped delivering on the promise of abundance and security. The bigger groups still worked with pythons for access to the property of knowledge that belonged to departed people. That way, some in the failed groups could reconstitute the respect that knowledge bore in scaling up the domain in which it would have value. Their knowledge contributed to other communities' abundance and security, through trade and mobility. But the local would never be immune from the risks and rewards of connecting to other localities. Failure brought tensions. Groups could resolve them by balancing accountability with forgetting, or those tensions could dissolve the group. Expansive clanship kept things complicated. It let people enjoy the benefits of having more options about which groups to join and which histories to shed. That took work, which the next chapter explores.

CHAPTER TWO

Possessing an Inland Sea

Making Mukasa, 1200s to 1600s

"There must have been some understanding among the gods because they
often gave identical prophecies." Information moved among shrines.
—Kagwa, *Customs of the Baganda*, 116

Mukasa never visited any of the other islands: all the people had to go to her
island when they wished the favour of the deity to be asked on their behalf.
—John Cunningham, *Uganda and Its Peoples*, 86

Balubaale b'e Ssese tebalina emiziro. "The lubaale's people of the Ssese [Islands]
have no avoidances." Healers from Ssese can have ties with anyone.
—Michael Nsimbi, *Amannya Amaganda N'Ennono Zaago*, 152

EXPANSIVE CLANSHIP had a littoral antiquity and a far-flung lateral
reach by the twelfth century. The Kintu figure represented a new kind
of expansiveness, built on the older kind. It was achieved by representatives of several clans coming together to reside at one place. Each representative brought access to different networks of herders, grain farmers, hunters,
bark cloth producers, ironworkers, and high-quality salt makers. Each clan
representative at each central place potentially had access to the networks of all
of the others there. These central places attracted people speaking different
languages and using different practices of mediumship and interpretation to
gain access to ancestral knowledge. The importance of access to ancestral
knowledge at these central places means we can call them shrines. Through
such connections, people imagined they belonged to this diverse community,
even as its constituent groups proliferated. But traditions about them reveal
that competition over access to networks and over the nodes that formed a

network could be pointed and unpredictable, paving the way for other groups to form. After the thirteenth century, these shrines blended spiritual and practical groupwork. By the sixteenth century, many existed.

A rich example emerged in the Ssese Islands at a shrine oriented to a figure called Mukasa (see map 3). This chapter tracks the sequence of Mukasa's growth from a territorial python spirit to a more expansive spiritual authority. Mukasa granted safe travel over the Inland Sea and successful fishing, which provided collective and individual well-being. People came to Mukasa to get these things because they were parts of the virtues of adulthood. Their desire for access to the hive of information created from assembling at the shrine drove its growth. Instead of Mukasa visiting them, people came to Mukasa. The idea and practice of Mukasa thus spread around the Inland Sea, and success bred competition. The number of titled clan representatives attached to Mukasa's place proliferated. Servants working there grew in number. People founded Mukasa shrines elsewhere in the region. Mukasa's shrine attracted successful clans from networks built around other centers and devoted to different authorities (sites in map 3). They earned new titled positions among Mukasa's networks. But not all of them came the shrine's way. In other words, Mukasa's people won some competitions and lost others.

The new clanships that Mukasa's shrine attracted reflected shifting relations between rich and poor, the well-connected and the isolated, the living and the departed. They brought new kinds of work and wealth, prompting debates about what people should do or think "in relation to kin and neighbors, patron and clients," the heart of a moral community.[1] These key vectors of belonging must be pulled from the sources with imagination and forbearance. They represent a durable groupwork uninterested in boundaries but capable of exclusion.

In building this far-flung network from modest beginnings in the Ssese Islands, healers developed a new spirit category, beyond those discussed in the last chapter. They called it *lùbaalè*. Mukasa's lùbaalè focused on the Inland Sea, drew different clans to it, and managed the consequences of success. Shrine leaders, and the clans they represented, rallied visitors to meet challenges to gendered social reproduction. Mukasa's people drew on python imaginaries, but they worked on a larger scale and in multiple rhythms of assembly (see chapter 3). To grasp their moral and practical depths, we need to think more carefully about how Mukasa's shrine exemplified the new kind of groupwork possible with lùbaalè.

Laterality, Depth, and Spirits

Careful thinking begins with assessing the influence of religions of the book on the shape of the sources beneath a history of spirit categories, like lùbaalè, and the practices of assembly they prompted. Joining such a group and assembling with them implied belief in the shrine's efficacy and faith in its managers' ability to prompt that efficacy. What one believed and the medium for one's faith mattered to religionists of the book. But framing lùbaalè practice as actions informed by belief and faith must include the practical aims guiding people to shrines like Mukasa's. Aspiration, not just belief, opens the way to thinking historically about the groupwork people carried out with lùbaalè.

Kagwa explained, "we understand very well that all the lubale were just people."[2] Kagwa defined lùbaalè as "just people" who "had particular skills" in part because nineteenth-century evangelism insisted on one true god who had both embodied and disembodied existence.[3] The material and spiritual aspects of lùbaalè confirmed that a common understanding of a living and spiritual Christian or Muslim god was possible precisely because such an understanding existed in Africa before missionaries arrived. Because lùbaalè had been "just people," they retained a likeness to the humanity of Christ or Mohammed. But in the long lists of named spirits, including lùbaalè, evangelists found an African understanding of god flawed by multiplicity. Hostility to that severalness drove it underground, defeated it in places, but did not erase its appeal as an alternative or supplement to religions of the book and forms of healing.[4] Some African catechists, colonial administrators, and European missionaries shared commitments to moral and intellectual independence that came to be known as "traditional religion."[5]

People made such figures durable. Lùbaalè was not an unchanging, timeless category. Stories about lùbaalè expressed change through genealogy and mobility. Kagwa's characterization implied that later persons and groups talked about, represented, and communicated with the figures and groups who lived in the distant past. Categories of spirit and body differed as historical products of lùbaalè practice, not as abstract givens.

Lùbaalè served genres of aspiration and need, including the need to offer social criticism through evanescent assemblies. Shifts in need and aspiration shaped the variety of people participating in those assemblies, but ensembles had a name, bàlubaalê ("they of the lùbaalè").[6] The local community hosting a lùbaalè shrine welcomed others to join their assemblies, and people came from every direction. This chapter's last epigraph recognizes that openness even though, as we shall see in chapter 3, exclusive belonging could emerge. Lùbaalè practice was a formula for moral belonging involving people from diverse origins.

Lùbaalè genealogies enclose a long sweep of time and reveal broad translocal networks. They disrupt stubborn images of small-scale, intimate polities as insular and isolated. Some lùbaalè are called Buganda's "national spirits" because

people held that the "efficacy" of a lùbaalè reached "beyond a particular territory or clan network and" ensured "the well-being of the entire kingdom."[7]
Their varied skills and knowledge created an enduring collectivity of people
interested in sustaining and expanding them.[8] A lùbaalè "has possessed for
many people," they say. Or, "lùbaalè chooses for himself or herself the medium
and for life time or till he or she chooses to stop using him or her because of old
age." Or, as reported by an octogenarian female medium in 1974, lùbaalè are
"spirits of the persons who gave evidence of supernatural powers during their
lifetime, and who manifested themselves after death not only, like other spirits,
for their personal ends but also in order to help the living."[9]

Lùbaalè numbered over a hundred; almost all had shrines in Ssese Islands.[10]
Mainland shrines had junior genealogical ties to a Ssese shrine. Like Mukasa,
some thirty-five lùbaalè were known across Buganda and beyond.[11] Two
lùbaalè related to Mukasa each patronized a shrine at the Buganda state's eastern and western borders.[12] But the vast majority of lùbaalè were not involved
in statecraft. Particular clans looked after some, and individual households
looked after others.[13] A few lùbaalè names also appear in a parallel category,
called *cwezi*, common in lands to the west and south (discussed below) or in a
category called énkuní, common in Buvuma and Busoga (map 3). The overlap
of lùbaalè with other categories of spirit reflects their long-standing importance and their mobility over great distances. A map of all the places people
used to access them would be unreadable.[14] Wherever lùbaalè ended up, they
began to travel by leaving an island.[15] Lùbaalè belonged to the Inland Sea.
They were mobile networkers making centers without boundaries before
states emerged.

When did people develop lùbaalè practice? Did they do so in one place and
spread it to others? Or did they develop lùbaalè in many places more or less
simultaneously, with mutual influence flowing through networks? Language
evidence, the concentration of engagement with lùbaalè practice in the islands,
archeology, and oral traditions all help address these questions. They point to
the thirteenth century as a period of interaction between shrines that exceeded
the scale and complexity of the python imaginaries animating the kind of
networks the Pangolin clan and Kintu mobilized to try to dislodge Bemba.

A few figures, such as Mukasa, were attended by many clans, had multiple
shrines, and were portable.[16] Some lùbaalè earned new names in the course of
traveling and establishing new shrines.[17] Others had no ancestors or offspring
and did not move. Lacking relatives and descendants, Katonda's three shrines
are found today in Kyaggwe. Ggulu had a couple of offspring associated with
particular places, but had neither parents nor a shrine.[18] Musoke, the Rainbow, had no shrine, residing in the sky and on the land.[19] Even the largest

group attending a shrine to a territorial spirit, like Bemba, was smaller than the groups attending the larger lùbaalè shrines. The new scale and form of groupwork echoed that of another, called *cwezi kùbàndwa*.

Lùbaalè genealogies mention figures named "cwezi," which have roots in the social history of the interior west. Their archeological background hints at their time depth. At Mubende Hill (map 3), about fifty miles from the Inland Sea, shrine activity was oriented to the first cwezi figure, Ndahura. Archeological research at Mubende has produced dates of initial use concentrated in the late thirteenth century (through the early eighteenth century).[20] If that occupation involved people making Mubende a shrine to Ndahura, then the people whom Ndahura rallied worked in the immediately preceding generations in the middle of the thirteenth century. The group of mediums and interpreters claiming descent from Ndahura formed later. They were the first to use the hill as a shrine, but they did not act alone. As we saw in chapter 1, one Lungfish clan history claimed Bukuku as an ancestor of Bemba. Bukuku was the father of Nyinamwiru, who gave birth to Ndahura. Father and daughter ran a shrine centered on Kisengwe, not far north of Mubende (map 3).

Archeological evidence from Ssese supports connections to the littoral, west of the archipelago, between 1000 and 1300.[21] Scheherazade Amin studied the attributes of excavated ceramics from sites on Bugala, Bukasa, Bubembe, and Bubeke Islands. She compared the structure of the clays used to make the pots, the materials introduced into the clays to make the pots stronger during firing and use, the object(s) used to decorate the pots, and vessel form. Using a new dating technique—optically stimulated luminescence—the results of Amin's analysis fall between 1000 to 1300. Amin found the attributes among the assemblages from Ssese varied much more than attributes in ceramic assemblages from mainland sites to the west. That difference pointed to interisland distinctiveness, but the islands were not cut off from the mainland. Amin also found overlapping, successively smaller sets of these attributes shared by Bugala Island sites and sites on the Kagera River, between Bugala and Bukasa Island to the east and between Bukasa and Bubeke Island to the northeast (see map 2). This chaining draws a map of an Inland Sea waterway linking islands in the archipelago and orienting its contacts with the littoral to the immediate west. Interisland communication and connection with lands to the west occurred while people were making Mubende Hill important, as the North Nyanza and Rutara speech communities came to the end of their lives.

Other bits of evidence link cwezi and lùbaalè figures. Eminent historian Semakula Kiwanuka first noticed that genealogies of cwezi and lùbaalè circulating in court settings made Mukasa and Ndahura contemporaries. The grandfather of each figure belonged to clans that avoided the Otter.[22] Genealogies from

Bunyoro name Mukasa as a sibling of Wamara, the last cwezi figure, and give
Mukasa a base in Ssese.[23] Other traditions, from southern regions of the Inland
Sea, put Mukasa "below" or after Wamara.[24] Cwezi figures, such as Wamara,
were commonly called lùbaalè in early twentieth-century Ganda traditions.[25]
Lùbaalè Mukasa also shared historical time with Kimera, a figure Ganda tradi-
tions link with mediumship, trade, and warfare.[26] So Mukasa's age depends on
where the question is asked, with the greatest time depth reserved for the islands.
The different antiquities accomplished by linking cwezi and lùbaalè histories
through genealogy echo in the archeological record at Mubende Hill or on
Ssese. Arguably, both practices emerged before the thirteenth century.[27]

Ganda traditions confirm this. They link lùbaalè to particular clans and
monarchs, but lùbaalè appear before the first Buganda royals.[28] Some accounts
place them after the struggles between mobile mediums like Kintu, Kintu's
Pangolin clan allies, and territorial spirits like Bemba, discussed in chapter 1.
Buliggwanga's Lungfish clan history places some lùbaalè still earlier than those
struggles.[29] Current scholarly consensus holds that the first royals of a Ganda
state whose domains exceeded the face-to-face emerged in the sixteenth century.[30] Chapter 1 argued that expansive clanship was clearly in play by the
twelfth century. Over the next four centuries, people developed the island
groupwork with the lùbaalè explored in this chapter.

Comparative linguistic evidence matches this broad timing. It shows that
people developed lùbaalè and cwezi in a creative tension unconcerned with
boundaries. Lùbaalè is younger than the òmùzimù or òmùsambwâ category of
spirit, discussed in the last chapter. The latter two words are broadly but discontinuously distributed in the Bantu languages of the region. That kind of
distribution develops over time, as some people replace old terms with new
ones. The first term, òmùzimù, shows patterns of regular sound correspon-
dence produced by people using it across the generations since a Proto-Bantu
speech community existed, five millennia ago, in the upland grassfields of
today's Cameroon.[31] The last chapter showed that the second term, òmùsambwâ, has skewed patterns of sound and morphology reflecting its repeated
transfer around the rim of the Inland Sea, with no clear point of origin. Examples of lùbaalè and of the figures and practices associated with lùbaalè shrines
concentrate in the northwestern littoral, where people established them.
They have moved, though not as far as èmìsambwâ. The world of lùbaalè clustered between Ssango Bay, the Ssese and Buvuma Islands, and the Kiyiira Nile
(map 1).

Terms connected with lùbaalè practice reveal a multilingual, multiregional
world, like the one Ssese ceramics suggested. The official who interprets what a
medium says and supervises the working life of a lùbaalè shrine is called kàbonà,

"seer-perceiver." The noun is derived from the verb *kùbonà*, "to see, perceive, find." Entries in Ganda dictionaries published between 1917 and 1967 explicitly describe this as a Nyoro verb. Throughout the Rutara language group (which includes Nyoro), spoken west and southwest of Buganda, and in Lusoga (spoken to the immediate east of Buganda), *kùbonà* is the generic verb for "see, perceive, find, or get." Luganda-speakers today use another verb, *kùlaba*, to talk about "seeing" and "perceiving." Other Luganda words, used in shrine settings like Mukasa's, bear traces of *kùbonà*. A derived form, *kùbonèka*, signifies "become visible; be new (of the moon)." Luganda inflections connect that kind of emergent visibility with affliction—*kùbonyà*, but usually *kùbonyààbonya*, "cause to suffer; torture" and *bonyèèbònye* (adj.) "tortured; afflicted; sorely tried."[32] These signs of spirit presence were linked with the official interpreter of a medium's pronouncements. Ganda-speakers used a Nyoro verb for "seeing" to name the most prominent manager of a *lùbaalè* shrine.

This suggests that shrines were multilingual contexts in which Ganda-speakers replaced *kùbonà* with *kùlaba*, as they used the first verb to discuss ritual, lunar cycles, and spirits.[33] Speaking in that way marked the shrines as oriented in part to landward centers—like Kisengwe or Mubende Hill—in regions home to the bulk of Nyoro- and other North Rutara–speakers, who continued to use the *kùbonà* form. Blending official duties with a local ritual calendar governed by lunar phases was a translocal practice. Other words for what happened and who worked at Mukasa's shrine belong solely to the shared lexicon of the North Nyanza subgroup. The bundle of terms points to diverse (if not clearly competing) glosses on the history of *lùbaalè*. Some glosses run deeply into the past of the Inland Sea's northern littoral, while the Rutara-inflected naming of *lùbaalè* officials as *kàbonà* looked inland. Each area provided important innovations in groupwork with departed figures in a thirteenth-century, multilingual world.

Blending need not presume that in the minds of the blenders, Nyoro-ness and foreignness and Ganda-ness and Ssese-ness were mutually constitutive references. One might be forgiven for thinking that was the case. After all, in the thirteenth century, Rutara and North Nyanza were dissolving into languages like Nyoro and Ganda. Yet to think of those languages as ethnic markers would be to take as given—yoking language to groupwork—what the historian must demonstrate. It is true that Ganda-speakers embraced the *kùlaba* form for "to see" or "to perceive" when a perfectly good verb, *kùbonà*, was already available. That datum suggests that some linguistic distinction was under way, not a little self-consciously oriented toward local people.

Cwezi practice was open. Afflicted adults with no kinship relation or shared clan identification with members of a healing group or to the spiritual authority patronizing the group could be initiated as a medium and join the group. People from pretty much anywhere in the greater region could participate. With deep roots in the area, this distinctive practice emerged among Rutara-speakers to the west before the thirteenth century.[34] Terms for its titled figures and material culture occur together only in the languages constituting this Rutara group. They were developed while that speech community existed. The cwezi spirits could return from the land of the dead through mediumistic acts, just like older spirits. But, to return, cwezi spirits did not need mediums to have a tie of descent or territorial identity with them. The premium on openness to newcomers contrasted with older, ongoing forms of healing oriented to lineage or territory.[35] The new healing scaled up participation by giving people access to a greater diversity of knowledge. Senior members of some groups assembled lateral connections that exceeded those of clanship by extending their spirits' efficacies beyond particular localities through mobile mediums.

In Buganda's shrines, by contrast, individual clans controlled the professionalization of new mediums, perhaps especially in the lùbaalè networks with great lateral scope, like Mukasa's.[36] Mukasa's medium, titled Nakangu, came from the Lungfish clan.[37] But Mukasa's officials came from a different clan. Formal initiation processes differed and were not always involved.[38] Yet the language of kùsamìra, "to possess by a spirit," discussed in chapter 1, showed that North Nyanza–speakers distinguished between established, professional possession experts from a particular clan and newcomers to the institution. In twentieth-century accounts of lùbaalè practice in Buganda, "many said that Lubale belonged to clans."[39] Senior lineages in clans chose a successor for a retiring medium. In a public ceremony, the lùbaalè in question possessed one of the lineage-mates or clanmates in attendance. The experienced, retiring medium taught the new one.[40] We have no accounts of how Mukasa's medium was replaced. Although each clan had a senior medium and a lùbaalè, clan members visited other shrines according to their needs.[41]

Shrines were meant to attract. People made the word lùbaalè from a noun signifying rocky ground, or a stony hill, like the granite outcroppings that dot the mainland and littoral and constitute many of the Inland Sea's rocky island prominences. A North Nyanza–speaker could use this word to refer to the kinds of stones you pick up and throw or to the pebbles in a rattle.[42] The singular prefix signifies spatial extension. Such a rock or patch of rockiness ranged in an otherwise different matrix. The vast majority of named lùbaalè spirits had island homes, so it is easy to understand the "extension" signified by the word's prefix as that of an island.[43] In a brief account of "Mukasa's stone," following his visits to Ssese in 1957, archeologist Ernest Lanning underscored its prominent location—"on the shore near the fishing port"—its white color making it "visible from Buggala Island, at Buswa, on bright days."[44] Officials meant their lùbaalè shrines to be seen, heard, and visited by many people.

The word bàlubaalê confirms that the semantic extension from a geographic feature to a type of spirit included the medium, interpreters, and others who engaged the spirit. This word is marked by a plural prefix reserved almost exclusively for people. In ordinary usage, the word refers to the people engaged with a particular lùbaalè.[45] So bàlubaalê is best translated as "the people of a lùbaalè," devoted to a spirit understood in part as a "flat, shiny stone," an island in a shifting, watery medium whose permanence as a place held a rich potential for wealth and health through assembly.

The terms lùbaalè and bàlubaalê were not in the lexicon of Proto–North Nyanza speakers between the eighth and twelfth centuries. They turn up in three of the four languages descended from that ancestral speech community. Only Ganda and Soga vocabularies have the rest of the terms associated with this kind of public healing. Material on lùbaalè is far richer in their littoral worlds, and Soga-speakers clearly distinguish their category of lùbaalè from figures like Musisi, Mukasa, and Kiwanuka, associated with Buganda and tied to the Ssese Islands.[46] The violence visited upon Ssese and Buvuma from the 1870s to the 1890s first by a Ganda monarch and then by a Ganda alliance with Stanley, dovetailed with the loss of life on the isles and the forced removals of people from the mainland littoral, after 1900. The violent rearrangement of the linguistic geography of the northern littoral foreclosed systematic study of the different languages or dialects associated with Ssese and other islands.[47] Some of them might have had lùbaalè and bàlubaalê in their lexicons, because oral traditions tell that lùbaalè shrines existed in each group of islands before they were depopulated. Lùbaalè practice generated figures with different names and overlapping authority. Mukasa does not appear on lists from Buvuma and Busoga, where a figure called Meru had a range of efficacy similar to Mukasa's.[48] In Luo-speaking littoral worlds, further east, a coiled-wire arm bangle–wearing island figure called Atego did the same.[49]

These hubs, oriented to figures like Mukasa, Meru, and Atego, shared an affinity for expanded scales of supplication, management, networking, and identification. Many shared some of the named spirits as authorities, some of the titled figures officiating at the shrines, and some of the language for talking about what was done there. However, details differed, including the relative importance of formal initiation of new mediums, their qualifications and clan identity, and the labels that described the genre of such work. Lùbaalè practice emerged in a corner of the region and spread to other hubs, but not under the editorial eye of a central authority.

This evidence suggests a few historical scenarios. Perhaps the so-called Proto–North Nyanza–speakers created lùbaalè. Their descendants abandoned it in the course of their dissolving that speech community but before Gwere and Shana developed distinct linguistic form. In this account, lùbaalè practice could have emerged as early as the eighth century, part of North Nyanza–speaking people's experiments in expansive clanship. Alternatively, the linguistic ancestors of Ganda- and Soga-speakers could have developed lùbaalè practice together—after all, lùbaalè practice is most diversified in Ganda and Soga speech areas. Shana- and Gwere-speakers have little to say about it. In this account, lùbaalè practice was elaborated over time by people living in different centuries. It emerged after the breakup of the North Nyanza speech community in the twelfth century and was elaborated during the breakup of the Proto–South Kyoga speech community in the sixteenth century, in the course of which the Soga language formed. Both accounts may be correct in some measure. Elements of lùbaalè practice emerged during North Nyanza times in the eighth and ninth centuries, and were developed into formal, shrine-centered practice later, between the thirteenth and sixteenth centuries. Whichever scenario is more accurate, authority moved among the shrine centers, never corralled by a single one. Sewn canoes bearing people, stories, and goods linked island centers to each other and to the mainland.

Reproducing lùbaalè practice mostly lacked the initiations that ushered novitiates from anywhere into the hierarchy of mobile cwezi mediums. Only a few lùbaalè became portable. But both healing practices grew the scale of community—and the diversity of knowledge that nourished competition and cooperation—beyond that of the communities built around territorial spirits, even the portable ones.[50] A plurality of the lùbaalè named in the sources comes from the Ssese Islands. Few cwezi figures have ties to the islands.[51] In the thirteenth century, lùbaalè public healing grew together with expansive clanship, but cwezi public healing moved in an even broader range of institutional and evanescent directions. Cwezi and lùbaalè public healing differed, even though their histories were deeply intertwined.

The differences may reflect a later stage in their interplay, when competition between public healing groups had grown fierce, raising political questions about their earlier histories and interrelations. Indeed, cwezi genealogies do not always mention Mukasa. Those that do disagree on the generation in which they lived or on the kind of kinship relation they had with a particular cwezi persona. Lùbaalè figures oriented to the Inland Sea, like Bukulu, Wanga, Musisi, and Wannèma, have littoral shrines but are not included in lists of cwezi figures. These ancestors of Mukasa were notable spiritual authorities, overseen by a single clan. These genealogies emerged during a period of debate about the nature and time depth of links between lùbaalè and cwezi figures that assumed the power and standing of each. Disagreements over that history—put into the idiom of genealogy—suggest the different histories at stake were distinct when debate about them began. It is thus fruitless to argue that one kind gave rise to the other or that both developed in a tighter frame of historical interaction than the frame created by trade and mobility, like the one Amin showed through her study of Ssese ceramics. Yet the genealogies tell us that as healers and ordinary people developed lùbaalè and cwezi, they produced new histories of places and groups to reflect more diverse communities of skill and knowledge. The workings of Mukasa's shrine exemplified that diversity. A clear sense of how that shrine worked will help unpack the story of its creation.

A Twentieth-Century Picture of Mukasa

Mukasa's shrine attracted people of different genders, ages, and statuses and of different regional and linguistic affinity. They assembled at the shrine to secure the means of social reproduction, the "assets that offered them self-mastery within their community of belonging."[52] Nineteenth- and early twentieth-century accounts of the shrine and the figure of Mukasa may be stitched together to show its reach and rhythms of life. With that in mind, we can use details of Mukasa's genealogy and stories told about Mukasa to reconstruct the steps people took to create that reach and establish its rhythms.

Mukasa's initial efficacy came from water and the Inland Sea.[53] Protestant missionary Robert William Felkin reported that Mugasa "lives in and rules over the Victoria Nyanza." Mugasa was consulted occasionally and he could "order or prevent war," bring or prevent illness, and hold back rain and cause famine. "Before the Waganda venture to undertake a voyage on the lake they place some food on a paddle, and say a short prayer, asking for protection on the way and a safe return; they then throw the fruit into the lake, and start on their journey."[54] Eugene Hurel, a Catholic missionary on Ukerewe Island in the far southeastern corner of the Inland Sea, does not gender Mugasa. He says that people there understood Mugasa to protect the fish and all things from the Inland Sea. People invoked Mugasa's name before traveling by water, and they offered Mugasa sacrifices before distributing the fish they caught.[55] Nicholas Stam, a Catholic missionary in South Busoga, 200 miles north of Ukerewe, gendered "Mukessa" male and called him the most important spiritual authority. He said "his habitat was Lake Victoria Nyanza." Fish workers crossing the lake "appeased the spirit by putting some bananas on the flat of their oars and tipping them into the water." Royals planning naval expeditions "used to consult the representative of the mighty" Mukasa and made offerings of "cattle, sheep, or goats, and sometimes, probably to show the disinterested-ness of the priest, even of men."[56] Men and women made offerings to Mukasa for help conceiving a child or for understanding a child's early death; Mukasa was also the source of twins.[57]

Accounts of Mukasa's shrine are rare but rich. One report says that a "canoe ferry service" to Bubembe Island, the shrine site, existed in 1955, with suppli-cants from Mawokota and Bulemeezi the most numerous patrons.[58] Earlier accounts described an elite place visited by chiefs from nearby islands or rep-resentatives of Ganda or Haya royals.[59] Ordinary islanders, and many others given to the shrine as slaves or as gifts of thanks for Mukasa's beneficence, were involved in its workings. Many buildings, a resident population, visitors, roads leading to ports, and unusual objects not reported from other lùbaalè shrines were found at Mukasa's.

Mukasa's ceremonial festivals resembled those at other shrines, including those oriented to departed Ganda royals.[60] A retinue of young women, given by elites as servants or slaves or by thankful parents who had enjoyed a spirit's efficacy, lived at any shrine of consequence.[61] Named drums, with particular beats played by titled officials, called people to assemble.[62] Tobacco, smoked in ceramic pipes over a special fire, instigated the medium's possession experi-ence.[63] The medium used a wand to emphasize the words she spoke while possessed. The waterproof wicker basket in which the senior shrine official collected sacrificed cattle blood for Mukasa was used at other shrines.[64] Large stones, some specific plants, and the attire of the managers and medium, would be familiar to visitors at other shrines. The male-only eating of sacrificed animals was also familiar. But when it came to building, labor, foods eaten, the choreography of sacrifice, seasonality, the importance of the phases of the moon's visibility, and fertility, there were contrasts.

Mukasa's shrine was the only place where the blood of sacrificed cattle (or goats) was conducted into the Inland Sea along an aqueduct made from the stems of mature fronds of a banana tree.[65] When refurbishing the shrine's buildings, a senior shrine official cut the necks of eighteen head of cattle sent from Buganda's mainland royal capital. The official then took a little of each animal's blood, put it in the waterproof basket, took the basket into the tem-porary temple, knelt, and asked Mukasa to accept it and "grant an increase in children, cattle, and food."[66] When the blood in the aqueduct reached the Inland Sea, those at the landing place chorused: "He has drunk it."[67] Cattle blood literally linked the shrine on the land to Mukasa's abode as the waters of the Inland Sea.[68] During rebuilding, all of the sacrificed cattle save one was "divided among the lower order of priests and workmen, but no woman was allowed to eat any of it."[69] The single animal—perhaps the one selected by the senior official and tied to Mukasa's temporary residence—"was the property of the priests, and might be shared only by members of their families and clans."[70] Mukasa's shrine was the only one where women cleared roads running to seven different harbors, their labor reviving a map of Mukasa's range.

The shrine came to life to different rhythms. At the sighting of a new moon, work on the island slowed markedly, as it did widely across the region, for varying lengths of time from four to ten days.[71] People did not even collect firewood or have sex. Every three months, "crowds of people gathered together" for twenty days while Mukasa appeared and possessed the female medium Nakangu, "and at this time only offerings and sacrifices were made."[72] During these gatherings, supplicants and gawkers shared the shrine with its managers, royal representatives, and estate-holding clan figures from other islands. Other gatherings were less rhythmic, prompted by a royal consultation or rebuilding the whole temple complex.[73] Food shortages or disease epidemics could prompt assembly.[74] No person or group saw all these events.

The shrine lay some distance from the shore, but its view shed included the waters.[75] Six pairs of roads radiated from it to different places. A seventh pair reached Musove harbor, controlled by the shrine.[76] The shrine consisted of at least four buildings; Mukasa's was the largest, enclosed by a living fence of strychnine trees.[77] Its unusual, hipped roof was topped by a bundle of objects that included "the iron blade of a hoe made for the purpose [of rebuilding] on each side of the pinnacle, and between the two hoe blades he placed two horns from one of the animals which had been killed on the previous evening," as part of the sacrifices overseen by the senior official.[78] Inside was a meteor-hammer, which the senior official turned twice each lunar month.[79] The open courtyard at the entrance to the enclosure held two other buildings. One belonged to Mukasa's chief wife, the other to Mukasa's medium. Mukasa's chief wife had her own medium. These important women's buildings sat between the entrance to Mukasa's enclosure and another set of houses for royal messengers. The crowd of dependents implied that many homes surrounded the main shrine.

Refurbishing the complex brought a swarm of visitors who built many temporary structures in a single day. Roscoe mentions eighteen such houses, each used by a group led by the representative of a different clan controlling land on one of the islands and having a particular refurbishing responsibility.[80] When Kagwa researched, beginning around 1890, at least seven clans had representatives with major responsibilities at Mukasa's shrine.

Oral traditions about the clanships connected to Mukasa at Bubembe tell of changed names, new clans, and one clan hiding inside another. They tell of interests in grain, exotic medicines, bark cloth, hunting, fish, and canoes. The

Inland Sea was a rich zone of wealth and health for groupwork with lùbaalè. Exploring how Mukasa's shrine became a central place attractive to broad constituencies shows the issues people debated in making moral communities uninterested in cultural difference.

Groupwork without Boundaries

Mukasa's genealogy reveals three stages of growth. Transitions between them point to moral and political dimensions of groupwork. Competition among shrines on one island drove the first stage, eventuating in Mukasa's departure. In the second stage, establishing a new shrine drew in mainland clans, creating a new central place. The third stage involved a growing number of parties seeking roles at the shrine. People disagreed over which groups had the senior ties to Mukasa because Mukasa and the islands had become reliable sources of gendered fertility. Accumulating interests in the shrine shaped political competitions, but each party's interests constituted a moral community of skill and the wealth it brought.

Claims about which figures populated Mukasa's unfolding genealogy are claims about range, authority, and ability. The meanings of the names of founder figures and the places they visited reflect those claims, describing the authority of effective, diverse networks.[81] Sometimes the names point to the sources of that authority by evoking the skills and knowledge each figure had. Itineraries layer the growth of range in generations, placing seniority in a longer, larger collective history. With these points of connection, people could imagine their belonging with Mukasa in historical terms.

Seedbead clan history exemplifies that dimension of belonging.[82] Kyaddondo, a grandparent founder of the clan, is said to have come with Kintu into Buganda. They shared time at Magonga, a multiclan central place that Kintu and leaders of other clans founded in Busujju (map 2). But Kyaddondo did not "build" anything until he went to a different hill in Busujju, called Busaaku. His independent power and the independence of the future Seedbeaders began to grow there. *Busaaku* means "the place of the first stage of bark cloth preparation." Those who adopted Kyaddondo and made him their ancestral figure of note did so soon enough after he actually lived for it to make sense to root involvement in an exchange economy as growing in Kyaddondo's lifetime. The bark cloth economy of Busujju was that economy.

A son, Kagoma, was born to an unnamed woman at Kawempe (today a northern suburb in Kampala), where Kyaddondo's life ended and Kagoma succeeded him. Kagoma's name means "little drum." Drums call people to assemble. Three generations and several stops later, a person named Mugambwa built on his great-grandfather's Kawempe estate, completing a circuit through

GUGU, OF BUBEMBE ISLAND
This young chief is the son and successor of the late high priest of the goddess Mukasa

Figure 4. Ggugu of Bubembe Island. "Ggugu" is the title of Mukasa's second official and the name of a kind of salt made from reeds that grow in the Inland Sea's shallows, which is used in the food eaten when "hatching out" children. Source: John Cunningham, *Uganda and Its Peoples* (London: Hutchinson, 1905), 83.

Busujju. Mugambwa's name means "be told," it refers explicitly to information exchange. Mugambwa's three children settled in different places. The eldest founded new estates and followings for the clan, one of which was in Busiro, to the west. Two of his great-grandchildren, Ggugu and Ssendege, founded estates and followings far away, on Bubembe and Bukasa in the Ssese Islands (figure 4). Ggugu's name refers to a kind of salt made from reeds growing in shallow waters of the Inland Sea, the kind of shallows where many species of sprat prefer to feed and breed. Ssendege's name means "owner of the bells." Bells are part of the musical performances accompanying assemblies.

Thus, in a compact form, the names in the genealogy provide the reasons Seedbead members created their historical belonging. From Busaaku, a small place rich with bark cloth trees, successful figures of later generations developed expertise in information management, bark cloth, and salt-making, expanding the reach of the Seedbead clan into the Ssese Islands. Why?

Information flowed through the islands, including Bubembe, at a higher velocity compared with inland centers to the west and north. In landlocked settings, information moved by short relays in lumpy networks. It had to pass through bottlenecks, like fords. Bottlenecks were weak ties because passage through them was easily controlled. Littoral centers, on the other hand, were connected by ports facing many other ports reached by canoes capable of long-distance runs. They could bypass the bottlenecks and promise access to larger arrays of other places and people.[83]

Wealth and knowledge attracted ordinary people, like the followers of Ggugu and Ssendege, to assemble repeatedly at island shrines. The information people went to Bubembe to get and share emerges from glossing the wealth and knowledge associated with clans, like the Seedbead, who were involved with the shrine. Mundane attractions included access to land suited to millet or bananas, access to different land races of these crops, and proximity to abundant fishing grounds. Specialized canoe and fish work, brewing, ironwork, bark cloth making, and potting were other magnets. Pursuing them entailed elements of moral community from the beginning because pursuit generated inequality and required discipline. Concern with boundaries and difference emerged clearly when mainland statecraft took active interests in the islands, from the late seventeenth century, addressed in chapter 3. Before then, difference and boundary appear fleetingly in making Bubembe a central place.

Here is a condensed account of Mukasa's emergence in that world.

On Bukasa Island, Nambubi Namatimba of the Lungfish clan bore a child she named Sserwanga Mukasa.[84] Nambubi also had ties to the Buvuma Islands and South Busoga.[85] Sserwanga disappeared from Bukasa Island as a child. But people in canoes passing Bubembe Island (due west from Bukasa) saw Sserwanga resting under a large tree. They told the elders of Bubembe and went to visit the sitting Sserwanga. In the course of their interview with the wayward child, they determined that "he" had come from Bukasa. One elder, Semagumba of the Seedbead clan,[86] "told his companions that he could not leave the boy on the shore all night, so he carried him up to a garden and placed him upon a rock, until they could decide where he was to go." Fearing a child who could travel between islands, no one took him in. As a result, "it was decided that a hut should be built for him near to the rock on which he was seated, and that Sema-gumba should take care of him." Bubembe's elders called the child "Sserwanga Mukasa" or just "Mukasa," to recognize "his" birth island. Semagumba and two clanmates built Mukasa's shrine at Bubembe. Semagumba was Mukasa's first medium.[87]

Mukasa, wives, and new mediums expanded the shrine's lateral range.[88] Nal-wanga, daughter of Kibonge, of the Bird clan, was the senior wife. She had her own medium.[89] Najemba of the Otter clan—or Najembe, daughter of Musumba, of the Monkey clan—are also mentioned.[90] Many accounts include Nakku, Nai-ruma, and Nanziri among Mukasa's wives.[91] The young slaves and servants entrusted to Mukasa as daughters took Nanziri's name.[92] Each name was also a medium's title. A woman called Nakangu, from one island south of Bubembe, replaced Semagumba as Mukasa's medium (figure 5).[93] Nakangu shared the Lungfish clan with Mukasa's mother, Nambubi Namatimba.

This account of Mukasa rests on histories of clans like the Seedbead. We saw in the last chapter the politics surrounding their compiling from the 1890s.[94] Authors focused on the figures involved in their founding, pinning the clan's most important accomplishments onto a genealogical and spatial lattice. Deep genealogy revived an aura of antiquity for clanship, using descent to connect groups of the living with their ancestors. It challenged chiefly title to landed private property, generated in the 1900 Agreement, lay the ground-work for legal struggles over rightful ownership, and promoted the value of distributed authority by providing alternative histories of the places and regions in question.[95] Authors organized clan histories around genealogy, mar-riage, and mobility. In the Seedbead example, place names, people, and the titles they held, adorned with vignettes, was an intellectual geography. Descent and movement marked time; marriage marked lateral connections.

This chapter blends the detail in such material with the descriptions of activity and actors at Bubembe, just discussed. The result recounts the stages of groupwork with Mukasa, dedicated to making a central place without boundaries, between the 1200s and the 1600s, in the time before expansionist states. People expanded Mukasa's shrine in the following steps. An established clan—the Seedbead—moved into the islands sometime after the thirteenth century as ambitious people settled places in its name, first at Bukasa Island, next at Bubembe Island. They made alliances with the Lungfish or Bird clans to do so. A new clan—Wild Date Palm Juice—emerged from this process. Over the following four centuries, as people from other clans invested in Bubembe and Bukasa, their interests opened the networks of belonging with Mukasa outward, far from the islands.

Figure 5. Cunningham's caption read: "The Goddess Mukasa and Her Court." But, Mukasa had more than one gender. Source: John Cunningham, Uganda and Its Peoples (London: Hutchinson, 1905), 75.

Leaving Bukasa

Mukasa emerged from a crowded field on Bukasa Island, a short canoe paddle east of Bubembe. A disorienting swarm of names constituted that field. Ties of marriage and descent defined their relations, lending historical depth and range to the networks interested in the islands. Behind each name in the swarm stood a shifting host of supporters. Supporters made the wealth and health in the islands accessible and gave it historical depth. Public actions to those ends can be called "healing" because they promoted open access to the resources of skill and knowledge promised by precedence and necessary for achieving social adulthoods. When circumstances required, those public actions prompted social critique within and between competing networks.

The swarm of names and relations tied to Bukasa Island reveal several shrines there, some of which were connected to other, distant centers. Semusulo-Wannèma, Bumbujje-Wamala, Musisi, and Sserwanga Mukasa had shrines on Bukasa Island. Nambubi Namatimba married Semusulo-Wannèma and Bumbujje-Wamala and, with Wannèma, bore Sserwanga Mukasa.[96] She established their shrines. Seedbead clan members with ties to mainland Kyaddondo officiated at Wannèma's shrine.[97] Seedbead and Civet Cat clan representatives looked after Wamala's shrine in Ssingo, in the west. They linked that shrine to Bumbujje-Wamala's, run by Nambubi Namatimba's people, on Bukasa Island.[98] As Musisi's children, Semusulo-Wannèma and Bumbujje-Wamala had networks that overlapped in time. People built shrines to Musisi in two other places, one in the islands, the other on the mainland. The Monkey clan provided managers at the island shrine; the Bird clan provided the managers at the mainland shrine.[99] Wannèma's people remained on Bukasa, but founded no new shrines (map 3).

These ties to Bukasa Island reveal desires for new knowledge. For example, many tales about Wannèma, Mukasa's parent, mention millet. One linked Wannèma to the grain's introduction to the islands, singling out the strange ways that islanders ate millet and the unusual requirement to plant during the short rains in December.[100] Another tale linked Wannèma to the invention of a new medicine, learned by traveling to Bunyoro. It was made with heated millet and easily eaten, like a delectable sauce. This medicine, brought back to Bukasa by a mother's brother, healed an ailing Wannèma.[101] Pleased and healthy, Wannèma ordered his mother's brothers to fetch millet to cultivate.[102] The praise name Semusulo Mairwe Lubâle Wannèma mixed lùbaalè and cwezi kubandwa practice.[103] The name blended lateral connections with historical depth, making shrines like Wannema's attractive to visitors. *Mairwe* translates as "return visits," evoking the spirits returned through the possession work of mediums and the travel between island and mainland. Stories and praise names connected mainland and littoral, crossed language boundaries, and framed alliances in an idiom of healing. Travel fostered respectable, innovative social adulthoods. But travel could also yield illness and injury, pointing out costs in making central places.

Creating new central places pushed mobility against staying put. Traditions expressed this tension literally. As a young child, Semusulo earned the jealousy of Musisi's senior wife, Nasenyama, who poisoned him with incessant coughing (a noise associated with a possessed medium's utterings). His mother, Namairwe Nsangi, introduced a competitive note into Musisi's shrine-household. One of Nasenyama's children, Bumbujje, healed Semusulo and then drove Semusulo away from Bubeke Island.[104] In some accounts, the two wrestled, Bumbujje gaining advantage when his dog bit Semusulo in the leg.[105] Another tale told that while departing, Semusulo broke his leg in a termite mound and cursed the island, saying that those who lived there would not mature, just like drone termites.[106] After this, Bumbujje was called Wamala and Semusulo was called Wannèma.[107] Friction over Bukasa Island's networks framed Sserwanga Mukasa's departure for Bubembe.

The Bumbujje-Wamala figure's ambition—and conflict with Semusulo-Wannèma—drove the move. But the movement seems contradictory. Bumbujje "wins" but "his" people leave the islands for Busundo (map 2), where Bumbujje becomes Wamala, while Wannèma's people remain on Bukasa. Two senior officials ran the Busundo shrine: one from the Civet Cat clan, and one from the Seedbead clan. One might expect the winner of a struggle for paramountcy on Bukasa Island to remain there. Instead, a new network emerged on the mainland, a clean break with island politics, which the name change expressed. The memory of Wamala's earlier history in the isles was not expunged. It was a political map orienting Ssese to the interior west, where Bunyoro was taking shape, and to the north, where Buganda was taking shape. In the tales compressed here, an island world of travel shaped the competitive interplay of lùbaalè and cwezi in which Sserwanga Mukasa lived. Though it cannot have been the only stake in play, the promise of a special millet agriculture was a major prize.[108] After seizing it, prominent islander figures—Bumbujje and Ssemusulo, to name two—operated in and beyond the islands, as Wamala and Wannèma.

The central places itinerant mediums of Wamala or Wannèma called home attracted ambitious persons—recalled as representatives of different clans—seeking expertise. Seedbead expansion into the islands was reflected in Seedbead figures running shrines in Ssese, many generations after Kyaddondo's sons established the clan on the mainland. Lungfish expansion across the islands was reflected in the figure of Nambubi Namatimba, who had a hand in Wannèma's, Bumbujje's, Sserwanga Mukasa's, and Mukasa's shrines. Her second title, Namatimba, echoed Sematimba, a key figure in establishing Lungfish people in settings west of the Kiyiira Nile with skilled canoe work and blacksmithing, who wore the copper wrist bangle of authority. During this time, people and collectivities had options in seeking the knowledge that healing provided, founding new networks in new places. Mukasa's shrine on Bubembe Island was one new place. It became the kind of place whose mediums stayed put.[109]

Taking Bubembe

When Semagumba of the Seedbead clan welcomed the child Sserwanga
Mukasa to Bubembe, two prominent public healing groups already worked
there.[110] In those first days, Semagumba ran the shrine alone. Then he invited
a woman from the Lungfish clan to take over as Mukasa's medium.[111] Together
they revitalized ties to the mainland and littoral through Seedbead and
Lungfish networks, probably over a long period.[112] Success attracted the ambitious to Bubembe to receive local responsibilities discussed in the next section.
Some Seedbead people made new clans, in a sequence that provides chronological markers and defines the stakes of groupwork. Their genealogies and the
identity of their clans reveals a history of competition and consolidation on
the Island.

Semagumba transformed a mobile territorial python spirit, Sserwanga
Mukasa, into a lùbaalè called Mukasa. Mukasa had authority over morally
appropriate access to the Inland Sea's mobility and fish. At that critical moment
in Mukasa's history, "Mukasa was said to have spoken directly to Semagumba,
and to have communicated to him what he wished to tell the people."[113] This
suggests the time when Sserwanga Mukasa was a territorial spirit on Bukasa
Island, possessing only people of a given descent group, before Semagumba's
public healing group converted the figure into a mobile lùbaalè with followings on Bukasa and Bubembe Islands. The Lungfish woman, Nakangu, who
replaced Semagumba as Mukasa's medium, opened the shrine still further.
Nakangu's arrival and her collaboration with the Lungfish and Seedbead clans
further transformed Mukasa into a lùbaalè with moral authority over access to
genres of health and wealth, such as children and crops, a broader appeal than
travel and fish protein.[114]

Nambubi Namatimba embodied the alliance with Lungfish people that
brought the littoral within range of Seedbead ambition. The Lungfish clan
shaped the rise of expansive clanship in the twelfth century, argued in the last
chapter. As we have seen, Lungfish people have a complex history. One strand
ran to the Ganda mainland and people there said that they "came with Kintu"
or that Kintu found them already there.[115] The other strand runs along the
littoral and through the islands of the northern Inland Sea and into the interior of western Kenya.[116] People say its founder figure was already in Buganda—
and Ssese—when Kintu arrived.[117] Seedbead expansion into Ssese must have
begun later, after mastering bark cloth making, in mainland Kyaddondo. As
the next chapter argues, a bark cloth economy emerged between the fourteenth and the sixteenth centuries. People from the Mushroom clan entered
next. They recall a founder figure who was a grandchild of Wagaba, a grandson of the grandson of Kyaddondo, founder figure of the Seedbead clan, with

estates on the mainland.[118] People formed the Wild Date Palm Juice clan still later, in the eighteenth-century reign of king Mulondo, in a time of military struggles with Buganda's peer polity, Bunyoro.[119] These interlocking genealogical threads and claims of association with major figures in mainland history expressed a relative chronology for the emergence of the clans as political players.

The shifting centers of their range tell us something about the stakes in play for the ambitious people who formed them. Wild Date Palm Juice nodes at Bubembe reoriented ties between the island-littoral and Kyaddondo mainland to focus on Busiro and Kyaggwe (map 2).[120] Half the titled positions held by Wild Date Palm Juice figures were based on land in Busiro and Kyaggwe. The rest were in the islands. The new landward gaze directed access to Bubembe's resources away from Kyaddondo, to two zones of conflict with Bunyoro, opened in the sixteenth century. Ganda royal tombs were concentrated in Busiro, which lay on Bunyoro's southeastern flank.[121] Kyaggwe gave access to the ports and market centers at Bulondoganyi, an important zone of trade with Bunyoro, Busoga, and points northeast, and a place best controlled with a fleet of canoes.[122] The competitive frictions between Seedbead brothers, a context in which the Mushroom clan expanded, followed by the emergence of the Wild Date Palm Juice clan, grew from Seedbead success in the islands. Sources of wealth moved from core lands, like Kyaddondo, to Buganda's borderlands. Opportunities for dignity and fame moved with them.

Kagwa reports that Ssendege, a Seedbead priest of Wannèma and father to Mwonda, "called himself a member of the Bugeme clan" because Seedbead "was not dignified because the people of Ssese did not know of it."[123] With this claim, Ssendege hid in the Bugeme clan. Seedbead figures like him valued the opinion of the audience at Ssese. After all, Ssendege was a close relative of Ggugu, the second of Mukasa's three officials. Seven of the ten tasks recognized by Ganda royals as belonging to Seedbeaders in the nineteenth century involved either shrine officialdom or canoes. Seedbead networks have linked mainland with island and littoral since at least the time of Ggugu and Ssendege.[124] As the sources of fame and dignity moved to eighteenth-century zones of conflict, islanders retained their prominence. Islanders took advantage of waterborne mobility to reorient that prominence by forming the Wild Date Palm Juice clan. Claims about which clans Mukasa's officials belonged to point to contingent histories, upsetting the just-so character of their official standing.

In sum, a Seedbead priest-interpreter and a Lungfish medium controlled a Bubembe shrine connected to the mainland from Buddu to Kyaggwe well before the addition of new managers and the creation of a broader set of links among groups, represented by Mukasa's later marriages and new mediums.

Semagumba was Mukasa's medium before Nakangu. Her involvement reflected the new scale of orientation. Members of the Seedbead clan, led by Semagumba, created lùbaalè Mukasa from òmùsâmbwa Sserwanga, in a public
healing network centered on Bukasa Island. Their decision to name the new
figure Mukasa revealed that at a time in the distant past, Bukasa Island was
known to generate such figures. This second phase, the one oriented to a
broader set of places on the mainland, began with Nakangu. Her mediumship
reflected the attractions to others, embodied in senior women, of what Seedbead clan members had accomplished with the Mukasa figure. They created a
new kind of network oriented to the Inland Sea, invested in canoes and, later,
in bark cloth making, with ties to the interior mainland, multiplying opportunities for pursuing fertility by visiting Bubembe. The first phase involved
establishing the shrine at Bubembe, in the wake of Sserwanga Mukasa's move
from Bukasa. The second phase built on the first, expanding the varieties and
rhythms of festive practice and attracting ambitious people to found new clans
with ties to Bubembe. Once established, Mukasa's shrine attracted many other
groups with no previous standing in Bubembe. Integrating them was a challenging, life-giving, and pleasurable dimension of island groupwork.

Growth

Mukasa's shrine grew by adding titled figures from elsewhere in the islands,
belonging to different clans and with different responsibilities. By late in the
nineteenth century, they numbered more than thirty. As the titled figures
invested in Bubembe, following Nakangu's arrival, they added chunks of
access and information to the mix. After 1700, a bellicose Ganda statecraft
loomed from the mainland with an interest in places like Bubembe. From
then on, Bubembe welcomed emissaries from royal capitals. That thread occupies the following chapter, here we tell the story of Bubembe's extraordinary
reach on its own terms.

Three kinds of networks emerged. Senior women, including those whom
sources call "Mukasa's wives," constituted the first. They came from clans
other than Seedbead and Lungfish. The titled chiefs who rebuilt Mukasa's
shrine made up a second network. They held estates on particular Ssese Islands
and came from still other clans. A third network consisted in shrines to
Mukasa established elsewhere in the region and in the use of the paddle as a
visual cue to signify engagement with Mukasa (map 3).[125] The roads radiating
from Bubembe, which women cleared during rebuilding, pointed to distant
destinations. As a metonym for Mukasa, the paddle spread.

This growth between the sixteenth and the eighteenth centuries distinguished Mukasa's Bubembe shrine. The parties creating the broad range of

efficacy were more diverse than at shrines oriented to other lùbaalè. Mainland royals took a regular interest in this shrine, investing in its rebuilding. At Bubembe, hoe blade, cattle horn, large retinues of young women, and the meteor-hammer (not a canoe paddle) represented Mukasa's provision of fertility. By exploring examples of each new network shift, the interplay of efficacy, constituency, metaphor, and intellectual work emerges, revealing an expansive but insular belonging in the islands.

Mukasa's wives increased the shrine's reach through their clans. At least seven resided at Bubembe, including a pair who were mother (Nakku) and daughter (Nanziri).[126] Nalwanga, daughter of Kibonge of the Bird clan, was the senior wife-official of Mukasa. Her accomplishments argued that women expanded Mukasa's range. Nalwanga provided children to those without them, adding a new power to Mukasa's groupwork. Her building stood on the main courtyard at Bubembe. She even had her own titled medium.

Nalwanga was held to have been a "pythoness, and to have come from the island of Banga."[127] Yet the officials at Mukasa's temple also ran Nalwanga's. The quote implies a period in the past when Bubembe expanded its brief beyond a core constituency of fishers, canoers, and the childless. These ties retained the interests in social reproduction embodied by Nalwanga's shrine and run by Mukasa's officials. The cliché that Nalwanga had been a pythoness—presumably prior to her involvement at Bubembe, perhaps when she was still on Banga Island—implied that when she brought her healing group to Bubembe she placed authority over childbearing in close proximity to the authority over life on the Inland Sea. Their joining at a single shrine most likely occurred sometime after the long fourteenth century, after Mukasa's people in Ssese had promoted their spiritual patron as a lùbaalè capable of delivering littoral-oriented prosperity from a center in the islands.

Nalwanga was an accomplished healer. She represented a Bird clan network with a history of skill and range. Most estates held by Bird clan founder figures lie in Kyaggwe, in southeastern Buganda. Kyaggwe's long littoral hosts ports close to many islands (map 3). Kakoto Mbaziira, an early founder figure, was a hunter-healer-artisan with knowledge of pharmacopeia and bark cloth trees.[128] Kakoto reached Bulondoganyi, the entrepôt connecting Bunyoro and central Uganda to the Inland Sea. When a holder of the Kakoto title died, the person's jawbone was removed and the new holder took possession by beating the drum battery called Mujaguzo, just like a *kabaka* did on accession.[129] Kakoto's first son, a forester, provided firewood to Kintu.[130] A second son herded for Kintu, and a third cooked for Kintu, introducing the chewing of coffee packets. A daughter ran Kintu's house at Magonga, offering hospitality to guests. Bird people began to move out of Kyaggwe when they went to Buvu

Island, off southern Kyaggwe. At Buvu, the clan's founder figure offered Kafuuma, the former cook who knew how to prepare coffee for chewing, as Kintu's doctor with a home near Magonga. A figure with the same name ran
Bufuuma, in Busujju, the mainland sister shrine to Musisi's shrines in Ssese.[131]
Magonga and Bufuuma are both in Busujju, connected to Buvu and Bubembe
by Kafuuma and Nalwanga, respectively.[132]

Nalwanga's name does not appear in the Bird clan histories I have consulted. Perhaps her historical significance lay outside the sequencing created
by patrilineal genealogy, in a time before powerful women were swept offstage
by the events of the nineteenth century. Or perhaps she belonged to a matri-
lineage, left aside by Buganda's male literati in their researches but a common
feature of descent in Ssese.[133] She falls into the period between initial Bird clan
engagement with the littoral, inaugurated by the move to Buvu Island (before
the founder figure died), and the violent attack on Bird clan people initiated
by Ganda king Semakookiro between 1800 and 1810. Engaging the littoral
revolved around Kafuuma, who enjoyed the same skill with healing that had
lent his father influence and position in Kintu's group. Nalwanga continued
that work, partly through her medium, Siriwao. Nalwanga's presence brought
Bird clan networks of healing and bark cloth preparation skills to the people
in Bubembe's networks. A similar story could be told for each senior woman
named as Mukasa's wife by juxtaposing their natal clan's history with nodes
they created by residing and working at Bubembe.

Other clans competed for access to Bubembe by drawing on different
strengths, embodied by the estate holders involved in refurbishment. They
constituted the second network. Estate holders of the Otter, Lungfish, Seedbead, and Monkey clans played key roles in refurbishment. They held land on
nearby islands, but their clans ranged widely.[134] The variety of their range
reflected the high value of the information and skill sets that came with a position there. Otter people have numerous links to littoral and island centers,
well to the south of Ssese. Sebwaato, or "Mr. Canoe," a Lungfish title with
estates in coastal Mawokota, was remembered as a senior bark cloth maker
there.[135] Otter and Lungfish prominence at Bubembe should come as no sur-
prise. Both clans were *ab'ebunnyanja*, or "people of the Inland Sea."[136]

Monkey clan figure Ssekayonga expanded links to mainland centers away
from the littoral. Ssekayonga organized building the temporary homes for
Mukasa, wives, and mediums during refurbishment. Ssekayonga's name means
"sooty man." It evokes the name Nyamiyonga, who captured Isimbwa in the
land of the dead. Through her innovative form of possession, Nyinamwiru
released Isimbwa from Nyamiyonga. Isimbwa and Nyinamwiru were the
parents of Ndahura, the famed "first" cwezi figure, whose followers made

Mubende Hill important in the thirteenth century. The "Sekayonga" central to refurbishing Mukasa's shrine was a landholder from Bunyama, an island famed for fishing and its parrots.[137] Ssemuggala, another Monkey figure with estates on Bugala Island, was the gatekeeper at Mukasa's Bubembe shrine.[138] The Monkey clan have close links to Kimera, a skilled integrator of diverse "bodies of knowledge for the benefit" of his community and an early fixture in Ganda king lists.[139] Mugema, one of their founders, was a member of the entourage that brought Kimera from Bunyoro into Buganda.[140] Mugema managed lands clustered in Busiro, but the earliest founder figures of the Monkey clan have links further west, where cattle and grain thrived. The cattle brought for sacrifice at Bubembe may have come through Monkey networks.[141] The hipped roof of Mukasa's house had an iron hoe blade and a cow horn at each end, making the networks their presence embodied metonyms of Mukasa's capacities.[142] The allusive links to cwezi tales, carried in the name Ssekayonga and in the Monkey clan's ties to Mugema, lent Ssekayonga's work a rich antiquity and an unusual range. Ordinary supplicants, the shrine's officials, and the landholding chiefs all held stakes in that range. Bubembe's reach grew vast as these figures, and the groups they represented, used the shrine.

Shrines and symbols of Mukasa constituted the last network embodying this growth. Mukasa's temple network extended to Dumu, in Buddu, and Kyange Hill, in Mawokota, on the littoral (map 3).[143] The destinations served by the roads and ports radiating from Bubembe offer another sense of scope. When Semagumba's senior wife picked up her hoe to work, other women began clearing the Bubembe road system. One road pair connected Musove port to the shrine. Other road pairs led from Bubembe to six locations around the rim of the Inland Sea.[144] Useful information exists for three of the locations. Butundu was in Kyamtwara, Buhaya. It was associated with the Batundu clan, who were leaders there before the seventeenth-century expansionist monarch Rugomora Mahe ruled. Some Batundu avoid the otter and thus may have deeper ties with Otter people from Buganda and Bwera. Others avoid the leopard and so may have had deeper ties with Leopard people from Bakka Hill in Busiro.[145] Mwesera, another of the six destinations, was the name of an òmùsambwâ based in Bubembe Island.[146] Musonzi port named a fishing ground rich with the catfish or mudfish. Local links crossed very distant destinations at Bubembe, fitting for a central place.

The broadest reach was marked by the use of canoe paddles as metonyms for Mukasa.[147] One paddle could be seen in the possession of the medium Nyakaima, who ran the shrine to Ndahura, the first cwezi figure, atop Mubende Hill, more than 100 kilometers from the Inland Sea.[148] Others were lodged in the ground

Figure 6. Nkulo, a medium of Mukasa. Note the copper paddle-spears, Mukasa's emblems. Source: Julien Gorju, *Entre l'Victoria, l'Edouard et l'Albert* (Rennes: Imprimeries Oberthür, 1920), frontispiece. Credit: Archivio Padri Bianchi, Rome.

or hung from the rafters in elite and ordinary dwellings in Buhaya, far to the southwest.[149] The "smaller temples built to him [*sic*] in all parts of the country," housed an emblem of Mukasa's paddle.[150] The paddle was often made of wood, but it could be made of metal, in which case it bore a striking resemblance to a spear. Catholic missionary Julien Gorju described one as an object of supplication "in order to ensure calm weather persons would plant a spear in the courtyard after having tied cowries or herbs just below the blade" (figure 6).[151] "The priests of the Uganda Neptune (Mukasa) carried a paddle as the emblem of their office or as a walking stick."[152] In Kiziba, Buhaya "fastened to a pole one step from the door hangs a single paddle as daua [medicine]."[153] This kind of paddle, "which had come from some particular place, and had received the blessing of the priest of that place," was never seen at the Bubembe shrine.[154]

The paddle implicated those who carried and encountered it in the network centered on Bubembe. By evoking the capacities and expectations of moral practice associated with the Mukasa figure, this unassuming object compressed time and space when each person encountered it planted at the edge of a camp or hanging inside a chief's house or spoke of it to others.[155] This kind of paddle made Mukasa's powers subjective processes of personal reflection as well as objective points or nodes in a network of shrines joined by canoes. Imagining Mukasa and gathering at Bubembe must not be conflated with each other, but they were obviously connected.

Mukasa's symbol repertoire—python, paddle, and the keels of sewn canoes—could exist "even where Mukasa was not known as a specific" figure of authority.[156] In the northeastern Inland Sea, people used this bundle to fashion groups of waterborne traders of salt and other commodities since at least the eighteenth century. The story of Atego and his two brothers, Sumba and Ugingo (both names also refer to islands; see map 2) closely resembles Sserwanga's transformation into Mukasa.[157] The similarities imply that groupwork at scales larger than those patronized by a territorial spirit was common on the littoral and involved similar conceptual building blocks from the thirteenth century onward.

By the eighteenth century, the range of skill and material wealth accessible through clanship—and the elasticity of its reach provided by long-distance canoe travel—fostered regular assembly. Ordinary people and Ganda state actors alike found what they were looking for at Bubembe. The attractions emerged in an earlier era of unprecedented creativity in healing practice, borne out of larger regional patterns of trade and competition and the opportunities for political-economic aggrandizement they carried.[158] But generating new skills, or reshuffling existing sets, was not the whole story of island groupwork. As we have seen, at Bubembe these practical skill sets nourished a central place whose main attractions related to social reproduction more broadly. Tracking skill sets and shifting networks over time reveals different historical trajectories, interwoven at different island shrines. They defy categorization by language, region, occupation, and so on.

The transformation of Mukasa from a territorial python spirit into an expansive lùbaalè began when enterprising figures from the Seedbead clan drew other networks their way in the fourteenth century. Mukasa's people moved into broader territory after the sixteenth century, forming clan alliances and new clans, augmenting information flows. Alliances between clans played key roles in early Ganda statecraft a century later, when different threads in Ganda sovereign knots sought to direct flows of wealth from and across the Inland Sea. Success appears in the respect and attention paid to Wannèma and Mukasa by Ganda royals from the eighteenth century onward. These centuries of groupwork with people of the Inland Sea began with Nakangu's arrival. She opened Bubembe and its information flows to other clans.

Groupwork did not emerge automatically out of island networks, as royals sought to control them. Access to information and fertility, provided to supplicants by shrine officials at Bubembe, gave the moral core of their relationships a beating heart. Success attracted the interests and machinations of mainland statecrafts. The Buganda state worked on Bubembe's moral communities to fashion new interests, oriented to boundaries and invested in difference, and aimed at new forms of material wealth, like the cloth made from the bark of *Ficus* trees. As chapter 3 explores, shrine officials responded by arguing for the shrine's unique efficacies, drawing lines between it, other shrines, and state interests. When a Buganda state took interest in the islands, Mukasa's people delivered much more than helping women and men fish in and travel over the Inland Sea.

CHAPTER THREE

Mukasa's Wealth

Belonging and Information, 1500s and 1600s

Ekyuma kitya omuwesi. "The iron fears the smith." Knowledge is power.
—F. Rowling, *A Guide to Uganda Prose Composition,* 113

Twagenda ne mandwa kulya enyama ge madu agata abalubale. "We went with the medium to eat meat, but that craving got the people of the lùbaalè killed."
—Apollo Kagwa, *Bakabaka Bebuganda,* 69, 70

ORIENTING GROUPS TO *cwezi* and *lùbaalè* figures paved the way for people to build larger networks with a central place, attractive to others, and unconstrained by boundaries. From the fourteenth century, the one oriented to Mukasa first ensured success in fish work and canoe travel and, from the sixteenth century, provided well-timed rains for fields and fertility for men and women. Access to salt, fish, and iron played long-standing roles attracting people to the islands. But the historical development of a vocabulary related to making cloth from the bark of *Ficus* trees reveals a long history of engagement with bark cloth. Iron fears the smith, as the first epigraph has it, in explaining that for those who know how to do something, it is easy. So, too, does bark cloth fear the bark cloth maker. This chapter explores that sequence of accumulating skill, information, and wealth that Mukasa's supplicants sought. It also explores the moral life of the gendered practices of assembly that made Mukasa's shrine a stable place, open to newcomers.

People attracted to this mix of material, information, and belonging came from many parts of the littoral and spoke different languages. They sought children and dealt with failures to have children; they managed information about and access to economic opportunity on the mainland and littoral, available through the places and people connected to Mukasa. Eating well as clan members running the shrine, celebrating skill sets as members of gendered groups, and enjoying timely sex resonated with the attractions of information and skill. Activities at Bubembe were compositional. Choreography highlighted the discreteness of the units that made Bubembe attractive. Each one controlled a particular body of knowledge, all were required to act in rebuilding the shrine, and no representative of a single group saw everything that occurred. Therein lay compositional knowledge at work.[1]

Expanded efficacy brought Mukasa's people new scales of constituents or supplicants. Competition for access to information prompted islanders and mainlanders to develop a cultural-historical boundary between them after the sixteenth century. Island success in keeping a distance from the mainland states prompted some on the mainland to promote ideas about islanders' cultural difference. Mainlanders may have held a lower rung on the ladder of opportunity. Ganda state actors, for example, wielded a judgmental language of cultural difference aimed at erstwhile islanders.[2] Their propensity to do so reflects an unseemly jealousy, not befitting those in power. But those were flashes of anomie, not permanent beams of light shined on difference, meant to reveal different histories of different groups.

Changes in ceramics reflected the new scales of social life. By 1500, the kind of pottery called Entebbe ware, used only in littoral settlements, disappeared from the archeological record.[3] At some point after that, Buvuma emerged as a regional source for water jars, serving bowls, and pipes.[4] Entebbe ware disappeared between 1240 and 1500, when people were making lùbaalè like Mukasa, Wannèma, and Wamara from territorial spirits like Sserwanga, Semusulo, and Bumbujje. Unique pottery found only around the rim of the Inland Sea was replaced by an entirely different kind of pottery called roulette that was used in homes on islands, littoral, and the far interior. The distinctive Entebbe ware disappeared as moral communities with centers on island and littoral built ties to dryland centers. People in each location used the new, rouletted wares. Surely, the relative uniformity of the rouletted pots reflected increasingly regular crossings between Island and littoral ports and to points in the interior.

The Virtues of Boundless Moral Community

The pursuit of lateral connections to wealth comes across clearly in traditions about island shrines. The principal official at Wannèma's shrine on Bubembe held the title Ssendege. The title honored one of the grandchildren of Lule Kasiriivu, a grandchild of Kyaddondo the Seedbead clan founder figure we met in chapter 2.[5] Ssendege traveled by canoe from his birthplace in Kyaddondo, stopping at four islands before reaching Bubembe. There, Wannèma gave Ssendege responsibilities at Mukasa's shrine. The arrival of two sons

Figure 7. A lùbaalè dancer, Busoga. Dancing was indispensable to assembling with possessed mediums. Source: Photograph Album of Dr. Albert Ruskin Cook, 46, CMS/ACC 244 Z1. Credit: Church Missionary Society Archives, Cadbury Research Library, University of Birmingham.

marked Ssendege's successful networking. One of them served Mukasa by fetching the water used to wash their face.[6] The excursions and the titled responsibilities they yielded linked Mukasa's network to specific island centers. Bark cloth production made those nodes worth linking to Bubembe. Other clan histories mention the places named as stopping points in Ssendege's journey.[7] A map of all of these journeys would be a confusing nest of interweaving itineraries. They were the itineraries of mediums and interpreters—healers— cultivating lateral groupwork with historical depth at multiple locations.

Lùbaalè, other public healing groups, and other kinds of groups used metaphors of descent, marriage, dance, dining, and travel to cultivate depth for the lateral connections made concrete by assembly (figure 7). Generations of Mukasa's people repeatedly brought Bubembe to life. Such accessible metaphors provided form to thinking about the groupwork represented in Ssendege's Seedbead story; they were good media for teaching and telling about

belonging. Everyone can relate personal circumstance to the duties and hierarchies of descent and ties of parenting, or to the risks and opportunities of
mobility and alliances like marriages. At Bubembe, the men and women discussed here drew on related sources of experience—gender, sex, and eating—
to mix the value of mobility into belonging through shrine practice. These
activities gave Bubembe its charge.

Gender, eating, and sex helped constitute moral belonging because they
articulated specific arrays of virtue in domestic and public life. They echoed in
the material, sociological, and kinesthetic scenes of assembly at Bubembe.
They likely figured prominently at other lùbaalè shrines specialized in gendered aspects of fertility about which we know frustratingly little.[8] Gender,
sex, and eating shifted the stakes in and techniques of groupwork. They promoted imaginative belonging in open registers and embodied the benefits of
that belonging.

Gender

Scholarship about gender and, to a lesser extent, sexuality, in this part of East
Africa has a familiar cast. It has been shaped by state interests in controlling
women's reproductive lives, partly through developing a masculinist notion of
public honor and aspiration fostering men's careers.[9] Nakanyike B. Musisi
showed that a Ganda court makes its residents socially male. When commoners enter, they enter a socially female status, no matter the biological details of
their bodies or their place in a socially defined life cycle.[10] This gendered ideology of Ganda royalty was spatial. Virtually all of the historical sources used
here formed with that reality. Rhiannon Stephens pushed these issues into
new territory by exploring how status and wealth in Buganda separated biological sex from sociological gender, with high-status women living life in a
male-gendered register. The increased value of biological motherhood after
the seventeenth century was a consequence of the growing number of captive
women a Ganda state's violent expansions brought into the domain (see chapters 4 and 5).[11] The point lies in recognizing that gendered state ideologies, not
just missionary or colonial ideologies of gender, inflect reading about Mukasa's
people.

Recent work has grappled with HIV/AIDS, generational divides, and
culturalist arguments about sexuality to dissolve the effects of colonial and
missionary ethnocentrism on our thinking about those topics.[12] It opens categories of male and female revealing the ideologies and changing economic
practices nourishing gender roles.[13] Simply noting the fluid relations between
gender and social life doesn't go far enough. Historians need to track those
relations into the gendered chambers at the heart of debates over the virtues

animating groupwork. What can be said along these lines for Bubembe and
Mukasa's people is often frustratingly abstract and disjointed, wanting in contextual detail, floating in a sea of precolonial time. One does the best one can
to sequence the shifting contents of gendered groupwork. The first move
reveals that Mukasa has multiple genders.

Genders crossed in particular social settings. One example, from Buhaya
(see map 1) illustrates links to Mukasa (called "Mugasha" there). In that part
of the western rim of the Inland Sea, a category exists of "men who behave as
women—greeting as women do." Such a person is called *muharambwa* in
Kiziba, a Haya language.[14] The muharambwa leads women in praising Mugasha's wife, Nyakalembe, for her powers over agriculture. The muharambwa
handles risky situations and materials. They dispose of dead animals or snakes,
remove burned bodies or the ash of burned bodies after deadly house fires.[15]
Smelters dressed in a woman's skirt to foster their furnace's fertility. They acted
like the muharambwa, the elder man who wore a skirt officiating at a village
shrine oriented to Irungu (called Ddungu in Buganda).[16] Crossing genders
was necessary for safe handling of these circumstances. Gender was a social
resource amenable to reconfiguration.

Gender crossing also unfolded over the course of a life cycle, prompted by
obligations binding leaders and followers in projects of civic virtue. The
muharambwa might act like a woman—by cultivating, for example—or act as
a man—eating grasshoppers and goat meat—with women. The "leader of the
women" should be a biological man, Nyakalembe argued, but he will act like
a man and like a woman in carrying out the responsibilities of that leadership.
August Kaindoa's tale claims that Nyakalembe gave the idea, the authority, and the paraphernalia of the muharambwa to Rugomora Mahe, a Haya
king. Kaindoa's history bound gender crossing with a king's rise to power.[17]
Nyakalembe's position in Ssese-centered networks brought gender-crossing
muharambwa practice to Buhaya. The patrilineal emphasis in lùbaalè genealogies doesn't mean that only men's pursuit and conceptualization of civic virtue
gave island groupwork its beating heart. Claims about Mukasa's gender, the
gender of the mediums Mukasa could possess, and the choreography of assembly on Bubembe reveals that island moral communities constituted themselves through varieties of gender, not just one form.

Mukasa bundled many kinds of existence at Bubembe, befitting a figure with
such a range of followers and managers. Mukasa was male, female, or both.[18]
Mukasa was the medium Nakangu, a senior woman of the Lungfish clan; a meteor
hammer; and the Inland Sea. Mukasa's genders reflected a shifting, composite
being, contingent on need and setting. Before Mukasa's medium was female, a
man played the part.[19] As a meteor hammer, Mukasa emitted a masculine aura of

metallurgical labor and sexual mechanics.[20] As a metonym of the Inland Sea, Mukasa embodied the femaleness of water as amniotic fluid and of some fish work. Mukasa received the projections of people at different stages of gendered life, making Mukasa relevant to individual and collectively gendered aspiration.

The choreography of assemblies to refurbish the buildings at Bubembe conveyed additional depth to the shifting fields of gendered aspiration. The blood of sacrificed cattle pointed to descent and lineage. Cattle formed parts of the wealth transferred from a man's lineage to a woman's in the course of them being married. Patrilineality predominated in crafting the genealogies for lineages. Men manipulated the blood in a way that emphasized its flow and capture as sources for mapping abstract qualities of descent enacted with sacrifice. Using cupped hands to accept something or catching liquid in a vessel is described in Luganda as *kùlembeka*. Its prepositional inflection, *kùlembe-kera*, describes the generic action of making an offering to a lùbaalè.[21] The blood Mukasa consumed as the Inland Sea crossed the boundary between the living and the dead invoking descent and belonging.

When it did so, the blood reenacted on a grand scale a central understanding of how to grow children. The key was the timely mixing of male and female fluids. Many in the audience—those who chorused "S/he has drunk it"—understood that in that time and place, the waters of the Inland Sea were amniotic fluids.[22] A common name for the Inland Sea in Luganda and Lusoga is Nnalubaale, "mother of the lùbaalè." Ordinary supplicants attending these festivals as part of fertility quests saw this ritual as high drama. Their personal travails or successes blended with something like a liturgy. The choreography expressed a theory of fertility, braided adult gender, and the possibilities of their abundance.

These passages defy careful chronological exploration. They may only be put into a generic "precolonial" period, divided by 1700, when Ganda state actors made their presence felt in the politics of refurbishing the Bubembe shrine, entailed by their interests in the isles. Yet these snippets reveal that gender crossing and gender braiding constituted key moral and instrumental dimensions of the groupwork at Bubembe. Led by the shrine's managers and enhanced by their august visitors and ordinary supplicants and gawkers, themes of sex and eating in assemblies at Bubembe illustrate the instrumental part.

Eating

Eating and sex (maybe not in that order) fit together easily. This was certainly true at Bubembe. But the heat and fluids of sex weren't the only things mapped metaphorically by eating and drinking. The entailments of sex and the complexities of ingestion were elaborated further. Using Mukasa and the Inland Sea as raw material, shrine officials evoked a bolus of experience, inviting

Kikoma Feast 1905

Figure 8. Feast at Kikoma, 1905. A taste of assembling, though on a smaller scale than those hosted at Bubembe. Source: "Photograph Album 1894–1900," H. B. Lewin?; CMS/ACC 276 F2. Credit: Church Missionary Society Archives, Cadbury Research Library, University of Birmingham.

reflection, relaxation, and pleasure. The anxieties, relief, and pride that supplicants experienced in pursuit of fertility, combined with the pleasures and majesty of Bubembe the place, gave officials thick cords to pull in creating groups from networks of moral belonging.

People ate well at Bubembe (figure 8). Ssebandidde, the title of one of the senior officials running the shrine, may be translated as "Head of they (whom), I have eaten." The phrasing is awkward in translation. It does not mean this official ate people. It means that the official's eating enacted the power and range sought by supplicants and attendees. With Ssebandidde, one could expect to eat expansively, to master one's aspirations.

The performative eating in Bubembe's festivals also contrasted with a python eating at other shrines and with claims of what Namatimba (Mukasa's mother) ate. Namatimba ate only ripe, uncooked *gònjâ* bananas, while everyone else boiled them or baked them over hot coals and sprinkled them with salt. Sserwanga Mukasa also ate uncooked food, in this case the heart, liver, and blood of hunted animals, but only after "he had been weaned" on Bukasa Island.[23] At Bulonge, resident pythons swallowed meals of whole animals and sipped milk mixed with kaolin.[24] At Bubembe, Mukasa ate blood and organ meat, while everyone else ate butchered meat, properly cooked. The entire animals that pythons swallowed but no person ever ingested in that condition were replaced at Bubembe with flesh, organs, and blood, materials everyone ingested from time to time, in ordinary eating.

The liver and heart of animals are nutritious and tasty. They also have linguistic associations with the palette of affect that communicates human intention. People often think of the body as a container for qualities of emotion.[25] But the details they add differ.[26] In Luganda, the zone of the body linked to desire is not restricted to a single organ in the chest. *Èmmemê* refers to the area around the sternum, extending to the heart and stomach. It is often a metonym for visceral emotion, distinguished in the course of the late nineteenth and twentieth centuries, from spiritual feeling.[27] Ethnographer-lexicographers were told that hearts housed courage and malice. The heart contained the life force after the body died.[28] Livers contained corrosive feelings of spite that drove a desire for revenge. The derivation of *kìbumba*, the Ganda term for liver, points to just such a detail. It is derived from a verb, *kùbumba*, "to mold (out of clay)." Ganda speakers ceased using other, widespread terms for liver. They are the only ones in the region to call the liver "kìbumba."[29] Baked or roasted goat livers were eaten during ceremonies naming royal children and in formal marriages, where property was exchanged.[30] A common metaphor in Luganda links potting to realizing the promise of things.[31] Scheherazade Amin, Ssese's archeologist, noted the prevalence of small jars among the islands' ceramic assemblages.[32] Mukasa's liver meal evoked ongoing labors required to grow the child in a well-contained space. In this case, linking organ and affect took on the gravitas of pointing to the risks to healthy children of envy, hidden in the livers of other people. Eating with Mukasa went beyond symbolic arcana. It staged moral arguments about the necessity of generosity and the risks of exclusion that watchers understood very well.

At Bubembe, people addressed those uncertainties. Under the gaze of officials, men of the same clan ate the beef Semagumba distributed during refurbishment. The animals whose blood Mukasa-the-Inland-Sea drank became food for people.[33] Sharing the flesh of sacrificed animals as separate groups of clanmates expressed their solidarities before an audience. Groups of female road clearers worked separately. Both kinds of assembly sustained and promoted Mukasa's efficacies.

Grandees and ordinary people rubbed shoulders at Bubembe, with consequences. The gifts of food left in Mukasa's house, near the meteor hammer, were ordinary things. Mukasa's priests ate ordinary things—a joint of beef, a rich liver, salty blood. But eating in public, on behalf of the others assembled, exposed the eaters to the ambivalent power of the past. Likewise, cattle blood flowing into the Inland Sea evoked ancestors and children and mixed anticipation with worry. Both kinds of eating connected the past and the future with the feelings that audience members brought. Whether solemn or pleasurable, the inner worlds these occasions evoked might limit the uncertainties of belonging. The creative skills, historical depth, and range in a clan's "network of knowledge," celebrated in a disciplined, public assembly of discrete social parts, made belonging worthwhile.

One tale from Bird clan histories emphasized the gendered, moral stakes in play when unseasoned youths ate at such public assemblies. At Njiwe's feast, the Bird clan founder figure Kakoto Mbaziira's sons and their friends mixed up bowls of beer and ox-blood pudding. They failed to properly clean the wooden bowls used for drinking each liquid. In the story, Kakoto Mbaziira used plant medicines to convert a lake without canoes into the flowing river of Nakinyanja that he could cross, a capacity the young men lacked.[34] The unmarked gender of the beer may be taken as blended male and female, because men likely made the beer from grain or bananas women had grown.[35] In Buganda (at least), the banana used to make such beer was gendered male.[36] The blood pudding carried strong associations of both genders. Oxen often formed part of the wealth transferred between marrying families, publicizing what were semi-private, drawn-out negotiations. The story warns about the limited capacities of young men to meet the moral and political rigors of correctly pursuing male fertility. In failing to clean the vessels that held the liquids, they failed to separate the conviviality of beer drinking from the access to future children promised by the ox blood. As youths, they lacked the specialized knowledge—how to make an uncrossable lake into a fordable river—that men needed in pursuing fertility. The tale of Njiwe's feast argued about moral community by linking oxen, facility on the Inland Sea, festive culture, and adult male self-control in Bird clan belonging. Inland Sea water and ox blood could blend to good effect because senior men and women of standing had correctly prepared to mix them. But blending beer with bovine blood reflected a moral laxness threatening the product of fertility's equation. Discipline made the assembly of groupwork productive.

Sex

Sex oriented the qualities of gender and the fuels of eating to the beneficial ends of life. The sex in groupwork had limits, if its great powers were to be good. The good powers of fertility took the form of adult children. Their presence suggested an adult's successful quest for self-mastery. An adult morally belonged in the group formed by the self-mastery they practiced through raising children. Semagumba judged Mukasa's acceptance of the animals offered for sacrifice. Animals who lowed or dropped dung during this moment were deemed unacceptable, and Semagumba often concluded that the cause was the failure of shrine personnel to control their sexual activity. Self-mastery created the efficacy of offerings, reflecting the ambivalent core of sex's power. It was efficacious if timed correctly, dangerous if not.[37] Sex echoed in Bubembe's festive life, suggesting that the place (as much as the timing) could shape its effects.

Sex fostered maturation, not just conception, making biology moral.[38] The head of a canoe-using fishing group explained to Kagwa the necessity of going home to one's wife to have timely sex—after a second, successful fishing expedition but not before. Kagwa wrote: "This task is called rearing the net."[39] The quote's transitive causative verb, *kùkuzà*, states that people have to help things mature—in this case, a fishing net—to be productive. Natural maturation is a fact of living things, but people must help objects mature, a theory of agency expressed in the verb *kùkulà*. That word expresses a natural progression of things to maturity. Hair, including the form it takes in horns, "grows" in this way, taking on additional qualities of individuated moreness over time as signs of aging. Fires and growth are linked in a proverb sung by women after burying their children's umbilical cord during the ceremony in which they name the children. "The rotten branch, it makes the fire run wild," which Kagwa rephrased as "The woman who bears a child's health is like the fire, and its mother is the little rotten branch." The mother's good behavior during pregnancy made the fire of healthy childhood run rampant.[40] Fertility quests and self-mastery echoed in the minds of those who chorused "S/he has drunk it," when the flow of ox blood reached the Inland Sea.

Human fertility was a central concern of the shrine and its rhythms of assembly. Fertility was a key aim of adult self-mastery and of the moral community that mastery formed. The phases of the moon provided Bubembe with a lively rhythm, aimed partly at winning children from the vagaries of life. The phases timed large gatherings of women and men. This reflected a theory of fertility aimed at tracking menstruation to increase the chances of pregnancy through well-timed sex. People linked lunar cycling with fertility. We can see this in the claims that sexual activity between official shrine couples was important to new moon celebrations and in the refurbishing festivals at Bubembe.

Kagwa and Roscoe wrote about sexual activity at such gatherings in coded language. Roscoe mentions that after the close of refurbishment, senior officials and "all the people who had taken part in the work" could "go to their homes."[41] The phrasing points to the resumption of sexual activity after the appearance of the new moon in the week after the twenty-day period of gathering and labor. Roscoe also mentions that Mukasa's female medium "might have as many slave-girls as she wished from those attached to the temple."[42] Shrine officials were susceptible to pressures on their responsibilities to shelter the young women in their care in keeping with the argument that they represented gifts of thanks to Mukasa from grateful (and wealthy) supplicants.[43] The young women given by island grandees and royals constituted a pool of potential unions and connections to the communities delivered from childlessness. Mukasa's female medium controlled their work, including "distributing them amongst the chiefs who were on good terms with her."[44] This points to fertility and vulnerability, matters of great concern to ordinary supporters of Mukasa. Sexual symbolism and activity are common features of songs sung during initiation into healing groups elsewhere in the region.[45] Even if it is dangerous under these limitations of information to say more on this topic, it is difficult to imagine Mukasa's shrine, a place engaged in mediumship, bereft of moon-influenced sex or spoken allusion to it.

People connected lunar cycles and fertility through mediumistic sanctioning of sexual activity among those at the shrine.[46] In Luganda, "to menstruate" is expressed by the verbal phrase *kùtuùlawô*, which means "be at ease, peace" or, "to relax, chill out." Another term is *kùsuùlumba*, "to menstruate" or "be a loafer, a homebody." Menstruation was supposed to be downtime for women. The idiom was "Wamirembe," a term sharing a semantic field with the "reigns" of royals but drawing most basically on the notion of an interval.[47] Lunar phases were named with other terms. Lunar waxing and waning conditioned far more kinds of activity than those entailed by the rhythms of a mature, healthy female body. The idea of an interval drew these fields together.

A period of sexual activity was opened by turning a large meteor hammer, kept in Mukasa's temple, to face east and then west, according to the phases of the moon.[48] Literally a place of potentially abundant fertility, Mukasa's shrine hosted practices designed to deliver on that promise.[49] They drew on female experience of their menstrual cycles in terms of the growth and decline of the moon. The language describing them suggests that people linked lunar cycles and fertility, perhaps hoping that fertility's uncertainties could be limited by tying them to the reliable phases of the moon. The word and phrase used in Luganda to describe the days of reduced work that followed a new moon contains an adjective signifying a delicate fragility.[50] One response to those uncertainties may have concentrated sexual activity around a particular moment in the lunar cycle, all across the land.

The idea of menstrual synchrony, hinted at in the practice of releasing everyone involved in refurbishment to "go home" sometime in the fourth week of their assembly, links fertility quests and shrine activity at Bubembe. But, the science of menstrual synchrony is equivocal. Some scholars find the evidence for it compelling, whereas others dispute it.[51] Be that as it may, the fact that menstrual cycles and lunar cycles are both about twenty-nine and one-half days long has prompted people the world over to think about menstrual timing and the moon's phases. That fit makes imposing circumstances of assembly an irresistible way to take advantage of causality. By keeping the temporal doubling in step, with rest and good food, differences between individual menstrual patterns might be reduced.[52] People understood that menstruation was a precondition for biological reproduction. The rhythmic assembly that occurred every twenty days might have had this practical orientation toward fertility, even though pregnancies were not guaranteed. Monthly menstruation may not have been the norm for lactating mothers and women on low-fat diets whose daily labor consumed many calories. It may have been so for younger women, not yet biological mothers, who rested and ate foods higher in fat, perhaps at celebratory assemblies like those at Bubembe.[53] Fertility quests clearly attracted supplicants of all statures to refurbishing events at Mukasa's shrine.

Naming Children

Bubembe's moral community echoed in other dramas in making groups on the Inland Sea littoral. Senior women, working in the public spaces of naming ceremonies, complemented the work at Bubembe.[54] The families of the children brought into a clan had their moral behavior and economic worth validated by emerging out of a local lineage. Success was often marked by a feast "prepared for the wives who had passed the test for their children." Their mothers-in-law, sitting across from them at the feast, held "a piece of cooked fish in her right hand and a piece of cooked plantain in her left." As she repeated the names of her son's male ancestors in the clan, her food-bearing hands rose up to her daughter-in-law's mouth, "into which she put first the boiled plantain and then the fish." The feeding emphasized the lateral connections forged by women in-laws. It included the fish "as a charm to effect rapid child-bearing, just as the fish swarm by thousands in the shallow waters of the lake."[55] Bubembe and local naming ceremonies were linked through Ggugu, a senior manager at Bubembe. That word-name also means the kind of salt made at home from reeds that grew in the shallows of the Inland Sea. That kind of salt featured prominently in the foods used in local naming ceremonies.[56] At Bubembe, Ggugu wore a distinctive hairstyle, called *èjjòbâ*, a cut reserved for fathers of twins, the embodiment of reproductive abundance.[57] Descriptions of naming ceremonies reveal that women used the gendered behavior of fish to elaborate the moral belonging in clans and lineages.

The fish in question were ènkejje, the abundant sprat discussed in chapter 1. As Jennifer Johnson has argued, their behavior informed thinking about the benefits of belonging to lineages and clans.[58] An ènkejje mother protects her young by taking them into her mouth when a threat appears and releasing them after it passes. The young she protects this way may include other kinds of fish.[59] Women fishing the shallow, inshore waters, where many kinds of ènkejje live and breed, could easily observe their behavior.[60] Many ceremonies, including those for naming twins or for "hatching out" children from a lineage and a clan, concluded with all the participants sharing a stew whose ingredients included the salt called èggùgù and the sprat called ènkejje enkasa.[61]

The ènkejje mother literally takes fry into her mouth, ejects them, and takes them back, as circumstance requires. The ènkejje mother's actions—and people eating ènkejje in naming ceremonies—reflects a theory of belonging in which one does not enter a group, one is hatched out of an existing group. In other words, groupness exists before individuation. But the ènkejje mother's mouth-brooding actions mix fry she bore with those from other mothers, belonging to other species. This allows people to distinguish "real" relatives, from the strangers, clients, and so forth, in any lineage or clan. The literal meanings possible with òkwàlula, summed up in "to hatch," express the core idea of groupwork producing individuals. Such practices orient people to categories like èssiga (hearth stone; large lineage) or èkìkâ (big homestead; clan) as the wholes out of which a group's individuals emerged.[62] This kind of hegemonic thinking shifts our attention from abstract principles of groupness, such as lineage or clan and so forth, to principles of individuation, such as life stage and the social production of gender. The time and place of actions touching on those enduring, abstract questions of belonging mattered a great deal in managing tensions between them. By glossing them with virtue or vice, gendered discipline in social behavior (including the intimacies of procreative sex) defined belonging.

Toby Kizito, a Catholic lay reader and prolific author, claimed that a close bond existed between Ssese and Muwawa, the name of the land that Kintu helped convert into Buganda. The bond was marked by the exchange of agricultural skills, manufactured goods (hides), and practices of social hierarchy and reproduction. It was from the clans of Ssese, Kizito explained, that people on the mainland learned to hatch their children, okwàlula abâna, using ènkejje ensese, the sprat found only around Ssese's rocky shores.[63] At the end of the nineteenth century, these "children" might have been rather up in years. "The naming of most children," wrote an anonymous contributor to a publication of the Church Missionary Society, "was curiously enough often left till they were quite young men and women."[64] The preceding decades of upheaval had perhaps made such ceremonies difficult to organize, leaving a pool of youths in urgent need of hatching out into adulthoods.

This ceremony tests and confirms a child's belonging to a particular family group and to a particular clan.[65] The matter of paternity, of the responsibilities to different communities born by a new mother, and of the character of a child, lie at the heart of this event. As will all issues of comportment and respect, those on display here are redolent of past and future actions expressing the moral character of a particular group, lineage, or clan. Commentators freely admit that character can remain an open question, regardless of what happened at this event.[66] A particular moment of drama came when the mother-in-law placed the child's umbilical cord (some clans first covered it in butter) on the surface of a waterproof wicker basket of milk, beer, and water. Whether a cord sank or floated when hatching the children was less important than a mother's and father's prior assessment of the risks their behavior represented in this public moment. Different clans used additional tests, cross-examinations, and so forth. Often, a later illness or bad behavior by the child in question raised doubts about parental fidelity. Women managed the anxieties about descent in this event.

Naming ceremonies differed in littoral settings. In Buganda, the details varied by clan.[67] In southern Busoga, only clans invested in fish work used the sprats.[68] In Busoga, *okúfulumyá omwáaná* is a fair translation of the naming ceremonies glossed by "to hatch the children."[69] On Ukerewe, in the southeast corner of the Inland Sea, *kuruka izima*, "to reach or jump over to maturity," named the equivalent practice there.[70] Senior women, made mobile by virilocal marriage (where the married woman goes to live at her husband's home), probably lent a family resemblance to these practices. The point lies in grasping women's centrality in the practice. A wife belonged to her natal clan and had intimate doings with her husband's clan. Mothers and grandmothers caught, processed, and served ènkejje as food.[71] The behavior of ènkejje—and the different parts of the Inland Sea in which they spent their lives—provided residents rich material for exploring gendered and aged dimensions of belonging.[72]

The distribution of these naming events and the importance of sprats in them crosses the Southern Ganda and Soga speech communities. It is tempting to conclude that these were practices passed down from North Nyanza times, set aside by Gwere- and Shana-speaking societies as they moved away from the littoral. That would put their development sometime between the thirteenth and the sixteenth centuries. But the variety of these names warns against inferring too much about their history from distributional evidence alone. A durable need to improvise locally in the public rituals of belonging that knit residential groups into a broader social fabric better explains the variety of names for doing so. The distinctive forms of reproducing clans— and of worrying about descent—by "hatching out" children and taking meals in which ènkejje or *enfúlú* and èggùgù salt were indispensable ingredients emerged with reliable access to these tiny fish and grass. This was littoral work.

Perhaps "hatching the children," practiced in settings dotting the Ganda, Soga, and Ssese littorals, represented a local echo of the gendered fertility in play on a grander scale at Bubembe. After all, many of the women at the heart of those naming rituals had probably visited Bubembe at some time in their lives. Without drawing bright lines connecting the intimacies of hatching the children with the pomp and circumstance of new moon ceremonies or rebuilding events on Bubembe, we can still think of them occupying the same conceptual space of fertility in people's minds. Canoes plying the Inland Sea brought news and pots, bark cloth, bananas, grain, and stacks of sun-dried sprats to mainland ports. Mainland news returned to the islands with iron goods, fine salt, cattle, and women slaves and "maids." Clan representatives working at the principal fertility shrine would relish hearing stories about the new children hatched out of their group. Mukasa's home represented the hope and the reality that life on the littoral was life in two zones. One formed where water met air, the other where island and littoral met mainland. By inhabiting the edges, men and women gained gendered prosperity and fertility.

Regional Economies, Information, and Groupwork

From the fourteenth century, Bubembe grew along with expanding regional trade links and technical specializations. These contexts lent its moral community a material current. In the sixteenth century, less rain, experiences of plague, experiments with select crops originating in the Americas, a sartorial revolution, and the hungry eye of mainland statecrafts converged. In that context, Mukasa's people expanded the range of efficacy Mukasa provided beyond safe canoe travel and abundant fish work. It came to include providing well-timed rains for fields and fertility for men and women. In the earlier contexts of trade in crops and medicines, fish work, and canoe travel, shrine managers fostered a moral community that payed scant attention to boundaries and difference. In the acute contexts of climate change, epidemic disease, agrarian change, and a firmer royal center, that openness shifted to reveal the edges of belonging.

From 1550 to 1700, it rained less on the mainland west and northwest of the Inland Sea.[73] The dry phase probably improved the exchange values joining landward farmers with littoral and island fish workers. In this period, food (including salt), iron bloom and finished hoe blades, pottery, female slaves and "maids" moved through island ports. Even cattle could be moved in a sewn canoe, and with them came balls of high-quality butter in standard sizes wrapped with banana leaf.[74] At the same time, plague may have begun to influence demographic process. By the eighteenth century, a degree of commodification may have emerged, as people used the dry season to produce for markets.[75] Smoked fish, like ènkejje, grew more desirable on the nearshore mainland, pulling the òlùkandà unit inland (chapter 1). Margins grew for canoe-borne traders and transporters who could move foodstuffs around the perimeter of the Inland Sea, responding to local shortages or surpluses. Prestige goods and illness moved along the same circuits.[76]

Island and littoral communities moving these goods required safe passage over the Inland Sea. But the new dry phase rearranged productive banana gardens and ènkejje and other fishing grounds in the mid-sixteenth century. Those effects of climate change enhanced the value of canoes for delivering surplus to places in need. They nourished new economic opportunities—illustrated by American crops and bark cloth—and new opportunities to collect information on grains, cattle, salt, and fishing grounds. Mukasa comes into play here.

The information moving with people in canoes between ports certainly included word of prosperous banana plantations. Investing labor in landed property planted with the tree, which could produce valuable calories for decades and even centuries, had emerged by the twelfth century. Scholars have noted the discontinuous availability of the perfect mix of soils and rainfall regimes favoring banana gardens in the northwestern quadrant of the Inland Sea.[77] Knowing where those different locations were and which banana cultivars would thrive where was work in progress as climatic and other conditions favoring them shifted. People could move banana tree suckers by canoe, but adaptation and innovation were local processes.[78] By moving around in sewn canoes people enjoyed access to more of such information simply by visiting more places than they could manage on foot. Assembling at shrines like Bubembe, people could share (or withhold) such information.

A period of agricultural improvisation began in the thirteenth century, just after the Proto–North Nyanza speech community dissolved. Similar terms for bananas, based on their use (including their ability to survive in drier environments), occur most numerously in the languages that formed as North Nyanza dissolved, near the Inland Sea. Experimentation has continued ever since, although the ingenuity of banana farmers is now sorely tested by the destructions of the banana blight afflicting the trees around the world.[79] Rhiannon

Stephens produced evidence for ongoing improvisations with the banana plant well after the twelfth century. The distribution of the new words demonstrates that people shared their knowledge. Proto–South Kyoga innovated only a single new term, as its speakers settled among others living east of the Nile.[80] By 1900, the Ganda language possessed more than eighty names for bananas, some of which thrived in very particular ecological zones, at the littoral and just behind.[81] It is not possible to order their entry into the language, but the diversity reflects active experimentation through cloning and shows that information exchange underlaid the development of named cultivars since the twelfth century.

Eating well begins with staples but requires sauce.[82] Good sauce needs salt. The specialized production of high-quality salt began at Kibiro, on Lake Mwitanzige, in northwestern Bunyoro (map 1), early in the second millennium.[83] Kibiro's salt was free of the ashy qualities of salt made by filtering water through the ash of burned grasses or plantain peelings. Fancy salts marked status differences. Commoners ate gifts of food seasoned with òmunnyù màwewùle or òmunnyù nsero. A pregnant woman ostentatiously avoided eating that second kind of salt.[84] Ordinary people made their own salt in the manner described already, a fact alluded to in the title Ggugu, one of Mukasa's three senior officials at Bubembe. Èggùgù is a swamp sedge that can be used to make this ordinary salt.[85] People clearly valued that kind of salt, in part for its associations with littoral place. They used it in the naming ceremonies just discussed. They also ate the gwà bìswazzi, the leavings of ashy salt of such poor quality that it was "insufficient to taste."[86] Salt fed a consuming body in many ways, and canoes provided access to fancy salts.

The phase of greatest growth at Kibiro occurred around the turn of the sixteenth century. It was marked by the appearance of smoking pipes made of clay.[87] While people likely used bowl-and-socket pipes before 1600 to smoke cannabis, increases in the number of pipes is commonly linked with tobacco smoking.[88] The "elbow-bend" design of these pipes reminded the archaeologist Graham Connah of links between tobacco smoking and similar pipes in West Africa. Tobacco had reached Kibiro, likely from links to Africa's Western Sudan.[89] Plants with origins in the Americas had clearly made their presence felt in this region. But they did not travel in a package and were unlikely to have been labeled as "American" by their consumers at Kibiro.[90] Kibiro's smoking pipes point to the fact that the wealthy salt-makers on the shores of Mwitanzige attracted information along lines running in many directions.

Kibiro lay at the northern end of the cattle-keeping zones revolving around Ntusi and Munsa. Katwe, another source of gourmet salt, was at the southern end (map 1). At the same time that Kibiro's salt gardens yielded their gourmet

product, metallurgists worked north of Ntusi. They improvised new techniques, drawing on local materials to develop a craft with deeper roots in the
lands of Buhaya and Mwenge, to meet the growing needs of herders, farmers,
and hunters.[91] The purchasing power provided by ivory, iron, cattle, grains,
and salt pulled some glass beads and cowries from the Indian Ocean coast and
copper from Katanga into settlements in Ssese and points west, where the
metallurgists worked (map 1). Bubembe's growth coincided with increased
scale of exchange linking specialized zones of production and skill across a
wide region.

Opportunities for additional artisanal labor may have expanded with the
onset of pronounced uncertainty over the timing of short rains in the region,
from the twelfth century, discussed in the first chapter. Dry seasons were periods of economic activity, especially where grains were important.[92] Free from
most farmwork, people used the dry season to make the sewn canoes to fish
and transport bark cloth, salt, cattle products, cattle, and plague.[93] In the
1930s, historian John Ggomotoka reported that men and women worked the
fields together on Bugaya Island in the Buvuma group.[94] This suggests
intensified, nongendered farm labor had lengthened the agricultural year and,
correspondingly, put a premium on the lower opportunity costs of dry season
labor. Potting on Buvuma and transporting the pots by canoe to mainland
markets were easiest in the dry season. The primacy of Buvuma as a source of
pots across the littoral may have contributed to the demise of Entebbe wares
in the fifteenth century.

Stories about millet, medicine, and the islands, explored in chapter 2,
revealed that trade and information exchange helped transform a territorial
spirit into a portable one. Stocks of seed, banana cuttings, salts, pottery, met-
alwork, and so on all joined Ssese and the mainland. The links converted a
network in which various crops went to Ssese in return for fish into a scaled-
up clearing house for information flow, with Bubembe as a central place. A
sartorial change from tanned hides to bark cloth swept the region from the
sixteenth century, adding fashion to the value of information. The history of
bark cloth exemplifies the equation that made the islands' network a magnet
for others.

New Clothes

Desire for bark cloth could multiply information velocities, especially about
fashion. The fig trees that produce the cloth are common near the littoral.
Like bananas, they grow easily from cuttings. People could move them around
an area on foot and by canoe.[95] As dressing with them grew popular in the
sixteenth century, people's desire for the different qualities and colors that a

particular variety yielded—or the aromas a particular style of fumigation gave the cloths—drew them around the region.

The Ficus trees that give bark cloth begin life as forest epiphytes, "becoming self-supporting after the death of their host, whose end is usually hastened by their strangulating embraces." They have been naturalized in plantain gardens and as living fences, "growing as an independent tree (raised from stakes)."[96] A tree can withstand being stripped of its bark some forty times, after three or four years.[97] In the nineteenth century, many species yielding cloths clustered on the Buddu and Mawokota littoral, inland along the Katonga and Lake Wamara corridors, in Ggomba, and in the Ssese Islands (map 2).[98] As people replaced the furry skins of hunted and domestic animals on their beds and bodies with sheets of bark cloth, the value of knowing where particular species thrived and what qualities of cloth they yielded grew.[99] This industry competed with tanners, whose products, if properly dressed, lasted longer and kept a person cleaner. Bark cloth drove a sartorial transformation.[100]

As Richard Reid and Emin Pasha noted, littoral centers of creativity in Buddu and Ssese attracted the attention of royals as they developed a culture of display, dress, extraction, and paternalistic shows of generosity.[101] Ganda royals promoted bark cloth in the late eighteenth century, carrying on a practice of using the material from the long sixteenth century. This implied an even earlier date for the development of the technology and style.[102] Language evidence confirms this inference.

At least two words for a kind of fig tree were arguably part of the lexicon of Proto–Great Lakes Bantu at least twenty centuries ago (RN 26.1). Words for production, the generic tree, the varieties of trees harvested, and the varieties of bark cloth they produced—sorted by weights, softness, color, and design—are densest and most specific in Luganda, Lusoga, Lunyoro, and Ruhaya.[103] People had used fig trees as sources of shade and fiber for rope centuries before making cloth from the bark.

Evidence for early bark cloth production clusters in Proto-Rutara, spoken around the turn of the first millennium CE. That vocabulary had a verb for "to beat out bark cloth," and a noun for "bark cloth" and "bark cloth tree" (RN 27–29) After Rutaran diverged into Northern and Southern groups (map 4) between the thirteenth and sixteenth centuries, people using those languages added to this tiny set of terms. The same sequence occurred a little earlier in Proto–North Nyanza. This grounds the claim that bark cloth took off as sartorial fashion in the region during the sixteenth century, as Rutara's and North Nyanza's last subgroups formed.

Some words differed from the Rutaran forms and concentrated in Ganda and Soga vocabularies. Particular species of Ficus, kinds of cloth, and weights of mallet used to finish the cloth were named as part of an explosion of terms related to the industry (RN 30–32). Ganda, Soga, and some Rutaran languages along the Inland Sea use a single word-stem to mean bark cloth and bark cloth tree. Nkore, Kiga, and Gungu (and Haya and Ziba) use a different, older term (RN 29). Its sound correspondences support reconstructing it to Proto-Rutara. This suggests a slightly greater time depth for bark cloth making in that speech community. It also suggests that the skill sets and fashion preferences spread around the western and southern rims of the Inland Sea as part of the dissolution of Rutara into its three main branches between the twelfth and the sixteenth centuries. The distributions of terms for bark cloth or bark cloth tree overlap between Buddu and southern Buhaya, a zone where artisans worked and trade occurred. The basic idea of bark cloth (RN 28) occurs around the Inland Sea rim, from Musoma to the Mpologoma River.

In each subregion where Ficus thrived, people worked up their own names for source trees, cloth types, and production, likely in the context of exporting and consuming their products. Specialized words clustered in the last subgroups to dissolve during the long sixteenth century or in the single languages that formed as those last subgroups dissolved into today's language map. People and fig trees have a long history together, but using them to make clothing is fairly recent and developed in distinct, intercommunicating zones of expertise not confined by differences in language. Connections are reflected in bundles of terms for technical work—and the botanical knowledge it presupposed—either clustering or displaying block distributions, without detectable sound changes.

The trees and finished product spread in Bunyoro, Nkore, and Bulemeezi by trade and imitation. The generic term for bark cloth (but not always for the bark cloth tree), just mentioned occurs well around the rim of the Inland Sea. This reflects a long-distance trade in finished cloth not later than the early nineteenth century, when Ssese canoes had established regular routes of travel to ports on the Inland Sea's southern littoral.[104] A generic term, *musara* (RN 32.1) for the finer cloth from a tree's first stripping, has a broad distribution with a notable gap between the Mpologoma River and Musoma that defines a separate zone of canoe-borne trade in the eastern half of the Inland Sea. The distributions of other names for kinds of bark cloth reveal their own zones of circulation (RN 32.1–32.5).

Like the distributions of banana and fish terms, the distribution of bark cloth terms hints at broad lateral reach, implying a premium on gaining information about the material that could have attracted persons to Bubembe's assemblies. Bark cloth was probably first produced on a small scale but became a domain of artisanal skill responsive to consumer demand for cloths of different colors, from white through every shade of russet red to black, including painted and stenciled cloths favored by the wealthy and royal.[105] Some cloths were dyed with silts and juices and fumigated with the sweet-smelling smoke of the *Albizzia* tree. Desirable cloths came from trees that thrived in different ecological zones, and anyone could travel with cuttings from new trees or try new manufacturing techniques. Makers may have protected their skill and knowledge from copiers to limit supply and enhance their wealth and standing.

When clan and dynastic histories claim that Otter or Seedbead, or other founder figures, controlled knowledge and skill related to bark cloth, they compress chronology in making the point. Otter and Seedbead clans are among the older clans to have formed, before the Kintu or Kimera figures rose to prominence.[106] Seedbeads have long-standing ties to Mukasa's shrine on Bubembe. But specialized bark cloth production worth celebrating in a clan or dynastic history has a shallower chronology than clanship, Kintu, or Kimera. The varieties of cloth, coloring and perfuming it, and the consumer culture that variety implies arguably had its beginnings much later, in the sixteenth century. Basic production and the initial circulation of finished bark cloth has a deeper past.

Comparing different sources of evidence in this way reveals an unsurprising chronological sleight of hand in the traditions. The importance of making and trading for bark cloth had distinctive regional histories, reflected in the unique terms used in each region. Canoes and islanders connected those regions. Seedbead or Otter people understood and ran bark cloth production, putting a stamp on a fashion revolution. Their work marked standing in a regional cosmopolitanism that could blend local and lateral connections with a color code. White cloths could be local, but special reds and blacks were from Kyaddondo, Buddu, or Busoga (figure 9). Fashion changed. In 1862, everyone in the capital dressed so smartly, Speke "could not discern the big from the small." In the 1870s, white cloth was reserved for courtiers.[107] By the 1930s, bark cloth was ubiquitous in mainland Buganda. Chiefs had to provide followers there with access to the material.[108]

Roads radiating from Mukasa's shrine to seven different ports mapped the routes by which information, people, and material wealth moved, including bark cloth. These routes connected people with sources for gendered forms of the social payments (e.g., hoes and cattle) required to produce a publicly recognized fertility embodied by children. Island assembly and naming ceremonies provided settings for weighing these moral terms of belonging. As Ganda statecraft nosed into those debates, just as plague spread, collective well-being fluctuated in new ways. Belonging with Mukasa gained an edge.

CHEOKWERI   KISOKO   SEWAYA
(from Bugaya)   (from Buziri)   (from Buvuma Proper)
(Showing manner of wearing bark-cloth robes)

Figure 9. Bark cloth style. These are "red" robes, pointing to Buvuma and Busoga styles. Note distinctive forms of tying the cloth. Source: John Cunningham, *Uganda and Its Peoples* (London: Hutchinson, 1905), 139.

The edge was expressed by distinguishing dry land (*olukalu*) from home on the water (*obunnyanja*). Late in the seventeenth century, at the close of the dry pulse that had opened in 1550, Ganda royals took strategic interest in Ssese. Perhaps at that time, the differences in the scale of mainland groupwork—slower, limited by bottlenecks—compared with the more open, quicker ones formed primarily with the Inland Sea, took on some of the cultural specificity the twinned terms could sum up. Kagwa and others report that when refurbishing the Bubembe shrine, gifts were given in sets of eighteen, double the usual number of nine. Mainland Ganda royals contributed this number in each of several categories: women, servants or slaves, cattle, and bark cloths.[109] The doubling paid respect to the two distinct centers of power, authority, and standing. One was on the mainland, wherever the ruling threads in a Ganda sovereign knot had their capital, and the other was in Ssese. The doubling might also be read as an attempt by mainland sovereign knots to perform a self-conscious superiority through ostentatious generosity. If so, that did not disrupt Ssese independence. Many titled figures from Ssese enjoyed exceptions from royal violence and displays of decorum, fitting marks of their standing as independent nodes of wealth, engaging with royals on their own terms. At the royal capital, these titled figures could not be assaulted, and they could stand in the presence of royals. Giving, excepting some from sovereign violence, and sovereigns expecting respect drew boundaries and expressed difference between mainland and island worlds. Perhaps primarily in the minds of those in a Ganda state, they constituted the two worlds.

The invention of words for the two categories defies precise dating. They were in play once mainland states formed, in the sixteenth century. Group-workers, at places like Bubembe, drew on ideas of descent, laterality, and gendered practices of eating, sex, and naming children in making central places with many clans. Concrete belonging and mobility, embodied by Bubembe's rhythmic assemblies and the behavior they modeled, were already moral forces when Ganda statecraft took interest.

Royals and Rats

Dynastic tradition compiled by Kagwa contains a thread of conflict between Mukasa's people and a sitting *kabaka*, Kyabaggu (r. 1780s). They disagreed over the civic virtue of some of Buganda's expansionist rulers. This chapter's second epigraph sums up the fractured state of relations of hospitality, respect, and personal ambition between royals and important shrines (like Mukasa's) in the eighteenth century. Kyabaggu was sick and needed Mukasa's healing. The islanders healed Kyabaggu, but the king received their healing rudely. Kyabaggu killed a lot of cattle in thanks for being healed. But he refused to give any of the cooked beef to his guests from the islands. They called him out for that meanness, as the epigraph makes plain. Embarrassed by the criticism, Kyabaggu executed the visiting healers from Ssese, then sent an expedition against Mukasa's shrine. Nanzigu, a titled royal wife and probably a woman of the Buffalo clan, led the expedition.[110] She and her soldiers killed Ggugu and plundered the islands to revenge the perceived insolence of criticism from Ssese. Resistance followed.

A plague of rats visited Kyabaggu's capital, killing people there, including "numbers of the King's wives," despite coordinated efforts to remove the pests.[111] The continued harm the creatures visited on residents perplexed Kyabaggu. He asked more questions. A "certain man" claimed that the rats were Mukasa's retribution for Nanzigu's war against the islanders. In his view, Mukasa "spoke from the sky" at a location in Vuuma belonging to Kinyoro (map 3), saying "I caused the epidemic because, by killing my people, the king made war upon me."[112] Kinyoro or, "the big Nyoro person," was the title of the second chief in the Monkey clan.[113] Mentioning the name brought a network oriented to Bunyoro into the story of Kyabaggu's rat plague. As we saw in chapter 2, Monkey clan networks centered on Ssingo, where dense banana plantations gave way to opener grasslands in the north, attractive to cattle. Whether they lived in Ssese or Ssingo, Mukasa's people found royal behavior unworthy of their support.

In response Kyabaggu called a council with "all the chiefs," in the course of which he chose peace after hearing Mukasa's people's criticism of royal selfishness. Kyabaggu instructed the Mukwenda, the titled *ssaza* chief of Ssingo, "to go and build Mukasa's shrine."[114] He did so with the assistance of Makamba, a chief at Buddo Hill, and the Ssaabaganzi, Kyabaggu's maternal uncle, of the Sheep clan. They refurbished Bubembe. Kyabaggu gave valuables to the shrine, including a daughter, Nakayiza. She may well have become a medium of Mukasa and a source of intelligence for her parents.[115] The rats no longer harassed and killed people in the royal capital as a consequence of royals showing Mukasa's people the respect warranted by their standing as a wealthy center supported by far-flung networks of followers. After all, that standing delivered health to Kyabaggu's sovereign knot through Sheep clan networks based at the littoral and Monkey and Yam networks in Ssingo, where cattle pastures interwove with banana plantations.

Scholars frame this vignette as an example of tensions between political and religious authority in a time of Buganda military conflict with Bunyoro and Busoga.[116] There is obvious appeal in reminding Kyabaggu's people that Mukasa's also wielded political authority, a reassuring restatement of the contingent character of a leader's following. Yet the story is steeped in pique. A senior royal woman plays an aggressive precipitating role in refurbishing Mukasa's shrine. But persistent killer rats suggest a plague event immune to existing techniques of control (hunting the rats) or on moving and rebuilding the capital.[117] Kyabaggu's court needed Mukasa's healing.

The aggressive role of the Nanzigu and the new position at Mukasa's shrine of a royal woman of the Sheep clan stand out. Nanzigu converted royal hubris into retribution. Nakayiza ennobled the refurbished shrine with a representative of the Sheep clan, Kyabaggu's mother's clan. The Sheep clan were powerful players on the littoral, famed as the principal managers of Kibuuka's shrine, a Ganda war lùbaalè based in Mawokota (map 3). She joined the Seedbead clan representative with the title of Ggugu. Mukasa's people had criticized Kyabaggu's behavior because it was blind to the obligation to reciprocate. That criticism precipitated the chain of events relayed in the story as conflicts between island, littoral, and mainland. Raising the profile of Sheep clan interests in relations between Ssese and a Ganda state, Nanzigu and Nakayiza reopened respectful lines of communication between them. In the 1780s, tensions swirled around the upsurge of war captives entering royal, chiefly, and even ordinary households, from distant corners of the region. This created openings for plague.[118] Constituents of centralized power executed their responsibilities to critique royalty in idioms of virtue.[119] Nakayiza and Nanzigu exemplified that work. They showed that critique reduced the vulnerability of a Ganda state to threats like epidemic illness or the designs of neighboring states by reviving a hospitable, moral politics of joining mainland and islands. From the lofty perch of a royal capital, noble women reformed that relationship.

Mukasa's people nourished regional prosperity because their fish and transportation nourished children and twins on the mainland. In the course of this history, people broadened the idea that Mukasa promoted the wealth and health of littoral communities, through fish and sewn canoe travel, into the idea that Mukasa promoted expansive, gendered categories of fertility and provided timely rainfall.[120] Information flows, not farming, were central to this project, a fact perhaps recalled in Kagwa's slur on the islanders: "And in the past Basese (people of the Ssese Islands) did not know how to cultivate crops, their women were lazy gossipers, excelling in visiting and entertaining, whereas the soil of Ssese was good, if it was cultivated it would yield very much produce."[121] Women ran the information networks that made island living a source of regional fertility, even if Kagwa could not appreciate the added value.

A pronounced, regionwide drought began in the middle of the sixteenth century. It prompted people to take new political risks and expand economic opportunity. With the Inland Sea, resources such as fish, salt, bloom, and bark cloth could be delivered to zones of need with incomparable precision, timeliness, and range. Little wonder, then, that Mukasa came to be associated explicitly with genres of experience of both littoral and dry-land economies. Mukasa's people had projected to the far reaches of the Inland Sea the connections they had grown from Ssese. They bound together royals, ironworkers, salt harvesters, canoe builders, paddlers, navigators, elephant and hippo hunters, (chewed) coffee preparers, fishers of all sorts, potters, bark cloth makers, herders, and relay traders connecting the Inland Sea to Indian Ocean and middle Nile Valley markets. Bubembe touched an increasing number of parties, generating friction between them. When Buganda took interest in the islands, Mukasa's people delivered much more than helping women and men fish in and travel over the Inland Sea.

Other spiritual authorities supported and competed with Mukasa. They await deeper study. In the northeast of the Inland Sea, people built them around figures such as Atego, Sumba, Namugonjo, Nkunda, Meru, and other mobile personages associated with the Inland Sea and its wealth and risks through canoes, islands, and pythons. Notwithstanding this diversity, Mukasa's power and its consequences for the Inland Sea's history are remarkable for their breadth. For nineteenth-century littoral residents, engagement with Mukasa's people was a fact of life. The idea that supplicants of all stripes traveled to Mukasa makes this point.[122] Shifting groups invested in the shrine's workings, but they shared an abiding interest in the things of the Inland Sea. Fish, transport, and the comparative advantage of access to more information brought fertility to students of the waters. The many other spiritual authorities in each of the island groups shows Mukasa's people succeeded in marking out with that figure an expansive territory of efficacy using the Inland Sea's resources and geographic processes. They did not dislodge and defeat all other shrines on the littoral.

The discipline of self-mastery lay at the heart of Bubembe's moral belonging. Mukasa's expanded efficacies were won when parts of new clans or representatives of older clans joined assemblies at Bubembe. They brought the new skills and information networks. The discipline of participation lent affective heft to assembling at the shrine, often choreographed to a lunar rhythm. Assembly involved separate zones of labor and knowledge—think of the women clearing the roads from the shrine, which led to different ports, simultaneously but separately. Visible wealth and adult children expressed the efficacy of all that, but the totality of Mukasa's expanded capacities were not controlled by a single figure.[123] They had been built up, over time, by many groups.

The conviviality and discipline of moral belonging were gendered. Men and women had different responsibilities to virtue. Living up to those responsibilities (or failing to do so) put everyone into the spotlight of social criticism. From ordinary people, to the followers of Mukasa, to the threads in a given sovereign knot, people debated and judged the moral belonging earned by acting with the virtues of self-mastery. They debated the discipline and conviviality of moral belonging—in a naming ceremony, a rebuilding event at a shrine, a feast given by a king, and so forth. Whenever they discussed such things, people were doing groupwork. Assessing grounds for difference and exclusion, or imagining those grounds have a common history, took on new weights with statecraft.

CHAPTER FOUR

Vigilant Python

A Bellicose Eighteenth Century
and Groupwork's Inner Edge

No greater power can be claimed by a political or military leader
than that he can conquer a territory and then himself become
the source of the fertility on which that territory depends.
—David Lan, *Guns and Rain*, 102

Akuweerera ekigambo, akira akuweerera envuma (ng'ogenda mu masengere).
"Advice on going to court is better than the gift of a slave."
—Edwin Scott Haydon, *Law and Justice in Buganda*, 334

T HE CONTENTS OF discipline and conviviality—and the groups they
animate—change with historical circumstance. This chapter explores
the territorial expansion of a Ganda state over the course of a long
eighteenth century. The expanders worked a local figure of the python, associated with fertility, into legal practices of winning justice through social critique to establish the authority of the expanders' fertility. Blending fertility
and justice this way revealed bodily and intellectual discipline as sources of the
gendered respectability worth arguing over and aspiring to. When violence
and territorial expansion became central facts of gendered respectability—
when men and women had to carry out and survive expansion and violence—
groupwork by exclusion on moral grounds took on new relevance.

Jural settings had long witnessed that kind of judgmental exclusion from
within. With bellicose state expansionism, exclusions from within highlighted
the labor of violence on behalf of expansion, setting new terms for belonging
with a Ganda state. The duties of expanding a state and the risks of carrying
out the violence sometimes indispensable for expansion raised questions about
the relationships between harming and healing, belonging and exclusion, justice and fertility. Without losing sight of the Inland Sea as part of that

expansion, this chapter focuses on the internal work of making statecraft moral in Buganda. Whom a group expels, why, and how tells a lot about moral struggles over belonging.

After 1670, the Ganda sovereign knot the queen mother Nnabuso and king Kateregga tied with their allies cleared fresh moral ground for their newly bellicose behavior. They sought to harness Sheep and Lungfish clan networks, linking the Inland Sea to the interior, by focusing on the dynamics of a shrine oriented to a clay-headed, rope-bodied python called Mbajjwe. The shrine was at Bweeya, in Butambala, immediately west of the young state's core areas (see map 3). At this shrine, clan representatives and royals crafted a variety of justices, pushing culpability for and moral bounds to male behavior—perhaps especially on a battlefield or in a raid. At Mbajjwe's shrine, men were judged as having departed from such mores in some manner. Those found wanting were executed, honing an internal edge to moral belonging. Influencing Mbajjwe's shrine, making an alliance of clans against others, and conquering a place called Butambala expanded the scope of royal justice into new territory where the state of Bunyoro had competing interests. Africa's historians of groupwork before 1900 have rarely looked at legal culture, moral belonging, political centralization, and territorial expansion in the same historical frame, over time.[1] A tight focus on a single reign and a single jural object reveals the detail needed to track the complex interplay of those themes.

A turn to bellicose statecraft had consequences for groupwork. But warriorhood was not the central fact of masculinity or of Buganda's political culture. To think that it was implies that studying the causes and consequences of violence will reveal the most significant elements of a history of groupwork with a Ganda state. But expansion was never only violent; it included the interplay of gendered self-mastery, politics, and legal practice. Exploring the historical field connecting Mbajjwe, Kateregga, and Butambala's clans reveals how gender, politics, and law shaped the course of expansionist statecraft and the groupwork it fostered. Statecraft's strategic embrace of violence to expand direct control over particular places called on legal culture. Gendered self-mastery bound the two.

Mbajjwe's shrine operators clothed royal justice with the trappings of collective well-being and fertility, and then judged men who did not measure up, executing them and the groups they represented. These removals unfolded in the context of a political alliance in which Mbajjwe played a key role. The moral valences of gendered self-mastery hung in the balance. An encounter with Mbajjwe shows two things. First, expansion involved royal attempts to exclude the Leopard clan, and Bunyoro, from the shrine.[2] Second, from Kateregga's time, the clay-headed python was involved in executions that marked an internal moral boundary by removing some men and the groups they led.

Encountering Mbajjwe

Canon Roscoe provided the most detailed description of Mbajjwe's shrine. Roscoe wrote in the moment when imperial military forces and missionary infrastructure had not yet given way to a Protectorate administration. But the base of land and people supporting *bàlubaalê*, royal women, and many clans had been reduced or was gone. His account is worth quoting at length.

Mbajjwe was the King's chief fetich, and had its temple, its priest, and a female medium through whom it was supposed to give oracles. This fetich was made of rope in imitation of a serpent, with the head formed of clay and fashioned like a serpent's head. The chief Katambala was its guardian, and it was his duty to place it in position in its temple, where it had a stool on which the head rested like that of a snake in repose. The man who carried the fetich belonged to the Kativuma [Seedbead] Clan, and the stool-bearer to the Yam Clan. The priest and the female medium were from the Leopard Clan; there were also two men attached, who beat the drums on special occasions, and who belonged to the Bushbuck Clan. Another man had charge of the coffee-berries which were supposed to be the food of the fetich. Mbajwe had a wife, who was a woman belonging to the Grasshopper Clan, and who had the care of the leopard skin rug upon which the fetich reclined. Only one man, a member of the Bird Clan, was allowed to thatch the temple; he resided in the temple-enclosure. In the temple there were two smaller fetiches, a drum named *Kisaja*, which was never beaten, and a fetich in the form of a knife handle, named *Namazi*; these, together with a bag belonging to Mbajwe, were placed before the fetich. Other objects belonging to the fetich were an axe (*Badukalulu*); a drum (*Talileka*); and a basket containing a kind of small millet called *bulo*, which was given with the coffee-berries as food to the fetich. When the King sent prisoners to Mbajwe for trial, as was his custom, the fetich was placed with its head pointing to the person whom the King had appointed to be the spokesman for the party. The medium stood by the stool, and as the prisoner made his statements, and tried to clear himself and his party, the medium who was possessed by the fetich replied: "It is so," after each statement. No prisoner was ever known to succeed in clearing himself or his party; nor did he live to go away from the place, he died as he knelt. The remaining prisoners were taken to the sacrificial place attached to the temple, where they were killed; and the body of the man who died in the temple was carried out, and thrown among the other corpses. The death of the spokesman in the temple was said to have been caused by fright, "Because he knew that the fetich wanted his blood." The medium, when possessed, addressed the King as *Matubwa*, and the chief guardian as *Nyabwe*. The fetich *Namazi* was sent from the temple on war-expeditions as the representative of Mbajwe, and was carried by a man of the Dog Clan.[3]

Mbajjwe was a principal in delivering royal justice. But the staging, the wide range of objects and clan representatives blended old and new. They projected the ancient relation between health and domination, expressed here by juxtaposing justice with objects and practices with legacies tied to fertility and prosperity. Drums were present. A medium worked there, whose utterings while possessed were interpreted by another person from the same clan. A woman consecrated to Mbajjwe but belonging to a clan other than the medium's or the guardian's also worked there. Mbajjwe was moved and tended—its head was rested on a stool that stood on a leopard skin rug. Mbajjwe was fed. All of that was part of working with pythons and objects found widely in the region.

Chapter 1 argued that this bundle existed by the last few centuries of the first millennium CE. These bodily movements, objects, and personnel were widespread in the region when Mbajjwe's shrine was established. The other objects and responsibilities described as "belonging to Mbajjwe"—such as the Namazi knife handle and the Dog clan's responsibility for carrying it on war expeditions—were unique or came along at some later time. Judging men before Mbajjwe involved weighing their courage, a practice that continued into the nineteenth century.[4]

In conquering Butambala, royals tried to control Mbajjwe's Bweeya shrine there. Leopard clan histories report that Kateregga persecuted them in Butambala for claiming royal identity.[5] Other histories do not make such claims, showing that people disagreed about the moral nature of the interplay of Mbajjwe's shrine with royal and clan interests. But they agreed that Mbajjwe's shrine delivered royal justice through trial and execution of groups in the aftermath of an initial territorial conquest by a Buganda royal. This chapter argues that blending violence, justice, and a new masculinity at Mbajjwe's shrine was an innovation nonetheless lent an aura of antiquity in an otherwise familiar setting for pursuing fertility. The new mix was conducive to affective groupwork because of its intimate ties to conquest. Weber's "particular pathos" of loss and the costs of success were weighed and debated in a medium of gendered work on behalf of expansionism, instigated by a python object.[6] If found wanting, men and the groups they represented were removed.

Mbajjwe reminded people of possibilities, a quality of vigilance with great emotional heft. The vigilance, to use David Doris's phrase, operated like a subjective mirror. Whoever came before Mbajjwe was forced into a complicated reflection on their actions.[7] Mbajjwe's constituent parts—shapes, materials, their arrangement, and the kinesthetics of using the object—were metonyms of gendered fertility. Roscoe worked closely with top officials in the kingdom, but he surely overstates the irreversible fates of the prisoners. For royal justice to work along these lines, inviting followers to avoid similar destinies, at least a few such prisoners must have been spared.[8] The point is that prisoners encountered Mbajjwe in an emotional state that shaped their fate.

Not only did one's future hang in the balance of what happened in that encounter, the groups one belonged to bore the burdens of the outcome. Blending justice and fertility in such a dramatic setting concentrated the state's arrogant claims to power, of being the source of fertility in a conquered territory. A male virtue floated between Mbajjwe, its operators, the deeds the prisoner men who came into its presence were accused of, and their fates. Violence, justice, and fertility made an expansionist statecraft. Inside thrummed the virtues of self-mastery in soldiering and the gendered fertility at stake in belonging with such a state.

Gendered Statecraft and Expansion

The region's well-known "monarchies" emerged from the new nexus of information flow, eclectic agropastoralism, trade and social payments connecting concentrated populations beyond the face-to-face, built around figures like Mukasa.[9] The scare quotes warn that these polities revolved around more than one sovereign. They were polycentric.[10] A queen mother, her (not necessarily biological) son, the king, and his queen sister (also not necessarily biological), knotted a sovereignty.[11] Other titled figures operated with high degrees of independence. Individually and together, they extracted from the expansive groupwork of clanship the ideological resource of reciprocal obligation. Sovereign knots of independent lines of authority established royal capitals through which flowed material and affective dimensions of patronage and clientship.[12]

Like older centers founded by Kintu, at Magonga, or founded with Mukasa, at Bubembe, or by Namatimba, at Bukasa, royal networks concentrated flows of wealth and followers. They helped people initiate their own patron–client relations with others in their community to behave like respectable adult men and women. If, as Kodesh put it, "kings gradually established the autonomy of the kingship by extracting royal ideology from the restrictive bonds of clanship," then, Hanson reminds us, that ideology "mediated the competition among chiefs for followers."[13]

This began during the long period of reduced rainfall mentioned in chapter 3.[14] Plague had arguably become endemic in the region by then, joining other agents of epidemic disease, like smallpox, yaws, and trypanosomiasis shaping the distributions of people and cattle.[15] Seventeenth-century regional food systems relied on different combinations of cattle, grains, bananas, and newer crops, like sweet potato, cassava, and American beans. Women worked the new crops into the older combinations. Differing access to raw materials like iron ore and bloom, bark cloth, or salt undergirded different political cultures, including states.[16] State formation likely began in Bunyoro, spreading by the necessity of imitation to regions like the one that became Buganda.[17] Late in the seventeenth century, Kateregga and Nnabuso initiated Buganda's territorial expansion. Expansion produced many female captives and many new chiefs. Leading chiefs tended to reside at the capital, and many captives ended up there as gifts.

Organized violence grew into a decisive feature of regional political economy in the eighteenth century. It may have made sweet potato and cassava appealing to banana and grain farmers. Hidden below ground, such crops could escape hungry army auxiliaries seeking food.[18] Auxiliaries looking to feed a group of soldiers would leave cassava in the ground. It took too long to remove the toxic skin and turn the tuber into food. Late in the eighteenth century, direct connections formed with trading emporiums at the Indian Ocean coast and in the middle Nile Basin.[19] At the same time, control over slaves increased the numbers of people unobligated to a royal center. Opportunities for establishing new centers grew with access to new markets and captives, disrupting royal authority over flows of wealth and knowledge.[20] That is one reason sovereign knots like Kyabaggu's, discussed in chapter 3, engaged centers like Mukasa's in a contentious register.

In this thumbnail sketch of what scholars call "state formation," the idea of centers is old. The innovation lay in expanding control over territory in two ways. First, through a practice and language of conquest, designed to direct resources of skill and material wealth to a single center. Second, in a language of justice designed to make the newcomers' fertility the source of the fertility on which people in the incorporated territory depended. Tradition makers in Buganda tied the new practices of conquest and delivering royal justice to the actions of a king named Kateregga. They claimed that Kateregga took control of Butambala through a collaborative conquest.[21] The aftermaths reverberated into the eighteenth century.[22]

When that happened suggests why it happened. Kateregga and Nnabuso reigned between 1640 and 1670, three generations before Mawanda, calculated by using an average generation length of thirty years, discussed in the introduction. Their knot reigned three generations beyond the plausible reach of reminiscences shared with the eldest of the oral historians who provided authors like Kagwa the material for *Kings of Buganda*.[23] Accounts of reigns at this remove cannot be taken literally as chronicles of events. They are thematic bundles, kept alive through repeated use by exegetical communities. Versions of what happened in their reign and in its aftermaths reveal shifting political imaginaries, struggles over them, and the aftermaths of struggle, but not calendar dates. It is wiser to set their reign in the larger period their expansionism disturbed. The second half of the seventeenth century will do. It was a prolonged period of reduced rainfall.

Kateregga and Nnabuso wanted to direct networks of wealth and food, centered on the Inland Sea and the grazing lands of the further interior, toward Butambala's centers. They succeeded in part by converting competition between groups in Butambala into an alliance oriented to their royal center. Dynastic traditions say Kateregga allied with figures in two clan networks, Lungfish and Sheep, in his conflict with the Leopard clan.[24] Tradition makers argued that Leopard people claimed nobility by descent from Kintu. Such a claim threatened to disperse nobility among any clan claiming a descent tie to Kintu.[25] With support from Lungfish and Sheep clan members, Kateregga hemmed in Leopard people and extended links to the wealth of the Inland Sea into the interior. He had his eyes on high-quality iron work and high-quality salt in the northwest, fish from the Inland Sea, and the canoes to move it around the littoral. It is worth noting that a long branch of the Katonga River reaches into Butambala, linking it by canoe to the Inland Sea.[26]

Lungfish groups had a broad presence in the isles and the littoral.[27] The Gabunga, a senior figure in the clan, had a principal estate at Bweeya, near Mbajjwe's shrine (map 3). Chapter 2 accounted for the clans invested in Mukasa's Bubembe shrine, where Seedbead, Lungfish, and Otter figures were senior. Bugala and other islands in the Ssese group had their own titled canoe fleet captains and titled officialdom of estate holders.[28] Some clans linked Buvuma and Busoga to Ssese and Buganda and to Buhaya. Late in the nineteenth century, Kagwa canvassed the clans with canoe fleet captains and titled clan estate managers in the islands. The range and orientation of the networks shifted as sovereign knots revised the territorial chiefship of clans.[29]

Access to the networks of knowledge embodied by Lungfish groups was one prize Kateregga and Nnabuso sought in their move into Butambala. They required power objects to succeed. Kiwanuka credited Kateregga with "appointing his successful generals to chieftainships." Many appointments became hereditary positions, including the Wakayembe ("horn-charm-person") title held in Butambala. Kiwanuka saw them as a compromise between royal rule and the weight of clan privilege.[30] But it is telling that power objects—so-called charms—were indispensable elements of successful conquest. They provided access to the knowledge outsiders needed to establish their fertility in the new territory.

Establishing newcomers' fertility had costs that those in the conquered territory bore unequally, reshaping the contents of gendered self-mastery. Wrigley noted that Kateregga was the first king with numerous wives.[31] Wrigley argued that entering into many marriages enjoined royals "to be constantly seeking new resources with which to compensate the groups that lost their daughters to them."[32] This pushed royals to develop an ideology of their right to appropriate wealth as a consequence of making access to women something ordinary people had to seek through "a political superior."[33] A concrete extension of this "right" is the credit given to "Kateregga and his chiefs" for taxing "prominent and wealthy chiefs . . . in the form of goods, to be given to the wives of the king."[34] The tax increased the flows of wealth set in motion by the growing numbers of royal wives. Wrigley treated such an equation as a model. Once established, following Kateregga's reign, it became an engine of militarization. Men's work in making war in areas outside royal control brought captive women into "circulation." It drew new volumes of material wealth to the royal center for bundling into the social payments cementing chiefly as well as royal marriages. Whether or not Kateregga intended it, having many wives provided wealth and honor to Buganda's royals.

Captive women—and the labor of capture—altered the ground for social constructions of gender. The masculinization of warfare implicit in conquest with power objects shaped that change. Soldiering embodied the new social realities of gender entailed by competition in increasingly complex networks, oriented to different centers. Some centers connected to the royal capital through a hierarchy of older, existing authorities of clanship and shrine work. An existing center like Mbajjwe's at Bweeya could lead directly to the capital via a new chief, like the Wakayembe, planted in a territory by one of the threads in the sovereign knot. Biologically female women and men shaped the contents of self-mastery through their public ritual work, taken up in the next chapter. But in the course of the events glossed here, elements of the soldiering behind the networks of conquest became gendered as sociologically male.

Musisi used the phrase "elite polygyny" to describe the outcomes of the new virtues of soldiering surrounding the expansion begun in Kateregga's reign.[35] Musisi recognized stratification in this new, instrumental use of women. On one plane stood men and ordinary women whose status resulted from proper exchanges of wealth. On another plane stood royal wives whose female descendants were recognized as princesses. Captive women stood on a third plane. The "circulation" of women inflated by organized violence was not only a technique of centralizing power at a royal center.[36] Royal women helped constitute themselves as sociologically male in part through controlling relationships between "princesses" and everyone else in a period of proliferating routes to the social payments that gave public standing to men and women as adult heads of families. Rhiannon Stephens built on Musisi's groundbreaking work to pull ordinary women's quest for motherhood in this period into the same frame as elite motherhoods. She revealed "an ideology of motherhood grounded in biology," such as that expressed by royal attempts to control access to women. This ideology provided opportunities for ordinary women to gain standing, should they bear an heir to a household.

Kodesh insisted that royals allied with clans to expand, fashioning alliances through public healing. The result wrapped notions of collective well-being around "generating support for military endeavors, and consolidating military victories." Kodesh implied that objects called *àmàyêmbe*, under royal control, were a novelty from Kateregga's reign that "highlights the impact of shifting notions of collective well-being on the state formation process." Kodesh refuted the idea that ritual and political power divided when states formed and that clans lost power as violent statecraft advanced.[37] The actual contents of the "shifting notions of collective well-being" in play with the creation of royal power objects, like Mbajjwe, remain to be explored. Power objects engaged a legal process, mixing soldiering, capital punishment, and tale-telling in which the moral behavior of men hung in the balance.

These views substantiate historical claims linking Mbajjwe, Kateregga, various clan networks, organized violence, and struggles over gendered fertility. Vernacular historians of Kateregga's reign highlight competition between clans and royalty at the beginning of Buganda's territorial expansion.[38] They agree that the Sheep clan held the titled chiefship Katambala, which Kateregga created after the conquest.[39] None dispute Kateregga's attacks on members of the Leopard clan in the conquered territory, although it is not mentioned in all accounts.[40] All agree successful conquest and administrative incorporation of the territory involved control over Mbajjwe.

Their debates reveal that conquest turned on controlling ancestral knowledge in the incorporated territory. The chiefly position of Katambala, created after conquest, was often given the additional moniker "Wakayembe," or "horn-charm-person," to honor the position's responsibility for Mbajjwe.[41] But accounts differ on the question of which clan controlled Mbajjwe before Kateregga and Nnabuso created the Katambala chiefship. The Protestant prime minister, Apolo Kagwa, said the Sheep clan had control of Mbajjwe.[42] But Lawi Wakibi Sekiti, writing in the Catholic newspaper *Munno*, disagreed. Sekiti reported that Maganyi of the Lungfish clan controlled the python object Mbajjwe first, followed by the Sheep clan. At the behest of the object itself, Kateregga took it, then returned it to the Sheep clan with instructions to found the shrine.[43] To consolidate the victory, Mbajjwe "foretold Kateregga" to cede control over itself to Mpungu of the Sheep clan and send both to Bweeya, the estate over which Mpungu had responsibility, where a Nyoro medium worked from a cave.[44] Sekiti implied a history for Mbajjwe before it was "one of the

King's principal fetiches."[45] He broke the "conquest" into two phases, only the first of which included support from Lungfish people. For Sekiti, consolidating conquest required building the shrine at Bweeya, prompted by Mbajjwe's request that Kateregga entrust it to the Sheep clan, excluding Lungfish people. Responsibility for Mbajjwe would henceforth be shared between Sheep clan representatives and Kateregga's sovereign knot. Their alliance then defeated a Nyoro group, under the leadership of one Kizunga or Luzunga, ensconced in a Bweeya cave.[46] Territorial expansion had many fronts.

Arguing about possessing a power object was arguing about the moral authority to rule, to provide fertility. These variations show the Sheep clan had grown in importance through the lineage established in service to Mbajjwe, working at their new shrine at Bweeya. That "moment" belonged to an individual, the first holder of the title "Maganyi." Descendants embodied that success, forming the group that gave Mbajjwe a substantive agency bound to the circumstances of military action. They moved against members of the Leopard clan and outcompeted Lungfish people already established at Bweeya, who sought alliance with Kateregga.[47] The Sheep clan succeeded. Maganyi was a title all agree belonged to Sheep clan people until early in Muteesa's reign. Whoever they were before their descendants invented the title, they succeeded with Kateregga and Mbajjwe in making Butambala part of Buganda.

Kateregga's alliances with the Sheep clan and a chastened Leopard clan embodied the importance of Butambala as a conduit for trade and transport between the Inland Sea and Bunyoro.[48] The freight borne by networks linking Buganda and Bunyoro made control over them important, even as the two states fought.[49] The prize of control over that conduit revealed tensions between clans, and royals shaped narratives about Mbajjwe's shrine at Bweeya. The Leopard people Kateregga persecuted represented networks of skill along the Mawokota littoral, reaching Butambala, and into Bunyoro, pushing aside Lungfish networks and elevating those of the Sheep clan. Kateregga sought increased access to littoral wealth and relied on clans with littoral roots—and roots in Bunyoro—to get it.

Reinventing Mbajjwe as the royal charm of justice and fertility, narrated by Sekiti in the context of a first territorial expansion undertaken by the state, reveals the importance of execution as an internal edge to moral belonging. Executing prisoners, with Mbajjwe, measured a moral community oriented to expansion and hierarchy, and the gendered fertility soldiers won. Executions pulled out the men and their groups found wanting, in some actual or accusing way, in the virtues driving expansion.

Guild accounts of Buganda's political history say little about objects like Mbajjwe or their entanglement in royal justice. They treat them as examples of mythic ritual practice lying outside of history or simply ignore them.[50] The few who treat objects as actors underscore their ability to attract multiclan alliances in running their shrines, exceeding what had been possible with a single clan or in a relation with a single chief. They see objects like Mbajjwe facilitating territorial expansion. Their portability helped distribute reciprocal obligation between royal and clan.[51]

Even these historians leave aside the intellectual sources of royal justice and the consequences of emphasizing group identification as an object of that justice, accomplished by groupwork with objects like Mbajjwe. But power objects like Mbajjwe have intellectual histories. Conquest and expansion had legal cultures. Jural process reveals moral and political dimensions to blending fertility, violence, and justice so dear to royals and consequential for allies and followers. A survey of that legal culture provides context for Mbajjwe's executions, revealing that debating gendered self-mastery meant debating belonging.

Legal Practice in Buganda: 1680 to 1880

Centralized, expansionist polities tend to link justice and authority with formal, legal shapes, as Jane Burbank and Frederick Cooper have argued.[52] States often have the interests and the means to limit disputes over principles of conflict resolution and forms of justice.[53] Legal culture in the Buganda state aspired to control what came before courts. Yet, the norms tested and tried in a legal process in Buganda were contingent rather than encyclopedic. With some idea of the general principles of legal culture before 1850, we may recognize the significance of Mbajjwe to groupwork with statecraft. Getting to those principles is easier said than done.

Imperial conquest, colonial rule, and the competing interests of various religious orientations toward the subject of justice comprehensively revised preexisting legal practice, creating "customary law."[54] Customary law claimed to draw a list of precolonial legal principles into colonial-era courts, masking the colonial realities shaping that process.[55] Customary law's educated, literate men composed that collage of precolonial principle and practice by using courts, writing, and working with colonial ethnographers and officials. Divides between subjects and citizens, colonial preoccupations with ethnicity, and the male gender of the voices in master sources—and of the magistrates in "native courts"—were common features across colonial Africa. Differences in the age, social position, and depth of memory of the people cited in customary law materials limited the details they provided.[56] Women used native courts a lot, shaping the application of law. Their legal strategy could transform the principles men put into the formal codes.[57] That tension helped make customary law varied, not monolithic.[58]

The challenge is to figure out what earlier, general principles existed and describe their interplay before these reconfigurations. The first step is to study sources composed in the decades ahead of conquest, evangelization, and colonial rule that include descriptions of legal process. The descriptions illustrate principles of legal standing and practice that bore directly on belonging, either as part of a punishment or as part of the standing to bring or defend a case.[59]

Some details reappear in sources from later periods, a redundancy suggesting a persistent usefulness.[60] For example, Kagwa reported in 1901 that Muteesa had one of his appointed chiefs (òmùtongòle) executed in 1862, just after Speke's sojourn in the queen mother's palace. His transgression lay in having acquired cloth from Karagwe but failing to turn it over to Muteesa.[61] The punishment reflected Muteesa's ongoing defense of the idea that wealth and status should flow into and out of a center he controlled. As we just saw, that system and its moral logic had been under threat since the eighteenth century by the increasing number of captives whose control by chiefs loosened their need to practice reciprocal obligation. Its logic was loosened even further from early in the nineteenth century by the ease with which commodities flowed into the centers controlled by unobligated, wealthy chiefs.[62] The fact that Muteesa still defended the imperative of a single center reveals that others in the realm might still subscribe to its logic. Thus, Speke's and Kagwa's accounts of legal culture early in Muteesa's reign, as well as in prior reigns, ring true, as far as they go. That legal world was largely gone by 1900. *Kabakas* and chiefs prosecuted, punished, and adjudicated in a divided field of courts. Royal women, who had done this work as recently as the 1870s, literally lost the ground beneath that responsibility. They disappeared as adjudicators of legal process.

Mbajjwe and its supporting cast worked in this shifting nexus of legal practice, but their relationships exceeded the reach and purpose of jural culture. Protectorate officials, missionaries, and African co-religionists of the book all sought to defeat such bundles of moral and political power, driving them underground. Mbajjwe's form, materials, and operators belonged simultaneously to other kinds of social action, including mediumship, making objects with occult life and historical weight, and so forth. In Buganda, while political hierarchy crossed over to the main stages of Protectorate rule, if radically changed, shrine and power object practices went offstage, into the hands of social critics.[63] Eighteenth-century Ganda legal culture may be treated as such, but doing so leaves dangling its ties to other parts of intellectual, political, and social life.

Principles

Legal standing turned on jural corporation, the idea that individuals and individualisms should be oriented to groups. Individuals could make their way in life because of groups, a fact so obvious and indispensable to social life that it lay beyond debate. In this vein, McCaskie distinguished between change-less custom and contingent, changeable legal practice in eighteenth- and nineteenth-century Asante.[64] The division has a close parallel in the Luganda concepts of *èmpisà*, "behavior, habit, manners," and *ètteekâ*, "regulation, law, edict."[65] Luganda has a verb, *kùsemba*, for the concrete practice of standing with and supporting one's close relations and friends in a dispute.[66] It was wise to support relatives in acting against a murderer, an adulterer caught in the act, "and a thief found with stolen goods in his possession."[67]

Exceptions prove this rule. They involve a person standing alone before justice and authority, a social atom cut off from the support of a group. A poisoner, often translated as "witch"—a person whose occult powers accusers judged dangerous—exemplified such a person.[68] As a social atom, a "witch" poisoned the domination of individualisms by groups, a domination ensuring that the exertions of questing people would serve larger domains of interest. The struggles of the most vulnerable—war captives, slaves, children—to min-imize exclusion proved its towering dangers. Male war captives or slaves could mitigate an atomic phase in their lives by making blood-friendship with a master's child.[69] The trick enjoined senior members of the child's clan to pay fines and protect its slave blood-friend. Captives understood that the moral weight of corporate belonging tipped the balance in their favor.

Transgressing the imperative to belong did not produce uniform techniques for judgment and punishment. In Shambaai, elder lineage-mates dealt with witchcraft. The subject of a witchcraft accusation and judgment was not brought into a chief's or royal's court, although lineage elders might hand over such a person to a chief to be rid of them.[70] The Asante state exposed and punished spirit mediums, treating them as atomic persons.[71] In Buganda, the figure of the witch embodied such an atom, reaffirming in the empty space around a singled-out person the sociality central to belonging. "A convicted sorcerer was burnt outside the village," wrote Lucy Mair in the early 1930s.[72]

When Speke sought to visit the mouth of a river, west of Entebbe, his staff warned against doing so without express permission from Muteesa. They wor-ried that moving around without such permission would provoke the people living there to accuse Speke of witchcraft "and would tell their king so."[73] They knew the risk to local people of giving hospitality and information to a stranger of evident importance. To protect themselves, locals washed their hands of this stranger by turning him over to Muteesa with a charge of nosing around without permission from the royal center, a kind of antisocial behavior. Chronic offenders might join witches and slaves as people a corporate group gave up on and sent away to a chief or the capital.[74]

The many connections to the social order left dangling by a narrow focus on principles of legal process accord quite well with legal practice itself. The idea of cutting from (*òkùsalà òmùsango*, "give a verdict, settle a question") a single lump of evidence or set of claims—and dividing out responsibility—lies at the heart of the language of judicial process in Buganda and elsewhere in the region.[75] The phrase described the moment of rendering a verdict. The trial was described with a different phrase, *kuwulisisya omusango* or "to hear a case" or with the verb *kùwozà*, "plead in court; seek justice from; render account of."[76] These processes often involved eliciting public testimony from witnesses (figure 10).[77] Audience opinion influenced the weighing of evidence. In some circumstances, torture could be applied to get confessions of guilt. A husband might torture his wife if he suspected her of infidelity. Authorities might inflict pain "to extract evidence" from a defendant.[78]

A sense of òkùsalà òmusango practice, before it was woven into Protectorate customary law, emerges in an account from 1862, given by Speke. Soon after entering Buganda, traveling in the province of Buddu under the protection of a group of soldiers and officials from Buganda and Karagwe, Speke reported a case in which a young man delivered a letter from his colleague, James Augustus Grant. The messenger wore the skin of a serval cat, a sign of royalty. Speke's minder, Nyamagundu, recognized sartorial pretense and applied force to win a confession of guilt. None forthcoming, he undertook òkùsalà òmusango. He took "up a long stick, and breaking it into sundry bits of equal length, placed one by one in front of him, each of which was supposed to represent one number in line of succession to his forefathers. By this it was proved he [the serval-clad letter-bearer] did not branch in any way from the royal stock." At Nyamagundu's suggestion, and after some debate, all who watched the proceedings agreed a fine of 100 cows was the best way to settle the matter. The pretender "quietly allowed the skin to be untied and taken off."[79] In this case, an individual was indeed the subject of a legal proceeding initiated by a representative of royalty. Genealogy provided the critical evidence in defense of the coherence of the corporate group his costume threatened.

Commoner women lacked standing before the legal principles (*ètteekà*) applied in a chief's court. Speke reported that women were disproportionately vulnerable to justice. "Some women, for misdemeanors, are sold into slavery; whilst others are flogged, or degraded to do all the menial labors of the house."[80] A woman may be the aggrieved, the aggressor, or the punished party to a case, but she did not appear in courts as plaintiff or defendant in the sources. Kagwa reported a circumstance that equated women to the large stones on which they cleaned the sponges a chief used when bathing. Women beat the sponges violently against the stone to clean them. Should an unmarried woman steal one of

AN IMPROMPTU COUNCIL

Kyuma—the landlord—seated in the porch ; Kaiso, his dispossessed brother,
in the foreground. Plaintiff and defendant standing in the centre. The *muruka*
chief on the right with his back to the camera ; next him the village "askari",
distinguished by his puttees.

Figure 10. An impromptu council. Legal process was public and the audience
mattered. Source: Lucy Mair, *An African People in the Twentieth Century* (London:
Routledge, 1934), opposite 200.

these stones, she risked seizure at the place of her theft. If married, her husband might (or might not) pay a fine to release her. The logic of this principle, according to Kagwa, insisted nothing distinguished the labor of the woman who used the stone to beat out the sponges from the stone itself. The only scope for "change" in applying this principle was conditional on the marriage status of the woman thief.[81] Legal culture was a sociologically male medium. It seems likely that the dynamics of a strategic bellicose expansion helped make it so.

Royals might subject entire groups to restrictions of movement and so forth based on the actions of a member or members. This logic guided the queen mother in denying food (but not beer) to Speke's party. She argued that because they "all came to Uganda in one body, so all alike were, by her logic, answerable to the offence."[82] Muteesa and Muganzirwazza regularly withheld this basic form of hospitality for reasons that escaped Speke but reflected the vulnerability of his atomic position at court (although royal withholding opened the way for others in the capital to provide Speke with food). Her reasoning also expressed the basic tenet of royal control over access to all forms of wealth in their domains. Both Muteesa and Muganzirwazza had granted Speke's party the right to "forage" or plunder for their supplies, but Speke found this "system" unsavory. Therein lay the misunderstanding.[83]

A variation that proved the rule of jural corporation emerged with the creation of the òmùtongòle, "a person who does not depend on a chief but upon the kabaka," as Stanislaus Mugwanya explained in 1906, looking back to "the old days."[84] Kagwa credited Mawanda with creating this kind of person, and Hanson explored its creation as a loosening of the reciprocal obligation that kept allegiance and wealth flowing in and out of a royal center.[85] The office was created during or just after the embrace of territorial expansion, taken up in this chapter.

An òmùtongòle belonged to an èkìtongòle, a group formed by ambitious figures including chiefs and royals, often composed of captives. A new chasm in status separated the leader from the captives/followers because the latter could not choose to serve another èkìtongòle. This reality eroded the reciprocity linking ordinary people and their social superiors. Individual èbìtongòle (plural) consolidated military victories, settled new areas, or addressed specific needs for labor or ecology control, in particular parts of Buganda.[86] The relations of àbàtongòle (plural) to legal process reveal the durability of jural corporation despite ambiguity in a person's relationship to a corporate group.

These new people exemplified the dislocations of bellicose, expansionist statecraft. When an òmùtongòle got into a legal process, the case was heard by the leader of the group, who conducted his court like any other chief. Roscoe called àbàtongòle "private servants" and noted that "the Queen and the King's

Mother tried cases among their own servants." In their account of "Court Customs," a self-contained section in Roscoe and Kagwa's 1906 "Enquiry into
Native Land Tenure," Kibare and Mesusala pointed out that an ordinary landed
estate holder and a leader of an èkìtongòle would each try cases in the same
manner as "a case of murder committed by one of his men upon a man of
another chief." If they found their man guilty, he "would have been handed . . .
to the chief of the murdered man who would have given him up to the relatives
to kill."[87] Even a powerful figure such as Teofiro Mulumba Kuruji, who had held
a number of positions, including one with control over land on which àbàtongòle already worked, was not free to drive them away. He "took them to the
Kabaka and he drove them away."[88] According to Hanson, the vast majority of
young men populating a given èkìtongòle were captives.[89] They had no ties to
the hierarchy of corporate authority in the locales where they worked. The èkìtongòle alone shielded them from the reality of an atomic existence. Its leader
strived to make such a group look corporate. Kuruji recalled that chiefs of established estates (òbùtaka) and of newly created estates (òbùtongole) parceled into
the same proportions their take in a round of tax collection.[90] They converted a
decidedly improvised group into something that looked more durable.

Folding the individual into a group, as the subject of a legal judgment, was
common in nineteenth-century Buganda.[91] This had been true earlier, following Mawanda's mid-eighteenth-century reorganization of the state's administrative structure into ten "counties" (àmàsaza) with a bewildering array of
chiefs, many of whom shared no ties of descent with the dominant clans in a
county. In 1906, Yusufu Nakanyero, the leader of a prominent lineage of the
Pangolin clan, explained that a sitting kabaka chose all the chiefs, save the
kàtikkiro, the chief of staff and justice, and the òmùsigìri, the stand-in for a
traveling chief.[92] Those two offices oversaw legal process at the county level
and below. They could keep control over the courts there in local hands, reinforcing the jural primacy of lineages and clans.[93]

By 1850, one could appeal judgments in a hierarchy of chiefly locations.[94]
Such courts were expensive, dangerous places. Knowing how to navigate them
was more valuable to their denizens than having a slave, as one of this chapter's
epigraphs explains. One entered only after failing to resolve disputes or to fix
compensation in the family, homestead, lineage, or clan.[95] One began in the
courtyard of a local chief (figure 10). Without a resolution, that chief could
send the dispute to a more important chief in the larger region, including the
chief of one of the named counties.[96] Beyond that lay the prime minister's
court, the queen mother's court, and the male kabaka's court in the capital.[97]

Kateregga's sovereign knot opened a new jural visibility for political leaders.
From Mawanda's through Muteesa's reign, new chiefships grew apace. Many

of the figures running the numerous courts named in 1906 were nineteenth-century creations.[98] By the 1890s, appeals rarely reached the ears and eyes of any strand in the state's sovereign knot.[99] In the three decades before, clan leaders and royal women had lost control of their lands, key material and ideological ground for their standing.[100] As a consequence, fewer cases reached them, and the katikkiro referred fewer to the kabaka's court.[101] The variety of legal spaces was matched by the variety of punishments meant to embody the gendered groupwork jurisprudence performed.

Punishment

Responses to deviance and crime included exile, fines, enslavement, confiscation of property, detention in stocks, mutilation, and death.[102] Incarceration apparently did not occur. Various stocks incapacitated transgressors.[103] Violating lines of gender and standing elicited the harshest punishments in the nineteenth century. When a social inferior was directly responsible for an action that displeased a superior—even kabakas—the social inferior was not punished. The party with the higher social station and responsibility for the transgressor was punished. Muteesa excused a page "tied by the neck and hands" for his role in seizing Speke's guard and assigned responsibility for the offense to the page's superior, the *Kamraviona* (the prime minister).[104]

Speke claimed some actions risked capital punishment. They included speaking of royal descent lines, conquests, or details of foreign lands, uninvited visiting with the kabaka's guests, any male gazing on women of the palace—"lest he should be accused of amorous intentions"—or possession of any foreign made object other than "beads and brass wire, exchanged for ivory or slaves."[105] Speke learned of royals and the capital, not what was going on elsewhere. Roscoe and Kagwa were told in 1906 that clan heads or county chiefs could exact capital punishment, although the practice "ceased in 1900."[106] Speke does not always distinguish when perpetrators or their responsible social superiors suffered punishment. But his vignette and list of transgressions show justice flowing down the ranks of hierarchy, implicitly reinforcing the jural corporation of clans and lineages even though he did not write in those terms. Legal culture reflected the social circumstances defining unequal access to justice and unequal vulnerability to punishment.

Capital punishment loomed large. Speke recounts a scene of reckoning. It occurred on return from a military operation in the east, in the presence of a thronging public and the drums, weapons, and power objects of war.

> Each regimental commandant in turn narrated the whole services of his party, distinguishing those subs who executed his orders well and successfully from those who either deserted before the enemy or feared to follow up their success.

The king listened attentively . . . ; when to the worthy he awarded pombé [beer],
helped with gourd-cups from large earthen jars . . . ; and to the unworthy, execution. When the fatal sentence was pronounced, a terrible bustle ensued, the
convict wrestling and defying, whilst the other men seized, pulled and tore the
struggling wretch from the crowd, bound him hands and head together, and led
or rather tumbled him away.[107]

Despite the fact that Speke understood little or nothing of what was said in
such a scene—his translator seems not to have been present at this event—he
painted a picture of tale-telling attended by people, drums, arms, and power
objects in which individual actors were indeed the subjects of this example of
a kabaka's legal process.[108]

Speke and Kagwa mention executions that apparently took place offstage,
at a location called èttâmbiro.[109] Rebels were executed there. Butambala had its
own èttâmbiro, at Bweeya, Mbajjwe's home.[110] Execution methods included
burning, clubbing, decapitation, drowning, choking, or being left for buz-
zards or Nile crocodiles. Ordinary people were executed at one place and
chiefs and nobles at another place. Burning was safest for the executioner and
perhaps for the person who decided the killing. Burning destroyed a person's
spirit, which otherwise came into existence with the death of the body.[111]

Many titled figures were exempt from royal violence, including the mass
arrests and executions that occurred from the mid-eighteenth century.[112] Their
titles were already prominent when Kintu and Kimera entered the picture.
Their exception honored that preexisting sovereignty. Others had courtyard
sanctuaries. Prisoners who reached such a courtyard could not be arrested
again. The last place on Kagwa's list of such safe havens was Mutawulira, at
Butawulira in Butambala.[113] The Mutawulira was one of the titles created and
held, with the approval of royals, by someone from a particular clan. In these
safe havens, a local face of the state smiled through the benevolence of hosting
clans. Ten of them existed in the nineteenth century. Chiefs from Ssese Islands
wore brass bangles (èbikomo), like the headless torsos in the Luzira Group, and
had special crests of hair atop their head (èjjòbâ, for one).[114] These adornments
signaled exemption from royal exactions, including execution.[115] In the case of
Gabunga, the title held by a member of the Lungfish clan who was the admiral
of Buganda's navy from early in the nineteenth century, these standards of
political independence echoed in the canoe's "crest" of waterbuck horns and
the èjjòbâ tuft of the gray parrot's coral-red tail feathers. These figures mapped
royal patronage in the polycentric landscape of clanship and public healing,
charting its limits during the long eighteenth century in which that landscape
took shape.[116] Of course, a few royals ignored the exemption.[117]

To sum up, three changes marked legal culture in the region between the latter seventeenth century and the 1880s. First, Kateregga, Mbajjwe, and its operators used power objects to judge and punish on behalf of royals. They pushed justice and territorial conquest into the ring with fertility. Second, the territorial expansions that continued through the eighteenth century produced many captives alongside the expansion of titled chiefships. An expanded officialdom doubled down on jural corporation. That created the third change: a sociologically male space for justice, shrinking the light between behavior (èmpisà) and regulation (ètteekà). In their courts, chiefs sought to increase the confidence of men to resolve disputes that affected the groups they represented. They sought to exclude those with little means from higher-level courts and to ensure that those with means entered for good reason.

Throughout, the legal process visited punishments on individuals, their responsible social superiors, and entire groups, constituted by a wide variety of criteria. In each case, a particular corporate group's integrity was at stake, not just the fate of an atomic individual. The state claimed to guarantee that integrity, even as it shuffled corporate group hierarchy. For example, the new installation rites, developed at Buddo Hill in the mid-eighteenth century, exhorted a new male kabaka to please his people when deciding cases.[118] Mbajjwe's shrine in Butambala represented an early chapter in that story. It blended capital punishment, conquest, clanship, and gendered respectability in a recursively creative formula shaping the moral terms of belonging from within.

Mbajjwe: A Vigilant Python Power Object

Power objects were indispensable for revising formulas of moral belonging in court and on battlefields. Recall that traditions compiled by African Christians ambivalent about (if not outright hostile toward) such power objects nonetheless narrated the "conquest" of Butambala by linking sovereign knot, clan, and the power object called Mbajjwe. That bundle, working through the Mbajjwe shrine, earned a victory against "The Totterer," a Nyoro medium and a political competitor in the struggle to establish the sources of fertility in the area to which residents would turn.[119] With the conquest of Butambala completed, Kateregga created a titled chiefship called "Katambala," held by Mbajjwe's guardian. From Kateregga's time until 1893, a member of the Sheep clan held the title.[120] Katambala's principal duty was to look after the kabaka's "charms," carrying them when a kabaka traveled.[121]

As is often the case, these names contain messages about the conditions of their creation. Kodesh derives "katambala" from the verb *kwàmbala* "to dress, clothe oneself; wear" plus the negative prefix, giving "place of poorly dressed people." The gloss emphasizes poverty and a kind of barbarism. One might also derive the term from *kutâmba* "slaughter, sacrifice; kill condemned person" plus the prepositional suffix *-ala*, giving something like "executing or sacrificing for, on behalf of." That derivation echoes in performances of traditions about Kateregga and Butambala linking the conquest of this county, the titling of its chief, and the responsibility of the shrine he oversaw to deliver this kind of justice. Another possibility, connected to the last, is that the county name and the chiefship's name are deverbatives of *kùtambala*, "stand up to, face (danger)." Both nouns, *katambala* and *butambala*, linked sacrifice and legitimate sovereign violence to facing the danger of such violence. The prominence of clans as objects of royal violence and as deliverers of justice at Mbajjwe's shrine is striking in this regard. Digging deeper into power objects reveals the salience of groupwork to the complexities of conquest.

Power Objects

The power objects Roscoe calls "fetiches" are called àmàyêmbe (sing. *èjjêmbe*) in the Ganda language. The Namazi knife handle, the Kisaja drum, and the rope-bodied, clay-headed snake Mbajjwe could each be called èjjêmbe. The term may be translated into English as "animal horn" or "charm."[122] They housed a spirit. In Buganda, specialists made them. Someone with a formal title, such as the *kaddulubaalè* ("servant of the lùbaalè"), tended them.[123] They could be made with whole horns, calabash, land snail shell, and other things.[124] Their inhabitation by a spirit, their mobility, and their use in divination and mediumship make it easy to think of them as "power objects." The set of qualities was spread discontinuously across the major branches (one of which includes Ganda) of a speech community with more than two millennia of time depth, suggesting the bundle is at least that old.[125] Even though we cannot tell from Roscoe's account if medicine had been put into its clay or rope, Mbajjwe belongs to this category.[126]

One way to think about power objects like Mbajjwe is to follow David Doris and conceive of them as both subject and object, because people shared an intersubjective world with them. Doris has argued that this is the way to understand *à:lè*, the vigilant things people in southwestern Nigeria use to keep thieves away. Their fashioning, placement, and materials prompt those who encounter them to reflect on the moral weight of the intentions that brought them into their presence. Because ordinary people already know something about the meaning of the object and its power, "it recalls the presence of moral law that is already inscribed within one's consciousness. . . . The efficacy . . . , then, regardless of any constituent medicinal power, ultimately resides in the eye—and in the consciousness—of the beholder."[127] Doris emphasizes an accessible language of visuality that binds person and object to moral concepts and strategies. Words spoken as an object was made, or over its finished state, activated the power of its constituent elements. Drum and flute music accompanied an object's use. Through these threads of meaning, objects and people worked together.

Power objects worked because makers and users shared with those who encountered them a single moral and political world, layered and networked in historical weight. The past called out from the fact that power objects differed in the scope of their efficacy and purpose. Some were personal. Others, like Mbajjwe, had a broader salience. The common ground lay in the fact that encountering such an object provoked an internal dialog about the world that focused on the consequences of one's intentions for one's place in it. The privacy of the reflective work prompted by encountering such objects lent them their supernatural air.

Similarities between the two classes of objects end there. Àmàyêmbe were not commonly placed and left in farms or houses, as are varieties of àalè.[128] Àmàyêmbe moved. They were often worn on specific journeys, like a visit to a powerful superior, a night of trying to make or grow a baby, or on a field of battle. Or they were worn when participating in a public event, such as the assembly Muteesa put on for Speke in late February 1862, probably during that month's new moon celebrations. Speke wrote that "the dressy Waganda . . . on their necks, arms, and ankles . . . wore other charms of wood, or small horns stuffed with magic powder, and fastened by strings generally covered with snake-skin."[129] When not in use, they were kept in a special part of the house—or royal precincts—and tended with beer and words. Muteesa and Muganzirwazza spent April 1, 1862, the "first day after the new moon" was sighted, "looking at and arranging their horns—mapembé, or fetishes, as the learned call such things."[130] Royals took power objects on military expeditions. They were made out of "long antelope horns, with iron spikes at the tips, the hollows of the horns being filled with ingredients known to the maker only." After a successful raid, these objects sat in the final rank of display at Muteesa's court.[131]

Specialists made àmàyêmbe. The way they worked, the things they said, the materials they used were central to the potency of the object. It is worth quoting Roscoe on this point.

Only the most skilled medicine-man could make fetiches; herbs had to be carefully selected, and other materials were needed, such as the hearts of lions, leopards, crocodiles, elephants, buffaloes, and other animals, which (it was supposed) would make the owner brave or strong. These materials were pounded together and stuffed into the horns, or they were mixed with clay, made into fetiches, and dedicated by the medicine-man to different gods. They thus became identified with a supernatural being, and in consequence they were possessed by the gods, and were powerful and effective. The secret of making these fetiches was confined to a small number of medicine-men who never divulged it to others, unless they themselves were to reap some benefit by the communication. The people believed that these objects had supernatural powers, they paid large sums of money for them, and treated them with the utmost respect and reverence.[132]

The clay and horn in Roscoe's account of preparation techniques held the chosen ingredients. Felkin notes in passing, "These powders are either placed in horns, *usually closed with python skin*, or else they are packed in small neatly made boxes covered by skin."[133] Edvard Schnitzel (a.k.a. Emin Pasha) reported a similar practice, while visiting Buganda in the 1870s. Mothers placed a bit of python skeleton, wrapped in bark cloth, on a child's body to prevent "colic and convulsions." In his Buganda house, Schnitzel hung a python's vertebral column "carefully wrapped up in bark cloth."[134] Pythons had a metonymic presence in àmàyêmbe.

Accounts of Mbajjwe say nothing about what might have been mixed into the clay before forming its python's head. That was secret knowledge and private work. Yet it seems likely that all who encountered Mbajjwe assumed that had been done in making the clay-headed python. That assumption contributed to the power of the object. Many remark on Mbajjwe's ability to provoke fear in the tale-telling prisoner kneeling before it.[135] Some àmàyêmbe circulated as commodities. A general knowledge of the capacities and symbolic meanings of their constituent materials and their origins in particular medical workshops underwrote that market. The àmàyêmbe in Butambala touched on fields of power, secrecy, and morality in which both ordinary and royal persons moved.

Mbajjwe

Dictionaries compiled early in the twentieth century translate Mbajjwe into English as "a royal charm, talisman; it transforms itself into a snake."[136] The noun derives from *kùbajja*, to chop wood into shape for use in carpentry, including joinery, or to work stone.[137] It is the most precise verb for describing the making of a dugout canoe.[138] The language of fashioning with clay or of plaiting with fiber is not involved in naming Mbajjwe, which was nonetheless constituted of clay and fiber. Lexically, the Mbajjwe was the roughly blocked-out wood or hewn stone thing. Materially, it was of clay and fiber. The derivation of the name, then, is not easily linked with the figure's materiality.

Its name may instead have emerged from the kind of things its mediums, priests, and guardians used it to accomplish. In a very general sense, blocking out was the work of culture making.[139] In this case, blocking out constituted a kind of political culture, properly dominated by removing unwanted parts, by executing royal prisoners after hearing a representative tale of their acts. The blocked-out thing—mbajjwe—evoked specific moral and political associations in the minds of viewers, especially the men it could block out from the living.

Mbajjwe's being exceeded facilitating the removals of execution. It was bound up in spirit possession, public healing, and the fertility they promised. Part of the struggle over which clan controlled the clay-rope serpent involved arguing about Mbajjwe's past, revealing that Kateregga's was not the first Mbajjwe to exist. At stake in those arguments was much more than which group would operate this powerful object. The winners would blend Mbajjwe's capacity to generate fertility with its capacity to judge the successes and failures of ordinary men and their groups, whose labors in the alliance between state and a set of clans would generate fertility. The details matter very much here. They reveal that the terms of a new masculinity could be used as moral grounds for removing those who fell short from access to webs of reciprocal obligation binding a young state to other centers of wealth and power. Mbajjwe carved out a sharp, internal edge to belonging.

A durable figure of female fertility informed historical arguments about Mbajjwe. Two generations before Kateregga's conquest of Butambala, Nakku, a royal grandmother of the Civet Cat clan, struggled with barrenness. Her name can be translated as "mother of descending."[140] She could go down beneath the earth, where ghosts resided. Nakku knew mediumship, she embodied the afflictions of reproductive disruption and other kinds of harm. According to Wrigley, Nakku was a title bestowed on a "woman who in each generation was reserved for a ritual marriage to the reigning king."[141] She commissioned doctors to make her an object called Mbajjwe that had the capacity "to enable people to beget children."[142] The three princes to whom she eventually gave birth, one of whom became kabaka, proved her Mbajjwe's efficacy.

The first Nakku belonged to Kimera's entourage, formed sometime in the fourteenth century.[143] Many historians find in the stories surrounding Kimera's group abundant evidence for a transition to a scaled-up political culture of trade and conflict, drawing on clans to compose groups with greater diversity of skills and knowledge.[144] She "married" (i.e., joined as a medium) Kimera's network and "bore" (i.e., was possessed by) a serpent.[145] Nakku was the daughter of Ntege, the founder figure of the Civet Cat clan, in Buganda.[146] This

Nakku "told" Kimera "all about the art of governing Buganda."[147] The first *cwezi* figure, Ndahura, conquered Ntege. Mukasa, Ndahura, and Nakku occupied overlapping temporal frames of competition.[148]

Through this language of marriage and birth, descriptions of the first Nakku fit her into Kimera's emergent public healing group. Marriage and birth also enfold the second Nakku, the one whom traditions claim fashioned a charm called Mbajjwe and, with its help, gave biological birth to a son in a ruling sovereign knot. Roscoe reported a tale about a third son of Kateregga's, Kayemba, whose mother was Lungfish. Kayemba wanted to marry his father's reigning Nakku, against divinatory warnings not to upset the orderly flow of generations. The occult messages signaled worry about the Nakku's power in a time of bellicose expansion: "she became the mother of a child without arms and legs," called "Kawumpuli," a name normally used for diseases of the skin, including plague.[149] The Nakku's fertility could produce extraordinary—and dangerous—results.

Fearful, Kayemba exiled Nakku and the monster-child "by canoe to Busoga." They were refused hospitality and refuge in Busoga and returned to Buganda. There, a "nurse" (a medium) called Nabuzaana (a cwezi kùbàndwa name) tended Kawumpuli until the misshapen figure's death. Kateregga's Nakku disappears from the story when Buganda built a shrine for the departed, limbless child in Bulemeezi, between the trading zone of Bulondoganyi and southeastern Bunyoro (map 2). Kawumpuli came to be known in the reign following Kateregga's as "the god of plague." A Nakku officiated at the shrine in Bulemeezi, which was similar in many ways to other lùbaalè temples except for "a deep hole in the temple, which was securely covered, in order to prevent him [Kawumpuli] from escaping and harming the country."[150] The Nakku's unbound fertility was dangerous, but she could control it by marshalling many interests.

Through discipline and assembly, the Nakku helped make rule powerful and efficacious. Kagwa recalled the Nakku as having key roles in the *okukula kwa basekabaka* ("to mature the kings" ceremonies).[151] She hosted the new kabaka, brought to her home by her brother.[152] The Nakku advised the new kabaka on managing all the royal wives in the palace.[153] In later reigns (presumably including Kateregga's), the woman who held the title of Nakku closed down the temporal break entailed by mourning the death of her spouse, the king, in a particularly gendered manner. She took up her hoe and began to cultivate, exhorting people that the funeral rites were concluded and they should get back to their usual work.[154] The same also happened at Mukasa's Bubembe shrine. There, the chief priest's kaddulubaalè, who was also one of Mukasa's wives, played the role.[155]

Thus, the Nakku who was Kateregga's grandmother echoed Mukasa's pythoness when she commissioned the first Mbajjwe, marking her power object with the swallowing and the coiling possession of the python. Nakku and the adult women of Buganda whom she represented restarted the time of the living interrupted by royal deaths and the darkness of new moons by bearing children and farming. Royal rituals like this one imposed order on the randomness of ordinary life. But this one was modeled on a Civet Cat woman's fertility, underscoring the labors of biological women in that order. The Nakku represented a creative, driven adult woman who overcomes impediments to fertility. She does so through her abilities and duties to "descend" or encounter occult domains of knowledge to resolve challenges above ground, in the land of the living. The Nakku's work expressed the challenges the living faced.

Bringing Kawumpuli into existence—with a name, a genealogy, and a shrine—marked the intensity of skin diseases, probably including plague, afflicting people late in the seventeenth century.[156] The embrace of violence in expansionist statecraft eased the plague's movement, increasing the threat of catastrophic epidemic. The Nakku's efficacies were all the more important in preventing and recovering from such events. As a royal wife, Nakku sometimes had no children.[157] Yet she embodied the woman, a daughter of the Civet Cat clan, who had produced the girls who would bring fertility to sovereign knots. As we saw already, captive women put that power, privilege, and responsibility very much in doubt after Kateregga's reign. This second Nakku, the one who fashioned the first Mbajjwe, was under construction as the burdens of expansion grew and the shapes of politics shifted. She helped guide the shift, underscoring the virtues of senior women's labor and fertility, when bellicose masculinity posed a dire threat to them.

We don't know the form or the materials constituting Nakku's Mbajjwe or how she operated hers.[158] Only the name links her Mbajjwe to the one at the center of this chapter. Yet the juxtapositions between python, Mbajjwe, and fertility were multiple. Kateregga's grandmother Nakku used her Mbajjwe to renew life by begetting a next generation. Access to the authority of departed persons was part of that work. No formula governed the fashioning of power objects. The original was uniquely efficacious.[159] This invited people to think about Mbajjwe as historically specific but recursively entangled with past versions. A power object with a history of efficacy—in Mbajjwe's case, its associations with the office of Nakku and the renewal of life after death—left a mark, represented in part by its name.

People made sense of Kateregga's Mbajjwe python's abilities by using their knowledge and experience of the older shrines. At those places, a guardian tended and fed a living python that embodied a spirit that possessed a medium. The python also had a stool on which to rest its head (figure 11). It was fed prepared foods and not just the offerings of live animals. A shrine official interpreted the possessed medium's utterings. An audience of supplicants had asked for assistance with their pursuit of fertility and prosperity. They wanted children and to raise them to adulthood, abundant catches of fish, rich yields from farming, and success in trade, and so forth.

At Mbajjwe's shrine people collaborated with objects similarly, but to different ends, in a context of royal violence and threats of plague. The Katambala had the "duty to place it [Mbajjwe] in position in its temple, where it had a stool on which the head rested like that of a snake in repose."[160] The stool was on a leopard skin rug. In this scene of encounter, Mbajjwe's operators elicited a prisoner's tale of transgression, told on behalf of a larger group of prisoners. This verbal performance differed from a supplicant's request for children or fish or safe passage on the Inland Sea. The practice at Mbajjwe's shrine mobilized associations between pythons, eating, and power, accumulated over the course of the python's involvement in spirit mediumship and the formation of clans. But the practice did so through a trial that could result in execution. Mbajjwe's shrine practice thus blended prosperity and fertility with judgment and capital punishment.

The tales of transgression Mbajjwe's fearful presence elicited with the assistance of a medium are unknown. But they were told by men, in a context of territorial expansion in which the moral content of royal violence was up for grabs, in a new place with new threats of disease. Mbajjwe's shrine worked a durable ideology binding affect, power objects, politics, and collective well-being. Mbajjwe's operators brought the failures of men's gendered self-mastery into the presence of a power object steeped in ideas about prosperity and fecundity. The new practice brought death and life together in a bundle of ritual work involving pythons and mediums that had been (and was elsewhere still) focused on the pursuit of fertility and fecundity. People used Mbajjwe to connect the groupwork of conquest, which associated harming and healing with justice, to executing men deemed to have fallen short in that work. Moral belonging with an expansionist state carried material risks of failure and internal, gendered edges of removal.

Wakes

Kateregga's bellicosity brought relations between shrines and royals into a new political territory bounded by tense matters of fertility, extractive power, the Inland Sea, and officialdom.[161] A famous example involved Ssese's entanglement with Buganda's militarism and the knot of sovereignty surrounding Nnakibinge (kabaka) and Nannono (a wife, of the Leopard clan), in the

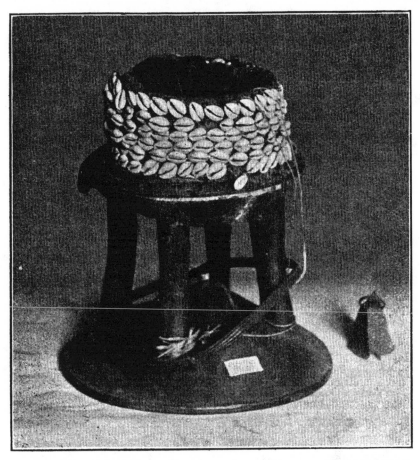

FIG. 49.—STOOL ON WHICH THE WAR-GOD KIBUKA WAS
PLACED.

Figure 11. Kibuuka's stool. Perhaps Mbajjwe's python head, resting on a similar stool, gazed at the man whose fate and that of his colleagues hung in the words of the tale he told? Source: John Roscoe, *The Baganda: An Account of Their Native Customs and Beliefs* (London: Macmillan, 1911), 289.

mid-eighteenth century, three generations after Kateregga.[162] Desperate for an answer to Bunyoro's military power, Nnakibinge sought the advice of mediums from one of the mainland centers founded by the Kintu figure. The mediums there told him to visit Mukasa's father, Wannèma, on Bukasa Island. Wannèma's children, Kibuuka and Mukasa, could help defeat Bunyoro. Wannèma offered Mukasa, but Nnakibinge preferred Kibuuka.[163] Kibuuka's military skill won a few battles but did not deliver lasting advantages to Buganda.[164] Nannono followed through. Her greatest success was supporting the establishment by Sheep clan leaders of a new shrine to Kibuuka, at Mbaale, equidistant from the littoral and Bunyoro's edges (map 3).[165]

Nnakibinge and Nannono addressed Buganda's military weakness through their alliance with an island lùbaalè shrine. Kibuuka embodied the necessary creativity and courage. Sheep clan leaders turned that alliance into a long-term solution. In establishing the Mbaale shrine, they attracted many young men and women from different clans to the possibilities of gain offered by involvement in an economy turning to organized violence.[166] Mukasa's network would have brought naval power to bear on the struggle with Bunyoro. Perhaps that is why Wannèma first suggested Mukasa to the desperate Nnakibinge.[167] But Nnakibinge, Nannono, and the networks that grew up around Mbaale's shrine to Kibuuka after his death were focused on ground action. Mbaale marked a martial boundary with Bunyoro.

Organized violence led to new royal installation rites at Buddo Hill, Bemba's former home. The move shifted the focus from the older rites, conducted near Bakka Hill, in Busiro (map 2), involving fewer clans. Mbajjwe had a role in the new rites.[168] The Katambala took Mbajjwe with him when he went to Buddo Hill. At a point, grandees lined up outside a shrine to hear the results of the lùbaalè's prophecy concerning the reign to come. They stood on a path oriented to Bweeya, home to Mbajjwe's shrine in Butambala.[169] Historians agree that the Buddo rites, worked out in the mid-eighteenth century, consolidated a new nationalism with a bellicose present by giving both a past.[170]

Mawanda's sovereign knot took up Nnakibinge's and Nannono's charge, blending militarism and administrative reform, in a period tied to Buganda's increasing aggression toward neighboring areas, like Bunyoro, Busoga, and Buhaya. Holly Hanson summed up that reform as a reimagined domain composed of ten counties, each run by a panoply of chiefs. Some chiefs shared deeper histories with the two or three clans already well established there. Other chiefs ruled at the pleasure of one thread or another in sovereign knots just before Mawanda ruled.[171]

The reforms included ordinary people, not just royals and nobles and bàlubaalê. A famous tale Stanley collected sums up the new dispensation after the 1760s, when a fresh generation of sovereign knots entered the picture. In 1875, the "Sabadu and the elders" told Stanley that Mawanda had encountered Kintu in Mabira forest (map 3) a century earlier.[172] A nameless peasant living close to Mawanda's capital had gone to the forest to cut wood for fuel and discovered Kintu. Exhausted from chopping wood, he built a temporary house, lay down to sleep, and dreamed. Three times a voice told him that he would win wealth and chiefship if he went "to a place in this forest, where the trees are very thick, round an open space near a stream running by." The dreaming peasant's Kintu was "a venerable old man, who reclined on a kind of throne." Two ranks of armed warriors sat on mats on either side of Kintu. Kintu learned from the peasant man that Mawanda then reigned. Aware of the ruler's desire for an encounter with him, Kintu instructed the peasant to return to the capital and tell Mawanda to meet in the forest, but that he must bring only his mother and the peasant man. Not even Mawanda's hunting dog was welcome at their meeting.

Mawanda had also had a dream, featuring the peasant man. While narrating his dream to his mother, the peasant arrived at the capital, demanding an audience. The three of them went off to Mabira forest alone. But everyone saw them leave the capital precincts. Mawanda's prime minister followed them into the forest. They found Kintu and had an interview, in the course of which Kintu saw the trailing prime minister. The three visitors looked over their shoulders to confirm their fears that Kintu had seen the uninvited man. When they turned back, Kintu and his warriors had disappeared.[173]

The peasant and Mawanda each dreamed parts of the story. A duly appointed official in the royal hierarchy—the prime minister who had until recently been a member of the Civet Cat clan—made it go wrong. The story introduced a new political culture where royals and commoners worked together directly. Less burdened by weighing official opinions and the constituencies they represented, they realized aspirations for wealth and power with correspondingly narrower—but more numerous—communities of beneficiaries. The new arrangement was ennobled with a patina of antique moral economies of networking, embodied in the figure of Kintu and grounded in ancestral authority. In case anyone missed that last point, Stanley was told that this new Kintu and his warriors were light-complected, almost certainly an image of the kaolin-rubbed faces of a bàlùbaalê group.

The martial bearing of the Kintu figure may have been a nineteenth-century flourish, but it was applied, after all, to a new kind of Kintu, one who had finally "returned" to this knot of sovereignty, now tied with lines from any number of clans and other groups. This reveals a renewed importance for public healing in the service of the state. The moral costs of territorial expansion were the reason. Expansion relied on values of courage, competition, creativity, and accountability, values promoted to core expressions of masculinity in a time of dislocation and enslavement. The growing number of captives upset the value of obligation to notions of obedience but were necessary components in struggles with neighbors.

Three elements of moral belonging developed together in the upheavals of the long eighteenth century. First, Mbajjwe blended royal justice with fertility in

judging the gendered respectability of men. Second, as an intended consequence of the first, the terms of royal fertility were reconfigured to open out,
displacing but relying on local ones. Third, bellicose boundary work formed
political others in the face of that violence. Some, like the Leopard clan, over-
came that othering. A broader range of "wifely" standings at royal and chiefly
courts pushed biological motherhood to the center of fertility. The opening of
royal fertility occurred in the course of an expansion that turned on royal alliances with Lungfish and Sheep clan members who held the Mbajjwe power
object. Those alliances conflicted with Leopard clan standing and with Nyoro
presence at Bweeya, Butambala, in what was becoming Buganda's west. There
is no need to conceive of Buganda in this long eighteenth century as a "war
machine" designed primarily to generate captive women to appreciate the
radical changes in gendered civic virtue begun by expansion.[174]

Kateregga initiated territorial expansion through violence and an alliance
with power object officialdom. In the following century, legal practice in
Buganda turned to promoting and defending the new masculinity. Mbajjwe
practice dramatized a gendered set of civic virtues offered as criteria for inclusion or exclusion. The authority to put them in motion originated with a royal
capital but required an object operated by representatives of several clans who
held the knowledge and standing needed to work the object. Kateregga and
his colleagues at Mbajjwe's shrine braided older lines that bound social reproduction and prosperity into royal violence against clans, like the Leopard and
shrines like the Nyoro Totterer's. Boundaries mattered in this new belonging.
They were moral and gendered, internal and external.

More people pushed more levers to influence the power unleashed by
eighteenth-century expansion. But to grow the realm, leaders attacked potential constituents, such as members of the Leopard clan. This revolutionized
group identification by activating the pathos of the risk representatives took
on its behalf as material for reconfiguring belonging through execution. Competition, fertility, self-mastery, and assembly—adulthood's virtues—took on
new weights. They reflected tensions between belonging in multiple, nested
groups and contracting a direct tie to a figure of wealth, standing, and ability.
Soldiering foregrounded men's anxieties, but women addressed the tensions of
expansion with their boundary work and othering, as we shall see next.

CHAPTER FIVE

Ladies and Slaves

Gendered Groupwork and a Long Nineteenth Century

Nnakawangiza-nkoto: ngʼomukazi aloota engʼoma ezirawa. "One who holds her neck straight up: Like a woman dreaming the war drums are being sounded."
—Ferdinand Walser, *Luganda Proverbs*, 287

Enzala mbi ekira obugumba. "Bad offspring are better than barrenness."
—F. Rowling, *A Guide to Luganda Prose*, 108

There are many tribes, I cannot say how many. I know a great number
but do not know them all. . . . I only know the customs
of my own clan, not those of others.
—Teofiro Mulumba Kuruji, in John Roscoe and Apolo Kagwa,
"Enquiry into Native Land Tenure," 36, 66

T HIS CHAPTER EXPLORES women's actions in a long nineteenth century of cultivating belonging and difference in broader social fields
than the statecraft explored in chapter 4. Men and masculinity were
central to soldiering, while women accompanied campaigns and kept households, markets, and other elements of daily life running when men were away.[1]
Noble men and women in Buganda set the terms of virtue, including the
embrace of raiding, the proliferation of chiefships, the captives it produced,
and the webs of obligation and opportunity they created. From at least the
early nineteenth century into the present, discourse on moral belonging with
a Ganda state has carried a clear patriarchal tone.[2] But commoner women did
the grassroots work. They cultivated boundaries between groups, nurturing them
with cultural practices legible to the captives within as statements othering

them. If nobles trumpeted the virtues of a Ganda statecraft, in registers of
masculine bravery and feminine propriety, commoners practiced them, lending intimacy to boundary work and cultural othering, painting them with an
implicit primordialism.

The combination of boundary work, cultural othering, and primordialism
was ripe for an ethnic formation. Yet seeing those dynamics through the lens
of ethnicity misrecognizes the richer picture of aspiration and respectability
that the protagonists in this story pursued. To resist reading all of that through
an ethnic lens, the broader fields shaping groupwork in the nineteenth century beckon. The consequences for groupwork of a turn to bellicose statecraft
must neither essentialize a warrior masculinity nor reduce political culture to
the dynamics of violence. Gendered experiences of that new world reduce
those risks but carry challenges of their own.

Senior men's and women's deeds and actions lay at the center of groupwork
with an expansionist state, but they are not equally accessible to scholars. Early
in the 1960s, Michael Wright interviewed two women, Rakeri Senfuma and
Zerida Nakibuka, among sixty-one others. The women provided Wright with
accounts of the past from Mukaabya Muteesa's time into the turbulence of the
1880s and 1890s. Nakibuka's brother, Kakungulu, was a major shaper of
Buganda's relations with imperial power in the 1890s. Regarding Nakibuka,
who was not a royal, and thus not a socially male voice, Wright had this to say
about her historical memory: "She was good on Kakungulu's career and the
antecedents of this man in the north." Ssenfuma, the daughter of Mukaabya
Muteesa's Kitunzi (a chief responsible for commercial ties to the royal center),
"remembered little," perhaps choosing silence from her perch as the wife of a
senior Protestant clergyman in regard to the upheavals of the 1880s, when the
two of them fled the violence.[3] Catholic priest and historian John Mary Waliggo
included thirteen women in his list of the oral sources beneath his account of
early Catholicism in Buddu. Waliggo spoke to religious Sisters, women who
cooked at various seminaries, and a few women whose lives included being
captured. Maria Kirofu, born in 1913, the daughter of "the last traditional ruler
of Bweera kingdom," had little to say "on the general history of Bweera" but
offered Waliggo "useful information on her own lineage."[4] Clearly, "women"
did not automatically absent themselves from history talk in interviews organized by men. The interplay of gendered historical knowledge with moral and
political threads of belonging is not a simple matter of women's presence or
absence.

When scholars study the histories African men made, they often find that
men's history talk dominated groupwork, especially ethnic formation.[5] The
worries and aspirations of men, and the contradictions men faced in living up

to them—imposed by their own failings and by economic and political factors beyond any individual person's control—are important topics.[6] They reveal how women worked lines of aspiration and competition in such a world, using its weaknesses and blind spots to their advantage.[7] But studying men's issues need not leave unexamined how women's words and deeds trafficked in history, in boundary work, and in cultural products.

In her magisterial study of the weave of property, movement, belonging, and ethnic formation in West Africa, Carola Lentz notes this problem and moves on, leaving male discourse at the core of her research.[8] Lentz built on Sandra Greene's groundbreaking blending of gendered social standing, mobility, and ethnic formations through clanship in the lower White Volta Basin's turbulent nineteenth century.[9] In formal colonial settings, Derek Peterson, Carol Summers, and Nakanyike Musisi have unpacked gendered discourses in East African history and politics, revealing dissenting men parrying "wordy women." They build on John Lonsdale and Luise White's foundational studies of masculinity and its discontents driving tensions of belonging to colonial breaking points.[10]

Jan Shetler argues persuasively that ethnic histories, guild history, and the experience of men say the same things about modern Africa's past differently. This can give the impression that the things women say about the past are neither historical nor related to political belonging. Shetler highlighted the moral value of knowing the social networks senior women and their grandmothers created when they married. Those networks were resources for addressing nineteenth-century crises, like drought and epidemics, or for navigating the pressures on men of colonial taxation. Shetler shows social network narratives are gendered "not because women told them" but because they "drew on gendered norms."[11] That insight guides this chapter's central argument that women helped compose those norms and used them for their own ends.

Gender, Groupwork, Buganda

This chapter digs into the entrepreneurial groupwork of noble and commoner women in Buganda. Their actions revise the scholarly consensus that the gendered indignities of bellicose statecraft and colonialism, falling more heavily on African women than men, left women's status in the twentieth century depleted in comparison with earlier times. That truism landed differently for different women because the ground of social hierarchy that separated noble from commoner and commoner from captive shifted.

The ground of social hierarchy shifted as women entered royal courts through the forms of "marriage" described in the last chapter. At court, biological royal women became sociologically male actors. They introduced key issues into civic virtue, lending coherence to royalist projects of enlisting followers. Many issues turned on tensions between sexual propriety and pronatalism. State-craft's obsession with such matters make them a rich territory of royal women's competition for political standing.[12]

On the other side of this gendered divide in social hierarchy, commoner women domesticated royalist entreaties. They occupied the contact zone between their men's ambition to work for a state or some other kind of center and the rewards and risks of that work. If things went well for him, he brought cap-tives, meat, and standing into the political economy of the "household" con-trolled by a senior wife. In performative and material ways, a senior wife applied—and revised—royalist ideologies of sexual propriety and pronatal-ism. She positioned herself as their embodiment, signifying that she was a Ganda lady and not a slave, by holding her neck straight up.

As we saw in chapter 4, Buganda dynasts and their colleagues undertook a strategic expansion westward late in the seventeenth century. It was aimed at linking the wealth of the Inland Sea to that of the interior west and directing it through centers controlled by the dynasts and their colleagues. The strategy developed a masculinist ethic of bellicose service in the region. Violence pro-duced new opportunities—and new standards—for men to pursue wealth and standing. A form of legal culture that blended justice and fertility used the new standards as grounds to remove the male-led groups that failed to meet them. Territorial expansion produced large numbers of female captives from different theaters of raiding or war and evictions from lands long held by par-ticular groups. The vulnerable and the secure could change places quickly.[13] Evicted families and captive women—often overlapping categories—brought loss and opportunity into their new homes, bridging the public politics of raiding with the private politics of making peace. The dynamics of violence grew central to groupwork but that violence neither erased earlier forms and their moral logics nor constituted the sole dimension of groupwork.

Men and women, nobles and commoners, in struggling over the shifting contents of civic virtue that would sustain their moral communities, settled on biological descent in drawing boundaries between statuses. Baganda women emphasized biological descent in constituting their motherhoods to brighten lines between them and outsiders. Stephens noted the irony in this move. Women who had been slave outsiders in youth and "reproductively successful" might aspire as elder widows to the status of having produced their master's heir.[14] An enterprising former captive woman from Bunyoro or Busoga who was taken to Buganda by a man, for example, could adopt gendered Ganda ways, positioning any children she had with him to distance themselves from the standing her life might have bequeathed to them otherwise. Tactics of absorp-tion unfolded in the shadow of men dominating the dynamics of enslavement.

But women pursued absorption by mixing biological reproduction with a cultivated, distinctive gendered comportment.

The interplay between state-involved violence and the increasing vulnerabilities of women occurred in several shifts. The first unfolded between the 1760s and 1810. A period of misrule created openings after 1760 to install a new layer of officialdom. Ssemakookiro's sovereign knot (r. 1800–1812) used the new chiefs to make a grand network linking the Inland Sea to the Nile Valley and the Indian Ocean coast (see map 1). In this period, successful territorial expansion exposed the reality (if not the idea) of a royal center to evasion by the ambitious. If political solutions to that uncertainty produced a familiar despotism, commoner men and women found openings in it for groupwork.

Their success drove the next shift, between the 1820s and the 1850s. Regional struggles erupted over the attractions and costs of the new long-distance mobility, unleashed by territorial expansion and upended gender relations, and central to success in trade for ivory, slaves, cloth, and guns. The struggles converged in Ssuuna II's efforts to revive Ssemakookiro's grand network linking the Inland Sea to points far and wide. As a Ganda state invested in naval power, gender and standing strained relations between established networks of knowledge and ambitious upstarts along the Inland Sea littoral.

In the 1880s, late in Mukaabya Muteesa's reign, the implications of religions of the book for a new politics of the subjective and the universal joined older, layered alliances. Many of the older networks—especially those managed by women—had been destroyed or rendered powerless. Civil wars between co-religionists and others had removed the landed base from beneath the power of royal women and many titled figures in clanship, domains that meant earlier groupwork had often crossed boundaries of language and location.[15] From the 1880s, new networks nourished latent, landed elements in the older ones, eventually replacing moral communities watered by a millennium or more of the practice and ideology of mobility. This last shift, taken up in chapter 6, unfolded in the decades on either side of the Buganda Agreement of 1900, which famously inaugurated a market in private property.

Royal women shaped the moral community these shifts presumed or entailed. Frictions between them and royal men produced the richest investments in biological descent and sexual propriety. Those tensions unfolded in the interplay between captives, commoners, and alternative centers unobligated to royal ones.

Royal Women: Virtues of Descent and Vices of Sex

Nakanyike B. Musisi's groundbreaking work on gender and Buganda state formation inspired historians to write about its eighteenth-century expansionism.

They focused on the effects a growing number of captives, especially captive women, had on gendered social standing.[16] Holly Hanson emphasized the disruptive effect these captives and their captors had on a flexible political logic of obligation. Hanson argued that unobligated persons had little need to treat followers with respect or seek the emoluments of a royal center. Their independence changed the social order, weakening the political institutions rulers and ordinary people used to generate obligation.[17] Rhiannon Stephens highlighted how captive women placed a premium on royal and free-born commoner women's biological motherhoods. In addition to changing the economy of expectations binding leader to follower, the captive women brought into Buganda through proliferating, unobligated centers might claim the standing of motherhood their ancestors (and neighbors) had enjoyed, but only if they bore children. Sylvia Nannyonga-Tamusuza added a flourish to this complex picture of socially and spatially contingent gendered standing. She argued that Ganda royal space—including any space occupied by an aristocratic body, wherever it might roam—was socially masculine.[18] When a biological commoner man entered an eighteenth-century royal capital, he became socially female. A turn to biology as an underpinning of socially powerful reproduction narrowed the politics of descent.[19]

These gender ideologies produced contradictions for people as their lives unfolded. In responding to the challenges of dislocation and enslavement, men and women embraced the idea that only biological descendants could be morally viable members of key groups.[20] More generally, as one of this chapter's epigraphs has it, even "bad offspring" offered a way forward into social visibility, something unavailable to a barren woman. Commoner and royal focused on the ideology of motherhood to debate social position in a shared language of sexual propriety, satisfaction, and pronatalism. If nobles promoted those values, commoner and captive women worked out their realities. They could take up "culture" and "ritual" in performing the virtues of belonging in a register that echoed noble women's actions, framing as outsiders those who could not behave like them. At each level, women made varieties of moral belonging separate aristocrat from commoner and commoner from slave. Noble women worked with the broadest repertoire.

Titled Royal Wives and Influence

Those repertoires emerge by following women—as categories and as actors—who populate aristocratic traditions. They connected the coalitions of clans and their allies, who helped bring a particular sovereign knot to power around one son and not another, to the royal domains that might reward the successful coalition's broader following for their support. As nodes in political networks, some royal wives, grandmothers, aunts, and mediums held power independent of their male co-rulers. But their ability to use their political power to steer men waned across the nineteenth century. From the domains controlled by queen mothers, which slipped from their grasp in the 1880s and 1890s, to the domains controlled by a wife, a grandmother, and their sisters, women responded to those threats. They were losing control for the same reasons that other chiefs and royals and senior shrine managers were losing their power. Newcomers and outsiders could compete with nobles; they had their own access to the riches and authority of the commodities, from cloth to guns, brought by ivory trading, warfare, and enslavement. With their landed base eroded, royal female power remained invisible to imperial, missionary, and colonial forces.[21] The swirl of things falling apart nonetheless opened new doors to gendered standing, authority, and wealth. People rebalanced the social responsibilities conferring virtue and risking vice against a shrinking capacity to meet them.

The smallest number of royal women held the title of queen mother, most often as a consequence of having groomed their sons with the support of their natal clan. The queen mother need not have been the sitting male *kabaka*'s biological mother, but she must belong to the same clan (or *èssigà* ["one of three hearth stones; lineage"] of a clan) as his biological mother.[22] Kagwa tells us that Nnamisango, the queen mother to kabaka Kamaanya, "was the youngest sister of Kamaanya's real mother."[23] Another small group of women held the title of queen sister (*lùbugà*). Rosoce was told the queen sister had a different mother than did the male kabaka.[24] She came from the group of aristocratic women called princesses (*àbàmbejja*). After her male kabaka died, a queen sister became a *nnaalinnya*, the senior manager of a new shrine complex built in Busiro and oriented to the jawbone and umbilicus (royal twin) of the departed male kabaka.[25] Royal wives were a much larger group. They held other ranked and titled positions, with a gaggle of chiefs beneath them.[26] One titled position, that of *kaddulubaalè*, was most often held by the first wife. She controlled power objects and conducted ceremonies with her male kabaka.[27] In chiefly houses, she also held the honorific *òmùkyâla*, or "lady," which carried a similar semantic charge of senior, respectable standing. Together with a male kabaka, these titled women formed the core political figures who blended lateral networks with the temporal depth of their landed titles to knot Buganda's sovereignty, creating its tensions.[28] Each gendered title holder hailed from a different clan, bringing new networks into the sovereign knot, increasing competition and intrigue among them.[29]

Musisi, Hanson, and Stephens revealed shifting gender relations and divisions as part of statecraft in Buganda, making royal women key players in choosing and cementing the alliances that mattered to a broad constituency. Stephens, in particular, identified "ideologies of motherhood" in the different speech communities she studied, examining parallels between political ideologies and economic life. It is a short step from there to note that such ideologies, and the social positions they sustained, were also subjects of debate in contests over the virtues of behavior and duty constituting moral communities.[30] If one asks about the political influence on particular clans or lineages of the shift in gender relations that informed motherhoods of one kind or another, the flavor of the debate emerges.[31] A political economy of dislocation, driven by competition for standing and followers, narrowed the scope of reciprocal obligation by creating large numbers of both unobligated people and captives. The political economy of dislocation fell disproportionately on women, limiting their scope of action and shrinking the moral ground beneath their actions. Senior wives or royal women limited their vulnerability to competition and dislocation by influencing matters of succession to titled position. They embodied a prevailing sense of virtue and standing in part through developing a language of vice to sway undecided followers to support a faction. A powerful woman had many in her hearthstone (èssigà) behind her, and she sustained that support by behaving correctly—or audaciously—as circumstances required. She could also reach beyond her natal clan for allies in the jumpy world of royal centers under threat.

The few women who became queen mothers crossed the bridge from commoner to royal standing. They began their lives in the court as in-marrying wives, reaching the height of their powers as one of the three kabakas that formed a knot of sovereignty. A queen mother moved in a capital and her own landed domains, formed alliances, rendered legal judgments, and collected information as she saw fit.[32] Princesses, on the other hand, were born into court culture. They grew up steeped in its intrigue and the opportunities for learning from visitors and through travel. Women in these categories held different kinds of power, position, and responsibility. They could use them to promote gendered notions of virtue and vice, as well as instrumental strategies for tending political boundaries. To the extent that others took up those prompts, royal women could be entrepreneurs of moral belonging, among other things.

Nassolo Ndege

Nassolo Ndege (r. 1730s–1760s) was the sister of Kagulu, who fought to reverse her brother's infamous transgressions of moral leadership. She shaped the transformative events of the generation of sovereign knots that Nagujja and her son, Kagulu, opened in the 1730s and that Nakkidde Luyiga and her son,

Mawanda, closed down in the 1760s. During those pivotal decades, Nnaki-binge and Nannono engaged Kibuuka to reverse Bunyoro's raiding, beginning the task of upgrading Buganda's military capacities (chapter 4). Royals of this generation reformed chiefship to bind military adventure to territorial control by increasing the variety and volume of wealth flowing through chiefships to royal centers.[33] One consequence was that the currents of captives and a grave note of bellicose masculinity would eventually undo the very innovations they helped create. But no one saw that coming when Nassolo Ndege took her position of influence as a noble woman who had to deal with Buganda's vul-nerability to Bunyoro's power. Buganda lacked access to key resources—iron bloom and sewn canoes chief among them—with which to attract followers and produce the means of destruction to ameliorate the vulnerability.

She led the rebellion against her uterine brother, Kagulu, whose onerous and mean-spirited expectations of followers in the wake of the struggles against Bunyoro had driven chiefs and retinues away from the royal center. In her open-ing move, she rallied her male relatives, convincing them to seek refuge with fellow nobles in Bunyoro.[34] They never arrived. A medium called Mawuba in-tervened, from a base of power in a region between the two polities. Mawuba used power objects to mobilize his regional networks and bolster the would-be rebels. The objects marshalled reciprocal obligations that reached across the vague boundary between Bunyoro and Buganda. Their reach outweighed those Kagulu had concentrated in his capital, where once again the mean king had unreasonably insisted people serve him, this time by calling them to grow crops in his private courtyard. Fortified with this alliance, Nassolo chased Kagulu into Kyaggwe (map 2), a key early source of iron bloom, bark cloth, timber, and access to numerous ports to points east. In convincing her brothers to seek Mawuba's help, Nassolo helped one of them, Mawanda, make a blood-friendship with the medium. After they defeated Kagulu, Mawuba leveraged the pact into a prime position as a leader of one of Mawanda's troops of professional sol-diers.[35] Mawuba clearly commanded a following of able fighters and skilled mediums, which Nassolo engineered into the stronger alliance. For his part, Mawuba used the opportunity to choose a side in a struggle over the royal center and, if victorious, move up in that world. These strategic moves restored a royal center after losses to Bunyoro, following Kibuuka's death, and after her brother's bad rule.

Nassolo's curriculum vitae embodied the emerging civic virtue of the so-cially male royal woman as a political and military operative whose diplomacy and righteous indignity relied on insiders as well as outsiders. She contributed to a suite of practices and values available to later entrepreneurs of moral belonging with Buganda, explored in the next chapter. Her strategies respected both biological descent and blood-friendship, keeping categories of belonging broad but bound by common cultural logics. In her life, violent conflict between two polities did not automatically prevent pulling on the aristocratic and public healing ties between them.

Nanteza

Nanteza (r. 1780s–1800s) was a royal wife to Kyabaggu and a queen mother with two of their sons.[36] She blended a shrewd sense of the persuasive powers in virtues of gendered sexual propriety with economic goals of expanding state interests east and southwest. A daughter of the Elephant clan, Nanteza delivered on the promise of Nannono's rule, creating regular supplies of iron into Buganda from three directions. She worried about descent and about sexual propriety in restoring her clan to high position late in the Ganda state's ascendant period. Kyabaggu, in the younger generation of the male relatives Nassolo Ndege had rallied, raided intensively but inconclusively in Busoga.[37] Early in their reign, the drama between Ssese and the royal capital unfolded, involving the plague of rats. Chapter 3 noted this story's unbecoming tone of royal pique and Ssese's critique of it and the senior royal woman who rebuilt Mukasa's shrine. Nanteza worked in their wakes. Royal traditions agree that during her son kabaka Jjunju's reign in the 1790s, Buddu—a rich source of iron bloom and bark cloth—came haltingly into the orbit of Buganda.[38] Such gambits pushed Ganda interests into a broad set of regions. Repercussions echoed from the Rwenzori mountains to western Kenya. Nanteza played key roles.

Ssemakookiro rebelled against his brother Jjunju with the pivotal help of the Abakunta, a "military regiment." People from many clans joined this version of an *èkìtongòle* chiefship, but it was dominated by members of the Lungfish clan and others from eastern Kyaggwe.[39] Those warriors killed Jjunju in a manner Ssemakookiro found abhorrent.[40] They removed his genitals and threw the body into the bush, affronts to virility and the politics of descent. Ssemakookiro needed the body to oversee a proper funeral, to conduct the previous male kabaka into the land of the dead, the correct domain from which a jawbone tomb might be constructed in Busiro. A ruined body was better than none. A search party located the severed genitals in the bush near Jjunju's last capital. They stored them inside a section of bamboo. In possession of these potent parts of his brother's body, Ssemakookiro and Nanteza could tighten a new knot of sovereignty.

Among his first acts was retribution against the errant Abakunta fighters. Learning of the royal plot against them, they fled west and east. Some were welcomed in the west, perhaps drawing on the trade networks that brought dried sprats into the interior. The main body fled far to the east, along the littoral, to Rusinga and Mfangano Islands and their immediate littorals, today in western Kenya (map 2).[41] Some accounts of the Abakunta populate them with people from many different clans.[42] Kagwa's sources insisted Lungfish were most numerous.[43] Accounts told on Rusinga and Mfangano Islands use genealogical links to particular littoral places, from southern Busoga to Mawokota; they don't use the "Abakunta" label.[44]

When scholars write about the Abakunta, they focus on the reasons for their flight and the details of the oral accounts of those who claim descent from the group members. They are fascinated by this history because it shows a sort of ethnic formation based on mixing people from different groups in the aftermath of a violent turn of fortune, with both literal and rhetorical elements of diasporic belonging. They note—but do not make much of—the fact that Nanteza and an unnamed royal wife of Ssemakookiro precipitated the conflict between Jjunju and Ssemakookiro. The two women made self-imposed exile a wise choice for the people of that ill-fated regiment.

These women used gendered comportment and sexual propriety as levers, pressing their male counterparts to act in a way that instigated the momentous Abakunta violence, a violence that picked up those very threads of gender, sex, and fertility. Nanteza sent Ssemakookiro seventy soldiers, asking rhetorically: "If you are a woman (or a commoner), get married to these men." She meant to goad Ssemakookiro to rebel against Jjunju, her other son, who had seized rule by dispatching two other brothers with Ssemakookiro's help. Nanteza impugned Ssemakookiro's noble standing and his masculinity. She showed their close bond at the same time that she suggested a broad threat to that bond.

This pithy vignette reveals the power and authority of queen mothers early in the nineteenth century, when warrior masculinities had been vital to an aristocratic Ganda moral community, since Kateregga and Nnabuso's rule, discussed in the last chapter.[45] But Nanteza's taunt brought to a head a string of events in which other royal women played key roles. Ssemakookiro's wives worried that he was losing standing in Jjunju's eyes, the brother he had helped to power. So, they began to grow maize and take it to Jjunju as a gift.[46] On one visit, Jjunju tried to seduce one of Ssemakookiro's wives. She refused his advances, saying she was pregnant. Jjunju insisted, claiming the child was his. The nameless aristocratic wife persisted in refusing him. Jjunju ordered his soldiers to disembowel her, to learn the sex of the fetus.

This outrageous act played on masculine anxieties about paternity, mixing them with royal ideologies about monopolizing legitimate violence. It was conveyed to Ssemakookiro by the co-wives of the murdered mother-to-be. Rather than act on his own behalf to avenge the murder, Ssemakookiro passed the news along to Nanteza. She gave him an estate in Mabira, on the eastern edge of the realm, on the approach to Busoga. Mabira was the same forest in which Mawanda, his queen mother, and the commoner pit sawyer had had their brief audience with a martial Kintu, a generation earlier. While Ssemakookiro was ensconced there, Nanteza sent him the seventy-soldiers taunt, signaling her growing support for him by manufacturing a shift in the biologically male part of the Ganda knot of sovereignty. She got rid of Jjunju in this crucial period when sustained ties to long-distance commodity trade were growing more important.

Nanteza's move had a local calculus as well. The son she began to favor had wives who bore more children than his brother's wives had borne. That difference in fertility shifted Ssemakookiro's fortunes and Nanteza's strategy for redistributing the balance of power in his favor. Nanteza also activated the masculinist core of bellicosity with her goading gift of the fighting men. With the soldiers, she rejected Jjunju's desperate, transgressive attempts to make up for his limited virility. But the goad also suggested a threat to the virtue of masculine bellicosity, as royal centers spun awry from plague, competitive tensions from Ssese, and proliferating chiefships. Those conditions undermined status differences between nobles and commoners, a divide at the core of a Ganda moral community. Nanteza sought to reestablish and conserve them in the promise of a next generation well populated by Ssemakookiro's children.[47] She was a model of the shrewd political strategist, reinvesting in a politics of biological descent to manage relations between royal and commoner.

Kamaanya

Kamaanya (r. 1814–1831) and the queen mother Ndwadewazibwa had to consolidate the expansions Nanteza had engineered.[48] They did so in part by focusing on the shifting standing of wives, in a time of conflict with politically small but militarily effective polities in Busoga and a full escalation of èbìtongòle chiefships.[49] Kagwa says that Kamaanya insisted that wives who stayed in their home compounds while chiefs—their husbands—went to fight had to provide gifts to him. Kamaanya also insisted the he was the "substitute" husband of all those women, absent their husbands (his chiefs). Kamaanya was given to exposing "his" men's genitals. Finding their endowments lacking, he derided their future prospects for respectable marriage owing to the likelihood they would not be able to satisfy the sexual desires of a wife. He gave "about twenty women" to well-endowed men, taunting them that even so large a number of wives would fail "to satisfy him."[50] Kagwa found these actions of Kamaanya's "odd," but they show a royal man fretting over relationships between heterosexuality, desire, and respectable marriage. These key domains for gendered standing were threatened as shifting political fortunes blurred the status separating royals from commoners and the salience of distinctive cultural practices—such as marriage—to moral community.

Appeals to sexual propriety, pleasure, and patriarchal control over it are ubiquitous in Kagwa's histories of Buganda's royals. Musisi notes radically different consequences for men than for women who breached their confines. In the late nineteenth century, men found guilty of seducing a married woman paid a fine. As we learned in chapter 4, a woman guilty of having seduced a married man could be physically harmed, even killed, by her husband, whose actions in that case could not expose him to legal jeopardy. The rigid gendered differences in access to justice were the flip side of stark differences in sexual propriety, presumptions about sexual satisfaction, and respectability flowing from one's biosocial gender and standing.[51] These claims and the experience beneath them are hard to pin down in earlier periods. Nonetheless, women were central sculptors of such ideologies.

They used the protections of paternalism to expand their scope of political activity. A princess resisted royal men's attempts to control her sexuality. When Kamaanya "forbade his sisters, the daughters of Ssemakookiro, to get married," he meant to prevent new aristocrats from competing with him for control of royal centers. One royal woman, Nabinaka, Ssuuna II's aunt, pushed back. She argued, "Because Kamaanya prevented us from getting married, I too shall do something nasty to his daughters." She played on Ssuuna II's aristocratic masculinist vanity, mocking him: "Why have you neglected all your sisters and left them to commoners? There is nothing to prevent you from making them your wives. Take them to your palace and marry them."[52] Ssuuna II obliged Nabinaka's request, but the aristocratic women about whom she spoke fought back. Ssuuna II executed Nabanakulya, the queen sister, and eight of her sister-princesses. The mortal risks of resisting Nabinaka's stratagem forced the younger generation of royal sisters to submit. But the story also shows Nabinaka engaging the core of patriarchal fantasy to the advantage of the groups royal women controlled. She embraced the patriarchal ideology animating the realpolitik of her day, turning it to her advantage. Her calculation cost women's lives.

Kamaanya designed the "odd" behavior glossed above to define the parameters of virility, recognizing limits. The improper gazing and sorting of men by the size of their genitals, his gifts of women to the larger group, and his warning that even this largesse would not satisfy them, were boasts about his wealth and the limits of that wealth to keep those "big" men stuck by his side. The account reveals the wealth in women at his capital was in question. Were "small" men the only ones who found foreign or captive women sexually—and by extension, socially—fulfilling? Late in the nineteenth century, Roscoe's teachers told him male kabakas desired women who looked like Hima herders from western Uganda.[53] Kagwa hinted at a hierarchy of sexuality—and pleasure—gendering moral community and lending it an ethnic air. Royal women's standing was under threat.

Muganzirwazza

Muganzirwazza (r. 1856–1882) was the queen mother with Mukaabya Muteesa. In different ways, they directed the long-distance connections to the Nile basin, Indian Ocean coasts, and Inner Congo basin in place since Kamaanya's and Ndwadewazibwa's time. She also navigated—and channeled—new currents of moral belonging with religions of the book swirling around her capital. Her life shows that the moral weight Kagwa lent to Kamaanya's obsessions did not mean royal women's standing had disappeared.

Muganzirwazza (figure 12) embodied the virtues and vices of gendered Ganda royalty from 1856, when she came into possession of the title of queen mother, to her death from typhoid in 1882.[54] A shrewd friend, Muganzirwazza abandoned old allies when the burdens of responsibility to them no longer served her purposes. Between 1901 and 1927, Kagwa fostered an image of her as a narcissistic kabaka whose ears are stopped up by the wonders of rule.[55] But

Speke introduces Grant to the Queen Dowager of Uganda.

Figure 12. Muganzirwazza, queen mother. Note the tale-singing harp player, her mirror, the smoking pipe being brought to her, and her distinctive attire. Source: John Hanning Speke, *Journal of the Discovery of the Source of the Nile* (Edinburgh: William Blackwood, 1863), opposite 424.

her prominent political life, nearly as long as her much-studied son's, exemplified royal visions of the moral cores to belonging in time of danger.

When political advantage lay with others, as it often did in a period of weakened Ganda military power, Muganzirwazza abandoned even her closest allies. They were disposable largely because their networks, crafted since the 1830s, had lost power by the end of the 1850s. Early in her career, she turned against her father, Kayiira, the prime minister who had put her and her son's line into the sovereign knot ahead of other sons of Ssuuna II with stronger records.[56] The choice of a weak prince lent fuel to a fire lit by factions desiring to wrest control of the royal center from Kayiira. They claimed his actions betrayed his true desire, which was to rule.

One faction supporting another of Ssuuna II's sons attacked the savvy prime minister by casting doubt on his genealogy. They suggested Kayiira had come into the country "while still a suckling," claiming his mother was "a Muhima or a Munyoro."[57] The matrilineal vessel carrying this affiliation revealed a defamatory attack using the logic of royal descent and perhaps of biologically male royal desire for the shapes and hues of a child descended from a Muhima mother.[58] Muganzirwazza did not refute the xenophobic claims of illegitimacy. She doubled down on the widely held perception that Kayiira was an "overmighty subject" whose accumulations of wealth and followers under Ssuuna II amounted to inappropriate designs on the sovereign knot she helped tie. These logics of belonging reveal the multifaceted threats to a ruling sovereign knot posed by contending factions. Some of them honed a rhetoric of patriarchal authority over sexual propriety. Having neutralized the moves against Kayiira and proud of his smarts, Mukaabya took a new name—Muteesa, or "deliberate."[59]

Muganzirwazza took advantage of the friction, making the right choices in a cutthroat environment. She tacitly backed the next move against Kayiira, led by three powerful princesses. They painted him as an "over-mighty subject" of their sovereign knot. They claimed he had mourned Ssemakookiro, despite that kabaka's having had a power object made with the aid of "Muslim medicine" to prevent such activity. The weight of the charge fell in three ways. Kayiira failed to honor a kabaka's wishes not to be mourned, arrogating to himself the public benefit of putting on mourning feasts and so on. He not only acted in a way reserved for the best-positioned aspirant to the vacated position, his mourning reopened the possibility that Ssuuna II might "rise from the dead," pulling him away from engagement with Islam and back into economies of spirit mediumship.[60] In leveling the charge, the princesses protected their positions of authority over power objects and the access to the authority of departed royals such objects allowed. Ssemakookiro's was made with medicines from afar. In 1812, when he died, the power object embodied the advantage brought by connections to Islam, connections likely read through trading ties to the Indian Ocean world. The ladies pressed their case in a third way. They named the people put to death by the prime minister. They were two of Mukaabya Muteesa's mother's brothers and all the senior chiefs whom Ssuuna II had left for the next kabaka to deal with. These actions, they claimed, made the prime minister an "over-mighty subject."[61] Even though Kayiira had supported Muganzirwazza and her son's bid to tie the sovereign knot of power after Ssuuna II, she saw a brighter future in abandoning an embattled prime minister. Things did not go well with the next prime minister, Kisomose. She drove him out of office by accusing him of poisoning her. Kagwa reports that he had refused Muganzirwazza's sexual advances. A scorned Muganzirwazza hurled the accusation of poisoning at a prime minister weakened by a series of military reversals.[62] Mukaabya Muteesa appointed Mayanja, who was prime minister when Speke visited in 1862.

The rhetoric of sexual power and propriety fits a pattern in the dynastic traditions in which Muganzirwazza pursued her ambitions through Mukaabya by weakening his prime ministers. At least one ambition was to promote her brothers' political fortunes. That bore fruit when Wamala Mulere became the prime minister after Mayanja's dismissal. Before he was promoted, Wamala had run one of the estates belonging to the queen mother's office. With Wamala as prime minister, Muganzirwazza had access to the numerous "expeditions" Mukaabya organized in the first few years of their reign. Kagwa makes plain that queen mothers raided on their own, although he does not describe any of Muganzirwazza's raids.

Her independent strength, knowledge of long-distance trade, aggressive courtly comportment, and influence on her son are amply documented in Speke's *Journal* and much discussed by scholars.[63] At Speke's first audience with Mukaabya Muteesa, during which he brought a rich basket of gifts, he had the royal women in attendance leave the hall before Speke presented each item.[64] At his first audience with Muganzirwazza, Speke noted the presence of four female "mabandwa" or *bàlubaalè*, "a mass of other women," many wealthy chiefs, fine beer and tobacco, and a troupe of musicians "dressed in long-haired Usoga goat-skins."[65] After listing three bodily complaints to Speke, Muganzirwazza submitted to a physical examination, causing some outrage among the few chiefs allowed to watch. In their exchange of gifts, Muganzirwazza included a "number of" rings of giraffe hair wound with iron and copper wire, a regional currency. Descriptions of the musical troupes' dress, orchestral composition, and dance steps suggest they had some responsibility for operating power objects connected with bàlubaalè practice.[66] Speke never misses a chance to remark on

Muganzirwazza's open enjoyment of beer, her stamina as a drinker, and her generosity in providing it to her courtiers. Near the close of Speke's second audience, Muganzirwazza's coterie of chiefs performed a mock charge, "as if they were to put an end to her for the guilt of loving" Speke. Her "calm indifference" nonetheless seemed to Speke to reveal that "she enjoyed" this dramatic defense of the propriety beneath her honor.[67]

Scholars often consider the moment when outsiders arrive in Buganda under the category of religion, both local forms and religions of the book. They focus on forces of commodification, particularly ivory and slaves.[68] Muganzirwazza's commitments to the intertwined logics of "chiefship" and bàlubaalè, however, reflect a broader northern littoral logic of moral community in the service of Ganda statecraft. The rhetoric of Muganzirwazza's actions reveal her as an entrepreneur of moral belonging, inviting her chiefs to police lines of biological descent, in an otherwise experimental era of aristocratic cultural politics. Investing in her chiefs and in *lùbaalè* practice, she distinguished herself from coastal Muslims; European Christians; her son, Mukaabya Muteesa; and neighboring polities like Bunyoro, Buhaya, or Busongora, who did not work with lubaalè.

The blend of freedom in bodily comportment and drinking, control over power objects, extractive expeditions, and alliance shifted against Muganzirwazza late in the 1860s. Kagwa reports that Mukaabya Muteesa "plundered all his mother's chiefs," executing her prime minister and ten others. The kabaka also executed some 100 "pages and royal wives" for being lovers.[69] Muganzirwazza seems to have been caught in a fit of male anxiety over the implications for his standing of his failure to control his wives' sexuality. Emboldened by that fear, he struck at the heart of her strength.

By the mid-1870s, Muganzirwazza struck back. A detailed story of princess Ndagire Malungu seducing one of Muganzirwazza's brothers, Tebakyagenda, while he held authority over commercial activity, is just the beginning.[70] Tebakyagenda also became the lover of one of Ssuuna II's widows, Ndimugambako. These incestuous tales ended with Muganzirwazza reversing her son's decision to pardon Tebakyagenda. Mukaabya Muteesa complained that Tebakyagenda's actions renounced their kin ties, but he was reluctant to punish that transgression and disturb a balance of power in which nonkin allies mattered for his success. Muganzirwazza had political territory to protect. She insisted that Tebakyagenda's actions went too far. By involving "daughters and their mothers," Tebakyagenda had threatened key resources that royal women—any women— used to pursue politics, economic opportunity, and security. In reversing her son's pardon, she defended biological descent, using its moral weight to force execution, pushing aside a man who held a position with authority over commerce. She blended sexual propriety with lines of biological descent, making their transgression a litmus test for a distinctively Ganda form of exclusion, the kind enacted at execution grounds (èttâmbiro). On his way to the execution grounds reserved for those found guilty of "grossly indecent crimes," Tebakyagenda tried to commit suicide. That act drained the spectacle of his execution of its moral and political value to a Ganda ethnicity. "Of what use is he now?" Mukaabya Muteesa asked, "He should be burnt."[71] At least that kind of death hindered the ghost from possessing anyone.

As centers proliferated in the 1870s from all these forces, exacerbated by a vicious attack of plague and by a resurgent Nyoro military, investments in controlling royal women's sexuality dissipated.[72] Mukaabya Muteesa's worries and weakness forced him to choose the intelligence he could get from his daughters and other princesses (as wives of chiefs) over the control of the sovereign knot he enjoyed by refusing marriage to those women. Kagwa writes about this in a matter-of-fact tone. Clearly, a vigorous queen mother's palace and a tight legal and moral control over princesses' sexuality only worked when a center functioned as the entrepôt of wealth and standing. Beyond a certain point, like the one reached after 1881, those luxurious expressions of the civic virtues of belonging became too risky. Muganzirwazza lived a few more months, her maneuvering within an ideology of propriety and patronage severely circumscribed.

Her death in March 1882 hit Mukaabya Muteesa hard. He had Alexander Mackay, the Protestant missionary, organize a proper English burial for royals.[73] Three thousand sheets of cotton (doti) and seven thousand bark cloths covered her body. She lay in four nested coffins, one of which was made of copper. Four thousand cowrie shells, ten loads of glass beads, and eighteen other bundles of unnamed material filled her tomb. "Eighteen" doubled the hegemonic "nine," marking abundance and indexed to human gestation. The funeral goods bundled multiple ages of commercial life.[74] Copper was oldest, then bark cloth, then cowries, then glass beads, then cotton cloth. Yet her influence quickly dissipated. Nnyika, who had navigated the unforgiving crosscurrents of the domain's dissolution with her, was dismissed from his titled position as Namutwe of Kyaggwe. Kaggwa does not even say as much, merely noting that a new holder of that title led a raid into Bukedi after Nnyika had returned, presumably unsuccessful, from yet another war in Budhola.[75]

In the 1880s, frictions erupted between co-religionists of various persuasions (Protestant, Muslim, Catholic), sovereign knots, and the chiefly hierarchies that had proliferated on the violent surface of territorial expansion. Domains of noble public power centered on royal women rarely echoed in the newly literate worlds of the victorious factions. Those men contended for control of the Ganda state in the wake of the civil wars precipitated by Mwanga's sovereign knot, which held the capital in 1884, following Mukaabya Muteesa's death in October. Mwanga turned on his youthful companions, the "readers" involved with missionaries since the latter 1870s, breaking with Mukaabya Muteesa's shifting embrace of their world.[76] By 1888, Mwanga's former comrades had cobbled together an alliance strong enough to chase him from the capital. It quickly dissolved along a Muslim-Christian fault line, with the Christian chiefs eventually returning Mwanga to a Ganda capital in 1889.[77] The faded politics of the center that nourished the drama of the 1880s had deeper roots, as we have seen. Those roots shaped the context in which Muganzirwazza sustained scurrilous attacks on her status.

Twenty years later, John F. Cunningham, an attentive lay ethnographer writing in the early years of the Uganda Protectorate, could repeat a demeaning slur on Muganzirwazza's name and Mukaabya Muteesa's standing. In 1881, the Catholic Father Lourdel was told that Mukaabya Muteesa's queen mother was a former slave who "his mother had recommended to him before she left Uganda" having been "sold to an Arab" in the 1850s by Ssuuna II.[78] Toli, a Muslim chief stirring the cauldron of criticism of the royal order under attack at the time, was probably the source of this information.[79] Just a year before her death, Muganzirwazza's influence had waned sufficiently to expose her to attacks on her biological relationship to sovereignty. Smearing the queen mother's genealogical status and social standing shows that biological women up and down the political hierarchy had suffered severe erosion of their former control over their own political fortunes as well as those of their "sons." It was a big change, for Muganzirwazza had shaped the course of events upended by the crises of 1884.

By the middle of the nineteenth century, a pronatalism shaped the royal center's interests in political stability in a shifting set of provinces. The matter crystalized in Mukaabya Muteesa's attitude toward succession for leadership positions. In short, leaving much else in this matter under the control of corporate groups, like lineages and clans, his capital elected not to recognize eldest sons as successors.[80] Mukaabya Muteesa and Muganzirwazza may not have been the first to enact such a policy, but the importance of intergenerational connections took concrete shape in the moment the first-born son ate a pumpkin seed from his dead father's palm.[81] The importance of pronatalism took shape in the fact that no pumpkin seed eater could succeed to his father's chiefly position. The only possible response that would make the pumpkin vines of linked generations continue to produce the fruit of official position lay in having more children. Stanislaus Mugwanya, the Catholic chief justice in 1906, confirmed that this was the intended result of a "custom" that "was adopted in order that the successor might have many children."[82] This politics of biological descent appears in Kagwa's discussion of Mukaabya Muteesa. He closes with

a story about Bukya and Namukundi, two men who came to prominence during Mukaabya Muteesa's time, whom he characterizes as *bafuusa*, "conjurers" or
people who change things. Kiwanuka calls these men "priests and mediums."
Kagwa noted that pregnant women asked these figures to tell them if they would
bear sons and that multitudes of them sought answers to this question.[83]

Royal women advanced their own political careers with and against those of
their men. They did so by developing a moral Ganda political culture oriented
toward descent, sexual propriety or sexual freedoms, divided between royal
and commoner. Kabaka Nnakibinge, in Nassolo Ndege's time, en route to Ssese
for help dealing with Bunyoro, left titled royal wives (*kabejja* and *nnanzigu*) at
Namiiro village in Buwaya.[84] Princesses resisted Kamaanya's attempts to shut
down their sexuality as an avenue to standing.

Threats to such women's standing, posed by the influx of captive women
from beyond Buganda, stimulated debates over the civic virtue (or lack thereof)
of the outsiders.[85] In taking up these debates, women sought to limit the pernicious effect on their own standing of the influx of captives. Moral community began to take on an ethnic cast, which women helped theorize. But if it
suited their male owners, captive women could seize the material requirements
for doing the cultural work ladies hoped to monopolize in performing their
standing as nodes of moral belonging. Publicly recognized commoner women
most urgently interested in renovating these traditions struggled to prevent
captive newcomers from eventually behaving in a similar manner. Promoting
biological descent was one of their moves.

All of this suggests reexamining the evidence that the standing of all women
fell as the eighteenth century turned to the nineteenth. In whose eyes was that
standing lowered, and by what criteria? Men and royals may have seen the
captive female as both opportunity and threat, to which they reacted with a
mix of defensiveness and repression. Perhaps commoner women—who were,
after all, threatened by this new reality but had few of the resources available
to royals for countering its corrosive effects on their position—moved in different directions. One thing they did was invest in the public rituals of adult
womanhood that their standing as wife and mother brought them. In doing so,
they intentionally started a new line of debate over moral community. They
emphasized a proper senior woman's comportment and responsibility to a husband and aimed it at outsider, captive women, wherever they may have called
home.

Commoner Women, Captives, and Respectability

Ganda intellectuals and scholars alike celebrate the ethos of competition running through the hierarchy.[86] Persons in one category could move to others

over the course of generations or in a single lifetime. Social gender and biological sex shaped options for promoting or crossing divides of social rank.
Scholars see the political economy of vulnerability, which had produced captives for two centuries by the time Kagwa and others wrote, as lowering wom-
en's standing. Thinking harder about labor and domestic scenes of cultural
performance occasioned by arrivals of captives suggests that women could shape
the interplay of social mobility, gender hierarchies, and childbearing to their
advantage. They could seize on their right to perform gendered cultural practices to defend their standing in the presence of captive outsiders. Captive
women who bore children for a household might claim a place on that platform if they knew the ropes. With commoner women distinguishing themselves from captives and captive women from other captives, otherwise widespread cultural practices could take on a Ganda cast.

Agricultural skill was a basic means for women to enact distinction. Women
integrated crops with origins in the Americas, such as maize, beans, cassava,
sweet potato, and peanuts. Maize planting and harvesting fit easily into agricultural calendars centered on millets or sorghum or on banana gardens but
introduced an unrelenting labor regime.[87] Returns to farm labor multiplied,
but people worked their farms for more months of the year. In high-rainfall
areas, such as the northern littoral, maize fields could give two yields. The burdens landed differently on different farm laborers. Maize's husks meant little
need for youths to keep hungry birds off mature cobs. The naked, ripe grain
heads of millet required a guard to minimize losses to birds. Maize plants must
be planted close together for cross-pollination to occur, enhancing the value of
intercropping them with ground-hugging plants, like beans and pumpkin,
which would be protected from the violence of convectional rains by their
maize canopies. The new crops revolutionized food production by spreading
yields of a greater diversity of foods over the agricultural calendar. Sweet potato
and cassava could be left in the ground, raising the opportunity costs for auxiliaries to feed a troop of raiders with the tubers.[88] The new crops reduced de-
pendency on banana gardens as calorie sources without displacing them as
sources of food and culturally appropriate materials. In the nineteenth century, ordinary households faced the threat of pillaging and the duty to fill the
larders of increased numbers of chiefs with banana bunches and beer more
often than noble houses. The new crops gave them flexibility to respond.

Weaving these crops into the fabric of agricultural life was ongoing in the
nineteenth century. Recall that Ssemakookiro's wives had sent Jjunju roasted
maize as a gift. Most likely, they came by it from fields they controlled on
which captive or commoner women worked or as gifts from followers. Women's
movements through marriage, pawnship, enslavement, or just plain visiting,

drew their knowledge of maize and other crops across the landscape.[89] The maize gift vignette singled out Ssemakookiro's "wisdom" in choosing it to mollify his brother the kabaka, who had grown jealous of Ssemakookiro's popularity.[90] The crop was a snack, not a staple, in noble circles by the turn of the nineteenth century, reflecting the reach of the networks Ssemakookiro's wives constituted. Perhaps their maize also signaled the ability of noble houses to take on tighter labor regimes. If low-status women figured out how to grow maize, their superiors treated it as a novelty. Commoner and noble women alike did not insert maize into the ceremonies they controlled. They kept it— and sweet potatoes and American beans, and so forth—at arm's length from that work. Bark cloth and banana gardens, millet, fish (like *ènkejje*), and collected foods like mushrooms held pride of place in ceremonies.

In the long nineteenth century, bark cloth reflected the reality of this political economy, but in subversive ways with respect to women's standing. In Luganda, the wood anvil on which bark cloth was beaten out was called *omuzzanvuma*, a compound noun meaning "welcoming the (scornable female) slaves." Making bark cloth was men's work. *Omuzzanvuma* meant an ordinary household enjoyed the benefits of a slave's labor, which could distribute farm work away from commoner men and women, allowing men to produce cloth throughout the year and not just in the cold, dry season. Having regained control of a labor regime from the unforgiving curve of an agricultural profile that included American crops, an ordinary household with a newly arrived female slave could afford to work bark cloth, dress well, and smell good.[91] By dressing well and smelling good, mothers (who may well have been former captives) with captive women in their household simultaneously remained aloof from the newcomers and shored up their status in the eyes of neighbors.

Noble and commoner wives had different standing, of course. A few women in both social worlds held ranked titles, such as the senior wife, separating them from other wives.[92] Senior wives were called kaddulubaalè ("little servant of a lùbaalè"), linking their primacy to the power objects giving access to lùbaalè. In commoner households, senior wives were also called *nnálúgóngó* ("mother of the spine"); a second wife took the title *nnasaza*.[93] Lists of the wives of kabakas Mulondo, Ssuuna I, and Ssekamaanya included *àbàsebeyî* (figure 13), or wives who traveled with them on their expeditions, and *àbàzaàna*, probably female pawns or young women placed in a court at the behest of her lineage or clan.[94] Such women lacked their own houses and precincts at the capital or in a wealthy court, unlike their titled counterparts, whose names and clans are recalled in dynastic tradition. Àbàsebeyî cooked and they prepared the warrior's body on military expeditions. When the raid was over, and everyone returned home, they receded into the background as the senior wife and her man per-

MTESA'S AMAZONS.

Figure 13. Mukaabya Mutesa's Amazons. These women likely belonged to the àbàsebeyî class of auxiliaries. Source: Henry Morton Stanley, *Through the Dark Continent*, vol. 1 (New York: Harper and Brothers, 1878), opposite 400.

formed the sexually inflected cultural work of "growing the battle" (see below).[95] The senior wife's proprietary public cultural work separated her from other adult women, noble and commoner alike. The chapter's first epigraph expresses the anticipatory pride such women could display.

The senior wife conducted herself in public in accordance with the civic virtues of her fertility. But the camp wife traveled and learned. The female servant remained in the court. The most vulnerable captive woman had access to the fewest (if any) kith and kin in pursuing their aspirations. Women fluent in the cultural work meant to garner the benefits of having borne children, possessed the richest capital for crossing out of slavery. Should children come, they changed their mother's choices for belonging and the political prospects they might cultivate.

The arrival of women pinned to these categories in noble and chiefly court life raised questions—and opportunities—about making and tending a clear fissure between the newcomers and women already in their husband's household. This opened some captive women to the dismissive scorn of strangerhood, of having no name or clan. Men and women, noble and commoner, used a derisive word to label the newest arrived and least powerful of slaves in a court or household in Buganda. The *ènvùmâ* were the scornable people.[96] As

Stephens has argued, "an òmùzaàna could aspire to be the mother of her master's heir and thus dramatically improve her social standing, but . . . this opportunity was not open to an ènvùmâ, even if she bore her master's children."[97] The lack of standing conveyed by scorn took concrete shape when the man of a household died. His wives with living relatives were escorted from the bereft house into the banana garden, home to the group's ancestors and full of the promise of food and security to come. They sat in the garden, on half of the house's central pole, which had been removed, placed on the hearth, and burned through. Kinless slave women were left to sit on the other half, which remained inside the destroyed home, their uncertain fates on dramatic display.[98] In a setting like this, free commoner ladies (àbàkyâla) could collude with female servants (àbàzaàna) to revise the latter's standing against that of the ènvùmâ. They used cultural work to achieve that goal. The simple act of being led away from a ruined house and into the fold of another set of relatives could not have expressed that more clearly. In a similar vein, camp wives (àbàsebeyî) found in the travel and vicissitudes of military life some scope for distinction and visibility (figure 13). With that, they pushed back on the image of rootless women by passing the effects of that image downward, helping create the ènvùmâ category by participating in the violence and striving that dislocated women in the first place.

Male slaves lived in a rather different reality. They could make blood-friendships with masters or sons of masters, at court, or in an ordinary household and buy their freedom. As we saw in chapter 4, slaves could not enter a clan.[99] Thus, at least in the turbulent mid-nineteenth century, clanship had an edge that applied most harshly to men, despite women's lack of access to legal process. The edge of viable social reproduction cut more deeply for enslaved men than for captive women whose scope for social visibility admittedly turned on their biology. But if children came, mothers could turn their knowledge of regional variations in respectable comportment to the task of eventually seizing respectability. Perhaps a male slave threatened a clan with his lack of an accessible patrilineal past and the networks it sustained. Be that as it may, the political edges to belonging in the turbulent nineteenth century were gendered.

The mix of vulnerabilities and opportunities in that world of violence and patronage created gendered openings, at every level of the hierarchy, for captives to improve their conditions. Captive women who married a commoner man and had children with him could seek to have the children recognized as members by his clan. A boy's matriline's "foreign" status did not automatically prevent him from inheriting property at his father's death. Yet Roscoe reported, "more frequently the children were passed over because of their foreign blood."[100]

The limited success of such multigenerational strategies for standing not only implied that commoners might suspend the norms of patrilineal descent when it suited them, it shows that pawns and captive women (other than ènvùmâ) could help them do so. These are common observations to make about the repercussions of slave presence in a community. More important for our purposes is the stage on which such negotiation and struggle unfolded. On that stage, captives and commoners alike doubled down on "Ganda ways" as media of moral community. They reshaped the virtues, breathing life into them by bending their gendered and descent-based obsessions.

The senior wife of a man who fought in a nineteenth-century battle organized by a kabaka, led by his appointed "general" or by a local chief, could confirm her fidelity to him while he was away fighting. The woman who could do this, the kaddulubaalè, tended the household's power objects and "it was with her that a man was bound to fulfill the taboos of journeying or of going to war."[101] She could confirm her fidelity to the house by receiving her returned husband in the road with a cup of water, taking his weapons, and spreading fresh grass over his footprints.[102] She prepared a meal of mashed plantain using fruit she cut from her trees, peeled, cooked, wrapped in leaves, and laid out for him to eat. If internal pains bit him after eating this meal, he could accuse her of having had sex with other men while he was away in battle. She could deny the allegation, in which case the man initiated a test. He instructed her to pick some leaves (used as a medicine to wash children when they were ill) and stir them into water for him to drink. His immediate recovery demonstrated his wife's infidelity and might move things into the legal realm of a case of adultery. He could charge that she did not leave his spirit alone while he was away fighting. However, if he seized up immediately upon drinking the infused beverage, then he was the adulterer and the wife was cleared. The wife was also cleared if the man's internal pains resisted healing over time, their persistence showing that his injury had not come from her.[103]

In courts and ordinary homes, resources like the ceremony just described bound paternal standing to biological descent. They could become tools of inclusion and exclusion by creating an impression of belonging and standing for audiences including people at very different points on the continuum under discussion here. The resources rose in value as security fell. Knowledge of these practices was the resource, and failure to follow them properly exposed a woman—and her man—to accusations of antisocial behavior, with legal consequences.[104] In the nineteenth century, this risky work put gendered reputation out for public consumption as a corollary to male mobility, especially raiding.

Much has been written about socially recognized soldiering in shaping masculinity.[105] Men pursued the resources of virility through this work. Among other things, it brought many of the captive women just discussed into Buganda's nineteenth-century households and chiefly courts. Because men worked in theaters selected by kabakas and nobles, they often raided and fought wars in parts of Bunyoro and Busoga but also from time to time in the domain of Buganda.[106] Those areas must have figured into the calculus of the wealthy seeking retribution on adversaries. Most often their leaders channeled commodities like cloth, guns, ivory, and captives in and out of the region. The salient point in this familiar equation lies in the close bond it created between gendered streams of social reproduction running over increasingly dangerous ground.

One danger lay in exposing men to fraught transactional economies of respect and honor, paid with currencies like courage and bravery or withheld in accusations of cowardice. Ali Mazrui argued that "the warrior tradition" constituted the nexus through which the lines of "culture, war, and politics" ran.[107] Richard Reid took up that point, insisting on the gender of the "courage" and "cowardice" in nineteenth-century East African military practices. Using Iliffe's approach to "honour," Reid highlighted the transactional qualities of these auras.[108]

Kagwa and Roscoe both reported punishments, from execution by burning to gender shaming, visited by higher-ups on men accused of cowardice and shirking in battle. A Nyoro soldier who failed to refute accusations of his cowardice "was made to wear the dress of a slave woman," serve food to his fellow soldiers, and clean up their celebratory feast.[109] In Buganda, superiors also gave such men women's work. But they dressed them with "a bit of the decayed pith of a plantain stem" at the lower back, "in imitation of a woman giving birth."[110] Like the drama of a fraught homecoming, this bit of theater linked food production, childbirth, warfare, and a palette of mood and comportment appropriate to sexed men and women as social reproducers. It's worth noting that the courage a mother-to-be should show in bearing a child was used here as the currency for withholding the honor won by courage, at the core of masculinity. Does using women's courage in childbirth to mock men for showing cowardice in battle betray a deeper male anxiety about the banality of female courage and the currency of honor it circulated among other women? "Camp women" (àbàsebeyî) went into the field with men, but our ethnographers say nothing about their bravery, courage, or cowardice.

Numerous stages for performing civic virtues were available to women. They included succession ceremonies, activities and duties pertaining to twins (figure 14), and negotiations over the inheritance of property.[111] Women won standing for these roles over the course of more than one lifetime. But the quest began with asserting access.

A woman joined a man as the lùbugà when he succeeded to a title, providing her with a public platform for celebrating her standing. Roscoe reported that commoner lùbugà were "ideally a near female relative of the deceased; if possible, the daughter of his brother."[112] Commoner lùbugà belonged to the same clan as the heir with whom they were paired in marking the birth of twins or enacting inheritance of (especially) landed property, affirming a single clan's interests in reproductive abundance and land.[113] The noun blended the speech of authority (*kùbugà*) with spaces of authority (*èmbugà*, "chief's compound"; *èkìbugà*, "town; royal capital").[114] Her title marked the integrity of a group constituted through patrilineal descent ideology.

Figure 14. At a twin ceremony. The play of emotion on their faces reflects a future of respect and responsibility brought by twins. Source: Lucy Mair, *An African People in the Twentieth Century* (London: Routledge, 1934), opposite 48.

In cases of noble descent—where a royal man or woman had established an estate in the past—standing as a lùbugà was curated and reserved for women who could claim descent from a particular patrilineage. On Mpata Island in Buvuma, this technique was used to circulate who among three groups on the island claiming descent from one of three sons of a nephew of Kyabaggu and Nnamayanja would be the lùbugà during succession ceremonies.[115] Before 1912, people on Mpata Island buried their estate holders (s. *omutaka*; pl. *abataka*) in a forest. At the head of each grave, they placed the number of cowries that marked how many had ruled before him. The next one in the cycle took the "omutaka" title with a lùbugà chosen from the same set of descendants. On Mpata, just like in the idealized, ordinary households Roscoe and Kagwa described, close attention to biological descent made it difficult if not impossible for outsider women to use any children they bore to assert standing as a potential lùbugà,[116] although one of those female children who had borne children of her own might use them to do so. Promoting "Ganda ways" could be part of belonging, including in places like Buvuma, only very recently incorporated into the territory of Buganda.

Women took up cultural practices of public salience because they helped bring into existence the many opportunities for doing so. Access to the cultural practices in question and their salience must have changed over the course of the nineteenth century. In recasting distinctive local variations in broadly familiar cultural work as their unique product, women's groupwork could be given an ethnic cast. It could be seen by witnesses as trading on a cultural practice's "timelessness" to establish a boundary beyond which cultural others lived. Examples occur in both vernacular and outsider ethnographic writing.

A sister, daughter, or wife could inherit one or more of "the women" under a deceased senior man's control, benefiting from their labor.[117] A man's descendants could include children of unions between a captive or slave woman and a commoner man. Men may have been the only "inheritors," but they might have had slave mothers.[118] That norm likely reflects many female slaves having slipped from their outsiderhoods by bearing children and garnering the public standing of motherhood. As we just saw, the senior wife tended power objects at home while her husband was away fighting.[119] This domain of cultural performance, including its connections with buried ancestors on a piece of land, was shared with settings in Busoga.[120] It was nonetheless resistant to captive women's attempts to engage it because operating the relevant power objects presumed a body of historical knowledge tied to the household in question. Women in those settings could embody a moral community, through biological motherhood and by operating power objects. They could express a cultural difference from lower-status women in their households through the ritual work their standing required. From the 1880s, religions of the book competed with that value, by dispersing the specificities of power objects into new universalisms. From the 1890s, this limited a power object's utility in the gendered play of power over a house's ancestral-historical past. A decade later, when the landed bases that embodied that spiritual heft were written into the hands of chiefs—or of the wrong lineages and clans—the scope of control over gendered ethnic comportments shifted again. Chapter 6 takes up those issues.

The powers of sex were not revised as easily as those of objects. Jumping over a person or a thing, often interpreted as a euphemism for the maturational powers of sexual intercourse, was distinctive in the region. Men of all social classes did this, in Buganda and beyond.[121] The evocation of sex accomplished by jumping points to capacious notions of well-timed, properly placed sex in promoting maturation, including the "growth" of wealth such as ivory and the washing away of the risks of plunder to the success of battle.[122] Certain moments required jumping, implicating certain persons. Roscoe reported that a man back from a journey "had first to jump over his chief wife, before he might go in to any of his other wives."[123] In a household where those women had different origins, performing this task underscored that fact. The senior wife, who tended the objects giving access to lubaalè networks, held the position of insider at that moment. She knew her house's relations with lùbaalè, allowing her to marshal that knowledge to particular ends. Her public receipt of symbolic sex from her husband kept her skill and knowledge growing and efficacious.

While jumping had long been a distinctive means to link the powers of sex and relations between people, in particular settings, the distinction could take on intimate edges in the long nineteenth century's world of mobility and dislocation. In Bunyoro, long a source of captives in Buganda, a military leader and a healer together readied men for battle. The healer sacrificed an animal to generate divinatory knowledge about the battle ahead and made the fighters engage the animal's dead body, sometimes by jumping over it.[124] In Busoga, men were said to avoid stepping over the seat a pregnant woman used while eating.[125] The point here lies in juxtaposing the ubiquity of a general practice with its distinctive elaborations by men and women in Buganda's public settings. What had been hiding in plain sight as a taken-for-granted current of moral practice—the gendered, symbolic charge of jumping—could take on a cast of boundary work and cultural othering with matters of descent at stake and an implicit primordialism on display.

Such educated guessing is sharpened by the (auto)ethnographies which took shape in the 1890s. The information they relied on came from prominent senior men—and a few senior women—whose personal experience of the

world reached into the early years of Mukaabya Muteesa's and Muganzirwazza's reign, when Speke was around. Roscoe's sources identified clan-specific
variations on practices surrounding pregnancy, birth, and raising and hatching
out young children. Members of the Bean, Genet, and Grasshopper clans took
different measures to ensure the birth of a healthy child or test a child's paternity.[126] Roscoe noted variations in naming ceremonies (see chapter 3), where
small groups of children were publicly recognized as members of their father's
clan, often in an event run at the clan's shrine at its principal estate.[127] Wives in
the Colobus Monkey clan colluded with their husbands to lord it over slaves
when hatching out the twins, making them stand in for sons in ritually dangerous roles.[128] When women restricted their actions in ways practiced in particular clans or more broadly in Buganda, they publicly expressed their proper
belonging.[129] In the chapter's last epigraph, Kuruji not only alludes to these
particularities, he perhaps implies that women, and not men like him, paid special attention to them.

     The set of possibilities reflects a gendered hierarchy in ordinary households
focused on sex, children, and domestic respectability. These were major components of renegotiating standing in a house in the wakes of war or colonial
contradictions.[130] Wives knew that preparing a welcome-home meal for a husband returned from raiding or general travel initiated a public accounting of
their respectability. It separated them from other, perhaps less knowledgeable
women, including those whom the husband might have brought with him as
his share of plunder, the scornable ènvùmâ, in this micropolitics of struggle
over standing. At fraught moments like these—returns from battle, travel, or
hatching out children with names—the reproduction of a bellicose statecraft
intersected with the social reproduction of the household. Women secure with
children—slave or free—widened and strengthened the divides between themselves and those without children, infusing moral belonging with the boundaries, othering, and implicit primordialisms of ethnicity.

In the region's long nineteenth century of dislocation, cultural work could con-
ceal and reveal, but it was always gendered. When it suited them, the powerful
used it to point to a person's past. Male slaves and newly arrived female slaves
were most vulnerable. Yet behaving in a way that conformed to—and helped
create—a local, clan-centered, or broader "Ganda" cultural practice could cloak
a foreign origin. Women slaves who succeeded in fertility quests could try to
do this as elders. The uncertainties matter less than noticing the centrality of
women to drawing boundaries, othering newcomers, and trafficking in taken-
for-granted or "primoridal" cultural practice—in short, ethnic formation—in
revising the makeup of lineage or a village. By colluding to exclude those who

had come from elsewhere as captives, payments for debt, or inherited property, sometimes those very outsiders worked ethnic formation as an instrument to parry forces of marginalization. New slaves might set aside the pasts their fellows only thought of in demeaning terms. Slaves who made blood-friendship or had a child might remember their pasts selectively to demonstrate a paternalist ideology claiming the "benefits" of a competitive Ganda field of social mobility to exiting slavery.[131] Their work domesticated noble obsessions with sexual propriety and biological descent.

Loss, stalemate, and success suffused the organized violence of the long nineteenth century. Its masculine cast—an effect of the male bias in the sources—blended with women's involvement as auxiliaries and with the women who remained at home but bore the losses of a husband killed or dishonored, or enjoyed the wealth his involvement in a successful operation might bring. Kagulu was an avatar of shame for Ganda rulers at least as early as 1875. Stanley reported a story about a battle between Ssuuna II's naval coalition and the able mix of infantry and naval forces assembled from Bunha and beyond in Busoga. Unnamed Soga warriors called out to Ssuuna II and his allies, who had failed in proper direct combat (they eventually prevailed by siege). They taunted him to "seek the graves of Kaguru and Kamanya, and bury himself there for very shame."[132] Buvuma and Kyaggwe had been theaters of Ganda ambition since Kagulu's and Nagujja's times. Success and failure cost dislocation and relocation. Those legacies of misrule were taken up in Kamaanya's time (see the introduction), giving a new texture to oral traditions about Ganda dynasts. From the 1910s to the 1930s, in the generation of private property (*mailo*), despotism again loomed. Men returned to the ruptures of the eighteenth century, debating them in a language of clan persecutions and clan hiding.

Stanley, Kagwa, and others planted a just-so ethnicity in this soil of loss and honor. They gave it territorial edges by mentioning crossings of the Nile at Jinja and of the perilous liminal offshore zones and islands. That kind of integrity also suffused Mukaabya's contentious but otherwise peaceful accession. After building his first capital, his first act as kabaka was to appoint someone to "take a burning stick to Bunyoro." Kagwa's translator, the historian Kiwanuka, gives the quoted gloss, but Kagwa himself explained that this stick was used to roast the meat consumed at funerals. Given that Ssuuna II actually lost his life during a military adventure to Busongora, not Bunyoro, the burning stick vignette takes on a different cast.[133] Delivering the stick to Bunyoro presupposed a boundary separating Bunyoro from Buganda, investing Bunyoro as fit territory for eliminating any dangerous power released during a royal funeral, embodied in the burning stick. In this way, "Bunyoro" stood in for all enemies of "Obuganda," in this case, a place embodied in the person of the new kabaka.

An aristocratic woman could avoid deadly political struggles over her sexuality, threats meant to prevent her from gaining the authority of motherhood, by joining a shrine. She could escape Kyabaggu's rats and the traps set for her in a capital. She could pursue her political ambitions (map 3). By the middle of the eighteenth century, those central places had wrought deep bonds between fertility and statecraft. Commoner women's work in the nineteenth century with "culture" or "ritual" brought the noble face of moral belonging into the household. They did so to protect their standing while so much of its material base was under threat from the wakes of commerce and raiding. Theirs was a virtue of senior or public motherhood, not a form of ethnic nationalism. In high Protectorate days, in the time of private property, men again marginalized it in their otherwise expansive political work with print culture.

CHAPTER SIX

Hiding Clans

Eighteenth-Century Misrule
and Twentieth-Century Groupwork

Abataka bagalana be balima Akambugu. "Clan-land guardians who
like each other cultivate couch grass (create difficulty)."
—P. M. Gulu, "Ekika: ab'effumbe n'ab'enjovu," 117

Amàlâ òkwekwèkà yè àtende bannê òkwakwaya. "The one who hides first blames
the noise the later hiders make (for all of them being found out)."
—Ronald Snoxall, *Luganda-English Dictionary*, 164

THIS CHAPTER EXPLORES the shifting terms of literate men's debates
over an era of eighteenth-century misrule in a time of high colonialism, when the morality of rule was in question. The stakes could
hardly have been higher. They involved struggles over which kinds of groups
and which members would shape rule. Beginning in the 1910s, the vernacular
history writing hitherto dominated by a few powerful men, opened outward
to include many more men. The era of print culture had dawned, shining
brightly through vernacular newspapers whose sectarian lenses distorted their
contents less than one might think. These newspapers put the middle layers of
the Protectorate's literati alongside the powerful few, highlighting the different
futures they sought by debating the past.[1]

Their work foregrounded the weight of descent and the insurgencies of in-
laws. They pined for the generous character of rule and warned against its
insecure hunger for deference, too often on display in the theater of legal
process. They promoted selfless responsibilities of hospitality and insisted on
recognizing a host's extroverted generosity. They even explored the relevance
of spiritual authority with deeper roots than religions of the book. In the pages

of *Munno* ("Your Friend") a Luganda-language Catholic newspaper, they wrote family histories as parables of a fixable royal and Protectorate rule led astray by overconcentrated power and redeemable by belonging with more than ideas of descent. They vetted these themes inside debates over shifting edges between parts of clans. Parts of some clans hunted others, some hid in hosting clans, and hiders reappeared as their former selves. That scaffolding surrounded an allegorical reign of misrule in the middle of the eighteenth century.

In the 1910s, writers focused on that misrule's precursors and aftermaths. They wrote about elite concerns with controlling access to royal centers by supplying daughters and holding titled positions. They wrote about commoners and nobles at the edges of a polity who instigated or sought to avoid relations of reciprocal obligation with a royal center. In the 1920s, debate shifted. The bad king's noble descendants, who had hidden in various clans to avoid retribution for their ancestor's misrule, came out of hiding.[2] They returned to public political presence when high tensions over land made increasing the points of access to reciprocal obligation particularly important. Given that so many points of access had been lost between the 1880s and the 1920s, reform hinged on open debate about the past.[3]

Though literate, they wrote from the wings of the stage run by literati such as the Protestant prime minister, Apolo Kagwa. They wrote about topics lodged in a taken-for-granted national topography of precolonial states, of ethnic groups identified from the perspectives of those states, of the many visitors to the region, and of sectarian religious communities. None of that prevented them from pushing lines of debate that exceeded and critiqued the boundaries that topography took for granted or that drew on categories like *lùbaalè* to make an argument. Writers felt their way toward a common future by arguing over a common past to tame the rancor of defeat or to domesticate the ambiguities of standing by insisting on the utility and promise of indigenous modes of rule in a colonial situation. In their writing, they arranged categories like gender, royal violence, noble standing, judicial process, landed belonging, and clanship to remake or revive them along the way. Some of their work generated exchanges that unfolded over decades.

One thread tying their arguments together focused on clan hunting or persecuting. These events caused the hunted in a clan to hide inside a second, host clan and raised questions about if and when their descendants would reappear. These dimensions of clanship had a noble cast. Overwhelmingly the hunters and hiders, if not always the hosts, had links to threads in a sovereign knot. Arguing over such events revealed tensions between groupwork and land. These tensions brought into the open the weight of gendered descent legitimating access to land. The tensions ran through competing practices of historical debate over the groupwork that could revive the morality of land tenure. It was a time of hardening material ground beneath Protectorate categories of exclusionary belonging, such as race, nation, and ethnicity. Yet these men worked out how the indeterminacies of belonging with clanship exceeded those descriptions of modern groupwork but were indispensable to a prosperous, moral future.

Clan Hiding as Groupwork with States

Hunting, hiding, and hosting elite parts of clans had shifted political alliances since Kimera's advent in Buganda. Kimera's entourage had included members of the Bushbuck clan, a clan with connections to the rulers of Bunyoro.[4] That connection raised explosive questions about the origins of Buganda. Were they authochthonous or foreign? The political risks of this association warranted hiding all Bushbuck girls in the Monkey clan. That way, if they married a sitting *kabaka* and had children with him, the children belonged to the Monkey clan, not the Bushbuck. In chapter 4, Kateregga hunted the Leopard clan members at Bweeya in the later seventeenth century, framing the story of Mbajjwe's judgments on respectable male behavior in battle.[5] These vignettes assume royal ideologies that clanship and descent go together.

Stories of clan hiding, hunting, and hosting set in the eighteenth century and after focused on the trials and tribulations of nobles seeking freedom from their ancestors' behavior. Vulnerable families hid; hospitable families hosted. But groups of descendants, the hearthstones (*àmàsigà*) and *Ficus* trees (*èmìtuba*) of a clan, accumulated over the generations. These groups took up the challenges of belonging and land tenure bequeathed by their ancestors. In daily life, a woman used hearthstones—lumps of sunbaked earth from a termite mound—to support the pots in which she cooked food or boiled water. Metaphorically, hearthstones were the dispersed group of extended families who claimed descent from a single man but existed only because women came out of their clans to marry into the hearthstones of other clans, "feeding" their members. The epiphytic Ficus trees were sources of bark cloth and the living fences around a homestead. Metaphorically, they emphasized the distinct roots of the groups that emerged out of *àmàsigà*, in clanship, growing in a particular place. Assemblies at the estate of a clan's founder figure enacted clanship's largest scale of identification. Hearthstones and Ficus trees embodied narrower scales at which people might strategize marriage alliances or open new lands. At least in the middle of the twentieth century, ethnographers and autoethnographers could write that at both scales, "authority follows lines of personal patronage and clientship; descent is, in principle, irrelevant."[6]

Hiding a given generation's hearthstone members (whose elders or recent ancestors had fallen afoul of a royal center) inside those of another clan created options. It left open the possibility that a hearthstone's "hidden" daughters might yet be inserted into the politics of royal reproduction under the cover of their adopted group.[7] Instances of such hiding abound because they followed attacks by royals, or attacks by appointed title holders on behalf of a royal, on a clan's members whom royals and officials deemed to be threats.[8] The sources speak of whole clans hiding, joining, or being hunted because the successes or failures of their hearthstone's leaders could redound to other hearthstones in the larger clan and to ones that formed later. If clan parts could change in the face of a moral outrage, perpetrated by royals or their officials, they could re-emerge at a later date, when circumstance allowed.

The practice helped the polity have a center in which different threads in a sovereign knot held authority. Titled royal wives, a queen sister, a queen mother, a male kabaka, the titled officials that each appointed, and leaders like the Mugema from important "counties" constituted independent nodes in the realm. Hunting, joining, hiding, and hosting clans occurred at the articulation point between these offices and between them and the followers who pressured higher-ups to do what they wanted. This was not about clans breaking apart as a result of struggles over leadership.[9] The point is that by hunting, hiding, and hosting clans, boundaries between groups could be temporarily revised.

Queen mother Muganzirwazza's standing exemplified this. In 1854, when she made a sovereign knot with her son, Muteesa, she pretended to belong to the Civet Cat clan. Her birth clan was the Elephant, which had been prevented from supplying royals six generations earlier in the 1760s. Among other things, in the 1730s that clan had produced Kagulu's and Nagguja's sovereign knot, whose violent misrule Kagwa featured in his histories.[10] In the 1850s, members of the Buganda court looked away from those facts in sustaining Muganzirwazza's position. Their collusive silence on her Elephant clan standing helped her and Muteesa come to power. The apparent boundaries between clans, the unique cultural work that distinguished one from the other, and the vernacular chronologies ordering their preeminence could be ignored, at least by royals and would-be royals.

Hiding elite hearthstones in another clan was not the only means by which people practiced fungible groupwork. As we saw in chapter 5, a nineteenth century of violent commerce put a lot of people in motion, sending them to places where they "were not well known," as Teofiro Kuruji put it in 1906. Kuruji was a commoner who had become a chief, responsible for Mukaabya Muteesa's property. He explained how a stranger could use "deception" to "get into a tribe."[11] Clans (or tribes, Kuruji used these words interchangeably) were permeable. But he described a dislocated individual's circumstances, not the collusive silence that let one clan's hearthstones to hide inside others. Elite re-formulations of ties of descent and alliance, intended to silence what precipitated the hiding and enable a later return to politics, had obvious consequences for commoner hearthstones in the persecuted or hosting clans. Elite hiding in plain sight, with the full knowledge of various publics, put those publics at risk, should later royals and their allies elect to renew the earlier conflicts.

A famous proverb explains the labor precipitated by hiding clans. "Abataka abaagalana be balima akambugu," or clan or hearthstone heads who get along dig out couch grass together. When a clan hides inside another, the deep roots of the past will have to be unearthed. But everyone knows it is impossible to rid a field of couch grass. Its roots spread underground, popping up in surprising places. The proverb points to tensions of belonging. Clan hiding revealed the solidity of the idea of clanship but promised challenges in making a shared history. Like that pesky grass, the details of genealogies, itineraries, and personas were hard to be rid of because people in distant places might remember them. It wasn't easy to clean the past to fashion futures less constrained by it.

Literate men found them irresistible devices in writing histories of a Ganda nation as rule took shape in the Protectorate in the 1910s and 1920s. Accounts of clan hiding underscored the ambiguous place of descent ideologies in a political culture of reciprocal obligation. Books about the Ganda monarchy often celebrate the open qualities of participation in its royal politics. There was no royal clan, at least after Kagulu's and Nagguja's misrule in the 1750s. As the ideology of competitive rank and its obligations would have it, any clan could send a woman to marry a sitting king. If she bore a son, then she, members of her hearthstone, people from other hearthstones in her clan, and any number of others could join her to support his succession. Her success obligated her to her supporters. She and her king-son met those obligations by filling offices with members of her clan and those of her supporters.[12]

Kagulu and Nagguja's despotism was a turning point.[13] In his earliest writings, Kagwa recalls Kagulu as having treated people exceedingly badly. Among other things, he burned them alive or required they approach him by crawling on beds of needles. When followers removed trees for Kagulu, he insisted they take out the root balls, too, which led to people being buried alive. After ordering the death of Sentongo, the Mugema of the Colobus Monkey clan, a locus of authority independent of the kabaka, "the whole country" supported his half-siblings' rebellion.[14] Such misrule revealed a rot at the heart of reciprocal obligation, in which the privileges of blind tradition concentrated power too much.[15]

In the first two decades of the twentieth century, Ganda male literati found tales of failure and rebellion by the high-born to be rich sources for weaving threads of gendered respect and social critique into histories of a permeable Ganda nation.[16] They used the distant misrule to debate the gendered, moral grounds on which a Ganda nation would blend the past with the "new things from Europe," the "advance of the way forward as the [Protectorate] Government has promised."[17] The region's history since that ill-fated reign reveals the depth of the conflict over access to wealth and respect embodied in clan hiding and hunting and the urgency of historical knowledge to making a better future.

Antecedents and Contexts

Before the upheavals of Kagulu's reign, the Civet Cat and Lungfish clans had royal wives in the capital more often than any other clan. Kagwa's list reflects a royal preference for women from clans with deep ties to Bakka Hill, "the highest point for miles around and the oldest center of kingship," according to Kodesh (see map 2).[18] Bakka Hill's clans supplied seventeen of the twenty-eight women who married into a capital from the time of Kintu until the reign before Kateregga's in the middle of the seventeenth century.[19]

In the eighteenth century, as royals expanded the titled positions with a stake in the fortunes of their court, they resisted the preeminent roles Civet Cat and Elephant clans had played in providing access to a royal center. Clans who acted like "royal" clans had been anathema since Kateregga attacked the Leopard clan, two generations earlier. The political culture of reciprocal obligation prided itself on competing for standing and wealth.[20] The ideology was embodied by the idea that sovereign knots could be tied with lines from any number of different clans, not just a select few. Dynastic accounts of Kagulu's misrule reflected the instability and intolerable exclusiveness of such an arrangement in a language of misdirection, one focused on his righteous punishment by his kin. Those accounts were shaped during Kamaanya's reign (1812–30; see introduction). Scrubbing "royalness" from clans pretended the field of play for power and standing had always been open. That editing occurred when slavery threatened the logic of reciprocal obligation.

A revived Nyoro militarism in the 1850s took advantage of things falling apart in Buganda. By the 1870s, royal factions in Bunyoro controlled a thick swath of territory north of Buganda, blocking off Egyptian geopolitical designs on the region. Buganda's century-old military advantage on land shifted to the Inland Sea as its naval power increased. The result funneled cosmopolitan, commercial forces toward Mukaabya Muteesa's increasingly polycentric polity from the south.[21]

Men engaged religions of the book, in the 1840s, with African Muslims from the Indian Ocean coast in the court of Ssuuna II.[22] Christian missionaries arrived in 1877. The 1880s saw fractious battles between Muslim and Christian blocs, watched closely by the kabaka Mwanga and a mistrusting cohort of chiefs and allies. The conflicts slipped outside the palace's reed walls in the 1890s, after the Christians had won the struggle over the royal center.[23] The ground of power shifted decisively in favor of Muslims and Christians and away from *bàlubaalè* assembly, royal women, commoner royal clients, and clan leaders. The dramatic shift produced Christian martyrs in the 1880s, and Bunyoro's defeat in the 1890s. From 1893 until 1962, Uganda was a Protectorate. From 1897, a regency ran Buganda until a child kabaka, Daudi Cwa, reached his majority in 1914. The partisan blocs that formed in and survived the religious wars of the 1880s and early 1890s rethought the moral and material ground of belonging in Buganda. Some sought continuities with the past while others wanted a radical break.[24]

Key parts of the results were codified in the 1900 Agreement between Buganda and the nascent British Protectorate of Uganda.[25] Buganda's regents, including Kagwa, the prime minister since 1889, negotiated the Agreement with a special commissioner, Harry Johnston. In the document, the British recognized the kabaka as king and the assembly of chiefs as his council (*lukiiko*) with the right to allocate land as gazetted square miles (*mailo*) with freehold title, and it recognized chiefs as a landowning class.[26] It gave to the kabaka—in effect, the regents—the power to select the chiefs who would rule the twenty counties constituting Buganda.

The regents took the lion's share of mailo for themselves, cementing Protestant control over the state.[27] This befit their position atop the coalition of Christian and Muslim chiefs who had worked with British imperial agents and their clients to defeat Bunyoro and other parts of the Protectorate. The rest of the mailo owners were overwhelmingly chiefs from the victorious factions in the religious wars. Allotments followed "the order of dignity," from kabaka to *èbìtongole* chiefs.[28] Most titled clan leaders, *lùbaalè* shrine managers, royal women and their male relatives, or individuals who had been given land by a past kabaka to commemorate a special relationship, lost their land or became the tenants of the new owner. Some 2,000 had already gone on record in 1902 as having been cut out of the initial land titling.[29] Ownership of land by royal tomb managers or by the descendants of clan founder figures became illegible. As Hanson has explained, British colonial law recognized only living individuals as owners of land, not departed persons or their collective following.[30] Through the 1920s, the council, acting in the manner accorded to it by the Agreement, nonetheless addressed the exclusions. The council revisited disputes over clan lands to protect them from rapacious chiefs or from control by the wrong branch of a clan or the wrong clan altogether.[31]

These were not the biggest obstacles to a peaceful political future. Without the appropriate array of landed, collaborating figures, a kabaka's ability to fashion the domain with them disappeared, replaced with unaccountable authoritarianism. The fact that clan founder figures were buried in these lands charged the loss of control over them with emotion. Without access to those graves, people could not organize funerals and engineer the succession of the next holders of leadership positions. This outrage fueled two decades of political struggle over land and power, framing this chapter's study of clan hiding, men's history writing, and Protectorate-era groupwork.

A period of in-migration to Buganda opened in 1904. People came to grow cotton and coffee and work in a newly waged world of industries, from transport and building to pit sawyer. Mailo owners exploited the opportunity.[32] Landlords practiced a social logic of reciprocal obligation that made working for them more attractive than working for other employers.[33] Desperate for labor, the British meant taxation to force Africans into waged labor. When that fell short, they resorted to compulsion. Responsibility for both fell on lower-level chiefs, making them exploiters, not providers of prosperity.

The first decades of mailo erased dense webs of obligation that flowed over a single piece of land. They were replaced by those flowing through a single owner, often with no connection to the bones of ancestors buried there, in a time of tax, migrant labor, forced labor, and fines. Conflicts between the logic of reciprocal obligation and Protectorate policy invited legal manipulation, exploitation of tenants by title holders, and the erosion of "the protective and sustaining capacities of chiefs" and clan networks.[34] The Agreement represented as settled politics the disappearance, since the 1880s, of thousands of positions of authority. For those who remembered the old political map, the former variety represented the diversity of authority gone by 1905.[35]

Kagwa's unbridled displays of power embodied the problem of imperious, unobligated rule.[36] His tarring Kagulu's descendants with the stain of that kabaka's misrule was not just cynical. It was also strategic, given that those descendants were prominent figures in the Catholic faction. In 1906, Kagwa had five graves dug up at Ssenge, a Grasshopper clan center he had received as mailo. The council forced him to rebury them to avoid splitting the Grasshopper clan.[37] Fifteen years later, in 1920, he embarrassed kabaka Daudi Chwa before the senior county chiefs without repercussions.[38] Many found this behavior emblematic of bad rule. Frustration unleashed a broad critique of the situation.

Dissent converged in a much-studied period of struggle over land, led by the Bataka Federation, from 1921 to 1926.[39] Hanson's exploration of this struggle pushed past opposing the power of chiefs to that of dispossessed clan leaders.[40] She analyzed testimonies provided to the Land Commission of Enquiry, conducted by the Protectorate, from 1924 to 1926. The inquiry was a response to the Bataka Federation's appeal in 1921 and 1922 to kabaka Daudi Cwa for justice. The inquiry contained a vast range of voices dissenting from mailo, not just those of clan leaders.

All sides resorted to selective historical argument to advance their cause. Regents argued they had successfully translated the beneficial changes brought by the British into "Ganda custom" by doling out mailo to chiefs and a few clan leaders. They argued that the absolute power they wielded as leaders of victorious blocs of chiefs flowed from the kabaka's authority. They claimed that the old oligarchy—which included clan leaders—had died slowly from the 1870s until the 1920s. The regents said the 1900 Agreement settled all that, it set aside "all the remembered relationships that had explained land allocation in the past."[41] The regents claimed that in resisting this, dissenters disrespected the kabaka's authority.

The dissenters agreed that the kabaka lay at the core of good rule. But they insisted that had made rule good because "kabakas had exercised power in interaction with other authority figures." The mailo arrangements, they continued, had destroyed that collaboration and "undermined the kabaka's power to create and realign relationships." Dispossession reduced the number of people with the standing to influence what higher-ups might do. The regents and mailo holders thus deprived the dispossessed of their preferred routes to respect. Dissenters were treated roughly when they brought cases before the council. Without access to ancestors' graves, they could not move on to the next generation with appropriate funeral and succession ceremonies. Disrespect amounted to being cut off from social reproduction by mailo owners who did not live up to their duties "to show concern for its [a piece of land's] residents."[42] Both sides drew explicitly on historical knowledge in this struggle, politicizing dispossession as a transgression against "tradition."[43]

When it came to clans and land, historical argument grounded disputes over which system of land control would put the country on the best footing for the future. Historical argument demanded an improved domination, more responsive to the needs of social lows.[44] In the two decades since the Agreement was made, the labor exactions pushed by chiefs at the behest of Protectorate policy had shrunken the capacity of ordinary people to act generously, perform gender deference, or provide hospitality and paternalist examples, embodied in the provision of assistance at regular clan and lineage gatherings. Dissenters argued that the problem lay with misrule, not with any incompatibility between commerce, religions of the book, and "civilization" and social practices in Buganda. If the older kinds of rulers could rule again, the moral

community of reciprocal obligation could invent a new future with a cosmopolitan and internationalist cast, grounded in a recognizable set of autochthonous virtues. Men's history writing mattered as a tactic for legal advantage,
sustaining the landed base of reciprocal obligation to pass it on to their children. It also created the imagined community of a Ganda nation as a parable
of responsible, modern rule for others in the Protectorate.

Newspapers, Misrule, and Literati

Newspapers hosted a lot of this writing. The rest of this chapter focuses on one
of them, the vernacular newspaper *Munno*. When its first issue appeared in
1911, it joined a growing world of readers, active for about a generation (figure 15).[45] People read to themselves, but they also read aloud to others. Newspapers had literal audiences who need not have been literate. Book shops were
lively spaces of public gathering, where reading and reading aloud could happen. They were dominated by men but not restricted to them. Women also
read. By the 1920s, there were nearly 200 literate Catholic professed nuns, the
bannabikira (figure 16).[46]

The breadth of *Munno*'s audience can be gauged in two ways. First, there
were Catholic mission stations across the Protectorate and beyond where *Munno*
would have been available. Second, the paper addressed topics with a wide

OUTSIDE THE BOOK-SHOP, MENGO.

Figure 15. Outside the bookshop, Mengo. Note the bark cloth–clad woman holding a
notebook. Source: J. D. Mullins, *The Wonderful Story of Uganda* (London: Church
Missionary Society, 1904), opposite 94, upper plate.

geographical range. By either measure, *Munno*'s core audience belonged to the Protectorate's southern tier of lands, broadly south of a line from Mount Elgon to Lake Mwitanzige, densest from Buddu through Buganda (map 1).[47] To put things this way is accurate but misleading. Authors published in *Munno* clearly saw themselves writing in and for a world far beyond the local or regional.[48] They assumed universal Christian settings, animated by shared features of modernity, especially progressivism. They felt no contradiction between that expansive sense of the future and the microhistorical details populating their writings.

Between 1911 and the 1920s, two priests edited *Munno*, Père Henri Le Veux and Bishop Julien Gorju. The prolific historian Alfonsi Aliwali was the associate editor. Le Veux completed his monumental Luganda-French dictionary while editing *Munno*. His notebooks cross-referenced articles under rubrics dominated by ethnographic topics.[49] Gorju studied the history of religious practices from Bunyoro to Burundi and from Buha to Busoga.[50] Aliwali was born in 1882 in Kyaggwe and left for Buddu as a ten-year-old in the aftermath of the religious wars. He attended seminary as a nineteen-year-old. He published in

Station de Notre-Dame de Roubaga.—Chez les Sœurs, le Dimanche.

Figure 16. Young women readers. A chance to gather, a performance of mission education, and a new skill set for debating. Source: Henri Le Veux, "Les Soeurs Blanches de Notre-Dame d'Afrique, Dans nos Missions chez les Nègres," *Les Missions d'Afrique des Pères Blancs* 7, no. 4 (1911), 100.

Luganda through the 1960s.[51] *Munno*'s editorial staff were scholars, not just priests.

Munno hosted a range of themes. Autoethnographies trafficked in a just-so ethnic world. Articles on marriage or cuisine assumed close bonds between language and groupwork, generating no threads of debate. This kind of feature appeared from the start, reflecting the paper reaching out to a popular audience.[52] Details of African engagement with Christianity figured prominently, with continuing features on its advent and current state of play in the Protectorate. Stories about the first missionaries and the first African readers and catechists accumulated as the issues appeared. But none of that prompted readers to write back, offering alternative accounts. If they did so, the editors hid their responses. Histories of the Protectorate's African states—Buganda, Bunyoro, Nkore—and their political cultures generated the most spirited and sustained exchanges. Clan hiding fits under that rubric.

Compared to the Anglican *Ebifa bya Buganda* ("News of Buganda"), *Munno* hosted vigorous debates over the past. African Catholic intellectuals wrote from the political margins of the sectarian arrangement of power drawn after the religious wars and the 1900 Agreement. A demographic majority in greater Buganda, Catholics nonetheless held about a third of mailo land, and their chiefs were paid lower salaries and held lower positions than Protestants.[53] Critique of that imbalance flowed from men writing in the public sphere of print culture. *Munno* published unheralded authors, like Viktoro Katula and P. M. Gulu, given no obituaries and absent from secondary histories of Christianity in Uganda. They argued with powerful grandees like Kagwa and John T. K. Ggomotoka. The editorial focus on historical and autoethnographic subjects revived a version of the public sphere that had long animated Ganda political life but had atrophied in the 1910s and 1920s in the shadows of Protestant writers, like Kagwa. The rich counternarratives developed by publishing arguments between heralded and unheralded figures in the Catholic intelligentsia revised those penned by Anglican literati, such as Kagwa.

These debates in *Munno* exemplify Karin Barber's idea of the exegetical community—that is, the group who lends textual traditions ongoing life by arguing over their meaning and structure. When community members wrote to one another debating details, and when texts reflected on themselves, they opened such traditions to the motives of others.[54] Membership in such communities was broad and complex in the Protectorate, dwarfing the few men so far named. Tracking them lies beyond the scope of this modest foray into African print cultures of the early twentieth century. Others, particularly Jonathon Earle, have shown the way forward, with keen sensitivity to their intellectual range.[55] But much remains to be done, especially outside Buganda, as shown by Caitlin Monroe's work on Akiiki Nyabongo and female historical knowledge in western Uganda.[56] The point is that discussions of and reflections on Kagulu's misrule and its aftermaths constituted a kind of exegetical community. They worked through and radically challenged groupwork, constituting an ethnography of larger ambitions for belonging by working out a parable for alternative shapes. But the parable was also a linear history of what had gone wrong.

Debates in *Munno* about Kagulu wrestled over the details of his actions and their consequences from 1913 to 1925. One group, organized by Ggomotoka, used the theme to reappear as descendants of the blighted kabaka. They narrate reappearing noble hearthstones, in times of political opportunity, including the 1920s. Gulu and Katula, on the other hand, expressed multiple views on hiding in clans, hosting hearthstones, and targeting them for attack. They share a tight focus on land and the grounds for claims over the people on it. All the articles highlight royal failure, even from the perspective of nobility, including the fraught responses to it led by Kagulu's relatives and in-laws. They passed judgment on schemes for realizing political ambition, the moral ground for accountability, and the threat of retribution fostered by failures of accountability. The consequences of Kagulu's misrule pointed to a similar geometry of the failed politics of land in Uganda's Protectorate and gave it a linear history with eighteenth-century roots.[57]

Ggomotoka was the Sabalangira, the official responsible for cutting or deciding cases involving nobles, from 1919 until 1941.[58] He was an accomplished field researcher and a prolific author.[59] In the later 1920s, he traveled to Mfangano and Rusinga Islands in western Kenya (map 1) to interview descendants of those who had fled after killing kabaka Jjunju at the close of the eighteenth century (chapter 5).[60] In the 1930s, he wrote up his interviews with elders on the populated islands in the Buvuma group.[61] P. M. Gulu was a son of the Elephant clan, likely a member of one of its littoral hearthstones.[62] Viktoro Katula wrote as a member of the Lungfish clan, claiming links to Bunyoro. He changed his name from "Kiwanuka," a Ganda lùbaalè of thunder, to "Katula," a bitter but edible red berry.[63] Like Gulu, he was an unheralded historian, literate but not a member of the literati.

Print culture placed the scholarship of noble elites like Ggomotoka alongside the likes of Katula and Gulu. In this way, the new medium revived and revised the public sphere of actual, physical assemblies at shrines or courts. But the print culture embodied in *Munno* and *Ebifa* was archly gendered. Only men's writing appeared in its pages. The formerly multigendered domain of historical knowledge narrowed tightly around men as they debated issues of virtue, vice, power, and accountability. It mattered, not least for gendering powerful knowledge, that noble and commoner men now wrote on the same platform.

When Ggomotoka debated the history of Kagulu, he had already taken a stand on a burning issue of the day: the matter of Kintu's origins.[64] He built on arguments that Kintu had come from outside Buganda. He accepted Tobi Kizito's view (shared by Nyoro and Soga historians) that Kintu had been the junior twin to Isingoma Mpuga Rukidi, the founder king of the Bito dynasty of Bunyoro.[65] His stance aligned with Kagwa's against clan historians, like Buliggwanga of the Lungfish, who had claimed Kintu as their own.[66] Ggomotoka's version implied that all Ganda princes, in effect, descended from the Ababito, the royal clan of Bunyoro, something Katula emphasized. Nobles solved that problem of legitimacy by adopting the avoidances "of their mothers' clans."[67] The gender of the lines to which one owed allegiance and respect were negotiable, not prescribed, even in a debate driven by the assumption that biological descent was the means to conceptualize belonging across time.

Ggomotoka's view muddied the ground for resisting Protectorate rule. If Kintu was a civilizing foreigner and the Buganda that Kintu brought into existence was not an autochthonous state, then European displacement of Buganda was just another step in Buganda's continuing embrace of the new. Ggomotoka noted that the British had migrated to their current home, refuting any primordial landed historical depth to their belonging. Ggomotoka instead insisted that the cultural vision of a patriarchal nobility—whether British or Ganda—with rather nomadic cosmopolitan inclinations, best expressed belonging with a state.[68]

The articles use elite hiding in—and reappearance from—firstcomer clan hearthstones to argue over the ambiguities of belonging, political standing, and access to property. They promote an intimacy between masculine respectability, responsive rule, and historical thinking. But they cultivate skepticism toward legal process as a source of justice.[69] Ggomotoka's team revived the voices of Kagulu's descendants, whom Kagwa treated as having been obliterated in the aftermath of his failed rule. Kagulu's vice was to place the deference of his followers above the generosity and responsiveness a good ruler should show followers. The moral balance sheet of Kagulu's reign—and much more— came back to life in African history writing of the 1910s and 1920s, shaped by the dramas of the 1908 Land Law, the agitation that eventuated in the Commission of Enquiry in 1924 and its immediate aftermath. These male historians celebrated virtues of inclusion by debating the moral ground of a future in terms of past injustice. They had been born into the violence of the 1880s and 1890s. In the 1930s, a new generation of writers, unburdened by the losses of that fractious period, turned away from a past of nations-become-tribes to make a future nation without tribes.[70]

The debates in *Munno* over Kagulu's legacy traverse these historical moments. But they are grounded in the last one, where access to land and learning continued to be essential aspirations nonetheless torn by the shifting social constructions of gender. Clan hiding pushed a Ganda political culture—the concrete social facts of competitive struggle between clanship, chiefship, bàlu-baalè, and royalty for followers and wealth—into renewed prominence. In a modern world taking ethnicity and race for granted as media of state power, Ganda political culture offered other vessels for social criticism. Writing from the margins of Protectorate power but writing as partners in progressivism, these Catholic men meant historical detail to resonate with a universal modernism, balancing the individual and groupwork.

Clan Hunting, Hiding, and Hosting Revisited in the 1910s

The focus in *Munno* on Kagulu's misrule settled on events in Kyaggwe, a bounteous, diverse land of smiths, ivory, fishing, timber, and trade, where much of the drama surrounding that misrule had unspooled. In 1916, P. M. Gulu argued that the consequences of Kagulu's misrule for clan hiding were to be found in blood-friendships between principal hearthstones of different clans. The bonds led one to hide inside the other, cultivating the couch grass later generations struggled to weed out. Blood-friendships were public events that enjoined the parties to loyalty and confidence, with penalties for shirking. Gulu narrated two moments in the past when an important hearthstone of the Elephant clan had joined the Civet Cat clan following a blood-friendship. The first occurred two generations before Kagulu's rule; the second occurred in the immediate aftermath of his misrule. In both cases, making a blood-friendship led to the decision to hide. The prompt to hide was escape from powerful royals hunting Elephant clan people. In both instances, hiding allowed a daughter of the Elephant clan to bear children with a kabaka, children who became kabakas themselves. Each party to the hiding enhanced their power. Gulu emphasized the strategic value of clan hiding, treating the betrayals of forced reappearance as a matter-of-fact breakdown of a blood-friendship.

Gulu wrote that nine sons of one mother founded the hearthstones composing the Elephant clan. One of them entered the first hiding arrangement with the Civet Cat clan's central hearthstone at Bakka Hill.[71] Bakka Hill evoked the vexed matter of "royal" clans, whose daughters had privileged sexual access to a sitting kabaka and whose mother's brothers had privileged access to titled positions inside the queen mother's palace. The Walusimbi was a titled founder figure of the Civet Cat clan.[72] The Mukalo was a grandchild of the Elephant clan's founder figure closest in seniority to the Walusimbi. The generational difference put the clans on unequal footing when they made the blood-friendships. The Elephant clan were clearly the needier party, even before they were hunted for Kagulu's misdeeds. It was this blood-friendship that prompted people to create the proverb about couch grass and stubborn memory.[73]

These elite machinations kept daughters of the Elephant clan in play as potential mothers of future male kabakas at a time when their standing to do so was vulnerable. Gulu's facts echoed in the meeting halls of the young Daudi Cwa, who had gained his majority just two years before Gulu's piece appeared in *Munno*. Readers would not miss the argument that maternal ancestry mattered in formulating a royal center. One outcome of the first blood-friendship was Nagujja giving birth to Kagulu. As soon as the first blood-friends saw that Kagulu could take control from his father and rule, they decided to hide the Elephant hearthstone inside the Civet Cat clan. That allowed Kagulu, whose mother came from an Elephant hearthstone, to jump over the ivory tusk used as the royal footrest when a kabaka sat on his banked throne in the so-called Ivory Court in the capital precincts.[74] Jumping over a tusk of ivory increased the number of tusks entering the domain. Any committed member of the Elephant clan would avoid such intimacy with this totemic material. If Kagulu refused to perform this basic public duty of his position, he would betray his loyalties to the Elephant clan. Hidden in the Civet Cat clan, Kagulu could foster ivory production without betraying his commitments to clanship. Once he was safely in power, the blood-friends divvied up which of their clans would supply the holders of powerful positions in the queen mother's palace. Their elevation of Kagulu produced the couch grass their descendants struggled to clean out from the 1730s well into the 1920s. As debates over the mistakes in mailo allotments grew louder in the 1910s, literate men like Gulu put under public scrutiny the fungibility of clanship as a technique of access to royal power.

Kagulu's misrule reverberated beyond Buganda. Gulu included an important Nyoro figure in efforts to overthrow Kagulu. When Kagulu's children tried to escape being hunted in retribution, they made the second blood-friendship with a Civet Cat son of Bakka Hill, so that he might "hide" them as they sought refuge in Bunyoro.[75] That instance of hiding produced the marriage that yielded a future queen mother (Nanteza, see chapter 5) and consolidated control of the queen mother's palace by her brothers. In each case, clan hiding produced near-term and long-term benefits to the hosts and the hiders.

Neither Kagulu's misrule nor the revisions of the past required of hosting and hiding were in dispute. In 1916, when Gulu wrote, kabaka Daudi Cwa, then in his majority for two years, had begun to push back on the regents' domination of Buganda. By returning to Kagulu's reign, Gulu showed that

Buganda had been through a similar period of discontent in which leaders departed from the moral strictures of reciprocal obligation. Evading account-ability was part of the problem.

Gulu refers to lùbaalè and *cwezi* practice, perhaps suggesting their value as forms of social criticism. He told readers that Kagulu threatened Kinyoro with a bag containing the head of his father's prime minister. Kinyoro threw it into the Inland Sea. Kinyoro linked Bunyoro and Buganda (map 3), as we saw in chapter 5. A titled figure of the Monkey clan, Kinyoro played prominent roles in tying the threads in a new sovereign knot. Kinyoro closed down a deceased kabaka's funeral by presenting the new one with a Monkey clan daughter and handed the new kabaka the scepter of royal justice. Kinyoro brought represen-tatives from all the shrines to greet the new king and, among other things, implore him to love them.[76] Gulu brought Kinyoro into his story to evoke the profound debts Ganda royalty owed to Bunyoro. The Kinyoro figure also un-derscored the need for respectful joining of all sources of power in a realm, including those run through shrines. He gestured to the influence of the fol-lowing on the figures around whom they assembled.

New assemblies were in the air when Gulu wrote this essay. Joswa Kkaate, the Mugema of the Monkey clan, founded his Malaki church in 1914 with a growing following of dissenters in the far corners of the Protectorate.[77] They saw a very different path to the future than the one presented by mailo, Pro-tectorate exactions, and biomedicine. Above all, they defended their duty to criticize rule to make it respond to the obligations of reciprocity, if necessary through reform. Their fidelity to the textual word of God turned them away from what they saw as the conceit of those who would interpret it, as healers of all types did when they sought to change the course of an illness. Yet they shared with public healers a commitment to social criticism on behalf of com-munities of belonging. Gulu agreed, in his own way. He refused to collude in silencing the checkered past of particular Elephant clan hearthstones by leav-ing them be inside the Civet Cat clan. Only the full details of complicity among the powerful to subvert the obligations of reciprocity between them and their followers constituted a forceful critique of that silence.

Gulu showed that proclaiming and persecuting people for ancestors' actions was publicly fungible and morally weighted. Boundary, difference, and shared history persisted by being reformulated, they were neither rigid nor primor-dial. Fungibility required openness to nourish a collective responsibility for suc-cesses and failures by individual members of a clan, especially those acting in high places. Metaphors of land and kinship worked in both registers, so what principles distinguished the rigid from the fungible? Virtues of reciprocity and criticism and vices of insecure selfishness were at stake in Kagulu's misrule.

They implied the fungibility of elite belonging was of greater consequence to responsive rule than arguing over rigid divides of nation and ethnicity separating Bunyoro and Buganda. Gulu highlighted Kagulu's despotic rule as destroying the balance of reciprocity with outrageous demands on supporters. The echoes with the dissenter's broad platform of complaints against mailo and the regents are loud. But Gulu gave that historical depth. He pushed the origins of despotism into the practices of his own ancestors, those of Kagulu's father's generation, exposing the elite niceties of Elephant clan hiding. Kagulu's misrule embodied the vices of deafness to criticism, pointless requests for followers' labor, and the costs of the violent reform that followed. But Gulu also showed the benefits enjoyed by the few near centers like Bakka Hill and royal capitals. The costs of the artifice of clan hiding and hosting were not borne equally by all they touched.

In the next reign, Kagulu's half-brother Kikulwe persecuted leading Elephant people, blaming them for Kagulu's bad deeds.[78] Kikulwe sanctioned the persecution of Elephant hearthstones through a legal process revealing their identity. He tried a case against the Walusimbi, who denied any relation to the Elephant clan, in effect betraying the duties of their blood-friendship. He exposed Mukalo's hearthstone to attack and saved his own. The winning argument turned on the fact that Mukalo's daughter had given birth to Kagulu.[79] Like the disputes over land before the council in the 1910s, in which contests over clan history shaped standing as landowners, Kikulwe's legal process refused to silence the past by hiding bad aristocratic hearthstones of one clan inside another. He showed that only in remembering the details of the past could a collective set right what had gone awry.[80] Kagwa's rough treatment of plaintiffs who did as much fell flat against Kikulwe's unflinching adjudication.

The decision produced a sentence of death against Mukalo and Nagujja, Kagulu's queen mother. They were thrown into a trench, a classic aperture through which departed spirits could travel between the land of the living and Ghostland, a process understood by people well beyond Buganda.[81] Kikulwe's vengeance thus embodied a return to order that highlighted respectful treatment, even of the group he sought to extirpate. Groups inside a polity that refused the reciprocal obligations of their standing would be dealt with firmly but honorably. Burial, rather than burning, left open the possibility that others in later generations might revive the questions addressed in court—or other places—through spirit possession and history writing. In Gulu's account, Kikulwe's sovereign knot replaced a fresh memory of misrule with a just and vengeful hunting of Elephant people.[82] As the kabaka's council tried to put right the wrongs of mailo allotments, Gulu's article warned that failure risked justifying continued retribution.

Gulu underscored the point in narrating the second joining of Elephant hearthstones inside the Civet Cat clan in the 1780s. This joining justified perpetuating the hunting of Elephant people by a kabaka of that day, Kyabaggu. The protagonists of the second blood-friendship descended from the Mukalo and the Walusimbi. But Gulu used personal names, not ancient titles. Serubale, the Walusimbi's descendant, proposed the blood-friendship with Lutabi, the Mukalo's descendant: "so that I may hide you in order that you won't fail to reach Bunyoro."[83] At their public making of blood-friendship, the woman Kasukusuku cooked the food for the feast. She married Lutabi. Gulu named all their children, one of which was Nanteza, the future queen mother of two nineteenth-century kings. This new hiding let Nanteza mask her "true" heritage as a daughter of the Elephant clan, allowing her to reenter royal politics as one of Kyabaggu's wives.

Gendered dimensions to the strains of hiding accomplished through public blood-friendships accumulated. Kasukusuku was the Walusimbi's daughter at Bakka and Serubale's sister. When Lutabi and Kasukusuku married, he gave his new wife a new name, Nabalimba. It marked a status change. Kasukusuku were a kind of mushroom growing abundantly in a plantain garden.[84] The name marked the sister, Kasukusuku, as a reliable provider of sustenance and children. Nabalimba means "mother of liars." It marked her new status as a wife entangled in silencing the past, a precondition for enjoying the benefits of hiding in a noble hearthstone. She helped plant the couch grass later generations struggled to weed from the past.[85] Gulu's history fit into the patriarchal world of Catholic circles in the 1910s, but echoed the pivotal actions of senior women using their sons and other male relatives to pursue their political aims. That older power had been driven from court and council into a domestic sphere long before 1916.

It is conventional to note that as the kabaka Daudi Cwa reached his majority in 1914, a younger generation criticized their elders, particularly Kagwa's Protestant clique. Catholic literati were particularly loud voices, keen to address the marginalization they had suffered since the 1890s. They offered a political culture of debate as an alternative to litigation.[86] But the range of intellectual opinion they expressed exceeds these narrower ambits. The dissenters, such as Joswa Kkaate, clearly understood their local politics in terms of universalist frames of individual and collective responsibility provided by reading the Bible.[87] Jonathon Earle has shown that literati built a larger frame in which regional struggles over respect, standing, and participation echoed in other histories, not just African ones.[88] The significance of historical debates about groupwork, hosted in *Munno*, go beyond their local frames. Authors revived a notion of responsible government to fix errors of rule in a present circumstance and as the path to a better future, a progressivism they took for granted as a modern phenomenon with deep regional roots. Debating the place of groupwork in that vision generated subtle, new ideas about the vicissitudes of belonging.

Nobility Reappeared and the 1920s

Seven years later, a formidable team picked up the threads of Kagulu's legacies. Between two pivotal moments in Buganda's and the Protectorate's history, they subjected the eighteenth century to thorough historical critique. In 1922, the Association of Baganda Ancestors or Bataka formally requested the Ganda king, Daudi Cwa, to hear their arguments against the mailo allocations engineered by Kagwa and the other regents.[89] In April 1924, the Protectorate formed the Bataka Land Commission, which misrecognized the friction as being about owning land, rather than the constitution of rule as a participatory undertaking, something that represented a promising, progressive approach to the narrow veins of power then in place.[90]

Ggomotoka's collaborators only revealed their names at the end of the last installment. Three claimed descent from Kagulu through his eldest son, Sematimba. As Sabalangira, or "head of the princes," the person responsible for litigation involving nobles, Ggomotoka had unparalleled access to the family traditions of the clans of the princes' mothers. Their essays abridge testimony about their noble standing that they had offered before Ggomotoka between 1918 and 1921 in his council chamber of the princes.[91] Ggomotoka was a prolific historian and held a position in the royal geography of knowledge upended by mailo. Exhaustive research marked their writing. The authors' names were the bibliography.

The team—let us call them the historians—narrated Kagulu's flight to Kyaggwe, his death there, and the genealogical history linking them to Kagulu's first son, Sematimba. The historians legitimated their claims to noble standing by proving their ancestors had buried Kagulu well.[92] They named his wife, Nnabbanja, and the six boys and three girls she bore.[93] They fled east to Kyaggwe (map 1).[94] After Kagulu's death, Sematimba took everyone to an island. The fugitives disagreed about next moves. Nnabbanja and the second son returned to where Kagulu had died and buried him properly. Sematimba went to another island off the eastern Kyaggwe coast.[95] He changed his name to hide from those seeking retribution for his father's misrule. He died on that island during the next reign. His three boys and two girls buried him like a noble, removing his jawbone and placing it with his father's. In the following reign, Sematimba's sons left for another part of Kyaggwe. With new names, they evicted the landowners of the hearthstones of their host clans. The next generation, Sematimba's grandchildren, planted Ficus trees. That is, they formed new groups, putting new tenants on the land they had taken from the hearthstones of the firstcomer clans who had hosted them. They converted Sematimba into the founder of a hearthstone. The historians named each founder of the hearthstones whose lands their ancestors had seized.[96]

During Ssemakookiro's reign (1800–1812) one of Sematimba's grandchildren rebelled by beating a drum called the Multitudes. The sisters-in-law of his place, the in-marrying women of the area, accused him of actually having beaten Ssemakookiro's royal drum battery. Sematimba's grandchild parried this accusation of rebellion by beating his drum in front of Ssemakookiro, who realized it did not sound like his royal battery but nevertheless had a sweet voice. He took possession of the new drum, asking if the grandson was a noble, publicizing what was known only among immediate family. Ssemakookiro then gave the grandson control over Kyaggwe's canoes and claimed to have given him the lands from which the firstcomer clan hearthstones had been evicted. In the next generation, those dispossessed hearthstones rose up to drive off the reappeared nobles. They pressed their case in Ssuuna II's court (1830–1856), and he supported them. Sematimba's grandchild left the region for a position among the queen mother's villages.

Tensions over standing continued. Mukaabya Muteesa settled the aggrieved firstcomer hearthstones in an èkìtongole chiefship run by another clan. Between 1885 and 1892, during the religious wars, a Muslim grandchild of Sematimba gained control of the lands his grandparents had taken in Kyaggwe. In 1889, when kabaka Kalema was chased out of Buganda, Protestant hearthstones regained control of the stolen land. The nobles who lost control went to court, pretending to belong to a hearthstone of the Lungfish clan, to push the Protestant hearthstones off the land their grandparent had seized. Those grandchildren of Sematimba, unlike their drum-beating cousin, hid their nobility throughout these legal efforts.[97] In 1911, the dispute between nobles and firstcomers went before the regents' council. The nobles lost. The historians said the decision against them was made in the king's dining room—not out in the open. In 1918, Kagwa gave Sematimba's grandson papers for the gazetted miles of the firstcomer hearthstone land.[98]

The historians rejected the miles because they were given under the pretense of their membership in firstcomer hearthstones. Sematimba's grandchild, Isaka Mayemba Sematimba, personally delivered to Kagwa a letter to that effect on September 26, 1918. It was his official reappearance as a noble, eventuating in a meeting with the kabaka Daudi Cwa. The kabaka referred Sematimba to Ggomotoka, in his capacity as the Sabalangira, the decider of legal cases affecting nobles. Ggomotoka convened his council and recognized the noble standing of these descendants of Kagulu, formerly hidden in the firstcomer hearthstones of Kyaggwe. The historians worked on this history until 1921. Some of Kagulu's descendants remained hidden to retain control over the evicted lands. The historians called them out as being unable to prove their blood connections to those hearthstones, the rightful landowners. In April 1922, the kabaka gave land in Busiro to Sematimba's reappeared children. They professed no grudge against those still hiding among the firstcomers. In the closing paragraphs of their history, Sematimba's living grandchild explained how noble standing survived from 1730 to 1922. When his ancestors hid among the firstcomer hearthstones of Kyaggwe's Spratfish clan, only their men avoided eating the tasty fish. Their daughters ate it, thereby keeping the noble line separate from Spratfish practices of belonging.

This complicated story was a parable about the rewards of history, meant for others in the *Munno* readership in the far corners of the Protectorate. It took on the corrosive entailments of clan hiding in large part by writing its history. They acknowledged Kagulu's misrule and the raw, instrumental power of evictions. But they argued that setting the record straight was the only way to address the suffering that Kagulu had visited on people in the past.[99] They displayed the value of different choices about historical narratives that "reappeared," or "outed," nobility from hiding in a clan. Open debate and nobility itself, the historians argued, revived the royal center's standing to create reciprocal obligation by gifts of land.[100] Naming Kagulu and Nnabbanja's nine children expanded the pool of people who could claim noble descent from Kagulu beyond the few or none that Gulu or Kagwa mentioned.[101] Ggomotoka had been writing about a princes' clan, composed of nobles who did not succeed to the throne, since at least 1913. The historians advanced this project with new terms—the terms of reappearance from hiding and the terms of reckoning with the injustices of the past—so that a richer future might be agreed.

They described the hearthstones they evicted as *nnansangwa*, a phrase built with the verb *kùsangwa*, "to be met or found already in a place." The label claimed being first to settle a place. By using the phrase, Kagulu's descendants underscored the continued salience of that argument. Being recognized as "first" had been difficult to accomplish, if not emptying of consequence, since the eighteenth century (see chapters 4 and 5), in part through the very processes being discussed in *Munno*. In the course of his eighteenth-century expansion into Kyaggwe, the pragmatic Mawanda allied with his disgraced father's descendants, hiding in the Spratfish clan. The hidden princes established themselves there with only the rights of force. They "ate" the lands of existing estate holders by evicting them. The historians found the raw instrumental power that had dominated Ganda politics since the eighteenth century troubling in the 1920s. The evictions transgressed the virtues of respect and honor won by those who first made an estate valuable by attracting and retaining tenants. The transgression echoed in the chaotic evictions entailed by the 1900 Agreement. In naming firstcomers and telling their clanship, the historians enabled the dispossessed of the 1920s to argue their loss—to king or Protectorate government—in those old terms of standing. Their research into the past actions of nobles and royals, from a time of misrule up to the present, revealed the dangers of concentrated instrumental power, then in the hands of mailo owners and a council run by regents.

Noble groupwork required land as a literal ground for belonging, but their rights could only come from a royal center. Confusing that with the moral imprimatur of first-ness guaranteed that disputes over the duties and responsibilities of having land would never end.[102] The historians revealed their claims to land in Kyaggwe had shallow roots. Only a few generations of children and grandchildren had lived under the Ficus trees of estates there. This looked like mailo, by the 1920s, as the first generation of title holders passed title to an elder child. By reappearing as nobles, the historians rejected such a politics of land and exclusion, rooted in a flawed responsibility to power. They revived the noble mobility layering such rights, a mobility lost to mailo's fixed placement of a title holder's rights. Such fixity limited removal by the kabaka, making it difficult for royals and nobles to respond properly to the complaints of tenants or dispossessed owners.[103] In the 1920s, rehabilitating Kagulu joined the spirit of dissent against mailo but insisted on the moral ground of royal control over land, a moral ground that made royals responsive to their subjects.

The reappeared nobles cleared their ancestor's taint through a public acceptance of responsibility. Accountability should not happen in a royal dining room. It should not have involved collusive silence, even though some nobles persisted in doing precisely that by continuing to hide in firstcomer hearthstones of the Lungfish. The historians argued that the past should reestablish royal responsibility for noble control over land, a control that made nobles deserving of subjects' generosity and responsive to their criticisms.

Reappearance could be forced by royals and sisters-in-law. The rebellious act of beating a named drum during Ssemakookiro's reign had, in effect, been "punished" by bringing Sematimba's descendants back into the public standing of nobility. Ssemakookiro's move simultaneously strengthened ties to ivory-rich Kyaggwe and displayed as virtuous restraint in treating a rebel.[104] Sisters-in-law of the hidden nobles instigated that event. They were *bàlamù* or commoner wives, some of whose parents may have been captives. Many female captives—and other displaced women—moved through Kyaggwe after 1800.

If they had children, those offspring joined the hearthstones affected by Sematimba's evictions. The bàlamù women, of whatever ancestry, questioned the
standing of Sematimba's interlopers, hiding in the hearthstones of their adopted
clan early in the nineteenth century. As in-marrying women, they had been
newcomers to a hearthstone; now they took up the mantle of local rootedness,
speaking in an idiom of first-ness that took moral control of a place. They
refused to join the noble silence about the past. The historians unearthed these
important facts, showing that in remembering truths about noble ancestry,
commoner women's knowledge kept rule good.[105]

Closing arguments about the value of reappearing and the moral risk of continued hiding distinguished commoner from noble but recognized their shared
acceptance of royal opinion.[106] Fidelity to a clan's avoidances created by nobility was gendered. It could be difficult to prove "blood connections," given the
open secrets of ancestry shared by family members. These means to include
and exclude were up for grabs in the 1920s as they had been earlier. One category stood out for its familiar nativist meanings. It was *nnàkabàla bannansangwa*—native-born, found already there—whose daughters avoided a clan's
distinctive totem.[107] In stating that noble women did not do so, the historians
connected the integrity of nobility to its women and connected the fungibility
of belonging to its men. They often add the phrase bannansangwa to qualify
Kyaggwe's clans as firstcomers, "they" whom the fleeing nobles "found already
there." That phrase first follows nnàkabàla when the historians explain who
did and did not eat sprats. Noble women did, but true daughters of the
Spratfish clan did not. The distinction emphasized the Spratfish clan's landed
formation compared with the mobility of fungible belonging that princes
should enjoy.

A labor theory of value had long breathed life into social networks, setting
terms for reciprocity and aspiration and grounding them in land. The theory
informed the modern, English gloss of "native-born person, aborigine" given to
nnàkabàla from the 1910s to the 1960s. The word is actually a phrase, "Mother
of the ground cleared of roots and ready to plant." It is not merely poetic to
note that the reference to a stage of agricultural labor glossed the blending of
land and belonging. A noun exists in Luganda for such cleared land, with the
soil broken and ready to plant. Ènkabàla, "newly broken-up land," resulted
from the hardest kind of agricultural labor.[108] An early gloss distinguished this
kind of heavy work, carried out by women, from that of men, who brought
down the trees on a future field.[109] In thickly forested regions, like Kyaggwe,
these kinds of labor required the efforts of more people than a single household could supply.[110] Nineteenth-century visitors noted the collective effort in
creating productive places, distinguishing men's labor from that of women.[111]

Across Buganda's twentieth century, glosses of nnàkabàla reveal that descent talk hid some sources of belonging—like labor—and promoted others—like descent and nobility. At a vexed moment in the fate of land tenure, gendered discourse and hierarchical alliances were embodied tensions between nobles and commoners. Noticing this is not to argue that the use of nnàkabàla in these ways marked the origin for nativist thinking in Buganda, casting doubt on the fungibilities of clanship in stating and defending blood ties. The difficulty of winning that kind of argument generated a phrase in Luganda, òmweboolerezê, which referred to "a relative whose blood connections cannot be proved genuine."[112] This word for the inconclusiveness of reckoning descent used the stem in the verb kùboòla, "to disown, expel from clan."[113] People in and beyond Buganda recognized that debates over biological descent might remain open, their tone more important than their resolution. Digging out this couch grass of clan histories—of any history told through a metaphor of descent—was never finished.

The family resemblance between clanship and ethnicity is clear enough. Indeed, early dictionaries glossed the quintessential colonial category "tribe" with the quintessential littoral category, èkìkâ.[114] But the historians under-stood clear differences. Nativist talk constituted commoners. The exclusive group of nobles held authority through biological descent from a mother who had borne children with a royal man. The investments in biological standing that emerged in Buganda's eighteenth century meshed well with European colonial notions of great similarity. Yet the historians' case that belonging with descent would revive rule responsive to a variety of interests could be pushed beyond those lines. It was the regents' insensitive attitude toward lost points of access to public airing of grievances that drove the case against mailo. The his-torians offered a larger parable of bad rule best fixed by reopening the ears of the powerful. Only detailed historical knowledge—drawing on both descent and pop-up groupwork—could sort out the moral from the immoral fungibil-ity of belonging, a precondition to press claims and make rulers respond.

Belonging in the 1920s with Lines from Above or Below?

Katula engaged the historians in six articles published in *Munno* from August 1924 through February 1925, as the Bataka Land Commission worked. The subtitle of the opening essay reads "to assert one's identity is not enmity."[115] Katula wrote about the vicissitudes surrounding the reappearance of families and hearthstones that were formerly hidden.[116] He wrote as a member of the Lungfish clan with noble standing reckoned through the maternal line. He insisted that weighing Kagulu's misrule and its aftermaths must include the role played by Nyoro connections. Nobles from Bunyoro and nobles from

Buganda were intertwined. Pushing that fact, Katula signaled that digging out the couch grass of the past would not be a simple matter. It would reveal that alliances of standing crossed those of ethnicity in the Protectorate between World War I and the Great Depression. Kagulu's fierce misrule had continued to affect Katula's ancestors, forcing them publicly to snuff out their noble Nyoro ancestry. But inside the hiding families, they had respected that ancestry by not accumulating wealth for commoner relatives in the clans hosting them, even though blood-friendships with them was what facilitated hiding.[117]

That divisive cost of clan hiding came due, in the 1920s, when so many noble groups, from small families to large Ficus trees, reappeared to stake their claims to land. Katula cataloged the travails entailed by hiding and hosting, weighing the actions of the historians' ancestors with pique.[118] He detailed the special burdens of hiding noble Nyoro cultural belonging. It took time to learn how to hide convincingly, to learn Luganda, and to hatch out children correctly. One relied on hosts not to call attention to their clumsiness.[119] He recalled these hardships of the eighteenth and nineteenth centuries: silence on genealogy, the indignities of fitting in, and the worry of persecution by those eager to curry favor with a royal center intent on using past misrule to justify rapacious power. He pointed to the maternal line as the stream down which the nobility flowed, carried by the names of daughters and how the names of sons cut them off from that standing.[120] Writing in a positivist register, as the historians had done, guaranteed a fuller picture. It restored to the kabaka the duty to bestow the respect of reciprocal obligation through the responsibilities of land ownership. But Katula argued that picture was partial, devoid of the historical experiences of outsider families whose travails nonetheless enriched the honor of landed obligation.

Katula had already waded into vexed relations between royal centers and the lands hearthstones stewarded in an essay published in *Munno* in 1913, with two other sons of the Lungfish clan.[121] They explained how Mawanda had placed Kagulu's sons, hidden in a Lungfish hearthstone, in his service, authorizing them to evict established families from their lands there. The historians told the same story ten years later, but they argued that the evicted hearthstones belonged to other clans. Katula's response in the 1920s defended his earlier claims by appealing to experience rather than historical research. The teller forgets things, Katula says, but the person to whom things are done does not forget.[122]

Katula agreed with all the other details of the account given by the historians, reviewed in the last section. He differed in centering the matter of Nyoro descent in the Kagulu story, raising pointed matters of ethnic loyalty. He claimed that Kagulu's wife, Nnabbanja, was a Nyoro noble. He repeated the detail that their daughters ate spratfish, proof that Nyoro ancestry passed through princesses. Katula's move converted all the nobles hiding in Kyaggwe's firstcomer clans, at the center of these exchanges, into men and women with both Nyoro and Elephant clan ancestry. In reviving the matter of a Ganda state's debts to Bunyoro, Katula suggested that loyalties of standing crossed the boundaries between the two states.[123] This muddied the historians' claims to land and their reappearance as nobles in Kyaggwe, by injecting Nyoro ancestry into the story.

In clarifying the terms of reappearance, Katula opened them outward, beyond Buganda. Fellow nobles from Bunyoro had helped a Ganda king by providing him a wife, just as they had helped their matrilateral relatives, Kagulu's half-siblings, who pushed back on his misrule. As a result, ordinary people in Buganda, the ones who hosted desperate, fleeing nobles, suffered evictions from their land. It was a cautionary tale. Do not just judge Kagulu's misrule, Katula implored, also recall the Nyoro ancestry of his children and the alliances his noble half-siblings made with Nyoro figures in vanquishing him. Hard lessons of experience pushed suppressed counternarratives into the present, and other interests came along with them. Sorting them out would have to involve more than Baganda and more than nobles.

Katula made his point with a proverb about mixing maturity and immaturity.[124] Kagulu's sons buried him respectfully, hiding the hideous wound inflicted by his pursuers. The successful attack by his half-siblings turned on making common cause with senior Nyoro princes. Their intent to persecute Kagulu's descendants drove the sons and their mother, Nnabbanja, to hide in the hearthstones along the Kyaggwe littoral. Katula likened the alliance of vengeful half-siblings and Nyoro nobles to the half-ripe fruit of the African incense tree (*Canarium schweinfurthii*), which gives off no aroma. Their violence left no scent trail of memory because they had hidden themselves—and their Nyoro ancestry—in Kyaggwe's Lungfish and Spratfish hearthstones, to avoid retribution for their father's misrule. The descendants of those hidden princes, who paid the price of dislocation for their ancestor's misrule, now enjoyed the intoxicating aroma of the ripe fruits of noble standing authorizing their critiques of mailo. Katula revealed the earlier vicissitudes of noble Nyoro ancestry hiding in the hosting hearthstones in order to humble rich reappearing nobles like the historians.

Echoes of Nyoro ancestry sounded different than they had in the 1730s. In the 1920s, Bunyoro was enfeebled by the aftermath of the collaboration of the victorious Ganda chiefs and regents with imperial forces that had laid waste to Bunyoro in the 1890s. Emptied of cattle and women and shorn of the lands that housed the shrines oriented to cwezi figures, Nyoro leaders had been replaced with those from a literate Ganda elite.[125] Jemusi Miti Kabazzi, a principal figure in the Bataka camp, had been one of those interloper chiefs. In the 1920s, the noble Nyoro of Kagulu's reign were distant figures of fear. Everyone knew that the instrumental power of the Nyoro state had been eclipsed, first by Buganda and then by the Protectorate.[126] The alliances Kagulu's half-siblings had made with Nyoro nobles might have emitted a sharp aroma of selfish collaboration in the 1760s. But the scent had dissipated as the central role Buganda enjoyed in an imperial situation eclipsed Bunyoro's tenuous hold on regional prominence in the mid-nineteenth century.

Katula's displeasure with the historians respected nobility but scorned its silence about past noble powerlessness in which connections to Bunyoro, with roots in Buganda, had been central to survival. Yet both Katula and the historians wrote against the regents' narrowed responsiveness to disputes over inappropriate mailo allocations. The burdens of past persecutions materialized as historical claims that land had been seized by force by nobles hiding in the hearthstones of accommodating clans. Lost lands were a deep taproot of the Bataka's case before the government in 1924.[127] The ferment behind that case opened the door for the hidden hearthstones to reappear on the political stage as proponents of a more responsive royal center.

Katula evoked dramatic moments of reappearing from the shadows, putting noble slipperiness on trial. One scene unfolded during the reign of Ssuuna II (1830–56). Katula recounted Kamuyange, his queen mother and a daughter of the Lungfish, policing the boundaries of male nobility in that time of dissolving centers.[128] Subtitled "the fourth persecution," Kamuyange attacked a son of the Lungfish for acting like a prince. His error lay in honesty. He said "we are not completely princes," insisting on the complexities of royal maternal descent by putting the fungibility of belonging with royalty out in the open.[129] His claim undercut Kamuyange's authority to favor members of her clan who were not nobles in filling positions in her palace. Flummoxed, Kamuyange chose the poison ordeal to settle this matter of identity legally and in public. Nothing less than rooting out the couch grass of nobles hidden in Lungfish hearthstones was at stake.

Katula highlighted the rowdiness of the proceedings. As the defendant prepared to swallow the liquid, the unruly audience forced the concoction down his throat. The crowd roared their approval when it "burned" him, a sign of his guilt. In choosing to apply the ordeal, Kamuyange admitted her inability "to cut the case," to sort noble from commoner families in her own clan. The ordeal delegated to the public a much greater role in shaping the outcome.[130] It reduced the dispute to a contest of stamina, not one of discerning persuasion. Under the psychopharmacological influence of a concoction both litigants swallowed, they competed to take the first step over a low bar tied between two banana stems. The winner won the case.[131] Katula cast a critical eye on this example of a public being heard by a royal authority. He noted that the time that had been allowed to pass between swallowing the poison and Kamuyange's judgment was too little for the drug to have had an effect. Guilt was decided precipitously; the ensuing death was unjust. The crowd of insiders at a royal court had too much influence because they were insulated from a world of commoner critique.

This vignette raised doubts about the moral integrity of the individuals and relationships constituting strands in a sovereign knot, when the benefits of chiefly standing had dwarfed the standing of everyone else. Anyone could buy land under the mailo system. As those initial mailo holders began to pass away in the 1920s, that is exactly what was happening.[132] The gap between chiefs and everyone else was moral because chiefs with land wove a political cloth smothering the critiques of the excluded. It is conventional in the literature to argue that clans struck back at this in part by steeping their authority to critique it in the raiment of antiquity and custom. Yet Katula wrote in an idiom of persecution broader than clanship, friendly to nobility but protective of commoners. He aimed his rancor at the plague of litigation the struggles over landed standing visited on people in his day. That is why he agreed with the historians, that incessant conflict had dogged Kagulu's descendants since his reign, something legal culture alone could not fix.[133] He insisted that historical research could balance deficits in character only by looking beyond nobility and ethnicity.

The remainder of Katula's essays focus on the need for his generation to interrogate their elders about the family histories their hiding had forced into the closet. He saw very well that not every clan in Buganda was one thing; "it didn't stay where it first entered" the country.[134] By forcing their fathers to speak about the noble Nyoro ancestry they shed by hiding among Buganda's clans, denying it to their children, youths would expose the fictions that a true ancestry sticks only to one line drawn with biological descent. Skeptical youth, acting bravely, unearthed the missing lines. Beneath the surface of silence, they found couch grass, roots knotted together but also separate; some roots were dispersed in a loam of loss.

For Katula, hiders fooled themselves because many around them knew the truth and when circumstances moved against them, they would be exposed. When hidden nobles reappeared, their blood-friends in the hosting clan could feel betrayed and angry. The poorest, the lowest among them, would not forget who belonged and who hid. They showed it by laughing at the partial histories hiding nobles pushed.[135] Unjust mailo allotment had multiplied such betrayals by emboldening nobles to reappear, as the historians had done, to get their due lands. The result was the endless litigation of Katula's day, by which people sought the respect and obligations entailed by responsibility for—ownership of—land. The hiders had grown rich but had forgotten their former difficulties, warned about in this chapter's second epigraph. Katula raised serious doubts about the value of the historians' claims that more knowledge of the past would resolve all at stake in the 1920s, unless it broke free from traps of descent. The Nyoro nobles in Buganda's princes clan were the former hiders whose wealth has made them forget their debts to the hosts who protected them. They were the ones against whom Ganda nobles brayed so loudly, preventing Daudi Cwa from calmly sorting fact from fiction and resolving disputes of respect and obligation that only responsibility for land allowed one to live up to.

Katula's honesty had roots in exclusions from royal prerogatives. But it paid the respect owed to a person who claimed his friends, his fellow clan members, particular sets of paternal and maternal ancestors, and his descendants yet to come. Claiming them—bringing them out of hiding—represented individual courage in a world of relentless litigation and the harsh derisions of social hierarchy. Katula celebrated social connection and obligation, earned through individual self-control in times of difficulty. He doubted that silence about the indignities of past vulnerabilities—and the entanglements of ethnically distinct men and women of standing—could revive rule responsive to those burdens. This was Katula's gloss on the limits of a liberal citizenship that the Protectorate's laws denied Africans and a Buganda state's administrators tried to harness.

In making the point that the biological cannot be separated from the social, Katula closed his response to the historians by arguing that names mattered. Names bore weights of descent in their literal meanings and they showed descent moving below ground, popping up like couch grass. He refused the idea that groupwork like hearthstones, Ficus trees, clans, nobility, or a nation rendered only by clean lines of kinship guaranteed a good future. Such lines of belonging always escaped a generation's knowledge. At the close of the last installment, Katula revealed that he used to be named "Kiwanuka." He invited readers into the fraught moment when he asked his father why he had been given that name. His father answered that "lubaale Kiwanuka makes himself known from high in the sky, from a great distance . . . Kiwanuka is the one who comes down from above to the Inland Sea . . . explaining how your ancestor . . . came out of the Inland Sea."[136] The name helped a son with distant roots fit in in a new home under conditions of vulnerability. It kept alive the fact that those roots had also grown from the Inland Sea. Katula invoked this lùbaalè spirit in a Catholic newspaper to pry open his fundamental point.

Belonging in Kyaggwe, in Buganda, in Bunyoro, in a Protectorate, in a progressive, modern world was a matter of character, openness to others, and historical knowledge about all the lines suspended in times of vulnerability by clan hiding and revealed in times of opportunity by reappearing.

Those qualities necessitated creative, public, historically contingent, not primordial groupwork. He and his people had their origins in the Inland Sea, a fact they embraced with the lùbaalè names. That metaphor of indigeneity included a far more expansive imagination of belonging with the defeated but formerly strong Nyoro world. In a time when colonial subjection and the promise of deliverance through liberal citizenship threatened to produce atomization, Katula argued that belonging should draw on an Inland Sea of possibility and reckon with the complexities of landed couch grass where old pasts popped up again and again.

Debates over Kagulu's historical legacies returned in the 1910s and 1920s as arguments over the vicissitudes of belonging in times of dislocation, the stresses on gender, respect, and land prompted by mobility, forced or chosen. Arguments contained the frictions created in the turmoil of applying the terms of the 1900 Agreement by giving the alternatives a deeper history, suggesting a less authoritarian future. The misrule of mailo and the onerous burdens of the Protectorate economy shifted the ability to live up to the requirements of land and threatened the virtues land was deemed necessary to performing. Hunting, hiding, hosting, and reappearing parts of clans were vessels for arguing over the future by revisiting the past.

Too much focus on instrumental circumstance masks how these historians make their arguments stick. The wealth of detail on display in the 1920s articles showed that Sematimba's people had kept them alive. Katula foregrounded the pathos of loss in his accounts of the limits of noble accountability. As conventional ethnicity became active during the 1920s, these authors reminded the reading (and listening) public that ethnicity coexisted with other forms of moral community. Their historical arguments on that issue unfolded in a measured idiom of comparison and critique. They recalibrated boundaries in two ways. In a colonial present, where the boundaries at stake were often landed, they presented facts that could be used to contest those boundaries. In the earlier past, where boundaries were often also about a more mobile belonging, they insisted on the fungibilities of noble and commoner hearthstones.

The implications of hiding affected later generations, and they bitterly debated the truths or falsehoods the act put in play. Prosperous descendants forgot the tribulations of their hiding predecessors. But hiding was a thing undertaken by individuals and passed through them to the others they represented. It was not only imposed by others on those whom the individual sought or was expected to represent. This quality of hiding runs through all who revisited the consequences of Kagulu's cataclysmic reign. It is hegemonic. Male individuals—including the sociologically male Kamuyange—shaped it. Biologically female people in hiding, lumped into sociological or kinship categories like the bàlamù, shaped it. This kind of gendered, individualized groupwork looks familiar and unusual all at once. Its instrumental belonging is familiar. Yet the public nature of the fungibility of the belonging at stake is unusual. In a colonial setting, public debating over the fungibility of belonging gave life and power to that element of groupwork.

Ethnic categories drawn with boundaries, oriented to difference, and filled with a rich affective history were indispensable but pernicious for the male intellectuals discussed here. Those defining elements of ethnicity had sources in both regional and colonial histories. For those who wished to operate beyond them, watched by a variety of officials interested in the outcomes of their arguments, ethnicity could be pernicious if it foreclosed public debate about its fungibility, preventing a more expansive set of moral claims about the scope of political belonging from shaping a better future.

Conclusion

THE NAMES OF the python accumulated over more than a millennium, as people from different corners of the region, speaking different languages, learned to share the riches and risks of life with an Inland Sea and precolonial states or a Protectorate. Their names for the great snake differed, but everyone thought about belonging, sometimes at crucial times, by thinking with pythons. With this metaphor, people balanced the gendered imaginaries of social reproduction, such as descent and growth, with the realities of material life, the twists of alliance, the pain of dispossession, the lure of information, and the surprises of innovation. With pythons, people imagined and made the ground of belonging moral, debating and using the past to create better futures.

This formula had consequences, which in turn transformed the names of the python themselves. Sometimes the python played a literal part in the story—actual snakes helped people think historically, offer social criticism, and chart a path forward. Other times, only a person bearing the name of the python had a part in making political life respond to the new by taking stock of the past. At still other times, a model of a python—a power object—elicited tales of the past and passed judgment on the moral behavior of the tellers. Or the bas-relief of a python, on a royal drum named "python," convened leaders and followers to discuss and debate. These different pythons show the great snake as a device, a technique of change and continuity in forms of belonging. It accommodated both inclusion and exclusion. That is one reason for its longevity as a conceptual resource for escaping what can become the tight corners of groupwork, especially perhaps when a state of any sort takes an interest in a group's wealth.

The first python in this story of belonging was called *ènzìramìre*, the swallower of offerings and avoidances. Ènzìramìre named the living python with whom people expanded their imagined worlds of belonging beyond the face-to-face a millennium ago. Bemba the snake had composed one of those worlds. The Kintu figure and their allies made it something bigger, composed of multiple kinds of groups, like Bemba's, but with different networks of knowledge.[1] Struggles over the past, summed up by the python's distinctive eating, were part of that expansion, but they were never resolved completely. Would Bemba's people have a history before Kintu's group, or would Kintu's ascent mark the beginning of historical time? Answers depended on context but always involved notions of insider and outsider, conqueror and conquered, primary and counternarrative. Working out the tensions in those binaries promised a moral future, better than a future oriented to just one term in the pairs.

From the fourteenth century, Mukasa's people made that larger scale into something boundless with the Inland Sea as the medium. Their ancestors—including their immediately preceding identity as healer, fashioner of social criticism, and seeker of new knowledge—included figures whose names referenced the python. Nambubi Namatimba bore Sserwanga Mukasa. She and the generation she led created the circumstances for enlarging the scale of social life. She had ties to points west, north, and east from the Ssese Islands. Dried fish, glass beads, copper bangles, and crops like millet and banana moved in that scale. Her first name translates literally as "mother of dappled gray cattle," pointing to the rich pastures and valuable herds of cattle, inland and west of the islands. Her second name, "mother of the enormous python," points to python centers like Bemba's and Sserwanga Mukasa's on Bukasa Island. Namatimba's range accommodated the debates Kintu's rise prompted, working them into even broader networks of knowledge.

Two pythons named Sserwanga and Nalwanga had homes in the islands and on the littoral. They embodied the connections through assembly and travel, which linked the forms of wealth represented by Mukasa's people. By the sixteenth century, bark cloth, ironwork, and salt moved through those connections, in addition to the older goods. Change in scale was represented by a change in name. "Mukasa" sloughed "Sserwanga," leaving a gender-blended figure on Bubembe Island. Mukasa's people grew into as expansive a community as Kintu's people did. But Mukasa's abode was the islands and the Inland Sea, where pythons—living ones, islands, and canoe keels—conducted flows of information about economic opportunity and political circumstance around the northern rim of the Inland Sea. As Mukasa's people attracted others to their shrine, from the far corners of the Inland Sea and its hinterland, the python slipped into the background but did not disappear from their groupwork.

In the seventeenth century, sovereign knots, based in the hinterlands and tied with threads of independent wealth, standing, and knowledge, expanded their networks to include the islands and points north and west. They started with a collaborative conquest of a region that connected the Inland Sea to the riches of iron and salt, in Bunyoro. A fabricated python lay at the core of that move. Mbajjwe, was a clay-headed, rope-bodied snake with its own shrine and retinue of officials. It was not a new object, but its powers changed once they were caught up in the novelty of territorial expansion. The Mbajjwe that already existed in the region to be conquered was steeped in producing fertility for people there. Once the *kabaka*'s local collaborators gave it to him, the operators of that Mbajjwe began using it to pass judgment on the behavior of men and the groups they led. When royals—and Mbajjwe's operators—found the actions of those men and their groups wanting, execution could follow. The new Mbajjwe changed the equation that bound fertility and belonging, introducing royal justice and the risks of death into its ambit. The python object helped the conquerors become the source of fertility in the territory they had taken. The dislocations of expansionist statecraft put a new importance on the labor of raiding and the enslavement it entailed. The changed python object, Mbajjwe, facilitated an ominous twist in the reciprocal obligations keeping leader and follower in a single field of debate, critique, and reform.

The consequences of enslavement in the successful territorial expansions caused a moral crisis for the state in the eighteenth century. Among other things, grandees revised their past to open avenues of reciprocal obligation beyond the small number of earlier ones, like those that had facilitated taking control of Mbajjwe. They tried to forestall the dissipation of centers unobligated to their royal one by forming networks that would funnel more opportunity and wealth to the royal domain, from the north, west, and the Inland Sea. They looked backward for inspiration and legitimacy. Among many other things, kabakas enlisted the python in that work. In the generation following territorial expansion, a drum called *ttimbà* ("python"; fig. 2) became the first one in a new creation: the royal battery of drums. Royals used the new drum battery when a kabaka undertook a complicated expedition, when one of the princes died, or when a kabaka sent an embassy to Bubembe to "confer with the spirit of Mukasa." Ttimbà was looked after by a grandee from Ssese. The python drum called people to assemble with kabakas. When the royal battery sounded, a voice from the islands—the voice of ttimbà, the python—spoke first.[2]

Across the nineteenth century and well into the twentieth, belonging was strained by the loss of the ground beneath many of its constituents caused by violent forms of wealth, such as enslavement. One result was heightened attention to biological descent as a measure of belonging and standing. Women outside the lines drawn by descent bore these burdens of vulnerability as subjects of enslavement and as the people who labored more as a result of having been raided. Some women shaped the gendered norms of that new world. They drew on the past as a resource to limit their vulnerabilities to dislocation. As elderly people, they might claim a place in that world, when one of the children to whom they had given birth and raised to adulthood became an heir to a named position in a clan or in one of the threads in a sovereign knot. These ladies and ambitious former slaves could seek out the networks of knowledge at shrines with living pythons (among other shrines), devoted to fertility quests, to reduce their vulnerability. They could visit Bukasa, in Ssese, Bulonge, in Buddu, Kisengwe, in Bugangaizi, or some of the *énkuni* shrines, spread densely over Busoga, or the shrine to Atego, off Rusinga Island.

Between the 1840s and the 1890s, the violent edges of commodification, overlapping with the universalist strains of humanistic imagination found in religions of the book, convulsed the Great Lakes region. The figure of the python split apart yet again over matters of virtue and vice. One part clung to a noble bearing its name. Another part formed around Abrahamic notions linking snakes to the problem of knowledge and evil. Sematimba, the "controller of an enormous python," was the eldest son of the infamous kabaka Kagulu, whose eighteenth-century misrule exemplified the challenges of belonging with a state. The trials and tribulations of the noble Sematimba represented a part of the python's new, twentieth-century world. Another part, not discussed in this volume, conceived of "the snake" (*omusota*) as "the devil" (*sitaani*), part of complex critiques of the social inequalities emerging after the 1880s.

In some ways, both names served essentially the same purposes. Those who debated the repercussions of—and lessons to be learned from—Kagulu's misrule charted a better future in which knowledge of the past was a precondition for balancing individualism and groupwork. Historical knowledge provided alternatives to biological descent as criteria for inclusion and exclusion. Those who wrestled with devil snakes highlighted the array of risks of knowledge and the importance of self-mastery in a moral future as challenges shared across time and place. It would be an error to think of Sematimba and Sitaani as unrelated. Each represented the difficult challenges of creating a moral, modern world. They prompted debate about living in a way that balanced the rights and duties of a gendered, atomized liberal citizenship and its colonial exclusions, with the rights and duties to debate the past, as members of larger groups, to revise the terms of belonging in a collective future. Each carried a weight of antiquity—one broadly regional, the other universal—bridged by the snake. The python remained present to that struggle, as a noble name and as an actual snake embodying the marginal and downtrodden.

Actual pythons returned to the fray of nationalist politics in Uganda in the 1950s as both devils and social critics. As Jonathon Earle has shown, the trade

unionist Erieza Bwete likely understood a tense encounter he had with a python as an encounter with a devil snake, that is, as a threat to the political
project of labor reform he was leading. Bwete and his comrades met the
python—and probably killed it—while hiding from police chasing them in
the aftermath of the 1949 general strike that affected nearly the whole of the
Protectorate.[3] But killing the python did not prevent Bwete from using it to
signal spirited resistance to colonial exclusions from lucrative cotton markets
and favorable access for Indians to managing cotton ginning. In this case, the
figure of the python evoked authochthony, perhaps racialized, given that Bwete's
resistance focused on racialized colonial exclusions from the cotton economy.
A decade later, another figure of social criticism, Kigaanira Kibuuka, took the
stage of social critique and debate with the help of a python. Kigaanira was a
Christian, but his Christianity was tuned to the promise of *lùbaalè* work in
fostering critique. In the 1950s, that critique included voices from beyond the
world of wages, work, and management. He used a two-headed python to
argue that violent struggle against injustice and healing were two parts of one
thing. "As Kibuuka, signified by one head of the snake, Kigaanira wielded an
ability to declare war against the colonial state; but as Mukasa's partner, the
other head, he embodied healing and blessing for the kingdom's exiled monarch and the subjects of Buganda."[4]

The names of the python did not—and do not—belong exclusively to a
Luganda world of communication. Ènzìramìre makes sense to people speaking languages from Bunyoro to Buzinza and Ukerewe. Atego is a Luo name
for the python. Mumbo named a serpent figure whose patronage promised
followers speaking many different languages the time and effort to devise a
proper way out of the racial and economic binds of colonialism in southwestern Kenya.[5] The names of the python worked in similar ways across the Inland
Sea's northern tier and far beyond. Python histories reveal that ideas about
exclusion and inclusion have changed a great deal over the past millennium. If
today's exclusions operating through class, ethnic, national, and racial categories will be tamed, thinking with pythons shows a way. Debate about the past
will be central to that project not just for excavating the causes and consequences of exclusion and dispossession but also for sustaining the value of
participation and justice in redressing them. The persistence of people's work
with pythons suggests hope.

Marginalized and vulnerable Ugandans continue to call on the python in
assembling and articulating social criticism of the grinding gears of growth.
The hunger of "development" for "growth" consumes healthy ecologies, dislo-
cating the poor from land, which population growth and private property
makes valuable. Adele Stock worked with a medium of Bemba Omusota,

resident in the Lubigi swamplands being swallowed up by Kampala's urban sprawl in the 2010s. Possessed by Bemba, the medium criticized the unresponsiveness of the kabaka to the obligation to protect followers, like her and those who live with her, devoted to inclusion and landed respect, from a rapacious statecraft beholden to the logic of private property.[6] Bemba's return reminds us that ethnicity's blinding certainties are vulnerable to alternative histories. Bemba's return also reminds us that those at the margins keep alternative histories alive.

The Names of the Python demonstrates the historical contingencies of a landed core to ethnic formation. Landed property was ancient, struggles over it were institutionalized, through inheritance and reciprocal obligation, but that did not translate into ethnic nationalisms until very late in the colonial period. That finding frays any straight narrative line from landed belonging to fractious ethnicities. As many have shown, promoters must work hard—even in conditions of heightened threat and inequality—to streamline people's normally complicated thinking about the world into identifying solely with narrower channels of ethnic, nationalist, or racial belonging in choosing a course of action.[7] Understanding those complexities requires bearing down on deep regional histories. One finds in them complimentary bundles of idea and practice for resisting fracture by debating and revising its premises.[8] Some ideas and practices, like python work, proved durable because they are changeable. Pythons do not exhaust these riches; many others await further study.

Appendix
Lexical-Semantic Reconstructions

A. Clan, Possession, Metaphors and Blends, Canoes, Fish, and Fishing Gear

Term	Gloss/Semantics	Proto-Language or Language	Sources
1. ngàndá	Heap, pile; clan, family.	Proto–Great Lakes Bantu	Schoenbrun (1997), RN 106
2. kùbândwa	Be knocked down; be possessed by spirit.	Proto–Great Lakes Bantu	Schoenbrun (1997), RN 271
mubàndwa	Spirit; initiated medium; lit. person mounted by a spirit.	Proto–West Nyanza	Schoenbrun (1997), RN 271
èmmandwà	Spirit; initiated medium; python; bull	Ganda	Schoenbrun (1997), RN 271
3. kùsambwà	Be kicked.	Circum-Lake	Schoenbrun (1997), RN 347
-sámbwa; noun, with different noun prefixes	Territorial location of a spirit; the spirit; its familiar.	Circum-Lake	Schoenbrun (1997), RN 347
4. èkikâ (s.); èbikâ (pl.)	Big homestead; clan, family.	Proto–North Nyanza	Stephens (2013), 187

Term	Gloss/Semantics	Proto-Language or Language	Sources
5. ènzìramìre, Polysemous noun	Python; lit. avoidance, offering swallower. From Ganda: *kùmira* (tr.) swallow; *kùzira* (tr.) not to allow, reject, forbid. Linguistic play in Ganda: *enzira* propitiatory sacrifice, offering. African rock python; *Python sebae*; lit. swallows big things.	Proto–West Nyanza	*Nkore, Kiga* (Taylor 1959); *Ganda* (Snoxall 1967), 204, 232, 265, 266, 355; (Le Veux 1917), 1037
miryamirye	*Python sebae*; lit. big swallower.	Proto–Great Lakes Bantu	Schoenbrun (2016), 221
6. kùlyâ	Eat, consume.	Proto–Great Lakes Bantu	
7. muzimu	Spirit of ancestor.	Proto–Great Lakes Bantu	Schoenbrun (1997), RN 278
8. énkuní	Spirit of first men of each clan arriving in Busoga; shrine site.	Soga, Nyole; Luo Areal	Cohen (1972), 21; Ogot (1967), 79; Schoenbrun (1997), RN 315
9. mùsamìze kùsamìra	Initiated medium. Be possessed by a spirit; lit. to snatch.	Proto–North Nyanza with areal spread to Nkore and Nyole	Schoenbrun (in progress), RN 21
10. ttimbà polysemous noun	Python; name of a tributary entering Mayanja R. downstream of the Wasswa-Kato confluence; lead drum in royal battery, a chief from Ssese Isles is its hereditary keeper. From Ganda: *kùtimba*, "bind, lash; hang (curtain or picture); decorate (room); drape, entwine."	Ganda	Snoxall (1967), 312; Nsimbi (1980 [1956]), "Maapu," (river name)

Term	Gloss/Semantics	Proto-Language or Language	Sources
11. lusuku	Banana garden.	Proto–North Nyanza	Schoenbrun (1993), 71 (RN 43)
12. ènkejje	Sprat; haplochromine.	Proto–West Nyanza	Schoenbrun (in progress), RN 18
òbùmùkene	Sardine; *Rastrineobola argentea.*	Proto–West Nyanza	Schoenbrun (in progress), RN 20
endagala	Sardine; often *Stolothrissa* spp.	Proto–East Bantu	Schoenbrun (in progress), RN 19
13. èryâto	Dugout canoe.	Proto-Bantu	Bastin and Schadeberg (2002), 3252
èyrâto; amaàto	Sewn canoe.	Late Proto–North Nyanza	Schoenbrun (in progress), RN 42
ènsanda	Front prow.	Late Proto–North Nyanza	Kagwa (1918), 284; Gonza (2007), 169
bùlumbâ; àkàlumbâ	Rear prow.	Late Proto–North Nyanza	Kagwa (1918), 284; Gonza (2007), 80
èmmânvu	Dugout canoe.	Proto–North Nyanza	Schoenbrun (in progress), RN 41
14. òlùkandâ	Sewn mat of up to 30 skewers of dried sprats.	South Rutara; Ganda, Vuma	Schoenbrun (in progress), RN 13
15. ekiragala	Beach seine net, up to 100 ft. by 10 ft, with net weights.	Ganda, Vuma Areal	Schoenbrun (in progress), RN 9
16. sambo	Beach seine net.	South Rutara; Buddu; Ganda; Vuma	Schoenbrun (in progress), RN 7
17. buligo, kabigo	Inshore fish fence.	South Rutara; Ganda Areal	Schoenbrun (in progress), RN 10
18. -cúí	Fish, generic.	Proto-Bantu	BLR III 751
19. -nyeeni	Fish, generic.	Proto-Luhyia	Schoenbrun (in progress), RN 17
20. -kye nyanja	Fish, generic.	Proto–North Nyanza	Schoenbrun (in progress), RN 18

Term	Gloss/Semantics	Proto-Language or Language	Sources
21. -suku	*Labeo victorianus* (lake fish).	Proto-Rutara, Proto–North Nyanza Areal	Schoenbrun (in progress), RN 9
22. -mamba	Lungfish (swampland fish).	Proto–Great Lakes Bantu	Schoenbrun (in progress), RN 32
23. -conzi	Mudfish (swampland fish).	Proto–Great Lakes Bantu	Schoenbrun (in progress), RN 39
24. -sinja	*Barbus* sp. (river fish).	Proto–Great Lakes Bantu	Schoenbrun (in progress), RN 30
25. -gege	Tilapia (Inland Sea fish).	Proto–East Bantu	Schoenbrun (in progress), RN 26

B. Bark Cloth

Term	Gloss/Semantics	Proto-Language or Language	Distribution
26.1 -kúyù 11/6; 3/4	Fig; *Ficus* tree.	Proto-Bantu	Bastin and Schadeberg (2002), 2086; *Tembo* (Kaji 1985), 236; *Wanga* (Anangwe and Marlo 2008), 23, 68; *Nyole* (Musimani and Diprose 2012), 26.
26.2 -bumu; -bumo 3/4	*Ficus* tree.	Proto–Great Lakes Bantu	*Rundi* (Meyer 1984 [1916]), 37; *Rwanda* (Coupez et al., 2005), 2751; *Nyole* (Musimani and Diprose 2012), 234.

Term	Gloss/Semantics	Proto-Language or Language	Distribution
26.3. -lumba 3/4 noun	Bark cloth tree; loin cloth.	Proto–Great Lakes Bantu	*Kwaya* (MacWilliams 1973), 52; *Shi* (Polak-Bynon 1978), 30; *Shi* (P[ères] B[lancs], n.d.), 109; *Rundi*; *Nande, Koonzo* (Mutaka and Kavutirwaki 2011), 248.
27. -kómaga (from -kóma "to fasten, tie" + contactive suffix)	Beat out bark cloth.	Proto-Rutara, with spread to Ganda	*Nyoro, Nkore, Kiga* (Taylor 1959), 62; *Haya, Ziba; Zinza. Ganda* (Le Veux 1917), 415.
28.1. rubugo or orubugu 11/10; [mubugu 3/4]	Bark cloth; bark cloth tree.	Proto-Rutara + spread to Ganda + Sumbwa	*Nyoro* (Maddox 1901), 106, *Nkore, Kiga; Haya* (Meyer 1914), 16; *Ziba* (Von Herrmann 1904), 159 and (Rehse 1914), 96; *Sumbwa* (Capus 1901), 80.
28.2. libugu 5	Bark cloth; bark cloth tree.	Southeastern Inland Sea Rim	*Kwaya* (MacWilliams 1973), 52; *Jita* (Mdee 2008), 70; *Sumbwa* (Kahigi 2008), 83.
28.3. òlùbugo; àmàbugo 11/6	Bark cloth (s.); grave clothes (pl.).	Ganda	*Ganda* (Wilson (1882), 48, 59; Pilkington (1899), 59; Le Veux (1917), 79; Snoxall (1967), 182.

Term	Gloss/Semantics	Proto-Language or Language	Distribution
28.4. kibugu or ekibugo 7/8	Bark cloth.	North Rutara Areal	*Nyoro, Nkore* (Davis 1952 [1938]), 66; *Nkore, Kiga* (Taylor 1959), 40.
29. mutôma 3/4; kitôma 7/8	Bark cloth tree, generic; latex tree, 3/4; bark cloth, 7/8.	Proto-Rutara or Proto–Great Lakes Bantu?	*Nande* (Fraas 1960), 113; *Nyoro* (Maddox 1901), 111, *Nyoro, Nkore* (Davis 1952 [1938]), 116; ***Nkore, Kiga* (Taylor 1959), 151; *Haya* (Meyer 1914), 111; *(Muzale 2006), 177; *Ziba; Gungu* (Businge and Diprose 2012), 201.
30. mutuba 3/4	*Ficus natalensis*, Bark-cloth tree; ranked leadership in a clan.	Pre-Ganda	*Ganda* (Wilson 1882), 133; (Pilkington 1899), 79; (Le Veux 1917), 680; (Snoxall 1967), 227; (Hamilton 1981), 102.
31.1. ensamo, 9/10 (noun)	Grooved mallet for beating *lubugo*.	Areal block distribution; North-Central Inland Sea Rim focus	*Ganda* (Pilkington 1899), 89; (Le Veux 1917), 752; *Soga; Nyoro, Nkore, Tooro; Nyole.*
31.2. empuuzo 9/10	Deeply grooved bark cloth mallet; flail.	Pre-Ganda	*Ganda* (Le Veux 1917), 415, 640; *Sukuma* (Literature Department, n.d.), 54.

Term	Gloss/Semantics	Proto-Language or Language	Distribution
31.3. impuuzu; akahuuzu 9/12	Bark cloth.	Proto–West Highlands	*Rwanda* (Coupez et al., 2005), 1809; *Rundi* (Meyer 1914), 47; *Ha* (Van Sambeek n.d.), 42; *Rufumbira* (Kisoro District Language Board 2009), 11.
32.1. musara 3/4	Bark cloth made after the first peeling (soft).	Inland Sea Rim (gap from Mpologoma River to Musoma), inland to Nkore and Kigezi	*Nkore* (Davis 1952 [1938]), 113; *Kiga*; *Haya* (Meyer 1914), 111; *Ziba* (Von Herrmann 1904), 159; *Ganda* (Kitching and Blackledge 1925), 71; (Hamilton et al. 2016), 110; *Soga* (Gonza 2007).
32.2. nserere 9; omuseerere; emi- 3/4	Bark cloth tree sp.; *Ficus brachypoda*; Rough type of bark-cloth.	Northwestern Inland Sea Rim	*Haya* (Meyer 1914), 43; Muzale 2006), 172; Ziba (Von Herrmann 1904), 159; *Nkore*; *Buddu* (Snoxall 1967), 255.
32.3. mugáyíre 3/4	Bark cloth kind.	Central Inland Sea Rim	*Gwere* (Nzogi and Diprose 2012), 175; *Soga* (Gonza 2007); *Nyole* (Musimani and Diprose 2012), 235.

Term	Gloss/Semantics	Proto-Language or Language	Distribution
32.4. kitentegere; kídhéndhébwa 7/8	Coarse bark cloth, taken from *F. brachyoda*.	Rutara–North Nyanza Areal	*Nyoro*, *Nkore* (Davis 1938), 79; *Haya*; *Ganda* (Le Veux 1917), 387, *Soga* (Gonza 2007).
32.5. endogo 9/10	Black bark cloth from Busoga.	Term of reference for consumers only; not in Lusoga	*Ganda* (Le Veux 1917), 548; *Nyoro*, *Nkore* (Davis 1952 [1938]), 123.
33. -tûmba	Bark cloth tree; headload, burden; load of cloth carried by porters.	Mashariki Areal	Schoenbrun (in progress), RN 206.
34. mutanda 3/4	Bark cloth clothing; any large coverlet of cloth; unit of sewn bark-cloth (approx. 15 feet long); piece of bark cloth from single tree.	Areal	*Ganda* (Le Veux 1917), 677; *Soga* (Gonza 2007), 152; *Nyoro*, *Nkore* (Davis 1952 [1938]), 115; *Nkore*, *Kiga* (Taylor 1959), 117; *Haya* (Meyer 1914), 131.

Notes

Introduction

1. Kifamunyanja, "Ssese: Gambuze nti agafudde e Mengo," *Munno* (October 1921), 159.

2. Andrew Apter, "Yoruba Ethnogenesis from Within," *Comparative Studies in Society and History* 55, no. 2 (2013), 356.

3. Jennifer L. Johnson, "Fish, Family, and the Gendered Politics of Descent along Uganda's Southern Littoral," *History in Africa* 45 (2018), 445–71; Helen Verran, *Science and an African Logic* (Chicago: University of Chicago Press, 2001), 234–36, applied in Apter, "Yoruba Ethnogenesis," 363–68.

4. N. S. B. Gabunga, "Okusala amagezi olwe njala mu Buganda," *Ebifa mu Buganda* 139 (August 1918), 153–55; Anonymous, "Obunyikivu bwokulima Pamba mu Saza lye Sese," *Ebifa mu Buganda* 143 (December 1918), 227.

5. Fredrik Barth, "Introduction," in *Ethnic Groups and Boundaries*, ed. Fredrik Barth (Boston: Little, Brown, 1969), 9–38; Jean-Loup Amselle, "Ethnies et espaces: pour une anthropologie topologique," in *Au Coeur de l'Ethnie: Ethnies, Tribalisme et État en Afrique*, ed. Jean-Loup Amselle and Elikia M'Bokolo (Paris: Le Découverte, 1985), 11–48.

6. Apter, "Yoruba Ethnogenesis," 356; Barth, "Introduction," 11–16.

7. Max Weber, *Economy and Society*, ed. Guenther Roth and Claus Wittich (Berkeley: University of California Press 2013), 395; Jonathon Glassman, "Ethnicity and Race in African Thought," in *A Companion to African History*, ed. William Worger, Charles Ambler, and Nwando Achebe (London: Wiley-Blackwell, 2019), 199–223.

8. John Lonsdale, "The Moral Economy of Mau Mau: Wealth, Poverty and Civic Virtue in Kikuyu Political Thought," in Bruce Berman and John Lonsdale, *Violence and Ethnicity*, book 2 of *Unhappy Valley: Conflict in Kenya and Africa* (Athens: Ohio University Press, 1992), 315–504.

9. Jan Bender Shetler, *Claiming Civic Virtue: Gendered Network Memory in the Mara Region, Tanzania* (Madison: University of Wisconsin Press, 2019), 12–28.

10. Lonsdale, "Moral Economy," 346–50.

11. Rogers Brubaker, "Ethnicity without Groups," *European Journal of Sociology* 43, no. 1 (2002), 167–75; John Comaroff, "The End of Anthropology, Again: On the Future of an In/Discipline," *American Anthropologist* 112, no. 4 (2010), 531.

12. Julie Livingston, *Debility and the Moral Imagination in Botswana* (Bloomington: Indiana University Press, 2005), 20.

13. Jonathon Glassman, personal communication, May 2018.

14. Lonsdale, "Moral Economy," 338–39.

15. Derek R. Peterson, *Creative Writing: Translation, Bookkeeping, and the Work of Imagination in Colonial Kenya* (Portsmouth, NH: Heinemann, 2004), 10–20.

16. Neil Kodesh, *Beyond the Royal Gaze: Clanship and Public Healing* (Charlottesville: University of Virginia Press, 2010), 14.

17. Steven Feierman, "Colonizers, Scholars and the Creation of Invisible Histories," in *Beyond the Cultural Turn*, ed. Victoria Bonnell and Lynn Hunt (Berkeley: University of California Press, 1999), 189–92, 196–203.

18. Holly Hanson, "Mapping Conflict: Heterarchy and Accountability in the Ancient Capital of Buganda," *Journal of African History* 50, no. 2 (2009), 179–202.

19. Holly Hanson, *Landed Obligation: The Practice of Power in Buganda* (Portsmouth, NH: Heinemann, 2003), 35–53, 65.

20. Anon. [Apolo Kagwa], "Basekabaka be Buganda nga bwebalirana, namanya ga Banamasole, ne Miziro gyabwe," *Ebifa mu Buganda* 63 (April 1912), 2–3. The list appeared through September 1912.

21. Steven Feierman, personal communication, September 24, 2019.

22. Julius B. Lejju, *The Influence of Climate Change and Human-Induced Environmental Degradation on Lake Victoria* (Addis Ababa: Organisation for Social Science Research in Eastern and Southern Africa, 2012), 26; Joseph L. Awange and Obiero Ong'ang'a, *Lake Victoria: Ecology, Resources, Environment* (Berlin: Springer, 2006).

23. Awange and Ong'ang'a, *Lake Victoria*, 23–24. Buvuma Islanders tell of "sinking" islands; John T. K. Ggomotoka, "History of Buvuma Islands," trans. David Kiyaga-Mulindwa (Kampala: Typescript, 1937–38), Buvuma, 3, 4, 14, 15.

24. Y. T. K. Ggomotoka, "Ab'Amasaza ge Buganda," *Munno* 16, no. 6 (1926), 103; M. S. M. Semakula Kiwanuka, *A History of Buganda: From the Foundation of the Kingdom to 1900* (New York: Africana, 1972), 26.

25. Colonel H. R. Bateman, "Research and Reminiscences: Uganda 1908–1910," *Uganda Journal* 15, no. 1 (1951), 26; Awange and Ong'ang'a, *Lake Victoria*, 9.

26. Kifamunyanja, "Ssese: Gambuze," 173.

27. Henry Morton Stanley, *Through the Dark Continent*, vol. 1 (London: Sampson Low, Marston, Searle & Rivington, 1878), 214; Franz Stuhlmann, *Mit Emin Pascha im Herzs von Afrika* (Berlin: Dietrich Reimer, 1894), 731; Kasirye Zzibukulimbwa, "The Beginning of Ennyanja Nnalubaale," trans. Robert Bakaaki and Jennifer Lee Johnson (Kampala: PDF, 2012), 12.

28. G. D. Hale Carpenter, *A Naturalist on Lake Victoria with an Account of Sleeping Sickness and the Tse-tse Fly* (New York: Dutton, 1920), 68; Edgar Barton Worthington, "Primitive Craft of the Central African Lakes," *Mariner's Mirror* 19, no. 2 (1933), 146–63.

29. Carpenter, *Naturalist on Lake Victoria*, 72. A six-foot tall person, gazing over a flat surface, sees a horizon three miles distant. The grayed ring around the rim of the Inland Sea in all maps depicts the normal range of travel by sewn canoe.

30. Alexander M. Mackay, "Boat Voyage along the Western Shores of Victoria Nyanza," *Proceedings of the Royal Geographical Society* 6, no. 5 (1884), 273–83; Anonymous, "The Bishop's Visit to Bubembe, Bukasa, and Kome," *Mengo Notes* 1, no. 2 (1900), 6–7; Ham Mukasa, *Uganda's Katikkiro in England* (London: Hutchinson, 1904), chap. 1.

31. Teofiro Mulumba Kuruji, in John Roscoe and Apolo Kagwa, "Enquiry into Native Land Tenure in the Uganda Protectorate," 1906, 33, Weston Library, Oxford, MSS Afr.S.17.

32. Michael Kenny, "The Powers of Lake Victoria," *Anthropos* 72, nos. 5/6 (1977), 726–27; Charles William Hobley, *Kenya: From Chartered Company to Crown Colony* (London: Witherby, 1929), 113–14; Harry Johnston, *The Uganda Protectorate*, vol. 2 (London: Hutchinson, 1902), 78–81.

33. Or the *nkŭngu*, a "mythical swordfish, king of the fish, can cut through a canoe, but is never caught"; see Capitein Von Herrmann, "Lusíba, die sprache der Länder Kisíba, Bugábu, Kjamtwára, Kjánja und Ihángiro, speziell der Dialekt der 'Bayŏssa' im Lande Kjamtwára," *Mitteilungen des Seminars für Orientalische Sprachen* 7 (1904), 161; Charles T. Wilson, *An Outline Grammar of the Luganda Language* (London: Society for Promoting Christian Knowledge, 1882), 124 (quote); Apolo Kagwa, *Ekitabo Kye Mpisa Za Baganda* (Kampala: Uganda Printing & Publishing, 1918), 280; Martin J. Hall, *Through My Spectacles in Uganda; Or, The Story of a Fruitful Field* (London: Church Missionary Society, 1898), 66.

34. Zzibukulimbwa, "The Beginning," 6.

35. Michael G. Kenny, "The Stranger from the Lake: A Theme in the History of the Lake Victoria Shorelands," *Azania* 17, no. 1 (1982), 7.

36. Kiwanuka, *History of Buganda*, 26–27.

37. Conrad P. Kottak, "Ecological Variables in the Origin and Evolution of African States: The Buganda Example," *Comparative Studies in Society and History* 14, no. 3 (1972), 351–80.

38. Christopher Wrigley, *Kingship and State: The Buganda Dynasty* (Cambridge: Cambridge University Press, 1996), 161, 167–68.

39. Henri Médard, *Le royaume du Buganda au XIX siècle* (Paris: Karthala, 2007), 182–91, 330 (map 25); Andrew D. Roberts, "The Sub-Imperialism of the Baganda," *Journal of African History* 3, no. 3 (1962), 435–50; Richard J. Reid, "The Ganda on Lake Victoria," *Journal of African History* 39, no. 3 (1998), 349–63.

40. Richard Reid, *Political Power in Pre-Colonial Buganda* (Oxford: James Currey, 2002), 64–68.

41. Reid, *Political Power*, 140–41; Michael G. Kenny, "Salt Trading in Eastern Lake Victoria," *Azania* 9 (1974), 225–28.

42. Kodesh, *Beyond the Royal Gaze*, 124–29.

43. Kiwanuka, *History of Buganda*, 114ff; Hanson, *Landed Obligation*, 80–81.

44. Reid, *Political Power*, 227–48, 233; Gerald Hartwig, *The Art of Survival in East Africa: The Kerebe and Long-Distance Trade, 1800–1895* (New York: Africana, 1976), 103–39.

45. Ceri Ashley, "Towards a Socialised Archaeology of Great Lakes Ceramics," *African Archaeological Review* 27 (2010), 135–63; Andrew Reid, "Recent Research on the Archaeology of Buganda," in *Researching Africa's Past: New Contributions from British*

Archaeologists, ed. Peter J. Mitchell, Ann Haour, and John Hobart (Oxford: Oxbow, 2003), 110–17.

46. Scheherazade Amin, "The Archaeology of the Sesse [*sic*] Islands and Their Contribution to the Understanding of Great Lakes Ceramics," PhD diss., University College of London, 2015, 427.

47. Andrew Reid and Ceri Ashley, "Islands of Agriculture on Victoria Nyanza," in *Archaeology of African Plant Use*, ed. Chris J. Stevens, Sam Nixon, Mary Anne Murray, and Dorian Q. Fuller (Walnut Creek, CA: Left Coast Press, 2014), 179–88; Merrick Posnansky, Andrew Reid, and Ceri Ashley, "Archaeology on Lolui Island, Uganda 1964–65," *Azania: Archaeological Research in Africa* 40 (2005), 73–100.

48. David Schoenbrun, "Early African Pasts: Sources, Method, and Interpretation," in *The Oxford Encyclopedia of African Historiography: Methods and Sources*, vol. 1, ed. Thomas Spear (New York: Oxford University Press, 2019), 10–17, 25–30. See also Koen Bostoen, Rhonda Gonzales, Birgit Ricquier, Constanze Weise, in the same volume.

49. Judith T. Irvine, "Subjected Words: African Linguistics and the Colonial Encounter," *Language and Communication* 28 (2008), 323–43; Sinfree Makoni, "Sociolinguistics, Colonial and Postcolonial: An Integrationist Perspective," *Language Sciences* 33 (2011), 680–88.

50. Dirk Geeraerts, *Theories of Lexical Semantics* (Oxford: Oxford University Press, 2010).

51. William F. Hanks, *Language and Communicative Practices* (Boulder, CO: Westview Press, 1996), 21–38.

52. Steven Feierman, *Peasant Intellectuals: Anthropology and History in Tanzania* (Madison: University of Wisconsin Press, 1990), 12.

53. Thomas Hinnebusch, Derek Nurse, and Martin Mould, *Studies in the Classification of Eastern Bantu Languages* (Hamburg: Helmut Buske, 1981); David L. Schoenbrun, *The Historical Reconstruction of Great Lakes Bantu Cultural Vocabulary* (Cologne: Rüdiger Köppe Press, 1997).

54. Rhiannon Stephens, *A History of African Motherhood* (New York: Cambridge University Press, 2013), 183–93.

55. Henry R. T. Muzale, *A Reconstruction of the Proto-Rutara Tense-Aspect System* (Ottawa: National Library of Canada, 1999); Rachel Angogo Kanyoro, *Unity in Diversity: A Linguistic Survey of the Abaluhyia of Western Kenya* (Vienna: AFRO-PUB, 1983). Western Nilotic rests on fewer studies; Richard T. Curley and Ben Blount, "The Southern Luo Languages: A Glottochronological Reconstruction," *Journal of African Languages* 9, no. 1 (1970), 1–18; Gerald Heusing, *Die Südlichen Lwoo-Sprachen: Beschreibung, Bergleich und Rekonstruktion* (Köln: Rüdiger Köppe Press, 2004).

56. Julie MacArthur, "The Making and Unmaking of African Languages: Oral Communities and Competitive Linguistic Work in Western Kenya," *Journal of African History* 53, no. 2 (2012), 151–72.

57. Benedict Anderson, *Imagined Communities*, rev. ed. (London: Verso, 1991), 22–36, esp. 32–36; Patrick Geary, *The Myth of Nations: The Medieval Origins of Europe* (Princeton, NJ: Princeton University Press, 2002), 41–63.

58. Roger Blench, *Archaeology, Language, and the African Past* (Lanham, MD: AltaMira Press, 2006), 16; Christopher Ehret, *History and the Testimony of Language* (Berkeley: University of California Press, 2011), 27–32.

59. Hanks, *Language*, 119.

60. Barbara Lewandowska-Tomaszczyk, "Polysemy, Prototypes, and Radial Categories," in *The Oxford Handbook of Cognitive Linguistics*, ed. Dirk Geeraerts and Herbert Cuyckens (Oxford: Oxford University Press, 2007), 153.

61. Koen Bostoen, "Semantic Vagueness and Cross-Linguistic Lexical Fragmentation in Bantu: Impeding Factors for Linguistic Palaeontology," *Sprache und Geschichte in Afrika* 20 (2009), 51–64.

62. Schoenbrun, "Early African Pasts," 4–11.

63. Hanks, *Language*, 239–67.

64. Glassman, "Ethnicity and Race," 212.

65. Though not argued in historical terms, see Michael Schatzberg, *Political Legitimacy in Middle Africa: Father, Family, Food* (Bloomington: Indiana University Press, 2001).

66. Carolyn Hamilton, *Terrific Majesty: The Powers of Shaka Zulu and the Limits of Historical Invention* (Cambridge, MA: Harvard University Press, 1998), 32–35; Naomi Quinn, "The Cultural Basis of Metaphor," in *Beyond Metaphor*, ed. James Fernandez (Stanford, CA: Stanford University Press, 1991), 56–93; Webb Keane, "Marked, Absent, Habitual: Approaches to Neolithic Religion at Catalhöyük," in *Religion in the Emergence of Civilization: Catalhöyük as a Case Study*, ed. Ian Hodder (New York: Cambridge University Press, 2010), 193, n3.

67. Thomas J. Csordas, "Embodiment as a Paradigm for Anthropology," *Ethnos* 18, no. 1 (1990), 5–47; Geeraerts, *Theories of Lexical Semantics*, 202–22; Rob Wiseman, "Getting beyond Rites of Passage in Archaeology: Conceptual Metaphors of Journeys and Growth," *Current Anthropology* 60, no. 4 (2019), 449–74.

68. Derek R. Peterson and Giacomo Macola (eds.), *Recasting the Past: History Writing and Political Work in Modern Africa* (Athens: Ohio University Press, 2009).

69. John Allen Rowe, "Revolution in Buganda, 1856–1884," PhD diss., University of Wisconsin–Madison, 1966, 220–60; Derek R. Peterson and Giacomo Macola, "Introduction: Homespun Historiography and the Academic Profession," in *Recasting the Past*, ed. Derek R. Peterson and Giacomo Macola (Athens: Ohio University Press, 2009), 20; Jonathon Earle, *Colonial Buganda and the End of Empire: Political Thought and Historical Imagination in Africa* (New York: Cambridge University Press, 2017), 23–37.

70. Robert W. Felkin, "Notes on the Waganda Tribe of Central Africa," *Proceedings of the Royal Society of Edinburgh* 13 (1885/1886), 764, noted an "almost identical sequence is followed, the same sentences and modes of expression being preserved as accurately as the incidents themselves," in contrast to "the same story told by an old man and a young one, although having one and the same main idea, yet varies considerably in detail and style."

71. John Hanning Speke, *Journal of the Discovery of the Source of the Nile* (Edinburgh: William Blackwood, 1863), opposite 424.

72. Omwami Semu Kasyoka Kakoma, Rev. Adoniya Musoke Ntate, P. T. I. Kayonga, and Mwami Musa Serukwaya, Kasolo, *Ekitabo Eky' Abakyanjove Ab'e Mamba Mu Siiga Lya Nankere e Bukerekere* (Kampala: East African Institute of Social Research, 1959), 4. *Ènnanga* is made from the same verb—*kùlanga*, "announce, give notice of"—which, in the prepositional (*kùlangira*) means "charge somebody with; proclaim," giving òmùlangira, "noble" or, more loosely, "proclaimer."

73. Speke, *Journal*, 246–453, 252.

74. Stanley, *Through the Dark Continent*, vol. 1, 380.

75. Kiwanuka, *History of Buganda*, 64–75, 114–20.

76. Stanley, *Through the Dark Continent*, vol. 1, 380.

77. Apollo Kagwa, *Bakabaka Bebuganda* (London: Headley Brothers, 1901), 31–65.

78. Speke, *Journal*, 252–56, named only kings but mentions titled chiefs and palace officials. Kagwa, *Bakabaka Bebuganda*, named holders of key titled positions, queen mothers and queen sisters, noting their clan.

79. M. S. M. Semakula Kiwanuka, "Introduction," in Apolo Kaggwa, *The Kings of Buganda*, ed. and trans. M. S. M. Semakula Kiwanuka (Nairobi: East African Publishing House, 1971), xxii.

80. Kagwa, *Bakabaka Bebuganda, passim*; Apolo Kagwa, *Ekitabo Kye Bika Bya Baganda* (Kampala: Uganda Bookshop, 1949 [ca. 1907], closes with a chronology, reprinted in *Uganda Journal* 16, no. 2 (1952), 148–58, translated by Abubakar M. Kakyama Mayanja.

81. See Wrigley, *Kingship and State*, 30, for other differences in reign order.

82. Muteesa had learned from traders familiar with Zanzibar that the bodies of his counterparts, the sultans, were buried whole. So he had the bodies of ten previous kings exhumed and reburied together with their jawbones; Apolo Kaggwa, *The Kings of Buganda*, ed. and trans. M. S. M. Semakula Kiwanuka (Nairobi: East African Publishing House, 1971), 160.

83. Wrigley, *Kingship and State*, 33 (quotes); Speke, *Journal*, 252, mentions "Kamanya." See Robert W. Felkin and Charles T. Wilson, *Uganda and the Egyptian Sudan*, vol. 1 (London: Sampson, Low, Marston, Searle & Rivington, 1882), 197; Felkin, "Notes on the Waganda Tribe," 740; Franz Stuhlmann, *Die Tägebücher von Dr. Emin Pasha*, vol. 1 (Hamburg: G. Westermann, 1916 [1876, 1877], 381; Stuhlmann, *Mit Emin Pasha*, 192–93; Kagwa, *Bakabaka Bebuganda*, the manuscript was complete by 1897 (Wrigley, *Kingship and State*, 32); Johnston, *Uganda Protectorate*, vol. 2, 681.

84. Kamaanya's sovereign knot reigned (1812–39) in the aftermath of a widespread drought; see David Anderson, "The Beginning of Time? Evidence for Catastrophic Drought in Baringo in the Early Nineteenth Century," *Journal of Eastern African Studies* 10, no. 1 (2016), 45–66.

85. For nuance, see Kiwanuka, "Introduction," xli–xlvi.

86. Martin Southwold, "The History of a History: Royal Succession in Buganda," in *History and Social Anthropology*, ed. Ioan M. Lewis (London: Tavistock, 1968), 127–51; Kiwanuka, *History of Buganda*, 273–79; Wrigley, *Kingship and State*, 20–42; Médard, *Le royaume*, 15–25.

87. David William Cohen, "A Survey of Interlacustrine Chronology," *Journal of African History* 11, no. 2 (1970), 177–99; Kiwanuka, *History of Buganda*, 281.

88. Kodesh, *Beyond the Royal Gaze*, 167

89. John T. K. Ggomotoka, head of the princes from 1919 to 1941, made analogies to European political charters, mentioning Clovis, in arguing that Kintu came from outside Buganda; see J. T. K. Ggomotoka, "Ebye Buganda: Ekika ky'Abalangira b'omu Buganda," *Munno* 10, no. 115 (1920), 121–22, 131–33 (analogies); J. T. K. Ggomotoka, "Ebye Buganda: Sekabaka Kintu nga bwe yajja," *Munno* 10, no. 116 (1920), 150–52.

90. Kagwa, in Roscoe and Kagwa, "Enquiry," 71; Kiwanuka, *History of Buganda*, 31–32 (clans from Ssese and Buddu as additional groups).

91. Sara Berry, "Marginal Gains, Market Values, and History," *African Studies Review* 50, no. 2 (2007), 60–61, 64–65.

92. Kodesh, *Beyond the Royal Gaze*, 20–26; Earle, *Colonial Buganda*, 45–67; Derek Peterson, *Ethnic Patriotism and the East African Revival: A History of Dissent, c. 1935–1972* (New York: Cambridge University Press, 2012), 1–36, 78–104; David William Cohen, *The Historical Tradition of Busoga: Mukama and Kintu* (Oxford: Clarendon Press, 1972), 28–69, esp. 30–32; Jan Bender Shetler, *Telling Our Own Story* (Leiden: Brill, 2003), introduction.

93. Karin Barber, *The Anthropology of Texts, Persons and Publics: Oral and Written Culture in Africa and Beyond* (Cambridge: Cambridge University Press, 2007), 1 (quote), 84–97 (exegetical communities).

94. Kagwa, *Bakabaka Bebuganda*; Kagwa, *Ekitabo Kye Mpisa*; John Roscoe, *The Baganda: An Account of Their Native Customs and Beliefs* (London: Macmillan, 1911); Alfonsi Aliwali, "Bwakamba Mukudde: 'Omudzukulu eyatta. Mukudde,'" *Munno* 4, no. 37 (1914), 7–9; Kiwanuka, *History of Buganda*, 18.

95. Jemusi Kibuka Miti Kabazzi, "A Short History of Buganda, Bunyoro, Busoga, Tooro, and Ankole," trans. G. K. Rock, CMS/ACC 728 Z1, Church Missionary Society Archives, Cadbury Research Library, University of Birmingham, Typescript, ca. 1947. Miti began writing in the late 1920s; Ham Mukasa, *Simudda Nyuma* (London: Society for Promoting Christian Knowledge, 1938); Bartolomeyo Musoke Zimbe, *Buganda ne Kabaka* (Mengo: Gambuze Press, 1939).

96. Ggomotoka, widely in *Munno*; and Ggomotoka, "History of Buvuma Islands"; John Ggomotoka, *Magezi Ntakke* (Bukalasa: White Fathers Press, 1934 [1931]). Ggomotoka helped excavate sites like Bigo, in Bwera. Kiwanuka, *History of Buganda*, 19; David William Cohen, *Towards a Reconstructed Past: Historical Texts from Busoga, Uganda* (Oxford: Oxford University Press, 1986).

97. Earle, *Colonial Buganda*, 223–40; Peterson, *Ethnic Patriotism*, 295–313.

98. Jan Bender Shetler, "Interpreting Rupture in Oral Memory: The Regional Context for Changes in Western Serengeti Age Organization (1850–1895)," *Journal of African History* 44, no. 3 (2003), 385–412.

99. Stephens, *History of African Motherhood*, 3–13.

100. Earle, *Colonial Buganda*, 143–57.

101. John F. Faupel, *African Holocaust* (Kampala: St. Paul Publications, Africa, 1984), 207–22; John Mary Waliggo, *The Catholic Church in the Buddu Province of Buganda, 1879–1925* (Kampala: Angel Agencies, 2010), 35–37.

102. Kiwanuka, *History of Buganda*, 18; Hanson, *Landed Obligation*, 93–163; Samwiri Lwanga Lunyiigo, *The Struggle for Land in Buganda, 1888–2005* (Kampala: Wavah Books, 2007), 10–19; Waliggo, *Catholic Church*, 16–99.

103. Holger Bernt Hansen, "The Colonial Control of Spirit Cults in Uganda," in *Revealing Prophets*, ed. David M. Anderson and Douglas H. Johnson (Oxford: James Currey, 1995), 143–63; Feierman, "Colonizers, Scholars," 200–202.

104. Neville Turton, John Bowes Griffin, and Arthur W. Lewey, *Laws of the Uganda Protectorate*, vol. 6 (London: n.p., 1936), 1372–84. A fourth regent, Noho Mbogo, signed the Agreement.

105. Buganda Lukiiko Archives (1894–1918), John Rowe Collector, Northwestern University Library, Film A2915; Michael Tuck and John Rowe, "Phoenix from the Ashes:

Rediscovery of the Lost Lukiiko Archives," *History in Africa* 32 (2005), 403–14, esp. 406–8; Neil Kodesh, "Beyond the Royal Gaze: Clanship and Collective Well-Being in Buganda," PhD diss., Northwestern University, 2004, 344–65.

106. Article 18, in Turton, Griffin, and Lewey, *Laws*, after p. 1384.

107. Lunyiigo, *Struggle for Land*, 40.

108. Hanson, *Landed Obligation*, 136–46.

109. Roscoe arrived in Uganda in 1891 and began a close relationship with Kagwa.

110. Apolo Kagwa, *Ekitabo Kye Kika Kya Nsenene* (Mengo: Privately published, 1905). The history resisted efforts to ostracize (òkùboòla) him from that clan.

111. Eriya M. Buliggwanga, *Ekitabo Ekitegeza Ekika Kye Mamba* (Kampala: Uganda Printing and Publishing, 1916); Kakoma et al., *Ekitabo Eky'Abakyanjove*.

112. John Rowe, "Myth, Memoir, and Moral Admonition: Luganda Historical Writing 1893–1969," *Uganda Journal* 33, no. 2 (1969), 218–19.

113. Mari Webel, *The Politics of Disease Control: Sleeping Sickness in Eastern Africa, 1890–1920* (Athens: Ohio University Press, 2019); Shane Doyle, *Before HIV: Sexuality, Fertility and Mortality in East Africa, 1900–1980* (Oxford: Oxford University Press, 2013), 80; A. J. Duggan Papers (concerning Cuthbert Christy) Report and 3 maps on sleeping sickness in Uganda, October 31, 1902, WT1/RST/G26/2, Wellcome Foundation Archives, London.

114. Webel, *Politics of Disease Control*, chap. 3. Forced removals in 1906 and 1907 did not affect the islands; see John Ford, *The Role of the Trypanosomiases in African Ecology: A Study of the Tsetse Fly Problem* (Oxford: Clarendon Press, 1971), 241.

115. Norma Octavia Lorimer, *By the Waters of Africa: British East Africa, Uganda and the Great Lakes* (London: Frederick A. Stokes, 1917), 83.

116. Ernest C. Lanning, "The Sesse [*sic*] Islands," 1957, Ernest C. Lanning Papers, MSS Afr.S.1329 (9), 2–3, Weston Library, Bodleian Libraries, University of Oxford.

117. Kifamunyanja, "Ssese," 159–61; 173–75; Kifamunyanja, "Ssese: Gambuze nti aga-fudde e Mengo," *Munno* (December 1921), 189–90; Kifamunyanja, "Ssese okufa kwe: Gambuze nti afagudde e Mengo, Ssese afa Mongota," *Munno* (January 1922), 7–9.

118. Lanning, "Sesse [*sic*] Islands," 4.

119. John Lonsdale, "Unhelpful Pasts and a Provisional Present," in *Citizenship, Belonging, and Political Community in Africa: Dialogues between Past and Present*, ed. Emma Hunter (Athens: Ohio University Press, 2016), 28–32.

Chapter 1. Python Imaginaries

1. Nakanyike B. Musisi, "Transformations of Baganda Women: From the Earliest Times to the Demise of the Kingdom in 1966," PhD diss., University of Toronto, 1991, 56.

2. David William Cohen, *Towards a Reconstructed Past: Historical Texts from Busoga, Uganda* (London: British Academy, 1986), 15; Ian Cunnison, *History on the Luapula* (London: Oxford University Press, 1951), 5–10.

3. David Newbury, "The Clans of Rwanda: An Historical Hypothesis," *Africa* 50, no. 4 (1980), 389–403; Jan Vansina, *How Societies Are Born* (Charlottesville: University of Virginia Press, 2004), 50, 88–97, 225–26.

4. Neil Kodesh, *Beyond the Royal Gaze: Clanship and Public Healing in Buganda* (Charlottesville: University Press of Virginia, 2010), 96; David William Cohen,

Womunafu's Bunafu: A Study of Authority in a Nineteenth-Century African Community (Princeton, NJ: Princeton University Press, 1977), 154–64.

5. Henry Morton Stanley, *Through the Dark Continent*, vol. 1 (London: Sampson Low, Marston, Searle & Rivington, 1878), 215.

6. Michael B. Nsimbi, *Amannya Amaganda N'Ennono Zaago* (Kampala: Longman's Uganda, 1980), 110; Renee L. Tantala, "Early History of Kitara in Western Uganda: Process Models of Religious and Political Chance, Part 2," PhD diss., University of Wisconsin–Madison, 1989, 601–2.

7. Kiseke kya munyumya, "'Amadzi gonna agali waggulu, mutendereze omukama' Ekika III, Ebitalina bulamu: Enkuba," *Munno* 7, no. 84 (1917), 192–93, here 193.

8. Kasirye Zzibukulimbwa, "The Beginning of Ennyanja Nnalubaale," trans. Robert Bakaaki and Jennifer Lee Johnson (Kampala: PDF, 2012), 7–8. Thanks to Jennifer Johnson for sharing this document.

9. Michael G. Kenny, "The Powers of Lake Victoria," *Anthropos* 72, nos. 5/6 (1977), 722–23; J. Adong and J. Lakareber, *Lwo-English Dictionary* (Kampala: Fountain, 2009), 7.

10. "Nsambya" names a tree, *Markhamia platycalyx*, on which the appearance of new leaves was sensitive to groundwater levels affected by short rains. An older term for long rains, *ituumbi*, came to refer in Luganda to the shorter, less certain rains (*ddumbi*). See David L. Schoenbrun, "A Lexicon for Affect, Violence, Vulnerability, and Dispute in Eastern Bantu," in progress, Root Numbers (RNs) 225, 227; J. Curt Stager, Brian Cumming, and L. David Meeker, "A 10,000-Year High-Resolution Diatom Record from Pilkington Bay, Lake Victoria, East Africa," *Quaternary Research* 59 (2003), items "g" and "h" in fig. 7, 179, 180.

11. David Lee Schoenbrun, *A Green Place, a Good Place: Agrarian Change, Gender, and Social Identity between the Great Lakes to 1500* (Portsmouth: Heinemann, 1998), 80; Holly Hanson, *Landed Obligation: The Practice of Power in Buganda* (Portsmouth: Heinemann, 2003), 28–36; Kodesh, *Beyond the Royal Gaze*, 39–66; Rhiannon Stephens, *A History of African Motherhood: The Case of Uganda, 700–1900* (New York: Cambridge University Press, 2013), 67–69.

12. Hanson, *Landed Obligation*, 37.

13. Kodesh, *Beyond the Royal Gaze*, 86–96.

14. Kodesh, *Beyond the Royal Gaze*, 181 (quote); Steven Feierman, "Healing as Social Criticism in the Time of Colonial Conquest," *African Studies* 54, no. 1 (1995), 73–88.

15. Andrew Reid and Ceri Ashley, "Islands of Agriculture on Victoria Nyanza," in *Archaeology of African Plant Use*, ed. Chris J. Stevens, Sam Nixon, Mary Anne Murray, and Dorian Q. Fuller (Walnut Creek, CA: Left Coast Press, 2014), 184–86.

16. M. McFarlane, "Some Observations on the Prehistory of the Buvuma Island Group of Lake Victoria," *East African Fisheries Resource Organisation Annual Report, 1967* (Nairobi: East African Community Printers, 1968), 51–52; Merrick Posnansky, Andrew Reid, and Ceri Ashley, "Archaeology on Lolui Island, Uganda, 1964–1965," *Azania* 40 (2005), 73–100; Michael G. Kenny, "Pre-Colonial Trade in Eastern Lake Victoria," *Azania* 14 (1979), 97–107.

17. Reid and Ashley, "Islands of Agriculture," 187.

18. Christopher Wrigley, *Kingship and State: The Buganda Dynasty* (Cambridge: Cambridge University Press, 1996), 233–34.

19. Richard J. Reid, *Political Power in Pre-Colonial Buganda* (Oxford: James Currey, 2002), 64–69, 227–48; Jennifer Lee Johnson, "Fishwork in Uganda: A Multispecies Ethnohistory about Fish, People, and Ideas about Fish and People," PhD diss., University of Michigan, Ann Arbor, 2014; Yuji Ankei, "Folk Knowledge of Fish among the Songola and the Bwari: Comparative Ethnoichthyology of the Lualaba River and Lake Tanganyika Fishermen," *African Study Monograph*, Supplement 9 (1989), 1–88; Patrick Mougiama-Daouda, "Phonological Irregularities, Reconstruction and Cultural Vocabulary: The Names of Fish in the Bantu Languages of the Northwest (Gabon)," *Diachronica* 22, no. 1 (2005), 59–107.

20. Schoenbrun, *Green Place*, 37–52; Stephens, *History of African Motherhood*, 20–26.

21. Apolo Kagwa, *Ekitabo Kye Mpisa Za Baganda* (Kampala: Uganda Printing and Publishing, 1918), 278–83; Harry Johnston, *The Uganda Protectorate*, vol. 2 (London: Hutchinson, 1902), 668.

22. P. J. P. Whitehead, "The Anadromous Fishes of Lake Victoria," *Revue de zoologie et de botanique africaines* 59 (1959), 329–63; Peter H. Greenwood, *The Fishes of Uganda* (Kampala: Uganda Society, 1966), 31; for details, see Fishbase.org; IUCNREDNET.org (accessed October 4, 2015).

23. Zzibukulimbwa, "The Beginning of Ennyanja Nnalubaale," 7, 9, 13, 14, 16, 17; John T. K. Ggomotoka, "History of Buvuma Islands," trans. David Kiyaga-Mulindwa (Kampala: Typescript, 1937–38), Buvuma Island, 45–46.

24. John Roscoe, *The Baganda: An Account of Their Native Customs and Beliefs* (London: Macmillan, 1911), 396; P. Otto Mors, "Notes on Hunting and Fishing in Buhaya," *Anthropological Quarterly* 26, no. 2 (1953), 93.

25. Peninah A. Aloo, "Biological Diversity of the Yala Swamp Lakes, with Special Emphasis on Fish Species Composition, in Relation to Changes in the Lake Victoria Basin (Kenya): Threats and Conservation Measures," *Biodiversity and Conservation* 12 (2003), 910; Kagwa, *Ekitabo Kye Mpisa*, 278–83; Roscoe, *Baganda*, 391–99.

26. Kagwa, *Ekitabo Kye Mpisa*, 281; Roscoe, *Baganda*, 396 (gives *buligo* [*sic*]).

27. Jennifer L. Johnson, "Eating and Existence on an Island in Southern Uganda," *Comparative Studies of South Asia, the Middle East, and Africa* 37, no. 1 (2017), 2–23; Paul Opondo, "Fisheries as Heritage: Indigenous Methods of Fishing and Conservation among the Luo fishers of Lake Victoria, Kenya," in *Conservation of Natural and Cultural Heritage in Kenya*, ed. Anne-Marie Deisser and Njuguna Mugwima (London: University College of London Press, 2016), 204 (fishing moratoria to protect spawning, *contra* Roscoe, *Baganda*, 396).

28. Robin L. Welcomme, "A Brief on the Flood Plain Fishery of Africa," *African Journal of Tropical Hydrobiology and Fisheries* 1 (1972), 67–76.

29. Wilson W. Mwanja, "The Role of Satellite Water Bodies in the Evolution and Conservation of Lake Victoria Region Fishes," *African Journal of Ecology* 42, Suppl. 1 (2004), 14–20.

30. Frans Witte, "Initial Results of the Ecological Survey of the Haplochromine Cichlid Fishes from the Mwanza Gulf of Lake Victoria (Tanzania)," *Netherlands Journal of Zoology* 31 (1981), 175–202.

31. Peter H. Greenwood, "Towards a Phyletic Classification of the 'Genus' *Haplochromis* (Pisces, Cichlidae) and Related Taxa. Part II; The Species from Lakes Victoria,

Nabugabo, Edward, George and Kivu," *Bulletin of the British Museum of Natural History (Zoology)* 39, no. 1 (1980), 1–101.

32. Johnston, *Uganda Protectorate*, vol. 2, 787–89, and Kagwa, *Ekitabo Kye Mpisa*, 279–80.

33. Roscoe, *Baganda*, 396. "*Abawomi be enkeje*," or "the sustainers of the sprats," took fewer sprats, with wicker traps, during lake fly hatches; Kagwa, *Ekitabo Kye Mpisa*, 283. Lake flies hatch just before a new moon; diatoms, a favorite food of other fishes, hatch during a full moon; Philip S. Corbet, "Lunar Periodicity of Aquatic Insects in Lake Victoria," *Nature* 182 (1958), 330–31.

34. Mors, "Notes on Hunting," 93.

35. David William Cohen, "Food Production and Food Exchange in the Precolonial Lakes Plateau Region," in *Imperialism, Colonialism, and Hunger: East and Central Africa*, ed. Robert I. Rotberg (Lexington: Lexington Books, 1983), 10–16.

36. John Hanning Speke, *Journal of the Discovery of the Source of the Nile* (Edinburgh: William Blackwood and Sons, 1863), 302; Ggomotoka, "History of Buvuma," Buvuma Island, 47; Charles Chaillé-Long, *Central Africa: Naked Truths of Naked People* (New York: Harper and Brothers, 1877), 165, in the west of Lake Kyoga, came upon a floating papyrus island with what was likely a Bakenye settlement, "before which was hung upon a frame of wood thousands of rotten fish."

37. Scheherazade Amin, "The Archaeology of the Sesse [*sic*] Islands and Their Contribution to the Understanding of Great Lakes Ceramics," PhD diss., University College of London, 2015, 424–33; Reid and Ashley, "Islands of Agriculture," 183; Peter Robertshaw, "Munsa Earthworks: A Preliminary Report on Recent Excavations," *Azania: Archaeological Research in Africa* 32, no. 1 (1997), 8, 13, 15, 16; Lucy Mair, *An African People in the Twentieth Century* (London: Routledge, 1934), 107, 130; Roscoe, *Baganda*, 439 (item's low cost); Edgar Barton Worthington, "The Life of Lakes Albert and Kioga," *Geographical Journal* 74, no. 2 (August 1929), 121.

38. Aloo, "Biological Diversity," 908–9.

39. Ankei, "Folk Knowledge of Fish," 77–78.

40. Ankei, "Folk Knowledge of Fish," 79.

41. Implied in Ankei, "Folk Knowledge of Fish," 61.

42. Mougiama-Daouda, "Phonological Irregularities," 59–107, for similar conclusions.

43. Keith E. Banister and Roland G. Bailey, "Fishes Collected by the Zaïre River Expedition, 1974–75," *Zoological Journal of the Linnean Society* 66 (1979), 206; M. Poll, "Zoogéographie ichthyologique du cours supérieure du Lualaba," *Publications de l'Université d'Elisabethville* 6 (1963), 1–191.

44. By specialized fishers called "Bakenyi" or "Bakenye"; T. K. Musana, "The Origin of the Bakenye," *Gambuze*, August 11, 1933; E. G. Katore, "The Origins of the Abakenyi Are Not Known," *Gambuze*, November 10, 1933, 33.

45. Martin J. Hall, *Through My Spectacles in Uganda; Or, The Story of a Fruitful Field* (London: Church Missionary Society, 1898), 64; Chaillé-Long, *Central Africa*, 137–38; Gerald Portal, *The British Mission to Uganda in 1893* (London: E. Arnold, 1894), 136, 274 (photograph).

46. Stephens, *History of African Motherhood*, 24–25.

47. Reid and Ashley, "Islands of Agriculture," 180.

48. Anonymous, "Steamer Service," *Uganda Notes* 4, no. 3 (1903), 13; Ham Mukasa, *Uganda's Katikiro in England* (London: Hutchinson, 1904), 1–7.

49. Including named canoes; Viktoro Katula, "Emmamba ye Namukuma: Kabaka Mawanda awangula e Kyagwe awa Nkutu e Namukuma," *Munno* 3, no. 31 (1913), 110–12; Nsimbi, *Amannya*, 151; David William Cohen, *The Historical Tradition of Busoga: Mukama and Kintu* (Oxford: Clarendon Press, 1972), 45–46; Yekoniya K. Lubogo, "Luba of the Nyange clan," in Cohen, *Towards a Reconstructed Past*, 118; Daudi Gahole Kaima, "History of the abaiseKaima," in Cohen, *Towards a Reconstructed Past*, 208.

50. Kodesh, *Beyond the Royal Gaze*, 67–97.

51. Apolo Kaggwa, *The Kings of Buganda*, ed. and trans. M. S. M. Semakula Kiwanuka (Nairobi: East African Publishing House, 1971), 5–6; Apolo Kagwa, *Ekitabo Kye Bika Bya Baganda* [*A Book of Clans of Buganda*], trans James D. Wamala (Makerere, Typescript, 1972 [1912]), 40–41; Omwami Semu Kasyoka L. Kakoma, Rev. Adoniya Musoke Ntate, Kayonga, P. T. I. and Mwami, Musa Serukwaya, Kasolo, *Ekitabo Eky'Abakyanjove Ab'e Mmamba Mu Siiga Lya Nankere e Bukerekere* (Kampala: East African Institute of Social Research, 1959), 4–5; Roscoe, *Baganda*, 475–77; Nsimbi, *Amannya*, 151–55.

52. Kodesh, *Beyond the Royal Gaze*, 30.

53. Benjamin Ray, *Myth, Ritual, and Kingship in Buganda* (Oxford: Oxford University Press, 1991), 84–86; Kodesh, *Beyond the Royal Gaze*, 135–38.

54. John F. Cunningham, *Uganda and Its Peoples* (London: Hutchinson, 1905), 173 (bones), 178 (laughter).

55. Brett L. Shadle, "Patronage, Millennialism and the Serpent God Mumbo in South-West Kenya, 1912–34," *Africa* 72, no. 1 (2002), 46–47; J. Cameron Monroe, *Precolonial State in West Africa: Building Power in Dahomey* (New York: Cambridge University Press, 2014), 57; Neil Norman and Kenneth Kelly, "Landscape Politics: The Serpent Ditch and the Rainbow in West Africa," *American Anthropologist* 104, no. 1 (2006), 98–110.

56. Alexander Mackay, by His Sister, *A. M. Mackay, Pioneer Missionary of the Church Missionary Society in Uganda* (New York: Armstrong, 1890), 172–77; John Roscoe, "Python Worship in Uganda," *Man* 9 (1909), 88–90; Speke, *Journal*, 394–96; Apolo Kagwa, *Customs of the Baganda*, ed. May Edel, trans. Ernest Kalibala (New York: Columbia University Press, 1934), 112–28; Kakoma et al., *Ekitabo Eky'Abakyanjove*, 4; Cohen, *Historical Tradition*, 44–45; Tantala, "Early History of Kitara," 601–3; Kodesh, *Beyond the Royal Gaze*, 73–75.

57. Captain Charles R. S. Pitman, "A Guide to the Snakes of Uganda, Part I," *Uganda Journal* 3, no. 1 (1935), 54–57, 61, 64–66; Captain Charles R. S. Pitman, "A Guide to the Snakes of Uganda, Part III," *Uganda Journal* 3, no. 3 (1936), 212 (quote); G. D. Hale Carpenter, *A Naturalist on Lake Victoria with an Account of Sleeping Sickness and the Tse-tse Fly* (London: T. Fisher Unwin, 1920), 188–89.

58. Pitman, "Snakes III," 217. Lunar cycles can influence python behavior, see Rachel Grant, Tim Halliday, and Elizabeth Chadwick, "Amphibians' Response to the Lunar Synodic Cycle," *Behavioral Ecology* 24, no. 1 (2013), 53–62.

59. Roscoe, "Python Worship," 88–90; Roscoe, *Baganda*, 320–22; John Roscoe, "Worship of the Dead as Practiced by Some African Tribes," *Harvard African Studies* 1 (1917), 42.

60. Roscoe, "Python Worship," 90; Cunningham, *Uganda and Its Peoples*, 218.

61. Roscoe, "Python Worship," 89; Apolo Kagwa, *Ekitabo Kye Bika Bya Baganda* (Kampala: Uganda Bookshop, 1949 [ca. 1907]), 112.

62. Eriya M. Buliggwanga, *Ekitabo Ekitegeza Ekika Kye Mamba* (Kampala: Uganda Printing & Publishing, 1916), 3; Mackay, *Mackay, Pioneer*, 168, 173; Roscoe, "Python Worship," 89; Speke, *Journal*, 395.

63. Ceri Z. Ashley and Andrew Reid, "A Reconsideration of the Figures from Luzira," *Azania* 43 (2008), 95–123; Andrew Reid and Ceri Z. Ashley, "A Context for the Luzira Head," *Antiquity* 82 (2008), 99–112; Tantala, "Early History," 630 (dead pythons buried).

64. Reid and Ashley, "Context for the Luzira Head," 104–8; Amin, "Archaeology of the Sesse Islands," 404 (cautions).

65. Tantala, "Early History," 613–15, first noticed this metonymy.

66. Nsimbi, *Amannya*, 153–54.

67. Stephens, *History of African Motherhood*, 23–24.

68. David Lee Schoenbrun, *The Historical Reconstruction of Great Lakes Bantu Cultural Vocabulary: Etymologies and Distributions* (Köln: Rüdiger Köppe, 1997), 78, RN106; Kodesh, *Beyond the Royal Gaze*, 10–14, 96–97. Great Lakes Bantu languages share the meaning "clan" or "family" with other Bantu languages; an innovation from a more widely distributed meaning of "group" or "bundle" or "heap." See Yvonne Bastin and Thilo Schadeberg (eds.), *Bantu Lexical Reconstructions* (Tervuren: Royal Museum of Central Africa, 2002), RN 1324; http://linguistics.africamuseum.be/BLR3.html (accessed August 28, 2014). Other terms in Great Lakes Bantu may be glossed as "clan."

69. John Roscoe, "Notes on the Manners and Customs of the Baganda," *Man: Journal of the Royal Anthropological Institute* 31 (1901), 118–19; Roscoe, *Baganda*, 56–57, 133; Kagwa, *Ekitabo Kye Bika*, 1; Nsimbi, *Amannya*, 170–82; Mair, *African People*, 42; Cohen, *Historical Tradition*, 6–7.

70. The verb yielded the noun, *mbàndwa*. *Kukwata mutwe*, "to seize the head," described the experience. *Èkitâmbo* was possession caused by a curse; Henri Le Veux, *Premier essai de vocabulaire luganda-français d'après l'ordre étymologique* (Algiers: Imprimerie des Missionaires d'Afrique [Pères Blancs], 1917), 630, 386.

71. Schoenbrun, "Lexicon," RN 212.

72. Le Veux, *Premier essai de vocabulaire*, 830; Schoenbrun, *Historical Reconstruction*, 225.

73. Julien Gorju, *Entre le Victoria, l'Albert et l'Edouard: Ethnographie de la Partie Anglaise du Vicariat de l'Uganda* (Rennes: Imprimeries Oberthür, 1920), 210; David L. Schoenbrun, "Conjuring the Modern in Africa: Durability and Rupture in Histories of Public Healing between the Great Lakes of East Africa," *American Historical Review* 111, no. 5 (2006), 1430–33.

74. Cohen, *Historical Tradition*, 21 and n 34; Bethwell Alan Ogot, *History of the Southern Luo*, vol. 1 (Nairobi: East African Publishing House, 1967), 79; Luo-Padhola people had the same discourses and practices named *kunu*.

75. Kagwa, *Ekitabo Kye Mpisa*, 285; Cohen, *Historical Tradition*, 45–46; Kenny, "Powers of Lake Victoria," 725–27; Kodesh, *Beyond the Royal Gaze*, 45.

76. Ashley, "Towards a Socialised Archaeology," 149–53; Posnansky, Reid, and Ashley, "Archaeology on Lolui Island," 73–100; Reid and Ashley, "Islands of Agriculture," 182.

77. Ashley, ""Towards a Socialised Archaeology," 154–56; Amin, "Archaeology of the Sesse Islands," 406–46.

78. New moons were calendar pivots beyond the littoral as well; see chapter 2.

79. J. Curt Stager, David Ryves, Brian F. Cumming, L. David Meeker, and Juerg Beer, "Solar Variability and the Levels of Lake Victoria, East Africa, during the Last Millennium," *Journal of Paleolimnology* 33 (2005), 247.

80. Ceri Ashley, "Ceramic Variability and Change: A Perspective from Great Lakes Africa," PhD diss., University of London, 2005, 177.

81. Reid and Ashley, "Islands of Agriculture," 182; Amin, "Archaeology of the Sesse Islands," 404–46.

82. Buliggwanga, *Ekitabo Ekitegeza*, 10; Yosia Njovutegwamukitimba, "Bemba," *Ebifa mu Buganda* (January 1920), 11–12; Wrigley, *Kingship and State*, 167–68 (littoral settings).

83. Kagwa, *Ekitabo Kye Bika*, 32–39 (no mention of Bemba).

84. Derisively: "Omusota gufuga gutya abantu?" or "How could a snake rule people?" See J. T. K. Ggomotoka, "Ebye Buganda: Sekabaka Kintu nga bwe yajja," *Munno* 10, no. 116 (1920), 150.

85. Kakoma et al., *Ekitabo Eky'Abakyanjove*, 3–4.

86. Ray, *Myth, Ritual, and Kingship*, 99–103.

87. Tobi Kizito, "Kintu ne Bemba," *Munno* 5, no. 54 (1915), 93–95; Lawi Wakibi Sekiti, "Abaganda abe Mbale," *Munno* 6, no. 61 (1916), 8–10; Ludoviko Kibatto, "Ennanga eya Kabaka mu Buganda," *Munno* 7, no. 80 (1917), 116–17; Daudi Bakika and Jemusi Bwagu, "Ekika ky'abalangira mu Buganda," *Munno* (April 1921), 62–63, esp. 63, (May 1921), 73; Nsimbi, *Amannya*, 151.

88. Buliggwanga, *Ekitabo Ekitegeza*, 12.

89. Kakoma et al., *Ekitabo Eky'Abakyanjove*, 9.

90. Buliggwanga, *Ekitabo Ekitegeza*, iii–iv (126 sources).

91. At more than 400 printed pages it would make readers tremble; M(ukunganya?), "Ekitabo Ekitegereza ekika eky'Emmamba," *Munno* 6, no. 62 (1916), 43.

92. Buliggwanga, *Ekitabo Ekitegeza*, 11, 12.

93. Kodesh, *Beyond the Royal Gaze*, 27–66; Schoenbrun, *Green Place*, 203–6.

94. Buliggwanga, *Ekitabo Ekitegeza*, 11.

95. Kakoma et al., *Ekitabo Eky'Abakyanjove*, 4.

96. Buliggwanga, *Ekitabo Ekitegeza*, 12; Bakika and Bwagu, "Ekika," 63, 73; Kakoma et al., *Ekitabo Eky'Abakyanjove*, 3 (Mukama, father of Kintu and Bemba). When Jjunju captured the region, at the turn of the nineteenth century, he gave the title Ppookino to the leader of Buddu; Kagwa, *Ekitabo Kye Mpisa*, 311.

97. Buliggwanga, *Ekitabo Ekitegeza*, 11.

98. Kodesh, *Beyond the Royal Gaze*, 38, 160–63; Steven Feierman, "Ethnographic Regions—Healing, Power, and History," in *Borders and Healers*, ed. Tracy J. Luedke and Harry G. West (Bloomington: Indiana University Press, 2006), 185–94.

99. Kagwa, *Ekitabo Kye Mpisa*, 5–8; Y. T. Kikulwe, "Ebye Buddo Ebikolerwa ku Basekabaka," *Munno* 5, no. 58 (1915), 156–59; *Munno* 5, no. 59 (1915), 173–76; *Munno* 5, no. 60 (1915), 188–91; Buliggwanga, *Ekitabo Ekitegeza*, 11; Audrey I. Richards, *The Changing Structure of a Ganda Village: Kisozi, 1892–1952* (Nairobi: East African Pub-

lishing House, 1966), 39–45; Ray, *Myth, Ritual, and Kingship*, 84–86; Wrigley, *Kingship and State*, 28–29, 211–14.

100. *Kùwuùla*, "lose wife through her going away; raid; beat hard, beat with a flail"; Ronald Snoxall, *Luganda-English Dictionary* (Oxford: Clarendon Press, 1967), 344. The stem *-twe* means "head" and the prefix *ka-* makes the noun diminutive.

101. Le Veux, *Premier essai de vocabulaire*, 1047*–1048*; Snoxall, *Luganda-English Dictionary*, 254. Echoed in possible glosses for Buwule.

102. Kagwa, *Ekitabo Kye Bika*, 38–39.

103. *Sema-* can make the noun phrase it prefixes enormous in size. The plural of "python" is *amatimba*, so the name Sematimba may be translated literally as "father of pythons" and figuratively as "enormous python"; Alan Hamilton, with Naomi Hamilton, Phoebe Mukasa, and David Ssewanyana, *Luganda Dictionary and Grammar* (Kampala: Gustro, 2016), 375.

104. Étienne Wenger, *Communities of Practice: Learning, Meaning, and Identity* (Cambridge: Cambridge University Press, 1998), 108–10, 128–31, 179–87.

105. Antoine Meillet, "Comment les mots changent de sens," *Année Sociologique* 9 (1906), 1–38; Andreas Blank, "Words and Concepts in Time: Towards Diachronic Cognitive Onomasiology," in *Words in Time: Diachronic Semantics from Different Points of View*, ed. Regine Eckardt, Klaus von Heusinger, and Christoph Schwarze (Berlin: de Gruyter, 2003), 37–65.

106. Scott Ortman, "Conceptual Metaphor in the Archaeological Record: Methods and an Example from the American Southwest," *American Antiquity* 65, no. 4 (2000), 613–45; Scott Ortman, "Bowls to Gardens: A History of Tewa Community Metaphors," in *Religious Transformation in the Late Pre-Hispanic Pueblo World*, ed. Donna M. Glowacki and Scott Van Keuren (Tucson: University of Arizona Press, 2013), 84–108; David Schoenbrun, "Pythons Worked: Constellating Communities of Practice with Conceptual Metaphor in Northern Lake Victoria, ca. A. D. 800 to 1200," in *Knowledge in Motion: Constellations of Learning across Time and Place*, ed. Andrew P. Roddick and Ann B. Stahl (Tucson: University of Arizona Press, 2016), 231–34; Axel Fleisch and Rhiannon Stephens, eds., *Doing Conceptual History in Africa* (New York: Berghahn Books, 2016).

107. Webb Keane, "Semiotics and the Social Analysis of Material Things," *Language and Communication* 23 (2003): 409, 419.

108. Zoltán Kövecses, *Metaphor in Culture: Universality and Variation* (Cambridge: Cambridge University Press, 2005); Scott Ortman, *Winds from the North: Tewa Origins and Historical Anthropology* (Salt Lake City: University of Utah Press, 2012), 203–25; David Schoenbrun, "Mixing, Moving, Making, Meaning: Possible Futures for the Distant Past," *African Archaeological Review* 29, no. 2 (2012), 297–300.

109. Kövecses, *Metaphor in Culture*, 68.

110. Ortman, "Bowls to Gardens," 89–96; Schoenbrun, "Pythons Worked," 231–39.

111. Rob Wiseman, "Getting beyond Rites of Passage in Archaeology: Conceptual Metaphors of Journeys and Growth," *Current Anthropology* 60, no. 4 (2019), 450–52.

112. Joseph Grady, Todd Oakley, and Seana Coulson, "Metaphor and Blending," in *Metaphor in Cognitive Linguistics*, ed. Raymond W. Gibbs Jr. and Gerard J. Steen (Amsterdam: John Benjamins, 1999), 101–24; Ortman, "Conceptual Metaphor," 618.

113. Edwin Hutchins, "Material Anchors for Conceptual Blends," *Journal of Pragmatics* 37 (2005), 1563 (quotes).

114. Webb Keane, "Marked, Absent, Habitual: Approaches to Neolithic Religion at Çatalhöyük," in *Religion in the Emergence of Civilization: Çatalhöyük as a Case Study*, ed. Ian Hodder (Cambridge: Cambridge University Press, 2010), 187–219.

115. Ideas developed from established ones "stick" more easily, see Karin Barber, "Improvisation and the Art of Making Things Stick," in *Creativity and Cultural Improvisation*, ed. Elizabeth Hallam and Tim Ingold (Oxford: Berg, 2007), 25–41.

116. Roscoe, *Baganda*, 327–28.

117. Aleksi Mukasa Bukya, "Engoma za Basekabaka be Buganda: Kabaka Mutesa ze yalina mu mirembe gye," *Munno* 6, no. 71 (1916), 180 (Ssese links); omitted in Anonymous, "Engoma za Kabaka Enkulu," *Munno* 3, no. 33 (1913), 142.

118. For use in a sentence, with a Ganda gloss, see Kagwa, *Ekitabo Kye Bika*, 106.

119. Michael Dietler (ed.), *Feasts: Archaeological and Ethnographic Perspectives on Food, Politics, and Power* (Tuscaloosa: University of Alabama Press, 2001).

120. Ggomotoka, "History of Buvuma," Buvuma Island, 30–31 (fifteen people drink beer from one pot).

121. David Parkin, *Semantic Anthropology* (New York: Academic Press, 1982), xlvi.

122. Spirits appeared as leopards, snakes, trees, stones, springs, and other bodies of water, a far richer conceptual world than explored here; see J. K. M. Kakondêre, "Okwesiga ebitalimu okw'Abaganda," *Munno* 16, no. 12 (1926), 204.

123. Roscoe, "Python Worship," 89.

124. Reid and Ashley, "Luzira," 104–8 (dating); Schoenbrun, "Pythons," 235 (blend).

125. Kagwa, *Customs*, 114; Roscoe, "Python Worship," 89.

126. Kagwa, *Customs*, 112–13; Tantala, "Early History," xix.

127. Kodesh, *Beyond the Royal Gaze*, 46–48; Buliggwanga, *Ekitabo Ekitegeza*, 10–12.

128. Wenger, *Communities of Practice*, 105.

129. Hanson, *Landed Obligation*, 37; Kodesh, *Beyond the Royal Gaze*, 86–96; Schoenbrun, *Green Place*, 200–206.

130. Kodesh, *Beyond the Royal Gaze*, 39–48.

Chapter 2. Possessing an Inland Sea

1. John Lonsdale, "Moral and Political Argument in Kenya," in *Ethnicity and Democracy in Africa*, ed. Bruce Berman, Dickson Eyoh, and Will Kymlicka (Oxford: James Currey, 2004), 78.

2. Apolo Kagwa, *Ekitabo Kye Mpisa Za Baganda* (Kampala: Uganda Printing and Publishing Company, 1918), 216–17; Apollo Kagwa, *Bakabaka Bebuganda* (London: Headley Brothers, 1901), 7; Teofiro Mulumba Kuruji, in John Roscoe and Apolo Kagwa, "Enquiry into Native Land Tenure in the Uganda Protectorate," 1906, 50, 52; MSS Afr.S.17, Weston Library, University of Oxford; Michael B. Nsimbi, *Amannya Amaganda N'Ennono Zaago* (Kampala: Longman's Uganda, 1980), 121.

3. Okot p'Bitek, *African Religions in Western Scholarship* (Kampala: East African Literature Bureau, 1970), 40–44; Henri Médard, *Le royaume du Buganda au XIXe siècle* (Paris: Karthala, 2007), 331–38; Paul Landau, *Popular Politics in the History of South Africa, 1400–1948* (New York: Cambridge University Press, 2010), 74–107.

4. Steven Feierman, "Colonizers, Scholars and the Creation of Invisible Histories," In *Beyond the Cultural Turn*, ed. Victoria Bonnell and Lynn Hunt (Berkeley: University of California Press, 1999), 200–202; David L. Schoenbrun, "Conjuring the Modern in Africa: Durability and Rupture in Histories of Public Healing between the Great Lakes of East Africa," *American Historical Review* 111, no. 5 (December 2006), 1435–39.

5. Holger Bernt Hansen, "The Colonial Control of Spirit Cults in Uganda," in *Revealing Prophets*, ed. David M. Anderson and Douglas H. Johnson (Oxford: James Currey, 1995), 157–58; Derek R. Peterson, "The Politics of Transcendance in Colonial Uganda," *Past and Present* 230 (February 2016), 201–3.

6. Henri Le Veux, *Manuel de langue luganda*, 2nd ed. (Algiers: Maison-Carrée, 1914), 271.

7. Neil Kodesh, *Beyond the Royal Gaze: Clanship and Public Healing in Buganda* (Charlottesville: University of Virginia Press, 2010), 143 (quote); John Roscoe, *The Baganda: An Account of Their Native Customs and Beliefs* (London: Macmillan, 1911), 273–74; Kagwa, *Ekitabo Kye Mpisa*, 209–37; John Roscoe, *Twenty-Five Years in East Africa* (Cambridge: Cambridge University Press, 1921), 135–41.

8. Nsimbi, *Amannya*, 123.

9. A. Mukanga, "The Traditional Belief in Balubaale," *Occasional Research Papers in African Religions and Philosophies* 17, no. 167 (1974), 1.

10. Kuruji, in Roscoe and Kagwa, "Enquiry," 50; Kagwa, *Ekitabo Kye Mpisa*, 209–28; Roscoe, *Twenty-Five Years*, 138; Franz Stuhlmann, *Mit Emin Pascha ins Herz von Afrika* (Berlin: Dietrich Reimer, 1894), 188.

11. Nsimbi, *Amannya*, 121–48, 122; Médard, *Le royaume*, 318–66.

12. Kagwa, *Ekitabo Kye Mpisa*, 218–25.

13. Eriya M. Buliggwanga, *Ekitabo Ekitegeza Ekika Kye Emmamba* (Kampala: 2006 [1916]), 10–12; Roscoe, *Baganda*, 134; Lucy Mair, *An African People in the Twentieth Century* (London: Routledge, 1934), 230, 241. Muganzirwazza recognized Speke's time-piece as a lùbaalè and Speke recognized lùbaalè as "a place of worship, the object of worship itself, or the iron horn or magic pan"; John Hanning Speke, *Journal of the Discovery of the Source of the Nile* (Edinburgh: William Blackwood & Sons, 1863), 307.

14. David William Cohen, *The Historical Tradition of Busoga: Mukama and Kintu* (Oxford: Clarendon Press, 1972), 18, 20, 22.

15. Except perhaps Bukulu; Kagwa, *Bakabaka Bebuganda*, 7; Timoteo Nakalya, byampebwa Luka Sejamba Semumira, "Bukulu ne Mukazi we Wadda Balubale gye bavwa," *Munno* 5, no. 57 (1915), 145–46; Nsimbi, *Amannya*, 121; Martin J. Hall, *Through My Spectacles in Uganda: Or, The Story of a Fruitful Field* (London: Church Missionary Society, 1898), 66; Médard, *Le royaume*, 322; Kodesh, *Beyond the Royal Gaze*, 79.

16. Kagwa, in Roscoe and Kagwa, "Enquiry," 4–5; Mukanga, "Traditional Belief," 1; Kodesh, *Beyond the Royal Gaze*, 131–73; Alfonsi Aliwali, "Ka Tulojje: Kabaka Mulondo," *Munno* 4, no. 38 (1914), 20; Apolo Kagwa, *Customs of the Baganda*, ed. May Edel, trans. Ernest Kalibala (New York: Columbia University Press, 1934), 152; Nsimbi, *Amannya*, 128, 291; Peter R. Schmidt, *Historical Archaeology: A Structural Approach in an African Culture* (Westport, CT: Greenwood Press, 1978), 95, 314.

17. Nsimbi, *Amannya*, 125; David Lee Schoenbrun, *A Green Place, a Good Place: Agrarian Change, Gender, and Social Identity between the Great Lakes to 1500* (Portsmouth, NH: Heinemann, 1998), 202–6; Henry Morton Stanley, *Through the Dark Continent*, vol. 1 (London: Sampson Low, Marston, Searle & Rivington, 1878), 386.

18. Lawi Wakibi Sekiti, "Abaganda abe Mbale," *Munno* 6, no. 61 (1916), 6–7; Nsimbi, *Amannya*, 137, 138–39.

19. Nsimbi, *Amannya*, 135–36, 132.

20. New dates (D-AMS 015188, D-AMS 015187, Beta-413015-Beta-413017), established in 2016, revising Peter T. Robertshaw, "Archaeological Survey, Ceramic Analysis, and State Formation in Western Uganda," *African Archaeological Review* 12 (1994), 105–31; Louise Iles, "The Development of Iron Technology in Precolonial Western Uganda," *Azania: Archaeological Research in Africa* 48, no. 1 (2013), 65–90.

21. This paragraph rests on Scheherazade Amin, "The Archaeology of the Sesse [*sic*] Islands and Their Contribution to the Understanding of Great Lakes Ceramics," PhD diss., University College of London, 2015, 399–446.

22. M. S. M. Semakula Kiwanuka, "The Traditional History of the Buganda Kingdom: With Special Reference to the Historical Writings of Apolo Kaggwa," PhD diss., University of London, 1965, 13; M. S. M. Semakula Kiwanuka, in Apolo Kaggwa, *The Kings of Buganda* (Nairobi: East African Publishing House, 1971), 9; Nsimbi, *Amannya*, 126; Schmidt, *Historical Archaeology*, 70.

23. John Nyakatura, *Abakama ba Bunyoro Kitara: Abatembuzi, Abacwezi, Ababito* (St. Justin, Quebec: W.-H. Gagne, 1947), 40, 45; Ernest C. Lanning, "Masaka Hill, an Ancient Center of Worship," *Uganda Journal* 18 (1954), 24–30.

24. Augustine Kaindoa, "Origins of Rugomora Mahe," in Schmidt, *Historical Archaeology*, 307; Hans Cory, "Bantu Religion of Tanganyika" (Typescript, n.d.), 5–6, Hans Cory Papers, Africana Section, University of Dar es Salaam, Paper no. 41.

25. Nsimbi, *Amannya*, 125–26; Nakalya, "Bukulu," 145–46; David William Cohen, "The Cwezi Cult," *Journal of African History* 9, no. 4 (1968), 651–57.

26. Kodesh, *Beyond the Royal Gaze*, 130.

27. Renee Louise Tantala, "The Early History of Kitara in Western Uganda: Process Models of Religious and Political Change," PhD diss., University of Wisconsin–Madison, 1989, 320, 425–31, 727 (cwezi dating); Iris Berger, *Religion and Resistance: East African Kingdoms in the Precolonial Period* (Tervuren: Musée royale de l'Afrique centrale, 1981), 85; Schoenbrun, *Green Place*, 204; Holly Hanson, *Landed Obligation: The Practice of Power in Buganda* (Portsmouth, NH: Heinemann, 2003), 61, 72; Kodesh, *Beyond the Royal Gaze*, 143–45, 173. Bukuku and Isimbwa preceded Ndahura's generation and were contemporaries of Musisi and Wannèma, who were Mukasa's parent and grandparent.

28. Buliggwanga, *Ekitabo Ekitegeza*, 10–12; Mukanga, "Traditional Belief," 7; Benjamin Ray, *Myth, Ritual, and Kingship in Buganda* (Oxford: Oxford University Press, 1991), 43.

29. Buliggwanga, *Ekitabo Ekitegeza*, 10–12.

30. M. S. M. Semakula Kiwanuka, *A History of Buganda from the Foundation of the Kingdom to 1900* (New York: Africana Publishing, 1972), 64–90; Christopher Wrigley, *Kingship and State: The Buganda Dynasty* (Cambridge: Cambridge University Press, 1996), 207–29; Kodesh, *Beyond the Royal Gaze*, 131–73 (consensus).

31. Yvonne Bastin and Thilo Schadeberg (eds.), *Bantu Lexical Reconstructions III* (Tervuren: Royal Museum of Central Africa, 2002), RN 1046. Zone J attestations not included (accessed February 27, 2016); Rebecca Grollemund, Simon Bradford, Koen Bostoen, Andrew Meade, Chris Venditti, and Mark Pagel, "Bantu Expansion Shows that Habitat Alters the Route and Pace of Human Dispersals," *Proceedings of the National Academy of Sciences* 112, no. 43 (2015), 13296–301.

32. Henri Le Veux, *Premier essai de vocabulaire luganda-français d'après l'ordre étymologique* (Algiers: Imprimeries des Missionaires d'Afrique (Pères Blancs), 1917), 67–68; Ronald Snoxall, *Luganda-English Dictionary* (Oxford: Clarendon Press, 1967), 24; Margaret B. Davis, *A Lunyoro-Lunyankole-English and English-Lunyoro-Lunyankole Dictionary* (Kampala: Uganda Bookshop, 1952 [1938]), 9; Yunus Rubanza, *Zinza-English-Swahili and English-Zinza-Swahili Lexicon* (Dar es Salaam: University of Dar es Salaam Press, 2008), 3; Richard Kayaga Gonza, *Lusoga-English Dictionary and English-Lusoga Dictionary* (Kampala: MK Publishers, 2007), 13.

33. Speke, *Journal*, 394–96, heard Mukasa's name as "Mgussa," a Ruhaya rather than a Luganda pronunciation, and recognized the dress of a male figure as in the "Wichwezi fashion"; Hans Cory, "The Buswezi," *American Anthropologist* 57 (1955), 924; Peter Ladefoged, Ruth Glick, and Clive Criper, *Language in Uganda* (Nairobi: Oxford University Press, 1971), 74 (Luvuma closest to Soga and Ganda, Lusese closest to Lutooro and Runyankore).

34. Berger, *Religion and Resistance*, 68–73; Tantala, "Early History," 318ff; Schoenbrun, *Green Place*, 203–6, 234–40, 265–69.

35. Schoenbrun, "Conjuring the Modern," 1430–33.

36. Kagwa, in Roscoe and Kagwa, "Enquiry," 4–5; Roscoe, *Baganda*, 296; Anonymous, "Mu Bugangazzi: Eby'obusamize n'obulaguzi," *Munno* 24, no. 12 (1934), 246; Cohen, "Cwezi Cult," 656–57; Peter Rigby, "Prophets, Diviners, and Prophetism: The Recent History of Kiganda Religion," *Journal of Anthropological Research* 31, no. 2 (1975), 129; Wrigley, *Kingship and State*, 184.

37. Kagwa, *Ekitabo Kye Mpisa*, 215. "Nakangu" elsewhere, see Kagwa, *Customs*, 27, 119; Kagwa, *Ekitabo Kye Mpisa*, 234.

38. Mair, *African People*, 238–41; L. B. Kaggwa and Frederick B. Welbourn, "Lubaale Initiation in Buganda," *Uganda Journal* 28, no. 2 (1969), 218–20.

39. Mukanga, "Traditional Belief," 7.

40. Nsimbi, *Amannya*, 122; Peter Hoesing, *Kusamira: Ritual Music and Wellbeing in Uganda* (Urbana-Champaign: University of Illinois Press, forthcoming).

41. Mair, *African People*, 231–41; Mukanga, "Traditional Belief," 8.

42. David L. Schoenbrun, "A Lexicon for Affect, Violence, Vulnerability, and Dispute in Eastern Bantu," in progress, RN 202.

43. John T. K. Ggomotoka, "History of Buvuma Islands," trans. David Kiyaga-Mulindwa (Kampala: Typescript, 1937–38), Buvuma 15; Peter Rigby and Fred D. Lule, "Continuity and Change in Kiganda Religion in Urban and Peri-Urban Kampala," in *Town and Country in Central and East Africa*, ed. David J. Parkin (London: Oxford University Press for the International African Institute, 1975), 217–18; Jennifer L. Johnson, "Fishwork in Uganda: A Multispecies Ethnohistory about Fish, People, and Ideas about Fish and People," PhD diss., University of Michigan, 2014, 226.

44. Ernest C. Lanning, "Some Brief Notes on Sesse [sic]," 1957, in Ernest C. Lanning Papers, Mss. Afr.S.1329 (9), 29, Weston Library, University of Oxford.

45. Kagwa, Ekitabo Kye Mpisa, 210–18, 229; Nsimbi, Amannya, 119–48.

46. Gonza, Lusoga-English Dictionary, 419; Kibedi Y. M. Zirabamuzale, "History of Bugweri," in Towards a Reconstructed Past: Historical Texts from Busoga, Uganda, ed. David William Cohen (London: Oxford University Press, 1986), 311–12.

47. Ggomotoka, "History of Buvuma," gives a few Luvuma names for fish, tools, and clothing. Snoxall, Luganda-English Dictionary, has "Buddu" names for fish and bark cloth; Timoteo Nakalya, "Empisa z'abantu: Emyezi gy'Ekisese," Munno 5, no. 52 (1915), 67, names the seasons in Ssese. Sir Harry Johnston, The Uganda Protectorate, vol. 2 (London: Hutchinson, 1902), 969–77, gives a "Lusese" vocabulary.

48. Johnston, Uganda Protectorate, vol. 2, 718; D. G. Maurice, "Buvuma Notes," Maurice Papers, mss. Afr.S.581, n.d., Weston Library, University of Oxford; Kagwa, Ekitabo Kye Mpisa, 209–28; Nsimbi, Amannya, 119–48; Cohen, Historical Tradition, 18, 20, 22.

49. Michael G. Kenny, "The Powers of Lake Victoria," Anthropos 72, nos. 5/6 (1977), 722, 723, 737 (Atego); Margaret Trowell, with Klaus Wachsmann, Tribal Crafts of Uganda (London: Oxford University Press, 1953), 299–301.

50. Schoenbrun, "Conjuring the Modern," 1427–33; Nsimbi, Amannya, 119–48; Kodesh, Beyond the Royal Gaze, 143–54. Both also attended individual lineages; F. Kibirige, "A Report about the Belief of the Baganda in Spirits," Occasional Research Papers in African Religions and Philosophies 19, no. 203 (1974), 13; J. M. Mawanda, "The Baganda Conception of the Ancestors," Occasional Research Papers in African Religions and Philosophies 19, 198 (1974), 1–2.

51. Cohen, "Cwezi Cult," 655–56; Médard, Le royaume, 322ff.

52. John Lonsdale, "Unhelpful Pasts and a Provisional Present," in Citizenship, Belonging, and Political Community in Africa: Dialogues between Past and Present, ed. Emma Hunter (Athens: Ohio University Press, 2018), 24.

53. Speke, Journal, 394; Nyakatura, Abakama, 45; Roscoe, Twenty-Five Years, 67, 137; Robert W. Felkin, "Notes on the Waganda Tribe of Central Africa," Proceedings of the Royal Society of Edinburgh 13 (1885/1886), 762; Nsimbi, Amannya, 127. Schmidt, Historical Archaeology, 63, 64, 70–72, 81, 301–2; Y. Bagenda, "Nzira mu bigambo bya B. Wakulira T. bye yawandika ku nsi Koki nga bw'efanana," Munno 15, no. 7 (1925), 111–12; Alex Arnoux, "Le culte de la société secrete des Imandwa au Rwanda," Anthropos 8 (1913), 767–78; Berger, Religion and Resistance, 145; Henry R. T. Muzale, Ruhaya-English-Kiswahili and English-Ruhaya-Swahili Dictionary (Dar es Salaam: University of Dar es Salaam Press, 2006), 159.

54. Felkin, "Notes," 762 (all quotes).

55. Eugène Hurel, "Religion et vie domestique des Bakerewe," Anthropos 6 (1911), 79.

56. Nicholas Stam, "Religious Conceptions of Some Tribes of Buganda (British Equatorial Africa)," Anthropos 3 (1908), 215 (quotes).

57. Roscoe, Baganda, 299 (twins).

58. D. G. Maurice, "Some Brief Notes on the Sesse [sic] Islands," Maurice Papers, MSS Afr.S.581, Weston Library, University of Oxford.

59. Speke, *Journal*, 395–96 (during a new moon); Kagwa, *Ekitabo Kye Mpisa*, 212–18; Roscoe, *Baganda*, 284, 290–91; Kifamunyanja, "Ssese: Gambuze nti agafudde e Mengo," *Munno* (October 1921), 159–61; Kaindoa, "Origins," 302–5.

60. Ray, *Myth, Ritual, and Kingship*, 124, 128, 143–44, 220, n7.

61. Kagwa, *Ekitabo Kye Mpisa*, 209–37; Roscoe, *Baganda*, 274–75, 300–301; Mukanga, "Traditional Belief," 7; Mary Consolate Nassiwa, "African Traditional Religion: Women and the Sacred in the Ganda Tradition," *Occasional Research Papers in African Traditional Religion and Philosophy* 7, no. 61 (1972), 5; Mawanda, "Baganda Conception," 5. Some joined shrines to escape unfavorable circumstances; for coeval West African parallels, see Sandra Greene, "Family Concerns: Gender and Ethnicity in Pre-Colonial West Africa," *International Review of Social History*, Supplement 44, S7 (1999), 19.

62. Betobanga ("those who get drenched"), Mukasa's senior drum, followed by Nabirye (mother of female twins), Nabikono ("mother of the lake's bays"), and Kikasa (drum rhythm in honor of a lùbaalè); Kagwa, *Customs*, 115; Roscoe, *Baganda*, 296, 297.

63. Roscoe, *Baganda*, 275–76. After the seventeenth century, Graham Connah, *Kibiro: The Salt of Bunyoro, Past and Present* (London: British Institute in Eastern Africa, 1996), 67, 69, 143.

64. Kagwa, *Customs*, 114, 115; Roscoe, *Baganda*, 62, 196, 294.

65. Roscoe, *Baganda*, 288.

66. Titled "Semagumba," or "controller of the bones." Kagwa (*Ekitabo Kye Mpisa*, 183) and Roscoe (*Baganda*, 54) describe Ganda women "breaking the bones," rubbing a mixture of butter and medicine on a pregnant woman's torso to ease childbirth. Synonymous with the adjective *gumba*, "barren," and with *kùgumba* (itr.) "gather in a group, muster," echoing the metaphor in "Lukumirizi," "the heaper; the fire tender," the gatekeeper's title at Bulonge; Snoxall, *Luganda-English Dictionary*, 91, 98.

67. John F. Cunningham, *Uganda and Its Peoples* (London: Hutchinson, 1902), 82, Roscoe, *Baganda*, 294; Kagwa, *Ekitabo Kye Mpisa*, 214. Roscoe says the gutter followed the path Mukasa took after first landing on Bubembe.

68. Roscoe, *Baganda*, 293–94; Kagwa, *Ekitabo Kye Mpisa*, 213; Cunningham, *Uganda and Its Peoples*, 82.

69. Roscoe, *Baganda*, 294.

70. Kagwa, *Customs*, 115; Roscoe, *Baganda*, 293–94.

71. Words for lunar phases differ in the subgroups of Great Lakes Bantu languages that formed after 1000 CE, suggesting that the practices they name emerged after that time. Paul Van Thiel, "Some Preliminary Notes on the Music of the Cwezi Cult in Ankole," *African Music Society Journal* 5 (1973/1974), 61–62; F. Lukyn Williams, "Hima Cattle, Part I," *Uganda Journal* 6, no. 1 (1938), 34; John Roscoe, *The Soul of Central Africa: A General Account of the Mackie Ethnological Expedition* (London: Cassell, 1922), 62; John Roscoe, *The Banyankole* (Cambridge: Cambridge University Press, 1924), 24, 45; Roscoe, *Twenty-Five Years*, 186; Aloysius Gonzaga Katate and Lazaro Kamugungunu, *Abagabe b'Ankole*, 2 vols. (Kampala: Eagle Press, 1955), 42.

72. Roscoe, *Baganda*, 299; Cunningham, *Uganda and Its Peoples*, 88 (every three months only); Yoanna T. K. Kasumba, "Eby' eBuddo," *Munno* 5, 60 (1915), 190.

73. Kagwa, *Ekitabo Kye Mpisa*, 215; Roscoe, *Baganda*, 196, 292; Elisa Jjumba and the Council of the Ssiga of Jjumba, *Ekitabo Eky'essiga lya Jjumba*, Africana Collection, Makerere University Library, 1964, 5, 11.

74. Mukanga, "Traditional Belief," 5.

75. John Musaazi, "Baganda Traditional Divination and Treatment of People's Troubles," Department of Religious Studies and Philosophy Occasional Paper No. 8, Kampala: Makerere University, 1966, 10, Vertical Files, Melville J. Herskovits Library of African Studies, Northwestern University; Mukanga, "Traditional Belief," 5; J. B. Nabaguzi, "Research Methods in Kyaggwe, Buganda Region," History Department Research Paper, Makerere University, Kampala, July, 13, 1970, 2, Vertical Files, Melville J. Herskovits Library of African Studies, Northwestern University; Julien Gorju, *Entre le Victoria, l'Albert et l'Edouard: Ethnographie de la Partie Anglaise du Vicariat de l'Uganda* (Rennes: Imprimeries Oberthür, 1920), 226–30; Roscoe, *Baganda*, 299, 320–22; Lanning, "Some Brief Notes," 29; Cunningham, *Uganda and Its Peoples*, 82–88; Kagwa, *Ekitabo Kye Mpisa*, 212–18.

76. Kagwa, *Ekitabo Kye Mpisa*, 213; Roscoe, *Baganda*, 293.

77. Roscoe, *Baganda*, 296. *Strychnos*'s shiny bark has "conspicuous white lines" and contains alkaloids used in medicine and poison, including in the poison ordeal, discussed in chapter 6; Alan Hamilton, *A Field Guide to Uganda Forest Trees* (Kampala: Privately Published, 1981), 172.

78. Roscoe, *Baganda*, 295.

79. Kagwa, *Ekitabo Kye Mpisa*, 214; Roscoe, *Twenty-Five Years*, 140; Gorju, *Entre le Victoria*, 222. The Sun and Moon rise and set at opposite cardinal points. Bubembe and Bukasa Islands lie just south of the Equator, making the length of day and night quite uniform. Manipulating the meteor locked terrestrial activities to a celestial clock.

80. Roscoe, *Baganda*, 293; Kagwa, *Customs*, 86, 155; Ipolito W. S. D. Lubalembera, "Enyanja yafe Nalubale," *Munno* (June 1922), 87.

81. Jan Bender Shetler, *Claiming Civic Virtue: Gendered Network Memory in the Mara Region of Tanzania* (Madison: University of Wisconsin Press, 2019), 58–61.

82. Apolo Kagwa, *Ekitabo Kye Bika Bya Baganda* (Kampala: Uganda Bookshop, 1949 [ca. 1907]), 53–61; Nsimbi, *Amannya*, 228–32.

83. Mark Granovetter, "The Strength of Weak Ties: A Network Theory Revisited," *Sociological Theory* 1 (1983), 201–33.

84. Kagwa, *Customs*, 114; Nsimbi, *Amannya*, 127, 128; Roscoe, *Baganda*, 290–91 (Bubembe); Cunningham, *Uganda and Its Peoples*, 79 (Bubembe); Roscoe, *Twenty-Five Years*, 138–39 (Bukasa).

85. Yekoniya K. Lubogo, *A History of Busoga* (Jinja: Cyclostyled, 1960), 102; Cohen, *Historical Tradition*, 90, 117ff. Nambubi Namatimba is "mother of the dappled grey cow; mother of the enormous python." Johnson, "Fishwork in Uganda," 176, mentions "Natende" or "mother of praises" and "Namukasa" or "mother of mukasa" as additional names for Mukasa's mother. Also, Cunningham, *Uganda and Its Peoples*, 82; Le Veux, *Premier essai de vocabulaire*, 622.

86. Nsimbi, *Amannya*, 127; Kagwa, *Ekitabo Kye Mpisa*, 212.

87. Roscoe, *Baganda*, 291 (quotes), 297; Kifamunyanja, "Ssese," 159–61; Nsimbi, *Amannya*, 125, 127; Cohen, *Historical Tradition*, 90. Ziba traditions recognize Mugasha's home as Isheshe Bubembe "village"; see Schmidt, *Historical Archaeology*, 72, 74.

88. Kaindoa, "Origins," 305 (Nyakalembe); Johnson, "Fishwork in Uganda," 152, names two others, including Nnakimû, recalled in the mid-twentieth century, as a "goddess, wife of Mukasa" and "person with a hare-lip"; Le Veux, *Premier essai de vocabulaire*, 705; Snoxall, *Luganda-English Dictionary*, 249.

89. Roscoe, *Baganda*, 301; Kagwa, *Ekitabo Kye Mpisa*, 216.

90. Kagwa, *Customs*, 116.

91. Kagwa, *Customs*, 29, 116; Roscoe, *Baganda*, 145–46. Nsimbi, *Amannya*, 194; Kodesh, *Beyond the Royal Gaze*, 100–102, 214 n3; Wrigley, *Kingship and State*, 178.

92. Nsimbi, *Amannya*, 140; Kagwa, *Ekitabo Kye Mpisa*, 216.

93. Kagwa, *Customs*, 115; Kagwa, *Ekitabo Kye Mpisa*, 211.

94. Jonathan Earle, *Colonial Buganda and the End of Empire: Political Thought and Historical Imagination in Africa* (New York: Cambridge University Press, 2017), 1–38.

95. Hanson, *Landed Obligation*, 139–43; Samwiri Lwanga Lunyiigo, *Struggle for Land in Buganda* (Kampala: Wavah Books, 2007), 10–19, 28–38; David L. Schoenbrun, "Ethnic Formation with Other-Than-Human Beings: Island Shrine Practice in Uganda's Long Eighteenth Century," *History in Africa* 45 (2018), 406–8.

96. Nsimbi, *Amannya*, 125, 231.

97. Kagwa, *Ekitabo Kye Mpisa*, 212.

98. Nsimbi, *Amannya*, 125. Wamala dropped the name Bumbujje when leaving Bukasa.

99. Kagwa, *Ekitabo Kye Mpisa*, 211.

100. Nakalya, "Ebya lubale Wanema," 150.

101. Nakalya, "Bukulu," 145–46.

102. Nakalya, "Ebya lubale Wanema," 150; Nsimbi, *Amannya*, 125–27. Haya women praised Nyakalembe, a wife of Mugasha, for her powers over agriculture, materialized in medicines she makes "for growing crops," Kaindoa, "Origins," 305.

103. Nakalya, "Bukulu," 145; Tobi Kizito, "Atalukugendere Akusibira ya Menvu," *Munno* 7, no. 74 (1917), 24; Buliggwanga, *Ekitabo Ekitegeza*, 11; Nsimbi, *Amannya*, 125.

104. Nakalya, "Bukulu," 145.

105. Roscoe, *Baganda*, 314; Kizito, "Atalukugendere," 24; Nsimbi, *Amannya*, 126.

106. Nakalya, "Bukulu," 145.

107. Nakalya, "Bukulu," 145; Nsimbi, *Amannya*, 125.

108. Cohen, *Historical Tradition*, 118 (Nambubi's "return for her millet to feed her hens.")

109. Roscoe, *Baganda*, 290; Tantala, "Early History," 612–13.

110. Kagwa, *Customs*, 123; Kagwa, *Bakabaka Bebuganda*, 6; Nsimbi, *Amannya*, 120.

111. Kagwa, *Customs*, 114, 156; Kifamunyanja, "Ssese," 159; Lubalembera, "Enyanja," 87; J. T. K. G[gomotoka], "Omuziro gw'Abalangira be Buganda: Omuziro si kiragiro," *Munno* (November 1922), 173.

112. Nsimbi, *Amannya*, 127, 231, 230 (Ggugu and Ssendege, children of Kasiriivu, a Seedbead figure from Kyaddondo); Kagwa, *Ekitabo Kye Bika*, 60 (Mwonda, a Seedbead figure, founded the Wild Date Palm Juice clan); Kagwa, *Customs*, 114, 121, 154; Anonymous, "Ab'obutiko," *Munno* 24, no. 7 (1934), 126 (Seedbead, Mushroom, Grasshopper, Buffalo, Colobus Monkey, and Civet Cat clan all descend from a power object, "Ssemugabi," which avoided sesame).

113. Roscoe, *Baganda*, 297.

114. Kagwa, *Ekitabo Kye Bika*, 61; Wagaba of the Seedbead clan, founded the Mushroom clan in Busiro, and named a canoe he had built Nakangu.

115. Kagwa, *Ekitabo Kye Bika*, 58; Omwami Semu Kasyoka L. Kakoma, Rev. Adoniya Musoke Ntate, Kayonga, P. T. I., and Mwami, Musa Serukwaya, Kasolo, *Ekitabo Eky'Abakyanjove Ab'e Mamba Mu Siiga Lya Nankere e Bukerekere* (Kampala: East African Institute of Social Research, 1959), 2, 4.

116. Cohen, *Historical Tradition*, 93–99; Ggomotoka, "History of Buvuma Islands," Buvuma, 2 (Ddolwe).

117. Kagwa, *Ekitabo Kye Bika*, 35; Nsimbi, *Amannya*, 252; Buliggwanga, *Ekitabo Ekitegeza*, 10–12.

118. Nsimbi, *Amannya*, 229; Anonymous, "Ab'obutiko," 126.

119. J. T. K. G[gomotoka], "Omuziro si Kiragiro," *Munno* (December 1922), 190; Kagwa, *Ekitabo Kye Bika*, 61; Kaggwa, *Kings of Buganda*, 30–32; Wrigley, *Kingship and State*, 210–15.

120. Nsimbi, *Amannya*, 230–31.

121. Roland Oliver, "The Royal Tombs of Buganda," *Uganda Journal* 23, no. 2 (1959), 127.

122. D. G. Maurice, "Bulondoganyi," Maurice Papers, MSS Afr.S.581, 1932, 7, Weston Library, University of Oxford.

123. Kagwa, *Ekitabo Kye Bika*, 61; Nsimbi, *Amannya*, 231; Roscoe, *Baganda*, 138–72, omits Bugeme.

124. Nsimbi, *Amannya*, 230, 231.

125. Roscoe, *Baganda*, 275.

126. Kagwa, *Ekitabo Kye Mpisa*, 216–17; Roscoe, *Baganda*, 301; Gorju, *Entre le Victoria*, 171, 219; Le Veux, *Premier essai de vocabulaire*, 705; Kaindoa, "Origins," 302.

127. Roscoe, *Baganda*, 301 (quote); Kagwa, *Ekitabo Kye Mpisa*, 216.

128. The "stooped sewer of bark cloths" carried skin bags for plant medicine that could convert a lake into a flowing river; Nsimbi, *Amannya*, 199–200.

129. Nsimbi, *Amannya*, 201.

130. Renamed Kyasanku Kakumirizi, or "chief of firewood, little heaper," by Kintu, echoing a shrine's "gatekeeper" or Lukumirizi; Kagwa, *Ekitabo Kye Bika*, 102.

131. Kagwa, *Ekitabo Kye Bika*, 98–101; Kagwa, *Ekitabo Kye Mpisa*, 211; Nsimbi, *Amannya*, 200–201 (Buvu not mentioned).

132. Kagwa, *Ekitabo Kye Bika*, 103; Kiwanuka, *History of Buganda*, 74–75.

133. Daneli Talika Kaganda, son of Lwamiti, and Tomasi Chakuambala Serumaga, son of Makatu, in Roscoe and Kagwa, "Enquiry," 102.

134. Kifamunyanja, "Ssese," 159–61.

135. Kagwa, *Ekitabo Kye Mpisa*, 309; Kagwa, *Customs*, 163–64.

136. Kagwa, *Ekitabo Kye Bika*, 7–13; Cohen, *Historical Tradition*, 82, 93–99; Kodesh, *Beyond the Royal Gaze*, 76–80.

137. Kagwa, *Customs*, 157. African gray parrot red tail feathers adorned sewn canoe prows.

138. Nsimbi, *Amannya*, 276; Kagwa, *Ekitabo Kye Mpisa*, 297.

139. Kodesh, *Beyond the Royal Gaze*, 120, 121 (quote); Wrigley, *Kingship and State*, 20–35.

140. Kagwa, *Ekitabo Kye Bika*, 18–20; Nsimbi, *Amannya*, 273–78; Wrigley, *Kingship and State*, 194–97.

141. Kagwa, *Customs*, 164; Kagwa, *Ekitabo Kye Bika*, 17–22; Nsimbi, *Amannya*, 273–78; E. W. S. Mukasa, "The Reason for the Creation of the Post of Mugema in Buganda," *Uganda Journal* 10, no. 2 (1946), 150.

142. Kagwa, *Ekitabo Kye Mpisa*, 213, 214.

143. Roscoe, *Baganda* 144; Byampebwa Kibâte and Alfonsi Aliwali, "Ka Tulojje: Kabaka Mulondo," *Munno* 4, no. 38 (1914), 20; Gorju, *Entre le Victoria*, 170; Kagwa, *Ekitabo Kye Mpisa*, 291. Dumu's location: Stanley, *Through the Dark Continent*, vol. 1, 213–14; Kifamunyanja, "Ssese," 175; Lubalembera, "Enyanja," 87.

144. Kagwa, *Ekitabo Kye Mpisa*, 213. Each road was part of a pair; two roads led from Musove harbor to the shrine site, the shorter one allowed officials to double back to the shrine before esteemed visitors arrived during festivals; Roscoe, *Baganda*, 293 (twelve roads), 298.

145. Schmidt, *Historical Archaeology*, 95, 96, 314, 317 (Batundu avoid the otter); Tomasi Semukasa Omukisi, son of Mukwanga and Ibrahim Gadukande Mwaziza, son of Mukwanga, in Roscoe and Kagwa, "Enquiry," 89 (Batundu avoided the leopard).

146. Kagwa, *Ekitabo Kye Bika*, 227.

147. Speke, *Journal*, 394–96, described a paddle in the consultation house and its use as a walking staff, he may have visited Dumu; Anonymous, "Mu Bugangazzi," 19; Anonymous, "Mu Bugangazzi: Eby'obusamize n'obulaguzi; emmandwa eyitibwa Kawuka," *Munno* 25, no. 2 (1935), 34.

148. Ernest C. Lanning, "The Surviving Regalia of the Nyakaima, Mubende," *Uganda Journal* 30, no. 2 (1966), 211.

149. Paul Kollmann, *The Victoria Nyanza*, trans. H. A. Nesbitt (London: Swan Sonnenschein, 1899), 73–78.

150. Johnston, *Uganda Protectorate*, vol. 2, 678; Roscoe, *Twenty-Five Years*, 138; Roscoe, *Baganda*, 290 (quote).

151. Gorju, *Entre le Victoria*, 222, caption opposite photo on 224.

152. Johnston, *Uganda Protectorate*, vol. 2, 678.

153. Kollmann, *Victoria Nyanza*, 76, and figs. 87 and 88.

154. Roscoe, *Baganda*, 290 (quote).

155. Extending David Doris, *Vigilant Things: On Thieves, Yoruba Anti-Aesthetics, and the Strange Fates of Ordinary Objects in Nigeria* (Seattle: University of Washington Press, 2011), 139–40.

156. Kenny, "Powers of Lake Victoria," 718; Ng'onga Odera and Odindo Ogema, Rusinga Island, October 10, 1977, in Michael G. Kenny (comp.) "Basuba Historical Narratives" (Typescript, 1978), 4–5, L VI398.2/420392, School of Oriental and African Studies Library, University of London.

157. Atego also names an island off Mfangano Island and a *Euphorbia* tree; Hamilton, *Field Guide*, 155.

158. Kodesh, *Beyond the Royal Gaze*, 158–73; Schoenbrun, "Ethnic Formation," 412–16.

Chapter 3. Mukasa's Wealth

1. Steven Feierman, "On Socially Composed Knowledge: Reconstructing a Shambaa Royal Ritual," in *In Search of a Nation: Histories of Authority and Dissidence in Tanzania*, ed. Gregory Maddox and James Giblin (Oxford: James Currey, 2005), 25–29.

2. Harry Johnston, *The Uganda Protectorate*, vol. 2 (London: Hutchinson, 1902), 693, 699; John F. Cunningham, *Uganda and Its Peoples* (London: Hutchinson, 1905), 80.

3. Ceri Z. Ashley, "Toward a Socialised Archaeology of Great Lakes Ceramics," *African Archaeological Review* 27, 2 (2010), 149.

4. Lucy Mair, *An African People in the Twentieth Century* (London: Routledge, 1934), 130; Margaret Trowell, "Some Royal Craftsmen of Buganda," *Uganda Journal* 8, no. 2 (1941), 59; Jürgen Jensen, "Töpferei und Töpferwaren auf Buvuma (Uganda)," *Baessler-Archiv, Neue Folge* 17 (1969), 53–100; Scheherazade Amin, "The Archaeology of the Sesse Islands and Their Contribution to the Understanding of Great Lakes Ceramics," PhD diss., University College of London, 2015, 415, 422.

5. Michael B. Nsimbi, *Amannya Amaganda N'Ennono Zaago* (Kampala: Longman's Uganda, 1980), 125, 228, 229.

6. Apolo Kagwa, *Ekitabo Kye Bika Bya Baganda* (Kampala: Uganda Bookshop, 1949 [1912]), 60–61.

7. Nsimbi, *Amannya*, on Bukunja: 203, 244, 248, 317, 308; John T. K. Ggomotoka, "History of Buvuma Islands," Translated by David Kiyaga-Mulindwa (Kampala: Typescript, 1937–38), Buziri Island, 3–4; Mpata Island, 7; Bugaya Island, 24; Buvuma Island, 3–4 (sank when Mubiru Kisanje came from Ddolwe); Buvuma Island, 20.

8. Each had female officials focused on adult women's issues; see Apolo Kagwa, *Ekitabo Kye Mpisa Za Baganda* (Kampala: Uganda Printing and Publishing, 1918), 226–29; Yolamu N. Nsamba, *Mystique in Sovereigns' Headgear: A Historical Journey via Bunyoro Uganda* (Wandsbeck: Reach Publishers, 2016), 118–30; Anonymous, "Mu Bugangazzi: Eby'obusamize n'obulaguzi," *Munno* 24, no. 12 (1934), 246–47.

9. Nakanyike Musisi, "Morality as Identity: The Missionary Moral Agenda in Buganda, 1877–1945," *Journal of Religious History* 23, no. 1 (1999), 51–74; Holly Hanson, "Queen Mothers and Good Government in Buganda: The Loss of Women's Political Power in Nineteenth Century East Africa," in *Women in African Colonial Histories*, ed. Jean Allman, Susan Geiger, and Nakanyike Musisi (Bloomington: Indiana University Press, 2002), 219–36.

10. Nakanyike B. Musisi, "Women, 'Elite Polygyny,' and Buganda State Formation," *Signs* 16, no. 4 (1991), 757–86; Sylvia Nannyonga-Tamusuza, "Female-Men, Male-Women, and Others: Constructing and Negotiating Gender among the Baganda of Uganda," *Journal of Eastern African Studies* 3, no. 2 (2009), 368; Sylvia Nannyonga-Tamusuza, *Baakisimba: Gender in the Music and Dance of the Baganda People of Uganda* (New York: Routledge, 2005), 7–21.

11. Rhiannon Stephens, *A History of African Motherhood: The Case of Uganda, 700–1900* (New York: Cambridge University Press, 2013), 133–44.

12. Stella Nyanzi, Justine Nassimbwa, Vincent Kayizzi, and Strivan Kabanda, "'African Sex Is Dangerous!' Renegotiating 'Ritual Sex' in Contemporary Masaka District," *Africa* 78, no. 4 (2008), 518–39; Sylvia Tamale, "Eroticism, Sensuality and 'Women's Secrets' among the Baganda: A Critical Analysis," *Feminist Africa* 5 (2005), 9–36.

13. Nakanyike B. Musisi, "The Environment, Gender, and the Development of Unequal Relations in Buganda: A Historical Perspective," *Canadian Woman Studies* 13, no. 3 (1993), 55; Stephens, *History of African Motherhood*, 65–71, 99–101; Christian Thibon, "Croissance démographique, paysage politique et diversification culturale dans la region des Grands Lacs," in *La diffusion des plantes américaines dans la region des*

Grands Lacs, ed. Elizabeth Vignati, special issue of *Les Cahiers d'Afrique de l'Est* 52 (2019), 151–240.

14. Alois Meyer, *Kleines Ruhaya-Deutsches Wörterbuch* (Trier: Mosella Press, 1914), 43, *muharámbwai*, "looks like a woman, does women's work, etc."

15. Augustine Kaindoa, "Origins of Rugomora Mahe," in Peter R. Schmidt, *Historical Archaeology: A Structural Approach in an African Culture* (Westport, CT: Greenwood Press, 1978), 305; John H. M. Beattie, "Initiation into the Cwezi Spirit Possession Cult in Bunyoro," *African Studies* 16 (1957), 150–61 (senior members of an initiatory group called "mothers" or "grandmothers" regardless of sex).

16. Peter R. Schmidt, *Iron Technology in East Africa* (Bloomington: Indiana University Press, 1997), 218; Hans Cory and Mary M. Hartnoll, *Customary Law of the Haya Tribe* (London: Percy Lund, Humphries, 1945), 114–20, 265–69. Irungu/Ddungu, a member of the cwezi group, helped with hunting and extracting forest resources, including those required for smelting iron.

17. Kaindoa, "Origins," 305; Edmond Césard, "Comment les Bahaya interprètent leurs origines," *Anthropos* 22, no. 3 (1927), 451 (Nyakalembe); Edmond Césard, "Le Muhaya," *Anthropos* 31, no. 3 (1936), 490 (mwarambwa).

18. Robert W. Felkin, "Notes on the Waganda Tribe of Central Africa," *Proceedings of the Royal Society of Edinburgh* 13 (1885/1886), 762; George Pilkington, *Luganda-English and English-Luganda Vocabulary* (London: Society for Promoting Christian Knowledge, 1899), 73, glossed Mukasa "a kind of female Neptune" and recorded a plural form as well, *bamukasa*. Julien Gorju, *Entre le Victoria, l'Albert et l'Edouard: Ethnographie de la Partie Anglaise de Vicariat de l'Uganda* (Rennes: Imprimeries Oberthür, 1920), 168 ("madame Neptune").

19. John Roscoe, *The Baganda: An Account of Their Native Customs and Beliefs* (London: Macmillan, 1911), 297.

20. Schmidt, *Iron Technology*, 215–23; Suzette Heald, "The Power of Sex," *Africa* 65, no. 4 (1995), 497–500.

21. Henri Le Veux, *Premier essai de vocabulaire luganda-français d'après l'ordre étymologique* (Algiers: Imprimeries des Missionaires d'Afrique [Pères Blancs], 1917), 527. Between 1150 and 1350 CE, jars dominated Amin's island assemblages but were absent in mainland assemblages. See Amin, "Archaeology of Sesse Islands," 401.

22. Jennifer Lee Johnson, "Fishwork in Uganda: A Multispecies Ethnohistory about Fish, People, and Ideas about Fish and People," PhD diss., University of Michigan, 2014, 6, 7, "Namayanja" or "Mother of the bodies of water," an unending pool of amniotic fluid; Johnston, *Uganda Protectorate*, vol. 2, 699.

23. Roscoe, *Baganda*, 291. In Kadu's story of Kimera (Henry Morton Stanley, *My Dark Companions and Their Strange Stories* [London: Sampson, Low, Marston, 1893], 149–50), Nakku welcomed Kimera by exchanging and eating uncooked bananas, showing that mediums and ordinary people "ate" differently. Pregnant women avoided eating roasted plantains, among other things; Kagwa, *Ekitabo Kye Mpisa*, 180–89; Mair, *African People*, 39; Stephens, *History of African Motherhood*, 93. Roscoe, *Baganda*, 291. Teofiro Mulumba Kuruji, in John Roscoe and Apolo Kagwa, "Enquiry into Native Land Tenure in the Uganda Protectorate, 1906," Kampala, 1906, MSS Afr.S.17, Weston Library, University of Oxford, 52; Kagwa, *Ekitabo Kye Mpisa*, 119.

24. John Roscoe, "Python Worship in Uganda," *Man* 9 (1909), 89.

25. Zoltán Kövecses, *Metaphor in Culture: Universality and Variation* (Cambridge: Cambridge University Press, 2005).

26. John R. Taylor and Thandi Mbense, "Red Dogs and Rotten Mealies: How Zulus Talk about Anger," in *Speaking of Emotions: Conceptualisation and Expression*, ed. Angeliki Athanasiadou and Elzbieta Tabakowska (Berlin: Mouton de Gruyter, 1998), 194.

27. Pilkington, *Luganda-English*, 68; Albert R. Cook, *A Medical Vocabulary and Phrase Book in Luganda* (Kampala: Uganda Bookshop, 1903), 39; Le Veux, *Premier essai de vocabulaire*, 624; Eridadi M. K. Mulira and G. M. Ndawula, *A Luganda-English and English-Luganda Dictionary* (London: Society for Promoting Christian Knowledge, 1952), 67. For usage, see Viktoro Katula, "Abadzukulu ba Sekabaka Kagulu: Ekiyigganyizo eky'okubiri," *Munno* 14, no. 9 (1924), 137 (omutima); Viktoro Katula, "Abadzukulu ba Sekabaka Kagulu," *Munno* 14, no. 11 (1924), 155 (emmeme).

28. Kuruji, in Roscoe and Kagwa, "Enquiry," 52: "We thought that after death one's heart traveled in the air and would kill other people, after death it was called muzimu."

29. Charles T. Wilson, *An Outline Grammar of the Luganda Language* (London: Society for Promoting Christian Knowledge, 1882), 70, gave "Liver, *kivumbu*"; Cook, *Medical Vocabulary*, 19, gave "*Kibumba*, liver"; Charles W. Hattersley and Henry Wright Duta, *Luganda Phrases and Idioms* (London: Society for Promoting Christian Knowledge, 1904), 85, *kibumba* "liver."

30. Apolo Kagwa, *Customs of the Baganda*, ed. May Edel, trans. Ernest Kalibala (New York: Columbia University Press, 1934), 71, 99. Thanks to Jon Earle for this. Roscoe, *Baganda*, 206, a royal wife closed down her experience of the funeral of a relative by eating a goat's liver.

31. Trowell, "Some Royal Craftsmen," 58, 61; Ronald Snoxall, *Luganda-English Dictionary* (Oxford: Clarendon Press, 1967), 206.

32. Amin, "Archaeology of the Sesse," 401; perhaps the *ènsumbi* (pitcher, small jar) type; Nsimbi, *Amannya*, 42.

33. Kagwa, *Ekitabo Kye Mpisa*, 214.

34. Nsimbi, *Amannya*, 200.

35. John Hanning Speke, *Journal of the Discovery of the Source of the Nile* (Edinburgh: William Blackwood, 1863), opposite 276; Roscoe, *Baganda*, 441.

36. Roscoe, *Baganda*, 440.

37. Roscoe, *Baganda*, 293 (sex too soon); Heald, "Power of Sex," 498–99.

38. Dancing, too; Le Veux, *Premier essai de vocabulaire*, 360, *kukiga* "dance, as was customary at the birth of twins."

39. Kagwa, *Ekitabo Kye Mpisa*, 280 (quote), 283.

40. Kagwa, *Ekitabo Kye Mpisa*, 186.

41. Roscoe, *Baganda*, 295.

42. Roscoe, *Baganda*, 298.

43. Kagwa distinguishes "slaves" from "women" in constituting such "gifts" in the nineteenth century; Kagwa, *Ekitabo Kye Mpisa*, 217–18; Roscoe, *Baganda*, 298, 300.

44. Cunningham, *Uganda and Its Peoples*, 86 (quote); Roscoe, *Baganda*, 276. Ggomotoka's sources in the Buvuma Islands also distinguished "slaves" from "maids," in listing what canoes carried; Ggomotoka, "History of Buvuma," Bugaya, 21.

45. Renee Louise Tantala, "Early History in Kitara in Western Uganda: Process Models of Religious and Political Change, Part I," PhD diss., University of Wisconsin–Madison, 1989, 181; A. B. T. Byaruhanga-Akiiki, *Religion in Bunyoro* (Nairobi: Kenya Literature Bureau, 1982), 54–55; John Nyakatura, *Aspects of Bunyoro Customs and Traditions*, trans. Zebiya Kwamya (Kampala: East African Literature Bureau, 1970), 71.

46. Or in a local banana garden; Roscoe, *Baganda*, 24–25; Johnson, "Fishwork," 253–55.

47. Kagwa, *Ekitabo Kye Mpisa*, 181; Snoxall, *Luganda-English Dictionary*, 205, 300.

48. Roscoe, *Baganda*, 290.

49. Gorju, *Entre le Victoria*, 222.

50. Different lengths at different shrines; the days involved were called *ènnakû za bwerendê*, lit. "delicate days"; Snoxall, *Luganda-English Dictionary*, 38.

51. Zhengwei Yang and Jeffrey C. Schank, "Women Do Not Synchronize Their Menstrual Cycles," *Human Nature* (2006), 433–47; H. Clyde Wilson, "A Critical Review of Menstrual Synchrony Research," *Psychoneuroendocrinology* 17 (1992), 565–91.

52. Martha K. McClintock, "Menstrual Synchrony and Suppression," *Nature* 229 (1971), 244–45; Martha K. McClintock, "Social Control of the Ovarian Cycle and the Function of Oestrus Synchrony," *American Zoologist* 21 (1981), 243–56; Winnifred B. Cutler, "Lunar and Menstrual Phase Locking," *American Journal of Obstetrics and Gynecology* 13 (1980), 834–39; Sung Ping Law, "The Regulation of Menstrual Cycle and Its Relationship to the Moon," *Acta Obstetricia Gynecologica Scandinavica* 65 (1986), 45–48.

53. Thomas Buckley and Alma Gottlieb, "A Critical Appraisal of Theories of Menstrual Symbolism," in *Blood Magic: The Anthropology of Menstruation*, ed. Thomas Buckley and Alma Gottlieb (Berkeley: University of California Press, 1988), 45–47.

54. Kuruji, in Roscoe and Kagwa, "Enquiry," 64–65; Roscoe, *Baganda*, 61–67; Kagwa, *Ekitabo Kye Mpisa*, 186–87; Eriya M. Buliggwanga, *Ekitabo Ekitegeza Ekika Kye Mamba* (Kampala: Uganda Printing and Publishing, 1916), 2–3.

55. Roscoe, *Baganda*, 64 (all quotes).

56. Kagwa, *Ekitabo Kye Mpisa*, 185; Roscoe, *Baganda*, 49, 62; Mair, *African People*, 56.

57. Kuruji in Roscoe and Kagwa, "Enquiry," 58–61; Roscoe, *Baganda*, 64–73; Michael B. Nsimbi, "Village Life and Customs in Buganda," *Uganda Journal* 20, no. 1 (1956), 27–36.

58. Jennifer Johnson, "Fish, Family, and the Gendered Politics of Descent along Uganda's Southern Littorals," *History in Africa* 45 (2018), 445–71.

59. Johnson, "Fish, Family," 455–56.

60. Johnston, *Uganda Protectorate*, vol. 2, 787–89; Kagwa, *Ekitabo Kye Mpisa*, 279–80; in Busoga, women caught and ate ènkejje; M. A. Condon, "Contributions to the Ethnography of the Basoga-Batamba, Uganda Protectorate," *Anthropos* 5, no. 4 (1910), 955.

61. Kagwa, *Ekitabo Kye Mpisa*, 185–86; Gomotoka, "History of Buvuma," Buvuma Island, 47, the wooden skewer sufficed as a metonym; Nsimbi, "Village Life," 31; John Roscoe, "Further Notes on the Manners and Customs of the Baganda," *Journal of the Royal Anthropological Institute* 32 (1902), 32, 33. Other ceremonies fell under this rubric, including *kùmenya òlùkanda*. Òlùkanda: a unit of dried fish—often ènkejje—traded since early in the second millennium (chapter 1).

62. Andrew Apter, "Yoruba Ethnogenesis from Within," *Comparative Studies in Society and History* 55, no. 2 (2015), 363–68, building on Helen Verran, *Science and an African Logic* (Chicago: University of Chicago, 2001), 234–36.

63. Toby Kizito, "Ensi Muwawa Buganda," *Munno* 5, no. 49 (1915), 7–8; Toby Kizito, "Kintu Anonebwa e Mangira," *Munno* 5, no. 52 (1915), 62–63; Nsimbi, *Amannya*, 152; Kasirye Zzibukulimbwa, "The Beginning of Ennyanja Nnalubaale," trans. Robert Bakaaki and Jennifer Lee Johnson (Kampala: PDF, 2012), 7 (and *mpwawa*, a deep-water sprat, echoes "Muwawa").

64. Anonymous, "Customs of Buganda," *Mengo Notes* 1, no. 4 (1900), 16.

65. Also, Elisa Jjumba and the Council of the Ssiga of Jjumba, *Ekitabo Eky'essiga lya Jjumba* (Typescript 1964), 25, Africana Collection, Makerere University Library; Nsimbi, *Amannya*, 181.

66. Roscoe, "Further Notes," 31–32; Nsimbi, "Village Life," 32; Mair, *African People*, 57.

67. Compare Roscoe, *Baganda*, 62–63 and Mair, *African People*, 56–59. Kagwa, *Ekitabo Kye Mpisa*, 187; Ggomotoka, "History of Buvuma," Buvuma Island, 48.

68. John Roscoe, *The Northern Bantu: An Account of Some Central African Tribes of the Uganda Protectorate* (Cambridge: Cambridge University Press, 1915), 215–16.

69. Stephens, *History of African Motherhood*, 121–22.

70. Eugène Hurel, "Religion et vie domestique des Bakerewe," *Anthropos* 6 (1911), 294.

71. Peter H. Greenwood, *Fishes of Uganda* (Kampala: Uganda Society, 1966), 117; Johnston, *Uganda Protectorate*, vol. 2, 787–89.

72. Johnson, "Fish, Family," 445–71; Jan Bender Shetler, *Claiming Civic Virtue: Gendered Network Memory in the Mara Region, Tanzania* (Madison: University of Wisconsin Press, 2019), 96.

73. David L. Schoenbrun, "A Mask of Calm: Emotion and Founding the Kingdom of Bunyoro in the Sixteenth Century," *Comparative Studies in Society and History* 55, no. 3 (2013), 635, n 3; Eurasian plague may have affected the region at this time; Monica Green, "Putting Africa on the Black Death Map: Narratives from Genetics and History," *Afriques: Débats, méthodes et terrain d'histoire* 9 (2018), 21.

74. Paul Kollmann, *The Victoria Nyanza*, trans. H. A. Nesbitt (London: Swan Sonnenschein, 1899), 87; Ggomotoka, "History of Buvuma," Bugaya, 21.

75. Y. T. K. G. S. Kajerero, "Eby'e Buganda: Entabalo za Ssekabaka Mawanda," *Munno* 10, no. 1 (1921), 10; Godfrey N. Uzoigwe, "Precolonial Markets in Bunyoro-Kitara," *Comparative Studies in Society and History* 14, no. 4 (1972), 444–49; Henry Okello Ayot, *A History of the Luo-Abasuba of Western Kenya, from A.D. 1760–1940* (Nairobi: Kenya Literature Bureau, 1979), 155–61; David W. Cohen, "Food Production and Food Exchange in the Precolonial Lakes Plateau Region," in *Imperialism, Colonialism, and Hunger: East and Central Africa*, ed. Robert I. Rotberg (Lexington, MA: Lexington Books, 1983), 1–18; Richard J. Reid, *Political Power in Pre-Colonial Buganda* (Oxford: James Currey, 2002), 141–48.

76. Graham Connah, *Kibiro: The Salt of Bunyoro, Past and Present* (London: British Institute in Eastern Africa, 1996), 152 (copper, glass beads); Peter T. Robertshaw, "Munsa Earthworks," *Azania: Archaeological Research in Africa* 32, no. 1 (1997), 16 (glass beads, 900–1200 CE); Andrew Reid, "Ntusi and the Development of Social Complexity in Southern Uganda," in *Aspects of African Archaeology*, ed. Gilbert Pwiti

and Robert Soper (Harare: University of Zimbabwe Press, 1996), 621–27 (twelfth-century glass beads at Ntusi); Andrew Reid and Ceri Z. Ashley, "Islands of Intensive Agriculture on Victoria Nyanza," in *Archaeology of African Plant Use*, ed. Chris J. Stevens, Sam Nixon, Mary Anne Murray, and Dorian Q. Fuller (Walnut Creek, CA: Left Coast Press, 2014), 179–88 (glass beads at Malanga Lweru, Ssese); Amin, "Archaeology of the Sesse," 424–33 (ceramic evidence for trade between Ssese and mainland littoral).

77. Andrew Reid, "The Lake, Bananas, and Ritual Power," manuscript, 2016, in author's possession; Conrad P. Kottak, "Ecological Variables in the Origins and Evolution of African States: The Buganda Example," *Comparative Studies in Society and History* 14, no. 3 (1972), 351–80; Christopher Wrigley, "Bananas in Buganda," *Azania* 24 (1989), 64–70; David Lee Schoenbrun, *A Green Place, a Good Place: Agrarian Change, Gender, and Social Identity between the Great Lakes to 1500* (Portsmouth, NH: Heinemann, 1998), 79–82; Stephens, *History of African Motherhood*, 65–70; W. K. Tushemereirwe, D. Karamura, H. Ssali, D. Bwamika, I. Kashaija, C. Nankinga, F. Bagamba, A. Kangire, and R. Ssebuliba, "Bananas (*Musa Spp*)," in *Agriculture in Uganda, Volume 2, Crops*, ed. J. K. Mukiibi (Kampala: Fountain Publishers, 2001), 281–319.

78. C. S. Gold, A. Kiggundu, A. M. K. Abera and D. Karamura, "Diversity, Distribution and Farmer Preference of Musa Cultivars in Uganda," *Experimental Agriculture* 38 (2002), 48–49; D. A. Karamura, "Exploiting Indigenous Knowledge for the Management and Maintenance of *Musa* Biodiversity on Farm," *African Crop Science Journal* 12, no. 1 (2004), 67–74.

79. Nathaniel Scharping, "The Banana As We Know It Is Dying . . . Again," *Discover*, December 27, 2017.

80. Stephens, *History of African Motherhood*, 100.

81. Tushemereirwe et al., "Bananas," 286–89; Stephens, *History of African Motherhood*, 66–70.

82. Jennifer Lee Johnson, "Eating and Existence on an Island in Southern Uganda," *Comparative Studies of South Asia, the Middle East, and Africa* 37, no. 1 (2017), 9–12.

83. Connah, *Kibiro*, 214. It may have been as old in Katwe, to the west; Ephraim Kamuhangire, "The Pre-Colonial History of the Salt Lakes Region of South Western Uganda, c. 1000–1900 A.D.," PhD diss;, Makerere University, Kampala, 1993.

84. Kagwa, *Ekitabo Kye Mpisa*, 180.

85. *Eggugu*, "type of sedge (in swamps; used for making mats and extracting salt) *Pycreus nitidus*"; *eggugu*; *amagugu*, "large load/bundle." See Alan Hamilton, with Naomi Hamilton, Phoebe Mukasa, and David Ssewanyana, *Luganda Dictionary and Grammar* (Kampala: Gustro Limited, 2016), 38.

86. Snoxall, *Luganda-English Dictionary*, 221–22; Kagwa, *Ekitabo Kye Mpisa*, 185.

87. Connah, *Kibiro*, 155.

88. Daphne Gallagher, "American Plants in Sub-Saharan Africa: A Review of the Archaeological Evidence," *Azania: Archaeological Research in Africa* 51, no. 1 (2016), 34–37 (tobacco).

89. Connah, *Kibiro*, 213; Christopher Ehret, "Dissemination of Tobacco in Africa," presentation to the Routes of Medieval Africa 11th to 17th Centuries conference, Université Paris I, Panthéon-Sorbonne, France, March 5, 2019.

90. Gallagher, "American Plants," 34–37, 42.

91. Louise Iles, "The Development of Iron Technology in Precolonial Western Uganda," *Azania: Archaeological Research in Africa* 48, no. 1 (2013), 65–90, here, 70; Louise Iles, "Impressions of Banana Pseudostems in Iron Slag from Eastern Africa," *Ethnobotany Research and Applications* 7 (2009), 286.

92. Gareth Austin, "Resources, Techniques, and Strategies South of the Sahara: Revising the Factor Endowments Perspective on African Economic Development, 1500–2000," *Economic History Review* 63, no. 1 (2008), 597–99, 608–9.

93. Kagwa, *Ekitabo Kye Mpisa*, 283–91.

94. Ggomotoka, "History of Buvuma," Bugaya Island, 16–17; Buvuma Island, 36.

95. Thibon, "Croissance démographique," 170 (nineteenth-century examples).

96. William J. Eggeling, *The Indigenous Trees of the Uganda Protectorate*, rev. Ivan R. Dale (Glasgow: Glasgow University Press, 1951), 238, 255 (quotes); Georg Schweinfurth, Friedrich Ratzel, Richard W. Felkin, and Gustav Hartlaub (eds.), *Emin Pasha in Central Africa: Being a Collection of His Letters and Journals*, trans. Mrs. Robert W. Felkin (New York: Dodd, Mead, 1889), 39–40.

97. John Roscoe, *The Bakitara or Banyoro* (Cambridge: Cambridge University Press, 1923), 236; Eggeling, *Indigenous Trees*, 253–55.

98. Roscoe, *Baganda*, 403–4; Roscoe, *Bakitara*, 236; J. T. M. Kikulwe, "Amagezi ag'okukomaga nga bwe gazulibwa," *Munno* 5, no. 57 (1915), 142–44; Richard Kayaga Gonza, *Lusoga-English Dictionary and English-Lusoga Dictionary* (Kampala: MK Publishers, 2007), 232. The number in Ssese and Buvuma is unknown.

99. Speke, *Journal*, 313–14; Roscoe, *Baganda*, 442; Kizito, "Kintu Anonebwa," 63. In the 1930s, on Bugala Island (Buvuma group), rich people and women wore bark cloth; ordinary men dressed with calf- and goat-skins and banana fiber; Ggomotoka, "History of Buvuma," Bugaya Island, 14.

100. John Roscoe, *The Bagesu and Other Tribes of the Uganda Protectorate* (Cambridge: Cambridge University Press, 1924), 113. Fumigation kept cloths free of insects like the fleas that carried *Yersinia pestis*; Wilson, *Outline Grammar*, 130; Roscoe, *Bakitara*, 237, 238.

101. Schweinfurth et al., *Emin Pasha*, 119–20.

102. Reid, *Political Power*, 72–76, claims production and circulation increased by controlling famed centers, not by establishing new ones.

103. Johnston, *Uganda Protectorate*, vol. 2, 648; John Roscoe, *Twenty-Five Years in East Africa* (Cambridge: Cambridge University Press, 1921), 99, 178, 182–83, 221. See also Marcos Leitão de Almeida, "The Deep History of the *Ficus thonningii Bl.* in Central Africa: Ontology, Settlement, and Environment among Lower Congo Peoples (Early Times to ca. 500 B.C.E.)," in *Historical Archaeology and Environment*, ed. Marcos Andrés Torres de Souza and Diogo Menezes Costa (New York: Springer, 2018), 188–91.

104. Reid, *Political Power*, 159.

105. Roscoe, *Baganda*, 297–98; 442; Mukasa wore two bark cloths, colored with fine silt; Anonymous, "Mu Bugangazi," 19.

106. Kagwa, *Ekitabo Kye Bika*, 11.

107. Speke, *Journal*, 315 (big from the small); Charles Chaillé-Long, *Central Africa: Naked Truths of Naked People* (New York: Harper and Brothers, 1877), 104 (white).

108. Mair, *African People*, 107: "'to plant bark-cloth trees for him' was used as a metaphor to describe the installation of a chief."

109. Kagwa, *Ekitabo Kye Mpisa*, 212–13.

110. Kagwa, *Customs*, 23, 32; Kyabaggu's Nanzigu is not named in *Ekitabo Kye Mpisa*, 54, or *Customs*, 36. Nanzigu honored the power object called Nampewo; Anonymous, "E Rubaga—Ebyedda," *Munno* 4, no. 23 (April 1933), 72.

111. Roscoe, *Baganda*, 224.

112. Apolo Kaggwa, The *Kings of Buganda*, ed. and trans. M. S. M. Semakula Kiwanuka (Nairobi: East African Publishing House, 1971), 84 (quote). Not in Apollo Kagwa, *Bakabaka Bebuganda* (London: Headley Brothers, 1901).

113. Nsimbi, *Amannya*, 274.

114. Kaggwa, *Kings of Buganda*, 83 (quote), 89; Kagwa, *Bakabaka Bebuganda*, 71. Roscoe, *Baganda*, 224–25, and Kagwa, *Bakabaka Bebuganda* say the events occurred early in Kyabaggu's reign.

115. Musisi, "Women, 'Elite Polygyny,'" 773; Kagwa, *Ekitabo Kye Mpisa*, 121. Nakayiza is not among the names of the children Kyabaggu had with any of the eighteen women recounted as royal wives in Kagwa, *Ekitabo Kye Mpisa*, 54, but Kagwa calls her an *omumbeja* in *Bakabaka Bebuganda*, 71.

116. Michael G. Kenny, "Mutesa's Crime: Hubris and the Control of African Kings," *Comparative Studies in Society and History* 30, no. 4 (1988), 600–601; Christopher Wrigley, *Kingship and State: The Buganda Dynasty* (Cambridge: Cambridge University Press, 1996), 247–48; Holly Hanson, *Landed Obligation: The Practice of Power in Buganda* (Portsmouth, NH: Heinemann, 2003), 74; Henri Médard, *Le royaume du Buganda au XIXe siècle* (Paris: IFRA-Karthala, 2007), 347, 354ff.

117. Kagwa, *Bakabaka Bebuganda*, 70–71; Green, "Putting Africa," 21; Jean-Pierre Chrétien, "Les capitales royales de l'Afrique des Grands Lacs peuvent-elles être considérées comme des villes?," *Journal des Africanistes* 74, nos. 1/2 (2004), 277–98; Kaggwa, *Kings of Buganda*, 222–24.

118. Kagwa, *Ekitabo Kye Mpisa*, 156–63.

119. Hanson, *Landed Obligation*, 45–46.

120. Mair, *African People*, 44, 234; Schmidt, *Historical Archaeology*, 63; Schmidt, *Iron Technology*, 37–38.

121. Kagwa, *Ekitabo Kye Mpisa*, 300; Kagwa, *Customs*, 158.

122. Cunningham, *Uganda and Its Peoples*, 86; Kagwa, *Customs*, 123; Roscoe, *Baganda*, 290, 300; Kifamunyanja, "Ssese: Gambuze nti agafudde e Mengo," *Munno* (October 1921), 159.

123. Feierman, "On Socially Composed Knowledge."

Chapter 4. Vigilant Python

1. But see Steven Feierman, "Concepts of Sovereignty in the Shambaa Kingdom," PhD diss., Northwestern University, 1970; Thomas C. McCaskie, *State and Society in Pre-Colonial Asante* (Cambridge: Cambridge University Press, 1995), 41, 87–88, 125, 132, 138, 140, 227–30. For legal process as a mechanism of removal see Ugo Nwokeji, *The Slave Trade and Culture in the Bight of Biafra* (Cambridge: Cambridge University Press, 2010), 132–40. As return to belonging, see Roquinaldo Ferreira, *Cross-Cultural*

Exchange in the Atlantic World (New York: Cambridge University Press, 2012), 98–125; Mariana Candido, "African Freedom Suits and Portuguese Vassal Status: Legal Mechanisms for Fighting Enslavement in Benguela, Angola, 1800–1830," *Slavery and Abolition* 32, no.3 (2011), 447–59.

2. Carola Lentz, *Land, Mobility, and Belonging in West Africa* (Bloomington: Indiana University Press, 2013), 163–65, for comparative complexities.

3. John Roscoe, *The Baganda: An Account of Their Native Customs and Beliefs* (London: Macmillan, 1911), 327–28; John F. Cunningham, *Uganda and Its Peoples* (London: Hutchinson, 1905), 218; Michael B. Nsimbi, *Amannya Amaganda N'Ennono Zaago* (Kampala: Longman Uganda, 1980), 85; Apolo Kagwa, *Ekitabo Kye Mpisa Za Baganda* (Kampala: Uganda Printing and Publishing, 1918), 228; Apolo Kagwa, *The Customs of the Baganda*, ed. May Edel, trans. Ernest B. Kalibala (New York: Columbia University Press, 1934), 123; Lawi Wakibi Sekiti, "Abaganda abe Mbale," *Munno* 6, no. 61 (1916), 7.

4. Roscoe, *Baganda*, 360–62.

5. Apolo Kaggwa, The *Kings of Buganda*, ed. and trans. M. S. M. Semakula Kiwanuka (Nairobi: East African Publishing House, 1971), 42; Apolo Kagwa, *Ekitabo Kye Bika Bya Baganda* (Kampala: Uganda Bookshop, 1949), 62–65; Roscoe, *Baganda*, 128, 140, 171; Nsimbi, *Amannya*, 209–10.

6. Max Weber, *Economy and Society*, ed. Guenther Roth and Claus Wittich (Berkeley: University of California Press, 2013), 1:33–36, 2:903.

7. David T. Doris, *Vigilant Things: On Thieves, Yoruba Anti-Aesthetics, and the Strange Fates of Ordinary Objects in Nigeria* (Seattle: University of Washington Press, 2011), 39–40.

8. Kagwa, *Customs*, 124–25; Roscoe, *Baganda*, 200, 361–62; Kagwa, *Ekitabo Kye Bika*, 21; Apollo Kagwa, *Bakabaka Bebuganda* (London: Headley Brothers Printers, 1901), 138. On mass execution, Henri Médard, "Exécutions et esclavage au Royaume de Buganda au XIXe siècle," in *Un demi-siècle d'histoire du Burundi: À Émile Mworoha, un pionnier de l'histoire africaine*, ed. Melchior Mukuri, Jean-Marie Nduwayo, and Nicodème Bugwabari (Paris: Karthala, 2017), 303–15.

9. Holly Hanson, *Landed Obligation: The Practice of Power in Buganda* (Portsmouth, NH: Heinemann, 2003), 59–91; Henri Médard, *Le royaume du Buganda au XIXe siècle* (Paris: IFRA-Karthala, 2007), 318–31; Yolamu N. Nsamba, *Mystique in Sovereigns' Headgear: A Historical Journey via Bunyoro, Uganda* (Wandsbeck: Reach, 2016), 92–173; Christian Thibon, "Croissance démographique, paysage politique et diversification culturale dans la région des Grands Lacs," in *La diffusion des plantes américaines dans la région des Grands Lacs*, ed. Elizabeth Vignati, special issue of *Les Cahiers d'Afrique de l'Est* 52 (2019), 170–91.

10. Yusufu Nakanyero, July 3, 1906, in John Roscoe and Apolo Kagwa, "Enquiry into Native Land Tenure in the Uganda Protectorate, 1906," Kampala, 1906, MSS Afr.S.17, Weston Library, University of Oxford, 79; Holly Hanson, "Mapping Conflict: Heterarchy and Accountability in the Ancient Capital of Buganda," *Journal of African History* 50, no. 2 (2009), 179–202.

11. Nakanyike B. Musisi, "Women, 'Elite Polygyny,' and Buganda State Formation," *Signs* 16, no. 4 (1991), 757–86; Rhiannon Stephens, *A History of African Motherhood: The Case of Uganda, 700–1900* (New York: Cambridge University Press, 2013), 112–44.

12. Jean-Pierre Chrétien "Les capitales royales de l'Afrique des Grands Lacs peuvent-elles être considérées comme des villes?," *Journal des Africanistes* 74, nos. 1/2 (2004), 277–98.

13. Neil Kodesh, *Beyond the Royal Gaze: Clanship and Public Healing in Buganda* (Charlottesville: University of Virginia Press, 2010), 137; Hanson, *Landed Obligation*, 65.

14. David Schoenbrun, "A Mask of Calm: Emotion and Founding the Kingdom of Bunyoro in the Sixteenth Century," *Comparative Studies in Society and History* 55, no. 3 (2013), 635, n3.

15. Kodesh, *Beyond the Royal Gaze*, 123–26; Monica Green, "Putting Africa on the Black Death Map: Narratives from Genetics and History," *Afriques: Débats, méthodes et terrains d'histoire* 9 (2018), 21.

16. Thibon, "Croissance démographique," 190–201.

17. Jan Vansina, *Antecedents to Modern Rwanda: The Nyiginya Kingdom* (Madison: University of Wisconsin Press, 2004), 38–66.

18. Thibon, "Croissance démographique," 179–81; Dennis Cordell, "Des 'réfugiés' dans l'Afrique précoloniale? L'exemple de la Centrafrique, 1850–1910," *Politique africaines* 85 (2002), 23–25.

19. Jean-Pierre Chrétien, *The Great Lakes of Africa: Two Thousand Years of History* (New York: Zone Books, 2003), 142–47, 154–58; Richard Reid, *Political Power in Pre-Colonial Buganda* (Oxford: James Currey, 2002), 177–205, 227–50.

20. M. S. M. Semakula Kiwanuka, *A History of Buganda: From the Foundation of the Kingdom to 1900* (New York: Africana Publishing, 1972), 148–52; Christopher Wrigley, *Kingship and State: The Buganda Dynasty* (Cambridge: Cambridge University Press, 1996), 230–51; Hanson, *Landed Obligation*, 75–91.

21. Kagwa, *Bakabaka Bebuganda*, 34–35 ("yagaba obwami" or "he shared authority" not "yalya," or "he ate authority"); Nsimbi, *Amannya*, 33; Kiwanuka, *History of Buganda*, 68–69, 99, 116; Wrigley, *Kingship and State*, 171–72; Hanson, *Landed Obligation*, 59–91; Médard, *Le royaume*, 47–62, 270–83, 313–67, 428–31; Kodesh, *Beyond the Royal Gaze*, 131–73; Stephens, *History of African Motherhood*, 112–15, 133–44.

22. Kiwanuka, *History of Buganda*, 112–26; Musisi, "Women, 'Elite Polygyny,'" 757–86; Stephens, *History of African Motherhood*, 133–35.

23. Wrigley, *Kingship and State*, 9.

24. Kagwa, *Ekitabo Kye Bika*, 64–65; J. T. K. G[omotoka] Sabalangira, "Atali Nanyini Mboli Asima Aliggula!," *Munno* (June 1921), 92; Kiwanuka, *History of Buganda*, 55, 69; Kodesh, *Beyond the Royal Gaze*, 38–39.

25. Kagwa, *Ekitabo Kye Bika*, 64. Anonymous, "Ekika ky'Ab'Akasimba," *Munno* 27, no. 2 (1937), inside back cover.

26. Nsimbi, "Maapu ya Buganda," inside the back cover of *Amannya*.

27. Kagwa, *Ekitabo Kye Mpisa*, 291–300.

28. Kagwa, *Ekitabo Kye Mpisa*, 298.

29. Kiwanuka, *History of Buganda*, 68–78, 112–22; Kweya, son of Sejemba and Apolo Kagwa, Katikiro, in Roscoe and Kagwa, "Enquiry," 86.

30. Kiwanuka, *History of Buganda*, 99 (quote), 116. The pre-prefix *Wa-* anthropomorphizes the object. Y. T. K. Ggomotoka, "Ab'Amasaza ge Buganda," *Munno* 16, no. 6 (1926), 103: "Till now a person of this county is called Wakayembe: because their

principal work involved carrying on the shoulders the èjjêmbe of the King called Mbajwe."

31. Kimbugwe, Kateregga's predecessor, had 9 wives, Kateregga had 309; Médard, *Le royaume*, 273; Kaggwa, *Kings*, 187–88, 203–21; Kagwa, *Ekitabo Kye Mpisa*, 26–89.

32. Wrigley, *Kingship and State*, 172, drawing on Conrad P. Kottak, "Ecological Variables in the Origin and Evolution of African States: The Buganda Example," *Comparative Studies in Society and History* 14 (1972), 374.

33. John Hanning Speke, *Journal of the Discovery of the Source of the Nile* (Edinburgh: William Blackwood, 1863), 361, 365, 369.

34. Kagwa, *Ekitabo Kye Mpisa*, 102.

35. Musisi, "Women, 'Elite Polygyny,'" 769, 777–78; Wrigley, *Kingship and State*, 171–74, for complexities.

36. Musisi, "Women, 'Elite Polygyny,'" 772–78; see also, Reid, *Political Power*, 120–30.

37. Kodesh, *Beyond the Royal Gaze*, 159–63; quotes, 161, 162. Also Koen Stroeken, *Medicinal Rule: A Historical Anthropology of Kingship in East and Central Africa* (New York: Berghahn Books, 2018).

38. Kagwa, *Ekitabo Kye Mpisa*, 40; Kaggwa, *Kings*, 38, 42–43; Roscoe, *Baganda*, 219; Sekiti, "Abaganda," 6–10; J. T. Kikulwe Gomotoka Kasumba, "Abalidde ku bwa Mukwenda n'emiziro gyabwe," *Munno* 7, no. 73 (1917), 10; Kiwanuka, *History of Buganda*, 69–70, 99–100, 116.

39. Teofiro Mulumba Kuruji, in Roscoe and Kagwa, "Enquiry," 40 ("The Ndiga's kitawi is Luoma, Katambala must be a Ndiga, but he is not the kitawi [the clanhead]"); Roscoe, *Baganda*, 154; Nsimbi, *Amannya*, 85.

40. John Roscoe, "Notes on the Manners and Customs of the Baganda," *Man: Journal of the Royal Anthropological Institute* 31 (1901), 127; Kagwa, *Ekitabo Kye Bika*, 64–65; Kiwanuka, in an editorial note, Kaggwa, *Kings*, 42; Wrigley, *Kingship and State*, 173.

41. Zachariah Kisingiri and Nuhu Mbogo, in Roscoe and Kagwa, "Enquiry," 12, 15; Y. T. K. Ggomotoka, "Ab'Amasaza," 103. During accession, royals could not seize lands controlled by the Katambala; Stanislaus Mugwanya, in Roscoe and Kagwa, "Enquiry," 9.

42. Kagwa, *Customs*, 123; Mugwanya, in Roscoe and Kagwa, "Enquiry," 7; Roscoe, *Baganda*, 154.

43. Sekiti, "Abaganda," 7; Kweya son of Sejemba, with Kagwa, in Roscoe and Kagwa, "Enquiry," 86. Tobi Kizito questions Maganyi's membership in the Lungfish clan but confirms Sekiti's claim that he stood below the Sheep clan members who founded the shrine at Bweeya; Tobi Kizito, "Atalukugendere Akusibira ya Menvu," *Munno* 7, no. 74 (1917), 26; Tobi Kizito, "Ensi Muwawa Buganda," *Munno* 5, no. 49 (1915), 6; Kaggwa, *Kings*, 43 (Mpungu and Degeya, titled figures of the Sheep clan, held the first Katambala chiefship); Kaggwa, *Kings*, 46, 53, and Kiwanuka, *History of Buganda*, 99 (Maŋanyi, a titled figure of the Sheep clan, was the Katambala after Kateregga's reign).

44. Sekiti, "Abaganda," 7; Yoanna T. K. Kasumba, "Eby'Ebuddo," *Munno* 5, no. 59 (1915), 173.

45. Roscoe, *Baganda*, 154.

46. Sekiti, "Abaganda," 7; Kizito, "Atalukugendere," 26; Nsimbi, *Amannya*, 85; Enocha Mupunga, in Roscoe and Kagwa, "Enquiry," 29. "*Kizunga* or *Luzunga*" are "the big, broad totterer." Tottering indexes the body in spirit possession. Banyoro lived in

Mawokota, a prominent member of the Bushbuck clan had an enclosure at Bweeya; see Kornelio Zerêse, "Gundi mugezi nga mubulire," *Munno* 16, no. 5 (1926), 80–81.

47. Roscoe, *Baganda*, 171; Kagwa, *Ekitabo Kye Bika*, 62, 64, 65; Anonymous, "Ekika Ky'Ab'Akasimba," inside back cover; Nsimbi, *Amannya*, 210–15.

48. Bark cloth and iron bloom were prominent; Kagwa, *Customs*, 155; Kagwa, *Ekitabo Kye Bika*, 65.

49. Nsimbi, *Amannya*, 85; Kodesh, *Beyond the Royal Gaze*, 38–39, 135–37.

50. Kiwanuka, *History of Buganda*, 116.

51. Hanson, *Landed Obligation*, 40, 45; Kodesh, *Beyond the Royal Gaze*, 160–65.

52. Jane Burbank and Frederick Cooper, *Empires in World History: Power and Politics of Difference* (Princeton, NJ: Princeton University Press, 2010), 24–31.

53. But see Okey Martin Ejidike, "Human Rights in the Cultural Traditions and Social Practice of the Igbo of Southeastern Nigeria," *Journal of African Law* 43, no. 1 (1999), 71–98; Ikenga K. E. Oraegbunam, "Crime and Punishment in Igbo Customary Law: The Challenge of Nigerian Jurisprudence," *Ogirisi: A New Journal of African Studies* 7, no. 1 (2010), 1–31.

54. Edwin Scott Haydon, "Legal Publications in an African Vernacular," *Journal of African Law* 6 (1962), 179–91; Sally Falk Moore, "Archaic Law and Modern Times on the Zambezi," *International Journal of the Sociology of Law* 7 (1979), 3–30; Simon Roberts, "Introduction: Some Notes on 'African Customary Law,'" *Journal of African Law* 28, nos. 1/2 (1984), 1–6; Martin Chanock, *Law, Custom, and Social Order* (Cambridge: Cambridge University Press, 1985); Sally Falk Moore, *Social Facts and Fabrications: "Customary Law" on Kilimanjaro, 1880–1980* (Cambridge: Cambridge University Press, 1986); Kristin Mann and Richard Roberts (eds.), *Law in Colonial Africa* (Portsmouth, NH: Heinemann, 1991).

55. Edwin Scott Haydon, *Law and Justice in Buganda* (London: Butterworths, 1960), 10, attempts a list.

56. Hamu Mukasa, in Roscoe and Kagwa, "Enquiry," 18.

57. Brett Shadle, *"Girl Cases": Marriage and Colonialism in Gussiland, Kenya, 1890–1970* (Portsmouth, NH: Heinemann, 2006).

58. Roberts, "Introduction," 1–6.

59. Steve Feierman, personal communication, April 6, 2010; also McCaskie, *State and Society*, 82–102. Speke and Stuhlmann took a greater interest in such matters than Grant, Stanley, or Chaillé-Long; Speke, *Journal*, 257, 268, 273, 275, 303, 319, 347–50; Franz Stuhlmann, *Mit Emin Pascha ins Herz von Afrika* (Berlin: Dietrich Reimer, 1894), 191–92.

60. Roscoe and Kagwa, "Enquiry," 54–67, 104–8. See also Sebald Rudolf Steinmetz, *Rechtsverhältnisse von Eingeborenen Völkern in Afrika und Oceanien* (Berlin: Springer, 1903); Andrew Lyall, "Traditional Contracts in German East Africa: The Transition from Pre-Capitalist Forms," *Journal of African Law* 30, no. 2 (1986), 91–129.

61. Kaggwa, *Kings*, 156–57.

62. Holly Hanson, "Stolen People and Autonomous Chiefs in Nineteenth-Century Buganda," in *Slavery in the Great Lakes Region of East Africa*, ed. Henri Médard and Shane Doyle (Oxford: James Currey, 2007), 161–73.

63. Steven Feierman, "Colonizers, Scholars, and the Creation of Invisible Histories," in *Beyond the Cultural Turn*, ed. Victoria E. Bonnell and Lynn Hunt (Berkeley:

University of California Press, 1999), 182–216; Jonathon Earle, "Political Activism and Other Life Forms in Colonial Buganda," *History in Africa* 45 (2018), 373–95.

64. McCaskie, *State and Society*, 87.

65. Henri Le Veux, *Premier essai de vocabulaire luganda-français d'après l'ordre étymologique* (Algiers: Imprimeries des Missionaires d'Afrique [Pères Blancs], 1917), 637, 990. Asante legislation ("hye mara"), altered judicial practice, no corollary existed in Ganda jurisprudence until after the religious wars of the 1880s, when chiefs, not royals, retooled jurisprudence to address dilemmas of *mailo* land (chapter 6); McCaskie, *State and Society*, 287.

66. "To form a line, be last to go"; George Pilkington, *Luganda-English and English-Luganda Vocabulary* (London: Society for Promoting Christian Knowledge, 1899), 99; Ronald Snoxall, *Luganda-English Dictionary* (Oxford: Clarendon Press, 1967), 280; Lucy Mair, *An African People in the Twentieth Century* (London: Routledge, 1934), 187–89.

67. Mair, *African People*, 186.

68. David L. Schoenbrun, "A Lexicon for Affect, Violence, Vulnerability, and Dispute in Eastern Bantu," in progress, RN 32 (*-dòg-*).

69. Kuruji, in Roscoe and Kagwa, "Enquiry," 43. Female captives applied their labor and reproductive power to similar ends.

70. Steven Feierman, *Peasant Intellectuals: Anthropology and History in Tanzania* (Madison: University of Wisconsin Press, 1990), 55–56; Wyatt MacGaffey, "Kongo Slavery Remembered by Themselves: Texts from 1915," *International Journal of African Historical Studies* 41, no. 1 (2008), 55–76.

71. McCaskie, *State and Society*, 123–25.

72. Mair, *African People*, 191.

73. Speke, *Journal*, 281.

74. Mair, *African People*, 185.

75. And *òkùsàlà òbulala*, "to reverse previous verdict"; Snoxall, *Luganda-English Dictionary*, 275; Robert Pickering Ashe, *Two Kings of Uganda or Life by the Shores of Victoria Nyanza* (London: Sampson, Low, Marston, 1890 [1889]), 55; Hanson, *Landed Obligation*, 67–68.

76. Broadly, *kùwozà* is "to make cold." Ideally, legal process cooled and calmed; Snoxall, *Luganda-English Dictionary*, 338–41.

77. Speke, *Journal*, 347.

78. Roscoe, *Baganda*, 263, 264.

79. Speke, *Journal*, 273.

80. Speke, *Journal*, 361.

81. Kagwa, *Ekitabo Kye Mpisa*, 244.

82. Speke, *Journal*, 420, 423.

83. Speke, *Journal*, 447.

84. Mugwanya, in Roscoe and Kagwa, "Enquiry," 109; Roscoe, *Baganda*, 257–58.

85. Kagwa, in Roscoe and Kagwa, "Enquiry," 4; Hanson, *Landed Obligation*, 82–85.

86. Médard, *Le royaume*, 301–4.

87. Zakaio Naduli Kibare, son of Sekamwa Luka & Kamya Mesusala, son of Balenkidi, in Roscoe and Kagwa, "Enquiry," 108.

88. Kuruji, in Roscoe and Kagwa, "Enquiry," 32.

89. Hanson, *Landed Obligation*, 84.

90. Kuruji, in Roscoe and Kagwa, "Enquiry," 33.

91. Kagwa, in Roscoe and Kagwa, "Enquiry," 71; Daneli Talika Kaganda, son of Lwamiti and Tomasi Chakuambala Serumaga, son of Makatu, in Roscoe and Kagwa, "Enquiry," 102; Naduli Kibare and Kamya Mesusala, in Roscoe and Kagwa, "Enquiry, 108; Kagwa, *Ekitabo Kye Mpisa*, 239, "friends" could take the poison ordeal if a party to the process was known to be susceptible to strong drink.

92. Yusufu Nakanyero, son of Kikongogo, in Roscoe and Kagwa, "Enquiry," 78.

93. Roscoe, *Baganda*, 266–67.

94. Roscoe, *Baganda*, 241ff; Aduloniko Lubebe, son of Semwaya, in Roscoe and Kagwa, "Enquiry," 98; Haydon, *Law and Justice*, 12. Kuruji, in Roscoe and Kagwa, "Enquiry," 54–55: "In the old days there were many more [courts], every man who had his own land decided cases on his land, and every elder of a butaka heard cases, now they don't. In the old days each of the men mentioned above had a katikiro etc. under them who heard cases, now they only take them up to the chief."

95. Kagwa, in Roscoe and Kagwa, "Enquiry," 2; Kagwa, *Ekitabo Kye Mpisa*, 238–39; Mair, *African People*, 187; Zakaio Naduli Kibare, son of Sekamwa Luka and Kamya Mesusula, son of Balenkedi, in Roscoe and Kagwa, "Enquiry," 104–5, gives costs for cases brought before an unnamed (i.e., unranked) chief, distinguished by the corporate standing of plaintiff and defendant.

96. *Èggombolola*: any location where disputes were settled; Haydon, *Law and Justice*, 15. *Kùgombolola* "to uncross, unravel," Le Veux, *Premier essai de vocabulaire*, 219.

97. Ashe, *Two Kings*, 54; Kagwa, *Customs*, 72, 129; Roscoe, *Baganda*, 241, 237, 258, 260, 266.

98. Kuruji, in Roscoe and Kagwa, "Enquiry," 54–55; Kiwanuka, *History of Buganda*, 124–26.

99. Roscoe, *Baganda*, 235; Hamu Mukasa, "The Rule of the Kings of Buganda," *Uganda Journal* 10, no. 2 (1946), 137.

100. Kagwa, in Roscoe and Kagwa, "Enquiry," 71: "The following women could ~~inherit~~ hold land the Nabikande, Namasole, ~~Lubuga~~, Bayomba (sister of the Nabikande) & certain other women and all Bambeja princesses" [editing in the original].

101. The number and titles of the members of the Kabaka's court changed in 1895; Apolo Kagwa, *Ekitabo Kya Basekabaka Be Buganda* (London: Sheldon Press, 1927), 206.

102. Robert W. Felkin, "Notes on the Waganda Tribe of Central Africa," *Proceedings of the Royal Society of Edinburgh* 13 (1885/1886), 723–24, 743–44; Kagwa, *Customs*, 130; Roscoe, *Baganda*, 260–66, 267.

103. Roscoe, *Baganda*, 262–63; 264; Mair, *African People*, 188. Kuruji, in Roscoe and Kagwa, "Enquiry," 50, mentions prison for a Kabaka's brothers, likely a structure Kabaka Mukaabya Mutesa had built on the Kisiinsi peninsula to confine his brothers, powerful political competitors; also Kagwa, *Bakabaka Bebuganda*, 131.

104. Speke, *Journal*, 326; Roscoe, *Baganda*, 247. Harry Johnston, *The Uganda Protectorate*, vol. 2 (London: Hutchinson, 1902), 683; Kagwa, *Customs*, 51; Nsimbi, *Amannya*, 72; Kiwanuka, *History of Buganda*, 140. Y. T. K. Ggomotoka, "Ab'Amasaza ge Buganda," *Munno* 16, no. 5 (1926), 88 ["*Katikkiro (kamala byonna)*"]."

105. Speke, *Journal*, 345.

106. Kaganda and Serumaga, in Roscoe and Kagwa, "Enquiry," 103.

107. Speke, *Journal*, 406; Henry Morton Stanley, *Through the Dark Continent*, vol. 1 (London: Sampson, Low, Marston, Searle & Rivington, 1878), 363.

108. Kagwa, *Customs*, 81, reports a "head captain" elicited a "report" from the accused about the details of the case: "Hopeless as was the situation, each proceeded to report."

109. Kagwa, *Customs*, 81–87; Roscoe, *Baganda*, 232–70, 331–38.

110. Roscoe, *Baganda*, 154, 266, 327 (connected to the Mbajjwe shrine), 338 (not connected to the Mbajjwe shrine).

111. Kagwa, *Customs*, 81–82; Roscoe, *Baganda*, 21, 202, 289, 306, 331. Èttâmbiro is derived from *kutambira* "immolate, sacrifice"; Le Veux, *Premier essai de vocabulaire*, 973*.

112. Kagwa, *Customs*, 83, 84–87; Stuhlmann, *Mit Emin Pasha*, 191; Médard, "Exécutions et esclavage," 307–9.

113. Kagwa, *Ekitabo Kye Mpisa*, 231; Kagwa, *Customs*, 124–25.

114. Kagwa, *Ekitabo Kye Mpisa*, 86–87. The same hair style worn by Ggugu, at Bubembe, and a sign of being the parent of twins.

115. Kagwa, *Customs*, 87.

116. Hanson, "Mapping Conflict," 191–201.

117. Kyabaggu, Ssemakookiro, and Ssuna II. The Kibaale, a titled position held by the Oribi clan, in a kabaka's absence, could hear cases against him, find in favor of a complainant, but not issue punishment; Zakaio Naduli Kibare, son of Sekamwa Luka, in Roscoe and Kagwa, "Enquiry," 81; Nuhu Mbogo, in Roscoe and Kagwa, "Enquiry," 15; Wrigley, *Kingship and State*, 175.

118. Kagwa, *Ekitabo Kye Mpisa*, 4–14, 19; Benjamin Ray, *Myth, Ritual, and Kingship in Buganda* (Oxford: Oxford University Press, 1991), 78–91; Kodesh, *Beyond the Royal Gaze*, 135–38, 157–58.

119. Kagwa, *Ekitabo Kye Bika*, 66; Kizito, "Atalukugendere," 26; but see Sekiti, "Abaganda," 7.

120. Kaggwa, *Kings*, 43; Kagwa, *Ekitabo Kye Mpisa*, 40; Nsimbi, *Amannya*, 85.

121. Stanislaus Mugwanya and Zacariah Kisingiri, in Roscoe and Kagwa, "Enquiry," 7, 11. Stanley, *Through the Dark Continent*, vol. 1, 311.

122. David Lee Schoenbrun, *The Historical Reconstruction of Great Lakes Bantu Cultural Vocabulary: Etymologies and Distributions* (Köln: Rüdiger Köppe Press, 1997), 218.

123. Anonymous, "Ekika Ky'Ab'Entalaganya," 222; John Musaazi, "Baganda Traditional Divination and Treament of People's Trouble," Religious Studies Occasional Paper No. 8, Kampala, Makerere University, 1968–69; Peter Rigby and Fred Lule, "Continuity and Change in Kiganda Religion in Urban and Peri Urban Kampala," in *Town and Country in Central and Eastern Africa*, ed. David Parkin (London: International African Institute, 1975), 213–27.

124. Medard, *Le royaume*, 323; Roscoe, *Baganda*, 323–29.

125. David Lee Schoenbrun, *A Green Place, a Good Place: Agrarian Change, Gender, and Social Organization between the Great Lakes to 1500* (Portsmouth, NH: Heinemann, 1998), 37–52.

126. Speke, *Journal*, 259, 372.

127. Doris, *Vigilant Things*, 1–58, 138 (quote).

128. Doris, *Vigilant Things*, 134. Other classes of object—*ekyonzira, ensiriba*—were so placed.

129. Speke, *Journal*, 285 (quote), 292.

130. Speke, *Journal*, 372.

131. Roscoe, *Baganda*, 324; Speke, *Journal*, 406.

132. Roscoe, *Baganda*, 325. People used exotic power objects to outdo adversaries because their histories of efficacy were unknown locally; A. Mukanga, "The Traditional Belief in Balubaale," *Occasional Research Papers in African Religions and Philosophies* 167 (1974), 9, Vertical Files, Melville J. Herskovits Library of African Studies, Northwestern University; Médard, *Le royaume*, 322.

133. Felkin, "Notes," 760–61; emphasis added.

134. Georg Schweinfurth, Friedrich Ratzel, Richard W. Felkin, Gustav Hartlaub, (eds.) *Emin Pasha in Central Africa: Being a Collection of His Letters and Journals*, trans. Mrs. Richard W. Felkin (Boston: Dodd, Mead, 1889), 47.

135. Roscoe, *Baganda*, 328; Sekiti, "Abaganda," 7; Nsimbi, *Amannya*, 85.

136. Le Veux, *Premier essai de vocabulaire*, 619 (quote, translation mine); Charles T. Wilson, *An Outline Grammar of the Luganda Language* (London: Society for Promoting Christian Knowledge, 1882), 129 ("a venomous species of snake"); Roscoe, *Baganda*, 327; Cunningham, *Uganda and Its Peoples*, 218; Snoxall, *Luganda-English Dictionary*, 202.

137. In the passive, plus -e as a suffix of manner: "carved thing" or "human-made wooden thing"; Le Veux, *Premier essai de vocabulaire*, 27–28, 619; Eridadi M. K. Mulira and G. M. Ndawula, *A Luganda-English and English-Luganda Dictionary* (London: Society for Promoting Christian Knowledge, 1952), 3.

138. Kagwa, *Ekitabo Kye Mpisa*, 283–92; Kasirye Zzibukulimbwa, "The Beginning of Nalubaale," trans. Bakaaki Robert and Jennifer Lee Johnson (Kampala: PDF, 2012), 4.

139. Doris, *Vigilant Things*, 183.

140. Derived from *kùkka* (itr.) "go down, descend; sink; be paralyzed (children)" by adding the prefix, *nna-*, "mother of," and the suffix /*ul*/, making a noun of quality.

141. Wrigley, *Kingship and State*, 178.

142. Kagwa, *Bakabaka Bebuganda*, 26; Kaggwa, *Kings*, 31.

143. Kagwa, *Ekitabo Kye Bika*, 26; Nsimbi, *Amannya*, 41–44, 194–95.

144. Wrigley, *Kingship and State*, 141–42, 144, 147–48; Kodesh, *Beyond the Royal Gaze*, 105–21.

145. Roscoe, *Baganda*, 275 and Kodesh, *Beyond the Royal Gaze*, 58–59, 63–64, 110.

146. Roscoe, *Baganda*, 145; Anonymous, "Ab'effumbe (Akabbiro: Kikere)," *Munno* 25, no. 4 (1935), inside front cover; Nsimbi, *Amannya*, 194; Kodesh, *Beyond the Royal Gaze*, 100–102, 214, n3.

147. Kagwa, *Ekitabo Kye Bika*, 26.

148. Renee Louise Tantala, "Early History of Kitara in Western Uganda: Process Models of Religious and Political Change, 2 Parts," PhD diss., University of Wisconsin–Madison, 1989, 143–44, 402, 707–8.

149. Roscoe, *Baganda*, 309.

150. Roscoe, *Baganda*, 309 (quotes).

151. Kagwa, *Ekitabo Kye Mpisa*, 24.

152. Kagwa, *Customs*, 17.

153. Kagwa, *Ekitabo Kye Bika*, 26; Roscoe, *Baganda*, 211; Kagwa, *Ekitabo Kye Mpisa*, 26.

154. Anonymous, "Ab'effumbe (Akabbiro: Kikere)," inside front cover; Nsimbi, *Amannya*, 52, 194–95.

155. Kagwa, *Ekitabo Kye Mpisa*, 213.

156. Green, "Putting Africa," 21–23.

157. Kagwa, *Ekitabo Kye Mpisa*, 27, 28, 30.

158. Kagwa, *Ekitabo Kye Bika*, 44, implies others existed; Pangolin clan history claims "Kabumba" from "Kavule" fashioned an èjjêmbe out of "clay" for a kabaka called "Mbajwe."

159. Mair, *African People*, 243, "copies never rival the potency of the original."

160. Roscoe, *Baganda*, 328; Kagwa, *Ekitabo Kye Mpisa*, 228.

161. Kiwanuka, *History of Buganda*, 109; Wrigley, *Kingship and State*, 182–229, esp.182–84; Reid, *Political Power*, 177–205, 227–48, esp.185–90; Hanson, *Landed Obligation*, 74.

162. Wrigley, *Kingship and State*, 182–214; Kodesh, *Beyond the Royal Gaze*, 143–54; Richard Reid, "The Reign of Kabaka Nakibinge: Myth or Watershed?," *History in Africa* 24 (1997), 287–97.

163. Kagwa, *Bakabaka Bebuganda*, 21–22; Henri Le Veux, *Manuel de langue luganda*, 2nd ed. (Algiers: Maison-Carré, 1914), 271–72, used the verb *okutunda* or to sell. Le Veux's sources described Kibuuka as having scarred shoulders and playing the lapharp (*ènnanga*). The Ènnanga represents tale singing, the scars were from smallpox.

164. M. S. M. Semakula Kiwanuka, "Introduction," in Apolo Kaggwa, *The Kings of Buganda*, ed. and trans. M. S. M. Semakula Kiwanuka (Nairobi: East African Publishing House, 1971), xxvii.

165. Kodesh, *Beyond the Royal Gaze*, 143–54, 225, n28.

166. Wrigley, *Kingship and State*, 210–15; Reid, *Political Power*, 181–85.

167. One version has Gabunga (Lungfish clan) initiating Kibuuka's recruitment, evoking the sewn canoe fleets Gabunga controlled; Le Veux, *Manuel de langue luganda*, 271–78. Isaiah Kunsa claimed that Mugema (Monkey clan) had controlled these networks, with Gabunga serving him, in Roscoe and Kagwa, "Enquiry," 93.

168. Y. T. Kikulwe Kasumba, "Ebye Buddo Ebikolebwa ku Basekabaka," *Munno* 5, no. 58 (1915), 156–59; Kasumba, "Eby'Ebuddo," 174, 175; Y. Kikulwe Kasumba, "Ebye Buddo," *Munno* 5, no. 60 (1915), 188–91.

169. Nsimbi, *Amannya*, 85 (Mpungu's estates in Bweeya). Enocha Mupunga and Luminsa, in Roscoe and Kagwa, "Enquiry," 29–30 (Gabunga's chief estate in Bweeya).

170. Ray, *Myth, Ritual*, 86–89; Wrigley, *Kingship and State*, 183; Kodesh, *Beyond the Royal Gaze*, 137–38.

171. Hanson, *Landed Obligation*, 81. Kweya, son of Sejemba and Apolo Kagwa, in Roscoe and Kagwa, "Enquiry," 86, include Kateregga in a sequence of kings who created counties (*àmàsaza*) ruled by members of clans other than those dominant in the territory.

172. Stanley, *Through the Dark Continent*, vol. 1, 344; Kodesh, *Beyond the Royal Gaze*, 138–43.

173. This account relies on Stanley, *Through the Dark Continent*, vol. 1, 351–58.

174. Holly Hanson, "Review of Christopher Wrigley, *Kingship and State: The Buganda Dynasty*," *African Studies Review* 42, no. 3 (1999), 139–40.

Chapter 5. Ladies and Slaves

1. Richard J. Reid, *Political Power in Pre-Colonial Buganda* (Oxford: James Currey, 2002), 179ff; William Fitzsimons, "Warfare, Competition, and the Durability of 'Political Smallness' in Nineteenth-Century Busoga," *Journal of African History* 59, no. 1 (2018), 58–59.

2. Rhiannon Stephens, *A History of African Motherhood: The Case of Uganda, 700–1900* (Cambridge: Cambridge University Press, 2013), 166–74; Richard J. Reid, *A History of Modern Uganda* (Cambridge: Cambridge University Press, 2017), 148–49.

3. Michael Wright, *Buganda in the Heroic Age* (Oxford: Oxford University Press, 1971), 222, 223; Michael Twaddle, *Kakungulu and the Creation of Uganda, 1868–1928* (Oxford: James Currey, 1993), 15–16, for complexities.

4. John Mary Waliggo, *The Catholic Church in the Buddu Province of Buganda, 1879–1925* (Kampala: Angel Agencies, 2010), 199.

5. John Peel, *Religious Encounter and the Making of the Yoruba* (Bloomington: Indiana University Press, 2003), 44–46; Derek R. Peterson and Giacomo Macola, "Introduction: Homespun Historiography and the Academic Profession," in *Recasting the Past: History Writing and Political Work in Modern Africa*, ed. Derek R. Peterson and Giacomo Macolo (Athens: Ohio University Press, 2009), 7–15; Carola Lentz, *Land, Mobility, and Belonging in West Africa* (Bloomington: Indiana University Press, 2013), 1–6; Jan Bender Shetler, *Claiming Civic Virtue: Gendered Network Memory in the Mara Region, Tanzania* (Madison: University of Wisconsin Press, 2019), 11.

6. Pamela Khanakwa, "Male Circumcision among the Bagisu of Eastern Uganda: Practices and Conceptualization," in *Doing Conceptual History in Africa*, ed. Axel Fleisch and Rhiannon Stephens (New York: Berghahn Books, 2016), 115–37.

7. Luise White, *The Comforts of Home: Prostitution in Colonial Nairobi* (Chicago: University of Chicago Press, 1990), 6–21; Heidi Gengenbach, "Living Ethnicity: Gender, Livelihood, and Ethnic Identity in Mozambique," in *Gendering Ethnicity in African Women's Lives*, ed. Jan Bender Shetler (Madison: University of Wisconsin Press, 2015), 57–83; Shetler, *Claiming Civic Virtue*, 12–28.

8. Caitlin Monroe noticed this, making its reconfiguration central to her work in Uganda. Caitlin Monroe, "Making History: Women's Knowledge and the Creation of a Historical Discipline in Western Uganda, 1800–1980," PhD diss., Northwestern University, in progress; Lentz, *Land, Mobility*, 23–24; Jan Bender Shetler, *Imagining Serengeti: A history of Landscape Memory in Tanzania* (Athens: Ohio University Press, 2007), 11.

9. Sandra E. Greene, "Family Concerns: Gender and Ethnicity in Pre-Colonial West Africa," *International Review of Social History* 44, S7 (1999), 15–31.

10. White, *Comforts of Home*, 185–220; Carol Summers, "Intimate Colonialism: The Imperial Production of Reproduction in Uganda, 1907–1925," *Signs* 16, no. 4 (1991), 787–807; John Lonsdale, "The Moral Economy of Mau Mau," in Bruce Berman and John Lonsdale, *Violence and Ethnicity*, book 2 of *Unhappy Valley: Conflict in Kenya and Africa* (Athens: Ohio University Press, 1992), 315–504; Nakanyike B. Musisi, "Gender and the Cultural Construction of 'Bad Women' in the Development of Kampala-Kibuga, 1900–1962," in *"Wicked" Women and the Reconfiguration of Gender in Africa*, ed. Dorothy L. Hodgson and Sheryl A. McCurdy (Portsmouth, NH: Heinemann,

2001), 171–87; Derek Peterson, "Wordy Women: Gender Trouble and the Oral Politics of the East African Revival in Northern Gikuyuland," *Journal of African History* 42, no. 3 (2001), 469–89.

11. Shetler, *Claiming Civic Virtue*, 5–12.

12. Linzi Manicom, "Ruling Relations: Rethinking State and Gender in South African History," *Journal of African History* 33, no. 3 (1992), 441–65; Sean Hanretta, "Women, Marginality and the Zulu State: Women's Institutions and Power in the Early Nineteenth Century," *Journal of African History* 39, no. 3 (1998), 389–415; Holly Hanson, "Queen Mothers and Good Government in Buganda: The Loss of Women's Political Power in Nineteenth-Century East Africa," in *Women in African Colonial Histories*, ed. Jean Allman, Susan Geiger, and Nakanyike B. Musisi (Bloomington: Indiana University Press, 2002), 219–36; Emily Lynn Osborn, *Our New Husbands Are Here: Households, Gender, and Politics in a West African State from the Slave Trade to Colonial Rule* (Athens: Ohio University Press, 2011), 1–20; Raevin Jimenez, "Rites of Reproduction: Gender, Generation and Political Economic Transformation among Nguni-Speakers of Southern Africa, 8th–19th Century CE," PhD diss., Northwestern University, 2017, 172–248.

13. Apolo Kagwa, *Ekitabo Kye Mpisa Za Baganda* (Kampala: Uganda Printing and Publishing, 1918), 152–63; Henri Médard, *Le royaume du Buganda au XIXe siècle* (Paris: IFRA-Karthala, 2007), 255–62; Reid, *Political Power*, 113–20, 177–205.

14. Stephens, *History of African Motherhood*, 134.

15. Neil Kodesh, *Beyond the Royal Gaze: Clanship and Public Healing in Buganda* (Charlottesville: University of Virginia Press, 2010), 98–130; David William Cohen, *Womunafu's Bunafu: A Study of Authority in a Nineteenth-Century African Community* (Princeton, NJ: Princeton University Press, 1977), 131–65.

16. Nakanyike B. Musisi, "Women, 'Elite Polygyny,' and Buganda State Formation," *Signs* 16, no. 4 (1991), 757–87, extending Karen Brodkin Sacks, *Sisters and Wives: The Past and Future of Sexual Equality* (Boulder, CO: Westview Press, 1979), 198–215.

17. Holly Hanson, "Stolen People and Autonomous Chiefs in Nineteenth-Century Buganda: The Social Consequences of Non-Free Followers," in *Slavery in the Great Lakes Region*, ed. Henri Médard and Shane Doyle (Oxford: James Currey, 2007), 161–73; Hanson, "Queen Mothers," 219.

18. Sylvia Nannyonga-Tamusuza, "Female-Men, Male-Women, and Others: Constructing and Negotiating Gender among the Baganda of Uganda," *Journal of Eastern African Studies* 3, no. 2 (2009), 371–75.

19. Apolo Kaggwa, *The Kings of Buganda*, ed. and trans. M. S. M. Semakula Kiwanuka (Nairobi: East African Publishing House, 1971), 147 (gendered bark cloth).

20. Damascus Kafumbe, *Tuning the Kingdom: Kawuugulu Musical Performance, Politics, and Storytelling in Buganda* (Rochester: University of Rochester Press, 2018), 80–94.

21. Hanson, "Queen Mothers," 226–31.

22. Isaiah Kunsa, son of Kyojo, in John Roscoe and Apolo Kagwa, "Enquiry into Native Land Tenure in the Uganda Protectorate, 1906," Kampala, 1906, 94, MSS Afr.s.17, Weston Library, University of Oxford.

23. Kaggwa, *Kings*, 104; Apollo Kagwa, *Bakabaka Bebuganda* (London: Headley Brothers Printers, 1901), 93.

24. John Roscoe, *The Baganda: An Account of Their Native Customs and Beliefs* (London: Macmillan, 1911), 111, 191 (different mother); Stephens, *History of African Motherhood*, 139.

25. Roscoe, *Baganda*, 283–84; Y[osia] N[jovu], "Ebyafa mu Kyagwe mu Mirembe gy'edda: Okuwangulwa kwa Kyagwe—N'okufa kwa kabaka Kimera," *Munno* 3, no. 31 (1913), 109.

26. Kaggwa, *Kings*, 201–2; Kagwa, *Ekitabo Kye Mpisa*, 102.

27. Roscoe, *Baganda*, 83.

28. Stanislaus Mugwanya, in Roscoe and Kagwa, "Enquiry," 9; Roscoe, *Baganda*, 66, 84, 187, 236–37; Kagwa, *Ekitabo Kye Mpisa*, 26–100; Holly Hanson, "Mapping Conflict: Heterarchy and Accountability in the Ancient Capital of Buganda," *Journal of African History* 50, no. 2 (2009), 179–202; Stephens, *History of African Motherhood*, 133–44.

29. Stephens, *History of African Motherhood*, 139; Martin Southwold, "Succession to the Throne in Buganda," in *Succession to High Office*, ed. Jack Goody (Cambridge: Cambridge University Press, 1966), 82–126, esp. 83–89.

30. Stephens, *History of African Motherhood*, 126, 133–44.

31. Hanson, "Queen Mothers," 223.

32. Christopher Wrigley, *Kingship and State: The Buganda Dynasty* (Cambridge: Cambridge University Press, 1996), 221–22; Stephens, *History of African Motherhood*, 116–30.

33. Kagwa, in Roscoe and Kagwa, "Enquiry," 3–4.

34. Kagwa, *Bakabaka Bebuganda*, 53–56; P. M. Gulu, "Ekika: ab'Effumbe n'ab'Enjovu Bagatta," *Munno* 6, no. 67 (1916), 118.

35. Kiwanuka, commentary, in Kaggwa, *Kings*, 65–66; Wrigley, *Kingship and State*, 187–88.

36. Kagwa, *Ekitabo Kye Mpisa*, 54–60; Apolo Kagwa, *Ekitabo Kye Bika Bya Baganda* (Kampala: Uganda Bookshop, 1949 [1912]), 54 (Nanteza bore Jjunju and Ssemakookiro); Alfonsi Aliwali, "Ka tulojje: Olutalo lw'Abakunta abatta Jjuunju," *Munno* 4, no. 39 (1924), 38 (Nanteza bore Ssemakookiro, Nnamisango bore Jjunju).

37. M. S. M. Semakula Kiwanuka, *History of Buganda: From the Foundation of the Kingdom to 1900* (New York: Africana, 1972), 80–81; David William Cohen, *The Historical Tradition of Busoga: Mukama and Kintu* (Oxford: Clarendon Press, 1972), 135.

38. Kagwa, *Bakabaka Bebuganda*, 77, 78; Alfonsi Aliwali, "Bwakamba Mukudde: 'Omudzukulu eyatta. Mukudde,'" *Munno* 4, no. 37 (1914), 7–9; Alfonsi Aliwali, "Ka tulojje: Kabaka Mulondo," *Munno* 4, no. 38 (1914), 20–23; Joseph S. Kasirye, *Abateregga ku Nnamulondo y'e Buganda* (London: Macmillan, 1955), 32; Kiwanuka, commentary, in Kaggwa, *Kings*, 91.

39. Kiwanuka, *History*, 88 (quote); Luyi Kaggwa, "Abakunta," *Munno* 20 [*sic*], no. 109 (1920), 7–8; John T. K. Ggomotoka, "History of Buvuma Islands," trans. David Kiyaga-Mulindwa (Kampala: Typescript, 1937–38), Bugaya Island, 26.

40. Kagwa, *Bakabaka Bebuganda*, 81; Apolo Kagwa, *Ekitabo Kya Basekabaka Be Buganda* (London: Sheldon Press, 1927), 69.

41. Roland Oliver, "The Baganda and the Bakonjo," *Uganda Journal* 18, no. 1 (1954), 31–32; Henry Okello Ayot, *A History of the Luo-Abasuba of Western Kenya, from A.D. 1760–1940* (Nairobi: Kenya Literature Bureau, 1979), 4–22.

42. Bethwell Alan Ogot, *History of the Southern Luo*, vol. 1 (Nairobi: East African Publishing House, 1967), 212–13; Aliwali, "Ka Tulojje: Olutalo," 38–40; Aliwali, "Ka Tulojje: Olutalo," *Munno* 4, no. 40 (1914), 57–58.

43. Kagwa, *Bakabaka Bebuganda*, 66–72.

44. Michael G. Kenny, "Basuba Historical Narratives" (n.p.: n.p., 1978), L VI398.2/420392, School of Oriental and African Studies Library, University of London, Testimony of Mzee Kakunglu [*sic*] Mmanye, Rusinga Island, 1969, 3 (Buvuma); Mzee Ekana Ochola, Kaswanga, Rusinga Island, 15 (Busoga); Kidera Ogaja, Wagimbe Mfangano Island, 1973, 49 (Jjinja, then Sigulu Island); and so forth.

45. Kiwanuka, *History*, 86; Hanson, "Queen Mothers," 223–24; Stephens, *History of African Motherhood*, 135–36.

46. Kaggwa, *Kings*, 91.

47. Ssemakookiro attacked relatives, including sons; Kagwa, *Bakabaka Bebuganda*, 85–91; Kiwanuka, *History*, 129.

48. Apolo Kagwa, "Chronology of Buganda, 1800–1907, from Kagwa's Ebika," trans. Abubakar M. Kakyama Mayanja, *Uganda Journal* 16, no. 2 (1952), 149.

49. Cohen, *Womunafu's Bunafu*, 73–79; Kiwanuka, *History*, 139–43.

50. Kaggwa, *Kings*, 108.

51. Musisi, "Gender and the Cultural Construction," 173–74; Roscoe, *Baganda*, 20, 23, 263.

52. Kaggwa, *Kings*, 136. Kagwa, *Bakabaka Bebuganda*, 128–29; Stephens, *History of African Motherhood*, 171. Nabinaka was Ssuuna II's father's sister (*ssèngâ*), a position of authority over her nieces and any junior woman.

53. Roscoe, *Baganda*, 111, 186. Ancient ties to Bunyoro (Kagwa, *Ekitabo Kye Mpisa*, 19–26) undergird this clearly post-Speke sensibility to phenotypical categories of royal male desire.

54. Kaggwa, *Kings*, 179, n53.

55. Kagwa, *Ekitabo Kya Basekabaka*, 118, "Obwakabaka bwa kitalo, anti buziba abantu amatu" or "Being a kabaka is a marvel, it stops up people's ears." It makes them selfish. He did not use the phrase in Kagwa, *Bakabaka Bebuganda*, 136–39.

56. Kiwanuka, *History*, 128–36 (details).

57. Kaggwa, *Kings*, 148.

58. Roscoe, *Baganda*, 93, 111, 186.

59. Around 1860; Kiwanuka, *History*, 134.

60. Kaggwa, *Kings*, 149 (quotes).

61. Kaggwa, *Kings*, 149–50.

62. Kagwa, *Bakabaka Bebuganda*, 137–38.

63. John Hanning Speke, *Journal of the Discovery of the Source of the Nile* (Edinburgh: William Blackwood, 1863), 312–13; John F. Cunningham, *Uganda and Its Peoples* (London: Hutchinson, 1905), 184, 189; Stephens, *History of African Motherhood*, 172–75.

64. Speke, *Journal*, 295; to prevent them from reporting its contents to Muganzirwazza.

65. Speke, *Journal*, 305, 305–7, 310–17, 333–34, 353, 360–63.

66. Speke, *Journal*, 308, 313, 314.

67. Speke, *Journal*, 316 (quote), 319.

68. Kaggwa, *Kings*, 157, on Mukaabya Muteesa's Islam; Wright, *Buganda in the Heroic Age*, 1–38. Holly Hanson, *Landed Obligation: The Practice of Power in Buganda* (Portsmouth, NH: Heinemann, 2003), 93–126; Médard, *Le royaume*, 432–45.

69. Kaggwa, *Kings*, 157.

70. Kagwa, *Bakabaka Bebuganda*, 145–46. "Kitunzi" ("the big seller"), a titled chief in Ggomba held by the Lion clan.

71. Kaggwa, *Kings*, 163.

72. Reid, *History of Modern Uganda*, 143–45.

73. Kiwanuka, *History*, 188.

74. Kaggwa, *Kings*, 179, 181–82.

75. Kaggwa, *Kings*, 180.

76. Kagwa, *Bakabaka Bebuganda*, 157–62; Robert Pickering Ashe, *Chronicles of Uganda* (London: Hodder and Stoughton, 1894), 66, 68; Reid, *History of Modern Uganda*, 154–60.

77. Samwiri Lwanga Lunyiigo, *Mwanga II: Resistance to Imposition of British Colonial Rule in Buganda, 1884–99* (Kampala: Wavah Books, 2011), 102–15.

78. Cunningham, *Uganda and Its Peoples*, 184. Her name was Gwolyoka ("it left") and the buyers were "Abalung'ana," or Waungwana caravan traders from the Indian Ocean coast; Ham Mukasa, "Ebifa ku Mulembe gwa Kabaka Mutesa," *Uganda Journal* 1, no. 2 (1934), 118–19; Stephens, *History of African Motherhood*, 173.

79. Wright, *Buganda in the Heroic Age*, 5.

80. The Pangolin clan could depart from this practice; Yusufu Nakanyero, son of Kikongogo, in Roscoe and Kagwa, "Enquiry," 79.

81. Lazaro Kanabi, son of Pokino, in Roscoe and Kagwa, "Enquiry," 72; Roscoe, *Baganda*, 117.

82. Stanislaus Mugwanya, in Roscoe and Kagwa, "Enquiry," 73.

83. Kagwa, *Bakabaka Bebuganda*, 156; Kaggwa, *Kings*, 182.

84. Kaggwa, *Kings*, 27.

85. Medard, *Le royaume*, 259; Stephens, *History of African Motherhood*, 133–34.

86. Teofiro Mulumba Kuruji, in Roscoe and Kagwa. "Enquiry," 31–67; Kiwanuka, *History*, 114–24.

87. Daphne Gallagher, "American Plants in Sub-Saharan Africa: A Review of the Archaeological Evidence," *Azania: Archaeological Research in Africa* 51, no. 1 (2016), 44; Emile Mworoha, "Monarchies, plantes, et rituels agraire dans l'Afrique des Grands Lacs est-africains (XVe–XIXe siècles)," in *La diffusion des plantes américaines dans la région des Grands Lacs*, ed. Elizabeth Vignati, special issue of *Les Cahiers d'Afrique de l'Est* 52 (2019), 68; Christian Thibon, "Croissance démographique, paysage politique et diversification culturale dans la région des Grands Lacs," in *La diffusion des plantes américaines dans la region des Grands Lacs*, ed. Elizabeth Vignati, special issue of *Les Cahiers d'Afrique de l'Est* 52 (2019), 190–94.

88. Kagwa, *Ekitabo Kye Mpisa*, 156.

89. Thibon, "Croissance démographique, 162, 170–71, 179.

90. Kagwa, *Bakabaka Bebuganda*, 78.

91. Roscoe, *Baganda*, 404; V. C. K. Nyanzi-Makumbi, "The Story of Barkcloth in Buganda," BA thesis, Makerere University, 1976.

92. Kuruji, in Roscoe and Kagwa, "Enquiry," 48; Kiwanuka, Table IX, in Kaggwa, *Kings*, 201–22.

93. Stephens, *History of African Motherhood*, 90–91; Henri Le Veux, *Premier essai de vocabulaire luganda-français d'après l'ordre étymologique* (Algiers: Imprimeries des Missionaires d'Afrique [Pères Blancs], 1917), 707; Roscoe, *Baganda*, 83, no mention of nnálúgóngó, 86, 135.

94. Kagwa, *Bakabaka Bebuganda*, 35–37; Roscoe, *Baganda*, 13; Apolo Kagwa, *Customs of the Baganda*, ed. May Edel, trans. Ernest B. Kalibala (New York: Columbia University Press, 1934), 89; Kagwa, *Ekitabo Kye Mpisa*, 155, àbàsebeyî a kind of woman or wife (òmùkazì) in describing military labor. Early in the twentieth century, the term meant women going to war to serve royals and chiefs; Le Veux, *Premier essai de vocabulaire*, 849. By the 1960s, the term also meant any woman who traveled with her husband; Eridadi M. K. Mulira and E. G. M. Ndawula, *A Luganda-English and English-Luganda Dictionary* (London: Society for Promoting Christian Knowledge, 1952), 98; Ronald A. Snoxall, *Luganda-English Dictionary* (Oxford: Clarendon Press, 1967), 278.

95. Kagwa, *Ekitabo Kye Mpisa*, 155–56.

96. Michael Twaddle, "Slaves and Peasants in Buganda," in *Slavery and Other Forms of Unfree Labour*, ed. Leonie Archer (London: Routledge, 1988), 118–29; Reid, *Political Power*, 124–30; David Schoenbrun, "Violence, Marginality, Scorn, and Honour: Language Evidence of Slavery to the Eighteenth Century," in *Slavery in the Great Lakes Region of East Africa*, ed. Henri Médard and Shane Doyle (Oxford: James Currey, 2007), 46–49, 60.

97. Stephens, *History of African Motherhood*, 134; Michael Tuck, "Women's Experiences of Enslavement and Slavery in Late Nineteenth- and Early Twentieth-Century Uganda," in *Slavery in the Great Lakes Region of East Africa*, ed. Henri Médard and Shane Doyle (Oxford: James Currey, 2007), 174–88.

98. Roscoe, *Baganda*, 121.

99. Kuruji, in Roscoe and Kagwa, "Enquiry," 41–42, 49.

100. Roscoe, *Baganda*, 14.

101. Roscoe, *Baganda*, 83.

102. Kagwa, *Ekitabo Kye Mpisa*, 153.

103. Kagwa, *Ekitabo Kye Mpisa*, 160–61.

104. Roscoe, *Baganda*, 324. If the kaddulubaalè outlived her husband, she ran the house built over his burial place, echoing a nnaalinnya; Alexander M. Mackay, by His Sister, *A. M. Mackay, Pioneer Missionary of the Church Missionary Society in Uganda* (New York: A. C. Armstrong, 1890), 196.

105. Dent Ocyaya-Lakidi, "Manhood, Warriorhood and Sex in Eastern Africa," in *The Warrior Tradition in Modern Africa*, ed. Ali A. Mazrui (Leiden: Brill, 1977), 134–65; Luise White, "Separating the Men from the Boys: Constructions of Sexuality, Gender, and Terrorism in Central Kenya, 1939–1959," *International Journal of African Historical Studies* 23, no. 1 (1990), 1–26; Dorothy Hodgson, "Being Maasai Men: Modernity and the Production of Maasai Masculinities," in *Men and Masculinities in Modern Africa*, ed. Lisa A. Lindsay and Stephan F. Miescher (Portsmouth, NH: Heinemann, 2003), 211–29; Fitzsimons, "Warfare, Competition," 51, 59; Jimenez, "Rites of Reproduction," 172–211.

106. Roscoe, *Baganda*, 14; Kagwa, *Bakabaka Bebuganda*, 85–144.

107. Ali A. Mazrui, "Introduction," in *The Warrior Tradition in Modern Africa*, ed. Ali A. Mazrui (Leiden: Brill, 1977), 2.

108. Richard Reid, *War in Pre-Colonial Eastern Africa* (Oxford: James Currey, 2007), 205–12; John Iliffe, *Honour in African History* (Cambridge: Cambridge University Press, 2005), 4–5; Rachel Taylor, "Crafting Cosmopolitanism: Nyamwezi Male Labor, Acquisition and Honor c. 1750–1914," PhD diss., Northwestern University, 2017, chap. 1.

109. John Roscoe, *The Bakitara or Banyoro* (Cambridge: Cambridge University Press, 1923), 312.

110. Kagwa, *Customs*, 93; Roscoe, *Baganda*, 361–62.

111. Roscoe, *Baganda*, 66; Kagwa, *Ekitabo Kye Mpisa*, 189–94.

112. Roscoe, *Baganda*, 83, 125.

113. Roscoe, *Baganda*, 66, 83; Le Veux, *Premier essai de vocabulaire*, 558; Lucy Mair, *An African People in the Twentieth Century* (London: Routledge, 1934), 212–14.

114. Stephens, *History of African Motherhood*, 141.

115. Gomotoka, "History of Buvuma," Mpata Island, 5–7.

116. Kagwa, *Ekitabo Kye Mpisa*, 171–80, esp. 171–77; Roscoe, *Baganda*, 82–97, 101–3.

117. Mugwanya, in Roscoe and Kagwa, "Enquiry," 73, "A woman never succeeded to land, except princesses."

118. Roscoe, *Baganda*, 14; Nuhu Mbogo, in Roscoe and Kagwa, "Enquiry," 14.

119. Roscoe, *Baganda*, 324; Kagwa, *Customs*, 89.

120. L. K. Bagimba, "Emizimu, Emisambwa, Enkuuni, Ebisweezi, Balubaale," Collected Texts of Busoga Traditional History, cited in Cohen, *Historical Tradition*, 19.

121. Kagwa, *Ekitabo Kye Mpisa*, 155; Roscoe, *Baganda*, 48, 144, 357.

122. Roscoe, *Baganda*, 48–49; Kagwa, *Ekitabo Kye Mpisa*, 155–56.

123. Roscoe, *Baganda*, 18.

124. Roscoe, *Bakitara*, 309.

125. John Roscoe, *The Bagesu and Other Tribes of the Uganda Protectorate* (Cambridge: Cambridge University Press, 1924), 120.

126. Roscoe, *Baganda*, 56–57, 69, 70.

127. Roscoe, *Baganda*, 61–64; Viktoro Katula, "Abadzukulu ba Sekabaka Kagulu," *Munno* 15, no. 1 (1925), 12–13.

128. Kuruji, in Roscoe and Kagwa, "Enquiry," 58–59, 61.

129. Roscoe, *Baganda*, 30, 48, 164, 289, 310, 402.

130. Cora Ann Presley, "Kikuyu Women and the Mau Mau Rebellion," in *In Resistance: Studies in African, Caribbean, and Afro-American History*, ed. Gary Y. Okihiro (Amherst: University of Massachusetts Press, 1986), 115–37; Luise White, "Matrimony and Rebellion: Masculinity in Mau Mau," in *Men and Masculinities in Modern Africa*, ed. Lisa A. Lindsay and Stephan F. Miescher (Portsmouth, NH: Heinemann, 2003), 163–87.

131. Dylan Penningroth, "The Claims of Slaves and Ex-Slaves to Family and Property: A Transatlantic Comparison," *American Historical Review* 112, no. 4 (2007), 1047; Sandra Greene, "Introduction," in *West African Narratives of Slavery: Texts from Late Nineteenth- and Early Twentieth-Century Ghana*, ed. Sandra Greene (Bloomington: Indiana University Press, 2011), 1–18.

132. Henry Morton Stanley, *Through the Dark Continent*, vol. 1 (London: Sampson, Low, Marston, Searle & Rivington, 1878), 365, 369.

133. Kaggwa, *Kings*, 140; Kagwa, *Bakabaka Bebuganda*, 130.

Chapter 6. Hiding Clans

1. Jonathon L. Earle, *Colonial Buganda and the End of Empire: Political Thought and Historical Imagination in Africa* (New York: Cambridge University Press, 2017).

2. Male nobility applied to descendants of a senior lineage in clan politics. Descent from a royal union produced the male noble called *mulangira*. See Apolo Kagwa, in John Roscoe and Apolo Kagwa, "Enquiry into Native Land Tenure in the Uganda Protectorate, 1906," Kampala, 1906, MSS Afr.S.17, Weston Library, University of Oxford, 3.

3. Holly Elisabeth Hanson, *Landed Obligation: The Practice of Power in Buganda* (Portsmouth, NH: Heinemann, 2003), 218.

4. From the Nsaamba branch; Apolo Kagwa, *Ekitabo Kye Bika Bya Baganda* (Kampala: Uganda Bookshop, 1949 [ca. 1907]), 20–21, 23; Michael B. Nsimbi, *Amannya Amganda N'Ennono Zaago* (Kampala: Longman's Uganda, 1980), 284–88; M. S. M. Semakula Kiwanuka, *A History of Buganda: From the Foundation of the Kingdom to 1900* (New York: Africana, 1972), 54–55, for complexities.

5. Kiwanuka, *History*, 54–55, 69; Christopher Wrigley, *Kingship and State: The Buganda Dynasty* (Cambridge: Cambridge University Press, 1996), 187–91; Hanson, *Landed Obligation*, 80.

6. Lloyd A. Fallers, assisted by F. K. Kamoga and S. B. K. Musoke, "Social Stratification in Traditional Buganda," in *The King's Men: Leadership and Status in Buganda on the Eve of Independence*, ed. Lloyd A. Fallers (London: Oxford University Press, 1964), 85.

7. John Roscoe, *The Baganda: An Account of their Native Customs and Beliefs* (London: Macmillan, 1911), 137; Kagwa, *Ekitabo Kye Bika*, 23.

8. Kagwa, *Ekitabo Kye Bika*, 24, 103–4; Apolo Kagwa, *Customs of the Baganda*, ed. May Edel, trans. Ernest Kalibala (New York: Columbia University Press, 1934), 39–40; Nsimbi, *Amannya*, 202; Kiwanuka, *History*, 53–55.

9. Michael B. Nsimbi, "Luganda Names, Clans, and Totems," *Munger Africana Library Notes* 52/53 (1980), 7–9; Kagwa, *Ekitabo Kye Bika*, 23.

10. Apollo Kagwa, *Bakabaka Bebuganda* (London: Headley Brothers, 1901), 53–54; Henri Médard, *Le royaume du Buganda au XIXe siècle* (Paris: IFRA-Karthala, 2007), 227–28.

11. Teofiro Mulumba Kuruji, in Roscoe and Kagwa, "Enquiry," 36.

12. Kagwa, in Roscoe and Kagwa, "Enquiry," 71, 75; Médard, *Le royaume*, 227.

13. Wrigley, *Kingship and State*, 187–91; Apolo Kagwa, *Ekitabo Kye Mpisa Za Baganda* (Kampala: Uganda Printing and Publishing, 1918), 47–48, and Kagwa, *Bakabaka Bebuganda*, 53–56, discuss Kagulu's rule but claim the mother of his two children is unknown.

14. Kagwa, *Bakabaka Bebuganda*, 53; Kagwa, *Ekitabo Kye Bika*, 29 (quote).

15. Nsimbi, *Amannya*, 164; Kyobe Sematimba accepted a chiefship from Kagulu.

16. Richard J. Reid, *A History of Modern Uganda* (Cambridge: Cambridge University Press, 2017), 299; Derek Peterson, *Ethnic Patriotism and the East African Revival: A History of Dissent, c. 1935–1972* (New York: Cambridge University Press, 2012), 28–32.

17. Hanson, *Landed Obligation*, 204 ("new things"); Daudi Basudde and Yuda Musa Mukasa to Chief Secretary, May 15, 1922, UNA SMP 6902 ("advance"), quoted in Hanson, *Landed Obligation*, 224.

18. Neil Kodesh, *Beyond the Royal Gaze: Clanship and Public Healing in Buganda* (Charlottesville: University of Virginia Press, 2010), 137.

19. Apolo Kaggwa, *The Kings of Buganda*, ed. and trans. M. S. M. Semakula Kiwanuka (Nairobi: East African Publishing House, 1971), 203–5; Kagwa, *Ekitabo Kye Mpisa*, 38–51; Anonymous, "Ab'effumbe (Akabbiro: Kikere)," *Munno* 25, no. 7 (1935), inside front cover; Wrigley, *Kingship and State*, 187–91.

20. Kiwanuka, *History*, 127.

21. Kiwanuka, *History*, 155–60; Reid, *History of Modern Uganda*, 127–28, 141–52.

22. Earle, *Colonial Buganda*, 143–51.

23. Samwiri Lwanga Lunyiigo, *Mwanga II: Resistance to Imposition of British Colonial Rule in Buganda, 1884–1899* (Kampala: Wavah Books, 2011), 37–90; Louise Pirouet, *Black Evangelists: The Spread of Christianity in Uganda, 1891–1914* (London: Rex Collings, 1978), 1–20; Earle, *Colonial Buganda*, 13–23.

24. Frederick B. Welbourn, *East African Rebels: A Study of Some Independent Churches* (London: SCM Press, 1961), 15–19.

25. Donald Anthony Low and R. Cranford Pratt, *Buganda and British Overrule: Two Studies* (Nairobi: Oxford University Press, 1970), 3–159.

26. Neville Turton, John Bowes Griffin, and Arthur W. Lewey, *Laws of the Uganda Protectorate*, vol. 6 (London: n.p., 1936), 1372–84. A fourth regent, Noho Mbogo, signed the Agreement.

27. Earle, *Colonial Buganda*, 16, table 1.1.

28. Low and Pratt, *Buganda and British Overrule*, 109; Welbourn, *East African Rebels*, 19.

29. Wilson to Sadler, January 2, 1902, cited in Low and Pratt, *Buganda and British Overrule*, 144–45; Hanson, *Landed Obligation*, 203–28.

30. Hanson, *Landed Obligation*, 139, 192.

31. Hanson, *Landed Obligation*, 142; Gardner Thompson, *Governing Uganda: British Colonial Rule and Its Legacy* (Kampala: Fountain, 2003), 45.

32. Mahmood Mamdani, *Politics and Class Formation in Uganda* (New York: Monthly Review Press, 1976); Victoire Chalin, Valérie Golaz, and Claire Médard, "Land Titling in Uganda Crowds Out Local Farmers," *Journal of Eastern African Studies* 9, no. 4 (2015), 561–62.

33. Hanson, *Landed Obligation*, 177–82.

34. Hanson, *Landed Obligation*, 203, 143–46.

35. Buganda Lukiiko Archives, July 10, 1905, 27–28, 39–42; Buganda Lukiiko Archives (1894–1918), John Rowe, Collector, Film A2915, Northwestern University Library; Hanson, *Landed Obligation*, 215.

36. Hanson, *Landed Obligation*, 138–43, 205–12.

37. Hanson, *Landed Obligation*, 141.

38. Michael Twaddle, "The Bakungu Chiefs of Buganda and British Colonial Rule, 1900–1930," *Journal of African History* 10, no. 3 (1969), 315.

39. Augustine Bikolo Mukwaya, *Land Tenure in Buganda* (Kampala: East African Institute of Social Research, 1953), 21; Welbourn, *East African Rebels*, 21; Donald Anthony Low, *The Mind of Buganda: Documents of the Modern History of an African Kingdom* (London: Heinemann Educational, 1971), xviii; Low and Pratt, *Buganda and British Overrule*, 233–36; Earle, *Colonial Buganda*, 103.

40. The following three paragraphs rest on Hanson, *Landed Obligation*, 203–28.

41. Hanson, *Landed Obligation*, 216.

42. Hanson, *Landed Obligation*, 216, 214, 221.

43. Derek R. Peterson and Giacomo Macola, "Introduction," in *Recasting the Past*, ed. Derek R. Peterson and Giacomo Macola (Athens: Ohio University Press, 2009), 1–28; Earle, *Colonial Buganda*, 13–21, 47–60.

44. Steven Feierman, *Peasant Intellectuals: Anthropology and History in Tanzania* (Madison: University of Wisconsin Press, 1990), 78–80, 82; Hanson, *Landed Obligation*, 167.

45. Earle, *Colonial Buganda*, 231–32, to which should be added *Matalisi* and *Munyonyozi*.

46. Antony Philippe, *Ouganda au Cœur de l'Afrique: un demi-siècle d'Apostolat au centre Africain, 1878–1928* (Paris: Editions Dillen, 1929), 156–57.

47. Marinus Rooijackers, *The Beginning of the White Fathers' Mission in Southern Uganda and the Organization of the Catechumenate, 1879–1914* (Rome: Society of Missionaries of Africa, 2008), 69. Catholic Mill Hill Fathers established a station in Bugisu, east of the Kiyiira Nile, after 1895.

48. Earle, *Colonial Buganda*, 92 and passim.

49. Such as "games," "execution sites," "emisambwa," and so forth; Henri le Veux, *Fonds le Veux*, Z47/1–5, Archivio Padri Bianchi, Rome.

50. Julien Gorju, *Entre le Victoria, l'Edouard, et l'Albert: Ethnographie de la Partie Anglaise du Vicariat de l'Uganda* (Rennes: Imprimeries Oberthür, 1920).

51. John Allen Rowe, "Revolution in Buganda, 1856–1884," PhD diss., University of Wisconsin–Madison, 1966, 249; John Mary Waliggo, *The Catholic Church in the Buddu Province of Buganda, 1879–1925* (Kampala: Angel Agencies, 2010), 196.

52. Echoing a turn to the popular in Nigeria's vernacular press; Karin Barber (ed. and trans.), *Print Culture and the First Yoruba Novel: I. B. Thomas's "Life Story of Me, Segilola" and Other Texts* (Leiden: Brill, 2012), 27–34.

53. Earle, *Colonial Buganda*, 183.

54. Karin Barber, *The Anthropology of Texts, Persons and Publics: Oral and Written Culture in Africa and Beyond* (Cambridge: Cambridge University Press, 2007), 4–5.

55. Earle, *Colonial Buganda*, esp. 1–38, 77–109, 177–210; Carol Summers, "Young Baganda and Old Boys: Youth, Generational Transition, and Ideas of Leadership in Buganda, 1920–1949," *Africa Today* 51, no. 3 (2005), 115–23.

56. Caitlin Cooke Monroe, "Searching for Nyabongo: Scholarly Categories and the Limits of Global History," unpublished essay, Northwestern University, 2020; Caitlin Cooke Monroe, "Making History: Women's Knowledge and the Creation of a Historical Discipline in Western Uganda, 1800–1980," PhD diss., Northwestern University, in progress.

57. Kagwa, *Bakabaka Bebuganda*, 53–56; Kagwa, *Customs*, 31–33; Kagwa, *Ekitabo Kye Mpisa*, 49; Kaggwa, *Kings*, 62–68; J. T. K. Gomotoka, "Kisolo jjajja w'ab'engonge," *Munno* 8, no. 96 (1918), 164–65; Y. Mabike Kato, "Ekitabo ke'ebyafayo by'ekika ky'effumbe," *Munno* 22, no. 1 (1932), 16; Anonymous, "Ab'obutiko," *Munno* 24, no. 7 (1934), back page; Anonymous, "Ab'effumbe," *Munno* 25, no. 4 (1935), back page; 25, no. 5 (1935), back page; 25, no. 6 (1935), back page; 25, no. 7 (1935), back page.

58. Joseph S. Kasirye, *Abateregga ku Nnamulondo y'e Buganda* (London: Macmillan, 1955), dedication; Nsimbi, *Amannya*, photograph of Ggomotoka, opposite 167.

59. He also authored *Makula* ("Wonders") a seven-volume manuscript, per John Rowe, notes April 15, 1964, given to author, October 1999. Waliggo, *Catholic Church*, 93–94, reports that vols. 1 and 2 are held in the Archbishop's House, Rubaga Mission Archives, and vols. 3 and 4 are held by Makerere University Library, probably the Africana Collection.

60. Kiwanuka, *History*, 19.

61. John T. K. Ggomotoka, "History of Buvuma Islands" (Kampala: Typescript, 1937, 1938), ed. David William Cohen, trans. David Kiyaga-Mulindwa; used with permission of the editor.

62. P. M. Gulu, "Ekika: ab'effumbe n'ab'enjovu bagatta," *Munno* 6, no. 67 (1916), 117. A Luganda word for "sky," "above," or "heaven," Gulu was the founder figure of an Elephant clan hearthstone at Busabala on the Kyaddondo littoral. Nsimbi, *Amannya*, 316–17, says the name was used by the Ènsumà (Elephant-Snout Fish) clan, whose founder figures came from Ddolwe Island; Jürgen Jensen, *Verwandtschaftlich-lokale Bindung und regionale Mobilität bei den Bavuma (Uganda)* (Berlin: Duncker & Humboldt, 1980), 186–90, 302–3; Ggomotoka, "History of Buvuma Islands," Buziri, 10; Elephant-Snout Fish people ran two busy shrines there; A. O. Jenkins, "Buvuma Notes," 12.10.1932, in D. G. Maurice Papers, MSS Afr.S.581, Weston Library, University of Oxford.

63. Henri Le Veux, *Premier essai de vocabulaire luganda-français d'après l'ordre étymologique* (Algiers: Imprimeries des Missionaires d'Afrique [Pères Blancs], 1917), 330.

64. Gomotoka, "Kisolo jjajja," 164–65. Kiwanuka, *History*, 94–96; John Rowe, "Myth, Memoir and Moral Admonition: Luganda Historical Writing 1893–1969," *Uganda Journal* 33, no. 2 (1969), 218; Benjamin Ray, *Myth, Ritual, and Kingship in Buganda* (Oxford: Oxford University Press, 1990), 102–3.

65. Tobi Kizito, "Kabaka lubo Kintu ne Kabaka Mpuga Lukidi owe Bunyoro," *Munno* 4, no. 41 (1914), 61–63.

66. Henry Wright Duta Kitakule, "Ebigambo bye mpisa za Basekabaka abe'da," *Ebifa mu Buganda* 33 (October 1909), 3–7; Eriya Buliggwanga, *Ekitabo Ekitegeza Ekika Kye Mamba* (Kampala: Uganda Printing and Publishing, 1916).

67. Ray, *Myth, Ritual*, 103.

68. J. T. Kikulwe Gomotoka, "Ebye Buganda: Ekika ky'Abalangira b'omu Buganda," *Munno* 10, no. 115 (1920), 121–22.

69. Earle, *Colonial Buganda*, 178.

70. Earle, *Colonial Buganda*, 102–9; Carol Summers, "Grandfathers, Grandsons, Morality, and Radical Politics in Late Colonial Buganda," *International Journal of African Historical Studies* 38, no. 3 (2005), 427–29; Peterson, *Ethnic Patriotism*, 13–27.

71. Also J. T. K. G. Kajerero, "Ekirungi kikayanirwa," *Munno* (June 1923), 100–101.

72. Wrigley, *Kingship and State*, 188, errs in calling Walusimbi "head of the Elephant clan."

73. Gulu, "Ekika: ab'effumbe," 117.

74. Charles Chaillé-Long, *Central Africa: Naked Truths of Naked People* (New York: Harper and Brothers, 1877), 103; Henry Morton Stanley, *Through the Dark Continent,*

vol. 1 (London: Sampson Low, Marston, Searle & Rivington, 1878), 394; Roscoe, *Baganda*, 168, 525. This meeting hall likely lay on the Lwajje road, tying ivory hunting to eastern Kyaggwe via Lwajje island, per Kagwa's map in Roscoe, *Buganda*, after 525. Kaggwa, *Kings*, 206; Ham Mukasa, "Ebifa mu Mulembe gwa Kabaka Mutesa," *Uganda Journal* 1, no. 2 (1934), 117; Bakumba na balamu and Petero Yoanna Sserwanga Ssebali-jja, "Ab'effumbe (Akabbiro: Kikere)," *Munno* 25, no. 4 (1935), inside the front cover; Kasirye, *Abateregga*, 23; Nsimbi, *Amannya*, 250, Nagujja "of" the Elephant clan.

75. Gulu, "Ekika: ab'effumbe," 118.

76. Kagwa, *Ekitabo Kye Mpisa*, 19–22; David L. Schoenbrun, "Ethnic Formation with Other-Than-Human Beings: Island Shrine Practice in Uganda's Long Eighteenth Century," *History in Africa* 45 (2018), 426.

77. Welbourn, *East African Rebels*, 46–47; Derek Peterson, "The Politics of Tran-scendance in Colonial Uganda," *Past and Present* 230 (February 2016), 197–225.

78. Gulu, "Ekika: ab'effumbe," 118; Kagwa, *Customs*, 33; Roscoe, *Baganda*, 221.

79. Gulu, "Ekika: ab'effumbe," 118.

80. Nsimibi, *Amannya*, 161–69 (noble descent reckoned through mothers).

81. Kikulwe's ally, Mawuba, was a healer. Gulu, "Ekika: ab'effumbe," 118.

82. Kagwa, *Bakabaka Bebuganda*, 57; Kaggwa, *Kings*, 67.

83. Gulu, "Ekika: ab'effumbe," 118.

84. Ronald Snoxall, *Luganda-English Dictionary* (Oxford: Clarendon Press, 1967), 122.

85. Gulu, "Ekika: ab'Effumbe," 119 (benefits to Lutabi and Serubale).

86. Summers, "Young Baganda," 109–28; Earle, *Colonial Buganda*, 179–90; Reid, *History of Modern Uganda*, 304–7.

87. Derek Peterson, "Nonconformity in Africa's Cultural History," *Journal of African History* 58, no. 1 (2017), 35–50; Peterson, "Politics of Transcendance," 217.

88. Earle, *Colonial Buganda*, 25–37; Peterson and Macola, "Introduction," 1–15.

89. Kabaka Daudi Chwa to Abataka, May 13, 1922, in Low, *Mind of Buganda*, 63–66.

90. Hanson, *Landed Obligation*, 203–32.

91. J. T. K. Gom[otoka], Sabalangira we Buganda, Isaka Mayemba Sematimba, Soli-mani Kiwanga, Aleksandre Kattaba, Seruwano T. Mawanda, Batulabudde ku lwa Lubanjwa, Matayo S. Gw'olirabajjo ku lwa Lukanga, Ibrahim Ntege Tamuzadde ku lwa Manyonyi, "Ebyafa mu Buganda: Edzadde lya sekabaka Kagulu; Ozayisanga n'otofisa [*sic*]," *Munno* 14, no. 2 (1924), 28–30.

92. They buried his umbilicus twin and his jawbone in Busiro, the land of royal tombs.

93. Anonymous, "II. Edzadde lya Sekabaka Kagulu: Ozayisanga n'otafisa," *Munno* (September 1923), 162–64.

94. J. T. K. G[omotoka] Sabalangira we Buganda, "Ebyafa mu Buganda: Edzadde lya Sekabaka Kagulu," *Munno* (December 1923), 207.

95. Lwajje, linked to the ivory trade. Ggomotoka, "History of Buvuma," Buziri, 9–17; "Lwajje," 5.

96. G[omotoka] Sabalangira we Buganda, "Ebyafa mu Buganda: Edzadde," 210 (Spratfish not Lungfish, as Katula had argued in 1913). Also, Anonymous, "Ekika ky'Ab'Enkejje," *Munno* 26, no. 7 (1936), 122; Ggomotoka, "History of Buvuma," "Lwajje Island," 5.

97. J. T. K. Gomotoka Sabalangira we Buganda and Isaka Mayemba Sematimba, Solimani Kiwanga, Aleksandre Kattaba, Seruwano T. Mawanda, Batulabudde ku lwa Lubanjwa, Matayo S. Gw'olirabajjo ku lwa Lukanga, Ibrahim Ntege Tamuzadde ku lwa Manyonyi, "Ebyafa mu Buganda: Edzadde lya Sekabaka Kagulu: Ozayisanga n'otafisa," *Munno* 14, no. 1 (1924), 13, exploiting local courts' ignorance of this history.

98. Gomotoka Sabalangira we Buganda et al., "Ebyafa mu Buganda," 28.

99. Gomotoka Sabalangira we Buganda et al., "Ebyafa mu Buganda," 29.

100. J. M. T. Kikulwe, "Olulyo lw'Abalangira be Buganda," *Munno* 3, no. 35 (1913), 177–81; Gomotoka, "Ebye Buganda," 121–22; Kagwa, *Ekitabo Kye Bika*, 110–11; Nsimbi, *Amannya*, 161–69.

101. Anonymous, "II. Edzadde" 164; J. T. K. [Gomotoka] Sabalangira, "Ebyafa mu Buganda: Edzadde," 207–11.

102. Carola Lentz, *Land, Mobility, and Belonging in West Africa* (Bloomington: Indiana University Press, 2013), 18–19, 109–10, 246–49.

103. Hanson, *Landed Obligation*, 215.

104. J. T. K. [Gomotoka] Sabalangira, "Ebyafa mu Buganda: Edzadde," 210–11.

105. Also Bakumba na Balamu and Ssebalijja, "Ab'effumbe"; Bakumba na balamu and Petero Yoanna Sserwanga Ssebalijja, "Ejjinja Kkungu awali obutaka bw'ab'empewo," *Munno* 25, no. 7 (1935), 132.

106. Gomotoka Sabalangira we Buganda et al., "Ebyafa mu Buganda," 13.

107. Le Veux, *Premier essai de vocabulaire*, 703; Eridadi M. K. Mulira and G. M. Ndawula, *A Luganda-English and English-Luganda Dictionary* (London: Society for Promoting Christian Knowledge, 1952), 81; Snoxall, *Luganda-English Dictionary*, 248. The 1900 Agreement forbade access to the kabaka's court "to any person not a native of the Uganda province"; see Turton, Griffin, and Lewey, *Laws*, Article 6, 1374–75.

108. Le Veux, *Premier essai de vocabulaire*, 729, 273; Mulira and Ndawula, *Luganda-English*, 85; Snoxall, *Luganda-English Dictionary*, 106, 242.

109. George Pilkington, *Luganda-English and English-Luganda Vocabulary* (London: Society for Promoting Christian Knowledge, 1899), 29–30.

110. Derek Peterson, *Creative Writing: Translation, Bookkeeping, and the Work of Imagination in Colonial Kenya* (Portsmouth, NH: Heinemann, 2004), 10–20.

111. Georg August Schweinfurth, Friedrich Ratzel, Robert W. Felkin, Gustav Hartlaub, *Emin Pasha in Central Africa: Being a Collection of His Letters and Journals*, trans. Mrs. Robert W. Felkin (New York: Dodd, Mead, 1889), 124; Kagwa, *Ekitabo Kye Mpisa*, 195–96; Roscoe, *Baganda*, 426–34; Lucy Mair, *An African People in the Twentieth Century* (London: Routledge, 1934), 155–57; Ggomotoka, "History of Buvuma," "Bugaya," 16.

112. Le Veux, *Premier essai de vocabulaire*, 66; Snoxall, *Luganda-English Dictionary*, 48.

113. D. W. Z. Zawaya, "Okubola abantu mu Bika," *Ebifa mu Buganda* 169 (January 1921), 47; Mulira and Ndawula, *Luganda-English*, 7; Snoxall, *Luganda-English Dictionary*, 25; Alan Hamilton, with Naomi Hamilton, Phoebe Mukasa, and David Ssewanyana, *Luganda Dictionary and Grammar* (Kampala: Gustro Limited, 2016), 19, *kuboola*: "to ignore, disregard (a family member)," reverses the direction of estrangement; see David L. Schoenbrun, "A Lexicon for Affect, Violence, Vulnerability, and Dispute in Eastern Bantu," in progress, RN 108.

114. Charles T. Wilson, *An Outline Grammar of the Luganda Language* (London: Society for Promoting Christian Knowledge, 1882), 87.

115. Viktoro Katula, "Abadzukulu sekabaka Kagulu: Okwetonda si bulabe," *Munno* 14, no. 8 (1924), 121.

116. Viktoro Katula, "Abadzukulu sekabaka Kagulu: Ekiyigganyizo eky'okubiri," *Munno* 14, no. 9 (1924), 136–37.

117. Viktoro Katula, "Abadzukulu sekabaka Kagulu," *Munno* 14, no. 11 (1924), 155–56.

118. Viktoro, Katula, "Abadzukulu sekabaka Kagulu: Ebivvunula," *Munno* 14, no. 12 (1924), 189–90.

119. Viktoro Katula, "Abadzukulu sekabaka Kagulu," *Munno* 15, no. 1 (1925), 12–13.

120. Viktoro Katula, "Abadzukulu sekabaka Kagulu," *Munno* 15, no. 2 (1925), 26–27.

121. Viktoro Katula, "Emmamba ye Namukuma. Kabaka Mawanda awangula e Kyagwe, awa Nkutu e Namukuma," *Munno* 3, no. 31 (1913), 110–12.

122. Katula, "Abadzukulu sekabaka Kagulu: Okwetonda," 122.

123. Kiwanuka, *History*, 102–6, discounts Nyoro involvement without discussing Ggomotoka's or Katula's writings on that subject.

124. Katula, "Abadzukulu sekabaka Kagulu: Okwetonda," 122.

125. Shane Doyle, "Immigrants and Indigenes: the Lost Counties Dispute and the Evolution of Ethnic Identity in Colonial Buganda," *Journal of Eastern African Studies* 3, no. 2 (2009), 284–302.

126. Shane Doyle, *Crisis and Decline in Bunyoro: Population and Environment in Western Uganda, 1860–1955* (Oxford: James Currey, 2006), 94–110.

127. Katula, "Abadzukulu sekabaka Kagulu: Okwetonda," 122; Henry W. West, *The Mailo System in Buganda* (Entebbe: Government Printer, 1965), 19–21.

128. Kaggwa, *Kings*, 115.

129. Katula, "Abadzukulu ba Sekabaka Kagulu: Ekiyigganyizo," 137.

130. Teofiro Kuruji, in Roscoe and Kagwa, "Enquiry," 37; Roscoe, *Baganda*, 289–90; Kagwa, *Ekitabo Kye Mpisa*, 148; Kagwa, *Ekitabo Kye Bika*, 26; Kaggwa, *Kings*, 22; Anonymous, "Ab'efumbe," 102; Mair, *African People*, 190–91, used "almost entirely for cases of sorcery."

131. Kagwa, *Ekitabo Kye Mpisa*, 239; Ferdinand Walser, *Luganda Proverbs* (Berlin: Dietrich Reimer Press, 1982), #4790, 429.

132. West, *Mailo System*, 20.

133. Katula, "Abadzukulu ba Sekabaka Kagulu," 156.

134. Katula, "Abadzukulu ba Sekabaka Kagulu," 155.

135. Katula, "Abadzukulu sekabaka Kagulu: Ebivvunula," 189.

136. Katula, "Abadzukulu sekabaka Kagulu," 27.

Conclusion

1. Neil Kodesh, *Beyond the Royal Gaze: Clanship and Public Healing in Buganda* (Charlottesville: University Press of Virginia, 2010), 69–81.

2. Allan J. Lush, "Kiganda Drums," *Uganda Journal* 3, no. 1 (1935), 10 (quote).

3. Jonathon Earle, "Political Activism and Other Life Forms in Colonial Buganda," *History in Africa* 45 (2018), 381–82, deduces the killing from the fact that Bwete reported its length down to the inch.

4. Earle, "Political," 389 (quote).

5. Michael G. Kenny, "The Powers of Lake Victoria," *Anthropos* 72, nos. 5/6 (1977), 722–23 (Atego); Brett Shadle, "Patronage, Millennialism and the Serpent God Mumbo in South-West Kenya, 1912–34," *Africa* 72, no. 1 (2002), 29–54. And well beyond this region.

6. Adele Stock, "In Lubigi There Is Freedom," honors thesis, Mount Holyoke College, 2019.

7. Jonathon Glassman, *War of Words, War of Stones: Racial Thought and Violence in Colonial Zanzibar* (Bloomington: Indiana University Press, 2011).

8. James H. Sweet, *Domingos Álvarez, African Healing, and the Intellectual History of the Atlantic World* (Chapel Hill: University of North Carolina Press, 2011); Jan Bender Shetler, *Claiming Civic Virtue: Gendered Network Memory in the Mara Region, Tanzania* (Madison: University of Wisconsin Press, 2019).

Bibliography

Unpublished and Archival Sources

Amin, Scheherazade. "The Archaeology of the Sesse [*sic*] Islands and Their Contribution to the Understanding of Great Lakes Ceramics." PhD diss., University College London, 2015.

Anangwe, Alfred, and Michael R. Marlo (eds. and comps.). *Wanga-English Dictionary.* Ann Arbor, 2008.

Ashley, Ceri Z. "Ceramic Variability and Change: A Perspective from Great Lakes Africa." PhD diss., University College London, 2005.

Buganda Lukiiko Archives (1894–1918). John Rowe, Collector. Film, A2915. Northwestern University Library.

Cory, Hans. "Bantu Religion of Tanganyika." (Typescript, n.d.). Hans Cory Papers, Africana Section, University of Dar es Salaam, Paper no. 41.

Duggan, A. J. Papers. WT1/RST/G26; Wellcome Foundation Archives, London.

Ehret, Christopher. "Dissemination of Tobacco in Africa." Presentation to the Routes of Medieval Africa 11th to 17th Centuries conference, Université Paris I, Panthéon-Sorbonne, France, March 5, 2019.

Feierman, Steven. "Concepts of Sovereignty in the Shambaa Kingdom." PhD diss., Northwestern University, 1970.

Fraas, Pauline. A. (comp.). *A Nande-English and English-Nande Dictionary.* Washington, DC: Cyclostyled, 1961.

Ggomotoka, John T. K. "History of Buvuma Islands." Trans. David Kiyaga-Mulindwa. Kampala: Typescript, 1937–38.

Jenkins, A. O. "Buvuma Notes." December 10, 1932, in D. G. Maurice Papers, mss Afr.S.581, Weston Library, University of Oxford.

Jimenez, Raevin. "Rites of Reproduction: Gender, Generation and Political Economic Transformation among Nguni-speakers of Southern Africa, 8th–19th Century CE." PhD diss., Northwestern University, 2017.

Jjumba, Elisa, and the Council of the Ssiga of Jjumba. *Ekitabo Eky'essiga lya Jjumba.* Kampala: Typescript, 1964. Africana Collection, Makerere University Library.

Johnson, Jennifer L. "Fishwork in Uganda: A Multispecies Ethnohistory about Fish, People, and Ideas about Fish and People." PhD diss., University of Michigan, Ann Arbor, 2014.

Kabazzi, Jemusi Kibuka Miti. "A Short History of Buganda, Bunyoro, Busoga, Toro, and Ankole." Trans. G. K. Rock. Kampala, Typescript, ca. 1947. CMS/ACC 728 Z1, Church Missionary Society Archives, Cadbury Research Library, University of Birmingham.

Kaggwa, Apolo. *Ekitabo Kye Bika bya Baganda* [*A Book of Clans of Buganda* (1912)]. Trans. James D. Wamala. Kampala: Typescript, 1972. Melville J. Herskovits Library of African Studies, Northwestern University.

Kagwa, Apolo. *Ekitabo Kye Bika Bya Baganda* [*Book of the Clans of the Baganda*]. Trans. John Allen Rowe. Unpublished typescript, n.d. In author's possession.

Kagwa, Apolo. *Ekitabo Kye Kika Kya Nsenene*. Mengo: Privately published, 1905. Miscellaneous Monographs, MF-566, Center for Research Libraries, Chicago.

Kamuhangire, Ephraim. "The Pre-Colonial History of the Salt Lakes Region of South Western Uganda, c. 1000–1900 A.D." PhD diss., Makerere University, Kampala, 1993.

Kenny Michael G. "Basuba Historical Narratives." Typescript, 1978. L VI398.2/420392, School of Oriental and African Studies Library, University of London.

Kibirige, F. "A Report about the Belief of the Baganda in Spirits." *Occasional Research Papers in African Religions and Philosophies* (Kampala: Cyclostyled, 1974) 19, no. 203. Vertical Files, Melville J. Herskovits Library of African Studies, Northwestern University.

Kiwanuka, M. S. M. Semakula. "The Traditional History of the Buganda Kingdom: With Special Reference to the Historical Writings of Apolo Kaggwa." PhD diss., University of London, 1965.

Kodesh, Neil. "Beyond the Royal Gaze: Clanship and Collective Well-Being in Buganda." PhD diss., Northwestern University, 2004.

Lanning, Ernest C. "Some Brief Notes on Sesse [*sic*]." In Ernest C. Lanning Papers, mss Afr.S.1329(9), Weston Library, University of Oxford.

Lanning, Ernest C. "The Ssese Islands." In Ernest C. Lanning Papers, mss. Afr.S.1329 (9), 1957; Weston Library, University of Oxford.

Le Veux, Henri. Fonds Le Veux. Z 47/1–5, Archivio Padri Bianchi, Rome, Italy.

Literature Department (comp.). *English-Kisukuma Dictionary*. Mwanza, Tanzania: Africa Inland Mission, n.d.

MacWilliams, Anita (comp.). *Kikwaya-English Dictionary*. Makoko, Tanzania: Cyclostyled, 1973.

Maurice, D. G. "Bulondoganyi." In Maurice Papers, mss.Afr.S.581, 1932; Weston Library, University of Oxford.

Maurice, D. G. "Buvuma Notes." In Maurice Papers, mss.Afr.S.581, n.d.; Weston Library, University of Oxford.

Maurice, D. G. "Native Administration." In Maurice Papers, mss.Afr.S.581, 21, f, 8; Weston Library, University of Oxford.

Maurice, D. G. "Some Brief Notes on the Sesse [*sic*] Islands." In Maurice Papers, mss. Afr.S.581; Weston Library, University of Oxford.

Monroe, Catilin Cooke. "Making History: Women's Knowledge and the Creation of a Historical Discipline in Western Uganda." PhD diss., Northwestern University, in progress.

Monroe, Caitlin Cooke. "Searching for Nyabongo: Scholarly Categories and the Limits of Global History." Unpublished essay, Northwestern University, 2020.

Mukanga, A. "The Traditional Belief in Balubaale." *Occasional Research Papers in African Religions and Philosophies* 167 (1974). Vertical Files, Melville J. Herskovits Library of African Studies, Northwestern University.

Musaazi, John. "Baganda Traditional Divination and Treatment of People's Trouble." Department of Religious Studies and Philosophy, *Religious Studies Occasional Paper* no. 8, Kampala, Makerere University, 1968–1969. Vertical Files, Melville J. Herskovits Library of African Studies, Northwestern University.

Musisi, Nakanyike. "Transformations of Baganda Women: From the Earliest Times to the Demise of the Kingdom in 1966." PhD diss., University of Toronto, 1992.

Nabaguzi, J. B. "Research Methods in Kyaggwe, Buganda Region." History Department Research Paper, Makerere University, Kampala, History Seminar, July 13, 1970. Vertical Files, Melville J. Herskovits Library of African Studies, Northwestern University.

Nassiwa, Mary Consolate. "African Traditional Religion: Women and The Sacred in the Ganda Tradition." *Occasional Research Papers in African Traditional Religion and Philosophy* 7, no. 61 (1972). Vertical Files, Melville J. Herskovits Library of African Studies, Northwestern University.

Nyanzi-Makumbi, V. C. K. "The Story of Barkcloth in Buganda." BA thesis, Africana Special Collections, Makerere University Library, Makerere University, 1976.

P[ères] B[lancs] (comps.). *Dictionnaire Mashi-Français*. Bukavu: Cyclostyled, n.d.

Reid, Andrew. "The Lake, Bananas, and Ritual Power." Unpublished manuscript, University College London, 2016.

Roscoe, John, and Apolo Kagwa. "Enquiry into Native Land Tenure in the Uganda Protectorate, 1906." Kampala, 1906. MSS Afr.s.17; Weston Library, University of Oxford.

Rowe, John Allen. "Revolution in Buganda, 1856–1884." PhD diss., University of Wisconsin–Madison, 1966.

Schoenbrun, David L. "A Lexicon for Affect, Violence, Vulnerability, and Dispute in Eastern Bantu." In progress.

Stock, Adele. "In Lubigi There Is Freedom." Honors thesis, Mount Holyoke College, 2019.

Tantala, Renee Louise. "Early History of Kitara in Western Uganda: Process Models of Religious and Political Change, 2 Parts." PhD diss., University of Wisconsin–Madison, 1989.

Taylor, Rachel. "Crafting Cosmopolitanism: Nyamwezi Male Labor, Acquisition and Honor c. 1750–1914." PhD diss., Northwestern University, 2017.

van Sambeek, J. (comp.). *Small Kiha Dictionary*. N.p: Typescript, n.d.

Zzibukulimbwa, Kasirye. "The Beginning of Ennyanja Nnalubaale." Trans. Robert Bakaaki and Jennifer Lee Johnson. Kampala: PDF, 2012.

Published Sources

Adong, J., and J. Lakareber (comps.). *Lwo-English Dictionary*. Kampala: Fountain, 2009.

Aliwali, Alfonsi. "Bwakamba Mukudde: 'Omudzukulu eyatta. Mukudde.'" *Munno* 4, no. 37 (1914), 7–9.

Aliwali, Alfonsi. "Ka Tulojje: Kabaka Mulondo." *Munno* 4, no. 38 (1914), 20–23.

Aliwali, Alfonsi. "Ka Tulojje: Olutalo lw'Abakunta abatta Jjuunju." *Munno* 4, no. 39 (1914), 38; 4, no. 40 (1914), 57–58.

Almeida, Marcos Leitão de. "The Deep History of the *Ficus thonningii Bl.* in Central Africa: Ontology, Settlement, and Environment among Lower Congo Peoples (Early Times to ca. 500 B.C.E.)." In *Historical Archaeology and Environment*, ed. Marcos Andrés Torres de Souza and Diogo Menezes Costa, 181–205. New York: Springer, 2018.

Aloo, Peninah A. "Biological Diversity of the Yala Swamp Lakes, with Special Emphasis on Fish Species Composition, in Relation to Changes in the Lake Victoria Basin (Kenya): Threats and Conservation Measures." *Biodiversity and Conservation* 12 (2003), 905–20.

Amselle, Jean-Loup. "Ethnies et espaces: pour une anthropologie topologique." In *Au Coeur de l'Ethnie: Ethnies, Tribalisme et État en Afrique*, ed. Jean-Loup Amselle and Elikia M'Bokolo, 11–48. Paris: Le Découverte, 1985.

Anderson, Benedict. *Imagined Communities*. Rev. ed. London: Verso, 1991.

Anderson, David. "The Beginning of Time? Evidence for Catastrophic Drought in Baringo in the Early Nineteenth Century." *Journal of Eastern African Studies* 10, no. 1 (2016), 45–66.

Ankei, Yuji. "Folk Knowledge of Fish among the Songola and the Bwari: Comparative Ethnoichthyology of the Lualaba River and Lake Tanganyika Fishermen." *African Study Monograph*, Supplement 9 (1989), 1–88.

Anonymous. "Ab'effumbe (Akabbiro: Kikere)." *Munno* 25, no. 4 (1935), back page; 25, no. 5 (1935), back page; 25, no. 6 (1935), back page; 25, no. 7 (1935), back page.

Anonymous. "Ab'obutiko." *Munno* 24, no. 7 (1934), 126 and back page.

Anonymous [Apolo Kagwa]. "Basekabaka be Buganda nga bwebalirana, namanya ga Banamasole, ne Miziro gyabwe." *Ebifa mu Buganda* 63 (April 1912), 2–3.

Anonymous. "The Bishop's Visit to Bubembe, Bukasa, and Kome." *Mengo Notes* 1, no. 2 (1900), 6–7.

Anonymous. "Customs of Buganda." *Mengo Notes* 1, no. 4 (1900), 16.

Anonymous. "II. Edzadde lya Sekabaka Kagulu: Ozayisanga n'otafisa." *Munno* (September 1923), 162–64.

Anonymous. "Ekika ky'Ab'Akasimba." *Munno* 27, no. 2 (1937), inside back cover; 27, no. 3 (1937), inside back cover.

Anonymous. "Ekika ky'Ab'Enkejje." *Munno* 26, no. 7 (1936), 122.

Anonymous. "Ekika Ky'Ab'Entalaganya." *Munno* 26, no. 11 (1936), 202; 26, no. 12 (1936), 222.

Anonymous. "Ekika ky'Ab'Omusu." *Munno* 27, no. 5 (1937), 97–98.

Anonymous. "Engoma za Kabaka Enkulu." *Munno* 3, no. 33 (1913), 142.

Anonymous. "E Rubaga—Ebyedda." *Munno* 23, no. 4 (1933), 71–73.

Anonymous. "Mu Bugangazzi: Eby'obusamize n'obulaguzi." *Munno* 24, no. 12 (1934), 246–47; 25, no. 1 (1935), 18–19.

Anonymous. "Mu Bugangazzi: Eby'obusamize n'obulaguzi; emmandwa eyitibwa Kawuka." *Munno* 25, no. 2 (1935), 34–35.

Anonymous. "Obunyikivu bwokulima Pamba mu Saza lye Sese." *Ebifa mu Buganda* 143 (December 1918), 227.

Anonymous. "Steamer Service." *Uganda Notes* 4, no. 3 (1903), 13.

Apter, Andrew. "Yoruba Ethnogenesis from Within." *Comparative Studies in Society and History* 55, no. 2 (2013), 356–87.

Arnoux, Alex. "Le culte de la société secrete des Imandwa au Rwanda." *Anthropos* 8 (1913), 754–74.

Ashe, Robert Pickering. *Chronicles of Uganda*. London: Hodder and Stoughton, 1894.

Ashe, Robert Pickering. *Two Kings of Uganda or Life by the Shores of Victoria Nyanza*. London: Sampson, Low, Marston, 1890 [1889].

Ashley, Ceri Z. "Towards a Socialised Archaeology of Great Lakes Ceramics." *African Archaeological Review* 27 (2010), 135–63.

Ashley, Ceri Z., and Andrew Reid. "A Reconsideration of the Figures from Luzira." *Azania: Archaeological Research in Africa* 43 (2008), 95–123.

Austin, Gareth. "Resources, Techniques, and Strategies South of the Sahara: Revising the Factor Endowments Perspective on African Economic Development, 1500–2000." *Economic History Review* 63, no. 1 (2008), 587–624.

Awange, Joseph L., and Obiero Ong'ang'a. *Lake Victoria: Ecology, Resources, Environment*. Berlin: Springer, 2006.

Ayot, Henry Okello. *A History of the Luo-Abasuba of Western Kenya, from A.D. 1760–1940*. Nairobi: Kenya Literature Bureau, 1979.

Bagenda Y. "Nzira mu bigambo bya B. Wakulira T. bye yawandika ku nsi Koki nga bw'efanana." *Munno* 15, no. 7 (1925), 111–12.

Bakika, Daudi, and Jemusi Bwagu. "Ekika ky'abalangira mu Buganda." *Munno* (April 1921), 62–63; (May 1921), 73.

Bakumba na balamu and Petero Yoanna Sserwanga Ssebalijja. "Ab'effumbe (Akabbiro: Kikere)." *Munno* 25, no. 4 (1935), inside front cover.

Bakumba na Balamu and Petero Yoanna Sserwanga Ssebalijja. "Ejjinja Kkungu awali obutaka bw'av'empewo." *Munno* 25, no. 7 (1935), 132.

Banister, Keith E., and Roland G. Bailey. "Fishes Collected by the Zaïre River Expedition, 1974–75." *Zoological Journal of the Linnaean Society* 66 (1979), 205–49.

Barber, Karin. *The Anthropology of Texts, Persons and Publics: Oral and Written Culture in Africa and Beyond*. Cambridge: Cambridge University Press, 2007.

Barber, Karin. "Improvisation and the Art of Making Things Stick." In *Creativity and Cultural Improvisation*, ed. Elizabeth Hallam and Tim Ingold, 25–41. Oxford: Berg, 2007.

Barber, Karin (ed. and trans.). *Print Culture and the First Yoruba Novel: I. B. Thomas's "Life Story of Me, Segilola" and Other Texts*. Leiden: Brill, 2012.

Barth, Fredrik. "Introduction." In *Ethnic Groups and Boundaries*, ed. Fredrik Barth, 9–38. Boston: Little, Brown, 1969.

Bastin, Yvonne, and Thilo Schadeberg (eds.). *Bantu Lexical Reconstructions*. Tervuren: Royal Museum of Central Africa, 2002. Online resource.

Bateman, Colonel H. R. "Research and Reminiscences: Uganda 1908–1910." *Uganda Journal* 15, no. 1 (1951), 26–40.

Beattie, John H. M. "Initiation into the Cwezi Spirit Possession Cult in Bunyoro." *African Studies* 16 (1957), 150–61.

Berger, Iris. *Religion and Resistance: East African Kingdoms in the Precolonial Period.* Tervuren: Musée royale de l'Afrique centrale, 1981.

Berry, Sara. "Marginal Gains, Market Values, and History." *African Studies Review* 50, no. 2 (2007), 57–70.

Blank, Andreas. "Words and Concepts in Time: Towards Diachronic Cognitive Onomasiology." In *Words in Time: Diachronic Semantics from Different Points of View*, ed. Regine Eckardt, Klaus von Heusinger, and Christoph Schwarze, 37–65. Berlin: de Gruyter, 2003.

Blench, Roger. *Archaeology, Language, and the African Past.* Lanham, MD: AltaMira Press, 2006.

Bostoen, Koen. "Semantic Vagueness and Cross-Linguistic Lexical Fragmentation in Bantu: Impeding Factors for Linguistic Palaeontology." *Sprache und Geschichte in Afrika* 20 (2009), 51–64.

Brachi, R. M. "Excavation of a Rock Shelter at Hippo Bay, Entebbe." *Uganda Journal* 26, no. 1 (1960), 62–71.

Brubaker, Rogers. "Ethnicity without Groups." *European Journal of Sociology* 43, no. 1 (2002), 163–89.

Buckley, Thomas, and Alma Gottlieb. "A Critical Appraisal of Theories of Menstrual Symbolism." In *Blood Magic: The Anthropology of Menstruation*, ed. Thomas Buckley and Alma Gottlieb, 3–50. Berkeley: University of California Press, 1988.

Bukya, Aleksi Mukasa. "Engoma za Basekabaka be Buganda: Kabaka Mutesa ze yalina mu mirembe gye." *Munno* 6, no. 71 (1916), 180–84.

Buliggwanga, Eriya M. *Ekitabo Ekitegeza Ekika Kye Mamba.* Kampala: Uganda Printing & Publishing, 1916.

Burbank, Jane, and Frederick Cooper. *Empires in World History: Power and Politics of Difference.* Princeton, NJ: Princeton University Press, 2010.

Businge, Makolome Robert, and Martin Diprose (eds. and comps). *Ntongoli gya Lugungu; Lugungu Dictionary.* Hoima: SIL International, 2012.

Byaruhanga-Akiiki, A. B. T. *Religion in Bunyoro.* Nairobi: Kenya Literature Bureau, 1982.

Candido, Mariana. "African Freedom Suits and Portuguese Vassal Status: Legal Mechanisms for Fighting Enslavement in Benguela, Angola, 1800–1830." *Slavery & Abolition* 32, no. 3 (2011), 447–59.

Carpenter, G. D. Hale. *A Naturalist on Lake Victoria with an Account of Sleeping Sickness and the Tse-tse Fly.* London: T. Fisher Unwin, 1920.

Césard, Edmond. "Comment les Bahaya interprètent leurs origines." *Anthropos* 22, no. 3 (1927), 440–65.

Césard, Edmond. "Le Muhaya." *Anthropos* 31, no. 3 (1936), 489–508.

Chaillé-Long, Charles. *Central Africa: Naked Truths of Naked People.* New York: Harper and Brothers, 1877.

Chalin, Victoire, Valérie Golaz, and Claire Médard. "Land Titling in Uganda Crowds Out Local Farmers." *Journal of Eastern African Studies* 9, no. 4 (2015), 559–73.

Chanock, Martin. *Law, Custom, and Social Order.* Cambridge: Cambridge University Press, 1985.

Chrétien, Jean-Pierre. *The Great Lakes of Africa: Two Thousand Years of History.* New York: Zone Books, 2003.

Chrétien, Jean-Pierre. "Les capitales royales de l'Afrique des Grands Lacs peuvent-elles être considérées comme des villes?" *Journal des Africanistes* 74, nos. 1/2 (2004), 277–98.

Cohen, David William. "The Cwezi Cult." *Journal of African History* 9, no. 4 (1968), 651–57.

Cohen, David William. "Food Production and Food Exchange in the Precolonial Lakes Plateau Region." In *Imperialism, Colonialism, and Hunger: East and Central Africa,* ed. Robert I. Rotberg, 1–18. Lexington: Lexington Books, 1983.

Cohen, David William. *The Historical Tradition of Busoga: Mukama and Kintu.* Oxford: Clarendon Press, 1972.

Cohen, David William. "A Survey of Interlacustrine Chronology." *Journal of African History* 11, no. 2 (1970), 177–99.

Cohen, David William. *Towards a Reconstructed Past: Historical Texts from Busoga, Uganda.* Oxford: Oxford University Press, 1986.

Cohen, David William. *Womunafu's Bunafu: A Study of Authority in a Nineteenth-Century African Community.* Princeton, NJ: Princeton University Press, 1977.

Comaroff, John. "The End of Anthropology, Again: On the Future of an In/Discipline." *American Anthropologist* 112, no. 4 (2010), 524–38.

Condon, M. A. "Contributions to the Ethnography of the Basoga-Batamba, Uganda Protectorate." *Anthropos* 5, no. 4 (1910), 934–56.

Connah, Graham. *Kibiro: The Salt of Bunyoro, Past and Present.* London: British Institute in Eastern Africa, 1996.

Cook, Albert Ruskin. *Medical Vocabulary and Phrase Book in Luganda.* Kampala: Uganda Bookshop, 1903.

Corbet, Philip S. "Lunar Periodicity of Aquatic Insects in Lake Victoria." *Nature* 182 (1958), 330–31.

Cordell, Dennis. "Des 'réfugiés' dans l'Afrique précoloniale? L'exemple de la Centrafrique, 1850–1910." *Politique africaines* 85 (2002), 16–28.

Cory, Hans. "The Buswezi." *American Anthropologist* 57 (1955), 923–52.

Cory, Hans, and Mary M. Hartnoll. *Customary Law of the Haya Tribe.* London: Percy Lund, Humphries, 1945.

Coupez, André, Th. Kamanzi, S. Bizimana, G. Sematama, G. Rwakabukumba, C. Ntazinda et collaborateurs. *Inkoranya y'ikinyarwaanda mu kinyarwaanda nó mu gifaraansá; Dictionnaire Rwanda-Rwanda et Rwanda-Français.* Butare: Institut de recherche scientifique et technologique, 2005.

Csordas, Thomas J. "Embodiment as a Paradigm for Anthropology." *Ethos* 18, no. 1 (1990), 5–47.

Cunningham, John F. *Uganda and Its Peoples.* London: Hutchinson, 1905.

Cunnison, Ian. *History on the Luapula.* London: Oxford University Press, 1951.

Curley, Richard T., and Ben Blount. "The Southern Luo Languages: A Glottochronological Reconstruction." *Journal of African Languages* 9, no. 1 (1970), 1–18.

Cutler, Winnifred B. "Lunar and Menstrual Phase Locking." *American Journal of Obstetrics and Gynecology* 13 (1980), 834–39.

Davis, Margaret B. *A Lunyoro-Lunyankole-English and English-Lunyoro-Lunyankole Dictionary*. Kampala: Uganda Bookshop, 1952 [1938].

Dietler, Michael (ed.). *Feasts: Archaeological and Ethnographic Perspectives on Food, Politics, and Power*. Tuscaloosa: University of Alabama Press, 2001.

Doris, David T. *Vigilant Things: On Thieves, Yoruba Anti-Aesthetics, and the Strange Fates of Ordinary Objects in Nigeria*. Seattle: University of Washington Press, 2011.

Doyle, Shane. *Before HIV: Sexuality, Fertility and Mortality in East Africa, 1900–1980*. Oxford: Oxford University Press, 2013.

Doyle, Shane. *Crisis and Decline in Bunyoro: Population and Environment in Western Uganda, 1860–1955*. Oxford: James Currey, 2006.

Doyle, Shane. "Immigrants and Indigenes: The Lost Counties Dispute and the Evolution of Ethnic Identity in Colonial Buganda." *Journal of Eastern African Studies* 3, no. 2 (2009), 284–302.

Earle, Jonathon. *Colonial Buganda and the End of Empire: Political Thought and Historical Imagination in Africa*. New York: Cambridge University Press, 2017.

Earle, Jonathan. "Political Activism and Other Life Forms in Colonial Buganda." *History in Africa* 45 (2018), 373–95.

Eggeling, William J. *The Indigenous Trees of the Uganda Protectorate*, rev. Ivan R. Dale. Glasgow: Glasgow University Press, 1951.

Ehret, Christopher. *History and the Testimony of Language*. Berkeley: University of California Press, 2011.

Ejidike, Okey Martin. "Human Rights in the Cultural Traditions and Social Practice of the Igbo of Southeastern Nigeria." *Journal of African Law* 43, no. 1 (1999), 71–98.

Fallers, Lloyd, F. K. Kamoga, and S. B. K. Musoke. "Social Stratification in Traditional Buganda." In *The King's Men: Leadership and Status in Buganda on the Eve of Independence*, ed. Lloyd Fallers and Audrey Isabel Richards, 64–116. Oxford: Oxford University Press, 1964.

Faupel, John F. *African Holocaust*. Kampala: St. Paul Publications, Africa, 1984.

Feierman, Steven. "Colonizers, Scholars, and the Creation of Invisible Histories." In *Beyond the Cultural Turn*, ed. Victoria E. Bonnell and Lynn Hunt, 182–216. Berkeley: University of California Press, 1999.

Feierman, Steven. "Ethnographic Regions—Healing, Power, and History." In *Borders and Healers*, ed. Tracy J. Luedke and Harry G. West, 185–94. Bloomington: Indiana University Press, 2006.

Feierman, Steven. "Healing as Social Criticism in the Time of Colonial Conquest." *African Studies* 54, no. 1 (1995), 73–88.

Feierman, Steven. *Peasant Intellectuals: Anthropology and History in Tanzania*. Madison: University of Wisconsin Press, 1990.

Feierman, Steven. "On Socially Composed Knowledge: Reconstructing a Shambaa Royal Ritual." In *In Search of a Nation: Histories of Authority and Dissidence in Tanzania*, ed. Gregory H. Maddox and James L. Giblin, 14–32. Oxford: James Currey, 2014.

Felkin, Robert W. "Notes on the Waganda Tribe of Central Africa." *Proceedings of the Royal Society of Edinburgh* 13 (1885/1886), 699–770.

Felkin, Robert W., and Charles T. Wilson. *Uganda and the Egyptian Sudan*, 2 vols. London: Sampson, Low, Marston, Searle & Rivington, 1882.

Ferreira, Roquinaldo. *Cross-Cultural Exchange in the Atlantic World*. New York: Cambridge University Press, 2012.

Fitzsimons, William. "Warfare, Competition, and the Durability of 'Political Smallness' in Nineteenth-Century Busoga." *Journal of African History* 59, no. 1 (2018), 45–67.

Fleisch, Axel. "The Reconstruction of Lexical Semantics in Bantu." *Sprache und Geschichte in Afrika* 19 (2008), 67–106.

Fleisch, Axel, and Rhiannon Stephens (eds.). *Doing Conceptual History in Africa*. New York: Berghahn Books, 2016.

Ford, John. *The Role of the Trypanosomiases in African Ecology: A Study of the Tsetse Fly Problem*. Oxford: Clarendon Press, 1971.

Gabunga, N. S. B. "Okusala amagezi olwe njala mu Buganda." *Ebifa mu Buganda* 139 (August 1918), 153–55.

Gallagher, Daphne. "American Plants in Sub-Saharan Africa: A Review of the Archaeological Evidence." *Azania: Archaeological Research in Africa* 51, no. 1 (2016), 24–61.

Geary, Patrick. *The Myth of Nations: The Medieval Origins of Europe*. Princeton, NJ: Princeton University Press, 2002.

Gengenbach, Heidi. "Living Ethnicity: Gender, Livelihood, and Ethnic Identity in Mozambique." In *Gendering Ethnicity in African Women's Lives*, ed. Jan Bender Shetler, 57–83. Madison: University of Wisconsin Press, 2015.

Geeraerts, Dirk. *Theories of Lexical Semantics*. Oxford: Oxford University Press, 2010.

Ggomotoka, J. T. K. "Ebye Buganda: Ekika ky'Abalangira b'omu Buganda." *Munno* 10, no. 115 (1920), 121–22, 131–33.

Ggomotoka, John T. K. "Ebye Buganda: Sekabaka Kintu nga bwe yajja." *Munno* 10, no. 116 (1920), 150–52.

Ggomotoka, John. *Magezi Ntakke*. Bukalasa: White Fathers Press, 1934 [1931].

Ggomotoka, Y. T. K. "Ab'Amasaza ge Buganda." *Munno* 16, no. 5 (1926), 88; 16, no. 6 (1926), 103.

Glassman, Jonathon. "Ethnicity and Race in African Thought." In *A Companion to African History*, ed. William Worger, Charles Ambler, and Nwando Achebe, 199–223. London: Wiley-Blackwell, 2019.

Glassman, Jonathon. *War of Words, War of Stones: Racial Thought and Violence in Colonial Zanzibar*. Bloomington: Indiana University Press, 2011.

Gold, C. S., A. Kiggundu, A. M. K. Abera, and D. Karamura. "Diversity, Distribution and Farmer Preference of Musa Cultivars in Uganda." *Experimental Agriculture* 38 (2002), 39–50.

Gomotoka, J. T. K. "Kisolo jjajja w'ab'engonge." *Munno* 8, no. 96 (1918), 164–65.

G[omotoka], J. T. K. "Omuziro gw'Abalangira be Buganda: Omuziro si kiragiro." *Munno* (November 1922), 171–73.

G[omotoka], J. T. K. "Omuziro si Kiragiro." *Munno* (December 1922), 190–92.

G[omotoka], J. T. K. Sabalangira. "Atali Nanyini Mboli Asima Aliggula!" *Munno* (June 1921), 90–92.

[Gomotoka], J. T. K. Sabalangira we Buganda. "Ebyafa mu Buganda: Edzadde lya Sekabaka Kagulu: Ozayisanga n'otafisa." *Munno* (December 1923), 207–11.

Gom[otoka], J. T. K. Sabalangira we Buganda, Isaka Mayemba Sematimba, Solimani Kiwanga, Aleksandre Kattaba, Seruwano T. Mawanda, Batulabudde ku lwa Lubanjwa,

Matayo S. Gw'olirabajjo ku lwa Lukanga, and Ibraimu Ntege Tamuzadde ku lwa Manyonyi. "Ebyafa mu Buganda: Edzadde lya Sekabaka Kagulu: Ozayisanga n'otafisa." *Munno* 14, no. 1 (1924), 12–13.

Gom[otoka], J. T. K. Sabalangira we Buganda, Isaka Mayemba Sematimba, Solimani Kiwanga, Aleksandre Kattaba, Seruwano T. Mawanda, Batulabudde ku lwa Luban-jwa, Matayo S. Gw'olirabajjo ku lwa Lukanga, and Ibraimu Ntege Tamuzadde ku lwa Manyonyi. "Ebyafa mu Buganda: Edzadde lya sekabaka Kagulu; Ozayisanga n'otofisa." *Munno* 14, no. 2 (1924), 28–30.

Gomotoka Kasumba, J. T. Kikulwe. "Abalidde ku bwa Mukwenda n'emiziro gyabwe." *Munno* 7, no. 73 (1917), 9–11.

Gomotoka, J. T. Kikulwe, Sabalangira wo Buganda. "Ebye Buganda: Ekika ky'Abalangira mu Buganda." *Munno* (1920), 121–22.

Gonza, Richard Kayaga. *Lusoga-English Dictionary and English-Lusoga Dictionary.* Kampala: MK Publishers, 2007.

Gorju, Julien. *Entre le Victoria, l'Albert et l'Edouard: Ethnographie de la Partie Anglaise du Vicariat de l'Uganda.* Rennes: Imprimeries Oberthür, 1920.

Grady, Joseph, Todd Oakley, and Seana Coulson. "Metaphor and Blending." In *Metaphor in Cognitive Linguistics*, ed. Raymond W. Gibbs Jr. and Gerard J. Steen, 101–24. Amsterdam: John Benjamins, 1999.

Granovetter, Mark. "The Strength of Weak Ties: A Network Theory Revisited." *Sociological Theory* 1 (1983), 201–33.

Grant, Rachel, Tim Halliday, and Elizabeth Chadwick. "Amphibians' Response to the Lunar Synodic Cycle." *Behavioral Ecology* 24, no. 1 (2013), 53–62.

Green, Monica H. "Putting Africa on the Black Death Map: Narratives from Genetics and History." *Afriques: Débats, méthodes et terrain d'histoire* 9 (2018), 1–45.

Greene, Sandra. "Family Concerns: Gender and Ethnicity in Pre-Colonial West Africa." *International Review of Social History* 44, S7 (1999), 15–31.

Greene, Sandra, Introduction. In *West African Narratives of Slavery: Texts from Late Nineteenth- and Early Twentieth-century Ghana*, ed. Sandra Greene, 1–18. Bloomington: Indiana University Press, 2011.

Greenwood, Peter H. *The Fishes of Uganda.* Kampala: Uganda Society, 1966.

Greenwood, Peter H. "Towards a Phyletic Classification of the 'Genus' *Haplochromis* (Pisces, Cichlidae) and Related Taxa. Part II; The Species from Lakes Victoria, Nabugabo, Edward, George and Kivu." *Bulletin of the British Museum of Natural History (Zoology)* 39, no. 1 (1980), 1–101.

Grollemund, Rebecca, Simon Bradford, Koen Bostoen, Andrew Meade, Chris Venditti, and Mark Pagel. "Bantu Expansion Shows That Habitat Alters the Route and Pace of Human Dispersals." *Proceedings of the National Academy of Sciences* 112, no. 43 (2015), 13296–301.

Gulu, P. M. "Ekika: ab'Effumbe n'ab'Enjovu Bagatta." *Munno* 6, no. 67 (1916), 117–19.

Hall, Martin J. *Through My Spectacles in Uganda; Or, The Story of a Fruitful Field.* London: Church Missionary Society, 1898.

Hamilton, Alan. *A Field Guide to Uganda Forest Trees.* Kampala: Privately published, 1981.

Hamilton, Alan, with Naomi Hamilton, Phoebe Mukasa, and David Ssewanyana. *Luganda Dictionary and Grammar.* Kampala: Gustro Limited, 2016.

Hamilton, Carolyn. *Terrific Majesty: The Powers of Shaka Zulu and the Limits of Historical Invention*. Cambridge, MA: Harvard University Press, 1998.

Hamilton, Carolyn, and John Wright. "Moving beyond Ethnic Framing: Political Differentiation in the Chiefdoms of the KwaZulu-Natal Region before 1830." *Journal of Southern African Studies* 43, no. 4 (2017), 663–79.

Hanks, William F. *Language and Communicative Practices*. Boulder, CO: Westview Press, 1996.

Hanretta, Sean. "Women, Marginality and the Zulu State: Women's Institutions and Power in the Early Nineteenth Century." *Journal of African History* 39, no. 3 (1998), 389–415.

Hansen, Holger Bernt. "The Colonial Control of Spirit Cults in Uganda." In *Revealing Prophets*, ed. David M. Anderson and Douglas H. Johnson, 143–63. Oxford: James Currey, 1995.

Hanson, Holly Elisabeth. *Landed Obligation: The Practice of Power in Buganda*. Portsmouth, NH: Heinemann, 2003.

Hanson, Holly. "Mapping Conflict: Heterarchy and Accountability in the Ancient Capital of Buganda." *Journal of African History* 50, no. 2 (2009), 179–202.

Hanson, Holly. "Queen Mothers and Good Government in Buganda: The Loss of Women's Political Power in Nineteenth Century East Africa." In *Women in African Colonial Histories*, ed. Jean Allman, Susan Geiger, and Nakanyike Musisi, 219–36. Bloomington: Indiana University Press, 2002.

Hanson, Holly. "Review of Christopher Wrigley, *Kingship and State: The Buganda Dynasty*." *African Studies Review* 42, no. 3 (1999), 139–40.

Hanson, Holly. "Stolen People and Autonomous Chiefs in Nineteenth-Century Buganda." In *Slavery in the Great Lakes Region of East Africa*, ed. Henri Médard and Shane Doyle, 161–73. Oxford: James Currey, 2007.

Hartwig, Gerald. *The Art of Survival in East Africa: The Kerebe and Long-Distance Trade, 1800–1895*. New York: Africana, 1976.

Hattersley, Charles W., and Henry Wright Duta. *Luganda Phrases and Idioms*. London: Society for Promoting Christian Knowledge, 1904.

Hay, Margaret. "Local Trade and Ethnicity in Western Kenya." *African Historical Studies* 2, no. 1 (1975), 7–12.

Haydon, Edwin Scott. *Law and Justice in Buganda*. London: Butterworths, 1960.

Haydon, Edwin Scott. "Legal Publications in an African Vernacular." *Journal of African Law* 6 (1962), 179–91.

Heald, Suzette. "The Power of Sex." *Africa* 65, no. 4 (1995), 489–505.

Heusing, Gerhard. *Die Südlichen Lwoo-Sprachen: Beschreibung, Bergleich und Rekonstruktion*. Köln: Rüdiger Köppe Press, 2004.

Hinnebusch, Thomas, Derek Nurse, and Martin Mould. *Studies in the Classification of Eastern Bantu Languages*. Hamburg: Helmut Buske, 1981.

Hobley, Charles William. *Kenya: From Chartered Company to Crown Colony*. London: Witherby, 1929.

Hodgson, Dorothy. "Being Maasai Men: Modernity and the Production of Maasai Masculinities." In *Men and Masculinities in Modern Africa*, ed. Lisa A. Lindsay and Stephan F. Miescher, 211–29. Portsmouth, NH: Heinemann, 2003.

Hodgson, Dorothy L., and Sheryl A. McCurdy. "Introduction." In *"Wicked" Women and the Reconfiguration of Gender in Africa*, ed. Dorothy L. Hodgson and Sheryl A. McCurdy, 1–24. Portsmouth, NH: Heinemann, 2001.

Hoesing, Peter. *Kusamira: Ritual Music and Wellbeing in Uganda*. Urbana-Champaign: University of Illinois Press, forthcoming.

Hurel, Eugène. "Religion et vie domestique des Bakerewe." *Anthropos* 6 (1911), 62–94; 276–301.

Hutchins, Edwin. "Material Anchors for Conceptual Blends." *Journal of Pragmatics* 37 (2005), 1555–77.

Iles, Louise. "The Development of Iron Technology in Precolonial Western Uganda." *Azania: Archaeological Research in Africa* 48, no. 1 (2013), 65–90.

Iles, Louise. "Impressions of Banana Pseudostems in Iron Slag from Eastern Africa." *Ethnobotany Research and Applications* 7 (2009), 283–91.

Iliffe, John. *Honour in African History*. Cambridge: Cambridge University Press, 2005.

Irvine, Judith T. "Subjected Words: African Linguistics and the Colonial Encounter." *Language and Communication* 28 (2008), 323–43.

Jensen, Jürgen. "Töpferei und Töpferwaren auf Buvuma (Uganda)." *Baessler-Archiv, Neue Folge* 17 (1969), 53–100.

Jensen, Jürgen. *Verwandtschaftlich-lokale Bindung und regionale Mobilität bei den Bavuma (Uganda)*. Berlin: Duncker & Humboldt, 1980.

Johnson, Jennifer L. "Eating and Existence on an Island in Southern Uganda." *Comparative Studies of South Asia, the Middle East, and Africa* 37, no. 1 (2017), 2–23.

Johnson, Jennifer L. "Fish, Family, and the Gendered Politics of Descent along Uganda's Southern Littoral." *History in Africa* 45 (2018), 445–71.

Johnston, Sir Harry. *The Uganda Protectorate*, 2 vols. London: Hutchinson, 1902.

Kafumbe, Damascus. *Tuning the Kingdom: Kawuugulu Musical Performance, Politics, and Storytelling in Buganda*. Rochester: University of Rochester Press, 2018.

Kaggwa, Apolo. *The Kings of Buganda*. Ed. and trans. M. S. M. Semakula Kiwanuka. Nairobi: East African Publishing House, 1971.

Kaggwa, Luyi. "Abakunta." *Munno* 20 [*sic*], no. 109 (1920), 7–8.

Kaggwa, L. B., and Frederick B. Welbourn. "Lubaale Initiation in Buganda." *Uganda Journal* 28, no. 2 (1969), 218–20.

Kagwa, Apollo. *Bakabaka Bebuganda*. London: Headley Brothers, 1901.

Kagwa, Apolo. "Chronology of Buganda, 1800–1907, from Kagwa's *Ebika*." Trans. Abubakar M. Kakyama Mayanja. *Uganda Journal* 16, no. 2 (1952), 148–58.

Kagwa, Apolo. *Customs of the Baganda*. Ed. May Edel; trans. Ernest Kalibala. New York: Columbia University Press, 1934.

Kagwa, Apolo. *Ekitabo Kya Basekabaka Be Buganda*. London: Sheldon Press, 1927.

Kagwa, Apolo. *Ekitabo Kye Bika Bya Baganda*. Kampala: Uganda Bookshop, 1949 [ca. 1907]

Kagwa, Apolo. *Ekitabo Kye Mpisa Za Baganda*. Kampala: Uganda Printing and Publishing, 1918.

Kagwa, Apolo. "Extracts from Kings of Buganda." Trans. Charles J. Phillips. *Uganda Notes* 3, no. 6 (June 1902), 44.

Kahigi, Kulikoyela K. *Sisumbwa-Swahili-English and English-Swahili-Sisumbwa Lexicon*. Dar es Salaam: University of Dar es Salaam Press, 2008.

Kaima, Daudi Gahole. "History of the abaiseKaima." In *Towards a Reconstructed Past: Historical Texts from Busoga, Uganda,* ed. David William Cohen, 203–14. London: Oxford University Press, 1986.

Kaindoa, Mzee Augustine. "Origins of Rugomora Mahe." In Peter R. Schmidt, *Historical Archaeology,* 298–312. Westport, CT: Greenwood Press, 1978.

Kajerero, J. T. K. G. "Ekirungi kikayanirwa." *Munno* (June 1923), 99–101.

Kajerero, Y. T. K. G. S. "Eby'e Buganda: Entabalo za Ssekabaka Mawanda." *Munno* 10, no. 1 (1921), 10–11.

Kaji, Shigeki. *Lexique Tembo 1.* Tokyo: Institute for the Study of Languages and Cultures of Asia and Africa, 1985.

Kakoma, Omwami Semu Kasyoka L., Rev. Kayonga Adoniya Musoke Ntate, and Kasolo Mwami Musa Serukwaya. *Ekitabo Eky'Abakyanjove Ab'e Mamba Mu Siiga Lya Nankere e Bukerekere.* Kampala: East African Institute of Social Research, 1959.

Kakondêre, J. K. M. "Okwesiga ebitalimu okw'Abaganda." *Munno* 16, no. 12 (1926), 204.

Kanyoro, Rachel Angogo. *Unity in Diversity: A Linguistic Survey of the Abaluhyia of Western Kenya.* Vienna: AFRO-PUB, 1983.

Karamura, D. A. "Exploiting Indigenous Knowledge for the Management and Maintenance of *Musa* Biodiversity on Farm." *African Crop Science Journal* 12, no. 1 (2004), 67–74.

Kasirye, Joseph S. *Abateregga ku Nnamulondo y'e Buganda.* London: Macmillan, 1955.

Kasumba, Y. Kikulwe. "Ebye Buddo." *Munno* 5, no. 60 (1915), 188–91.

Kasumba, Yoanna T. K. "Eby'Ebuddo." *Munno* 5, no. 59 (1915), 173–76.

Kasumba, Y. T. Kikulwe. "Ebye Buddo Ebikolebwa ku Basekabaka." *Munno* 5, no. 58 (1915), 156–59.

Katate, Aloysius Gonzaga, and Lazaro Kamugungunu. *Abagabe b'Ankole,* 2 vols. Kampala: Eagle Press, 1955.

Kato, Y. Mabike. "Ekitabo ke'ebyafayo by'ekika ky'effumbe." *Munno* 1, no. 22 (January 1932), 16.

Katore, E. G. "The Origins of the Abakenyi Are Not Known." *Gambuze,* November 10, 1933, 33.

Katula, Viktoro. "Abadzukulu ba Sekabaka Kagulu: Ekiyigganyizo eky'okubiri." *Munno* 14, no. 9 (1924), 136–37.

Katula, Viktoro. "Abadzukulu ba Sekabaka Kagulu." *Munno* 14, no. 11 (1924), 155–56.

Katula, Viktoro. "Abadzukulu sekabaka Kagulu." *Munno* 15, no. 1 (1925), 12–13.

Katula, Viktoro. "Abadzukulu sekabaka Kagulu." *Munno* 15, no. 2 (1925), 26–27.

Katula, Viktoro. "Abadzukulu sekabaka Kagulu: Ebivvunula." *Munno* 14, no. 12 (1924), 189–90.

Katula, Viktoro. "Abadzukulu sekabaka Kagulu: Okwetonda si bulabe." *Munno* 14, no. 8 (1924), 121–22.

Katula, Viktoro. "Emmamba ye Namukuma. Kabaka Mawanda awangula e Kyagwe awa Nkutu e Namukuma." *Munno* 3, no. 31 (1913), 110–12.

Keane, Webb. "Marked, Absent, Habitual: Approaches to Neolithic Religion at Çatalhöyük." In *Religion in the Emergence of Civilization: Çatalhöyük as a Case Study,* ed. Ian Hodder, 187–219. New York: Cambridge University Press, 2010.

Keane, Webb. "Semiotics and the Social Analysis of Material Things." *Language and Communication* 23 (2003), 409–25.

Kenny, Michael G. "Mutesa's Crime: Hubris and the Control of African Kings." *Comparative Studies in Society and History* 30, no. 4 (1988), 595–612.

Kenny, Michael G. "The Powers of Lake Victoria." *Anthropos* 72, nos. 5/6 (1977), 717–33.

Kenny, Michael G. "Pre-Colonial Trade in Eastern Lake Victoria." *Azania: Archaeological Research in Africa* 14 (1979), 97–107.

Kenny, Michael G. "The Relation of Oral History to Social Structure in South Nyanza, Kenya." *Africa* 47, no. 3 (1977), 276–88.

Kenny, Michael G. "Salt Trading in Eastern Lake Victoria." *Azania: Archaeological Research in Africa* 9 (1974), 225–28.

Kenny, Michael G. "The Stranger from the Lake: A Theme in the History of the Lake Victoria Shorelands." *Azania: Archaeological Research in Africa* 17, no. 1 (1982), 1–27.

Khanakwa, Pamela. "Male Circumcision among the Bagisu of Eastern Uganda: Practices and Conceptualization." In *Doing Conceptual History in Africa*, ed. Axel Fleisch and Rhiannon Stephens, 115–37. New York: Berghahn Books, 2016.

Kibâte, Byampebwa, and Alfonsi Aliwali. "Ka Tulojje: Kabaka Mulondo." *Munno* 4, no. 38 (1914), 20–23.

Kibatto, Ludoviko. "Ennanga eya Kabaka mu Buganda." *Munno* 7, no. 80 (1917), 116–17.

Kifamunyanja. "Ssese: Gambuze nti agafudde e Mengo." *Munno* (October 1921), 159–61; (November 1921), 173–75; (December 1921), 189–90.

Kifamunyanja. "Ssese okufa kwe: Gambuze nti agafudde e Mengo, Ssese afa Mongota." *Munno* (January 1922), 7–9.

Kikulwe, J. M. T. "Olulyo lw'abalangira be Buganda." *Munno* 3, no. 35 (1913), 177–81.

Kikulwe, J. T. M. "Amagezi ag'okukomaga nga bwe gazulibwa." *Munno* 5, no. 57 (1915), 142–44.

Kikulwe, Y. T. "Ebye Buddo Ebikolerwa ku Basekabaka." *Munno* 5, no. 58 (1915), 156–59; 5, no. 59 (1915), 173–76; 5, no. 60 (1915), 188–91.

Kiseke kya munyumya. "'Amadzi gonna agali waggulu, mutendereze omukama' Ekika III, Ebitalina bulamu: Enkuba." *Munno* 7, no. 84 (1917), 192–93.

Kisoro District Language Board. *English-Rufumbira Dictionary*. Kampala: Fountain, 2009.

Kitakule, Henry Wright Duta. "Ebigambo bye mpisa za Basekabaka abe'da." *Ebifa mu Buganda* 33 (October 1909), 3–7.

Kitching, Arthur Leonard, and George Robert Blackledge (comps.). *A Luganda-English and English-Luganda Dictionary*. Kampala: Uganda Bookshop, 1925.

Kiwanuka, M. S. M. Semakula. *A History of Buganda: From the Foundation of the Kingdom to 1900*. New York: Africana, 1972.

Kiwanuka, M. S. M. Semakula. "Introduction." In Apolo Kaggwa, *The Kings of Buganda*, ed. and trans. M. S. M. Semakula Kiwanuka, xii–xlviii. Nairobi: East African Publishing House, 1971.

Kizito, Tobi. "Atalukugendere Akusibira ya Menvu." *Munno* 7, no. 74 (1917), 22–26.

Kizito, Tobi. "Ensi Muwawa Buganda." *Munno* 5, no. 49 (1915), 6–8.

Kizito, Tobi. "Kabaka lubo Kintu ne Kabaka Mpuga Lukidi owe Bunyoro." *Munno* 4, no. 41 (1914), 61–63.

Kizito, Tobi. "Kintu Anonebwa e Mangira." *Munno* 5, no. 52 (1915), 62–64.

Kizito, Tobi. "Kintu ne Bemba." *Munno* 5, no. 54 (1915), 93–95.

Kodesh, Neil. *Beyond the Royal Gaze: Clanship and Public Healing in Buganda.* Charlottesville: University Press of Virginia, 2010.

Kollmann, Paul. *The Victoria Nyanza.* Trans. H. A. Nesbitt. London: Swan Sonnenschein, 1899.

Kottak, Conrad P. "Ecological Variables in the Origin and Evolution of African States: The Buganda Example." *Comparative Studies in Society and History* 14, no. 3 (1972), 351–80.

Kövecses, Zoltán. *Metaphor in Culture: Universality and Variation.* Cambridge: Cambridge University Press, 2005.

Ladefoged, Peter, Ruth Glick, and Clive Criper. *Language in Uganda.* Nairobi: Oxford University Press, 1971.

Lan, David. *Guns and Rain: Guerrillas and Spirit Mediums in Zimbabwe.* Berkeley: University of California Press, 1985.

Landau, Paul. *Popular Politics in the History of South Africa, 1400–1948.* New York: Cambridge University Press, 2010.

Lanning, Ernest C. "Masaka Hill, an Ancient Center of Worship." *Uganda Journal* 18 (1954), 24–30.

Lanning, Ernest C. "The Surviving Regalia of the Nyakaima, Mubende." *Uganda Journal* 30, no. 2 (1966), 210–11.

Law, Sung Ping. "The Regulation of Menstrual Cycle and Its Relationship to the Moon." *Acta Obstetricia Gynecologica Scandinavica* 65 (1986), 45–48.

Lejju, Julius B. *The Influence of Climate Change and Human-Induced Environmental Degradation on Lake Victoria.* Addis Ababa: Organisation for Social Science Research in Eastern and Southern Africa, 2012.

Lentz, Carola. *Land, Mobility, and Belonging in West Africa.* Bloomington: Indiana University Press, 2013.

Le Veux, Henri. "Les Sœurs Blanches de Notre-Dame d'Afrique, Dans nos Missions chez les Nègres." *Les Missions d'Afrique des Pères Blancs* 7, no. 4 (1911), 97–101.

Le Veux, Henri. *Manuel de langue luganda,* 2nd ed. Algiers: Maison-Carrée, 1914.

Le Veux, Henri. *Premier essai de vocabulaire luganda-français d'après l'ordre étymologique.* Algiers: Imprimerie des Missionnaires d'Afrique (Pères Blancs), 1917.

Lewandowska-Tomaszczyk, Barbara. "Polysemy, Prototypes, and Radial Categories." In *The Oxford Handbook of Cognitive Linguistics,* ed. Dirk Geeraerts and Herbert Cuyckens, 139–69. Oxford: Oxford University Press, 2007.

Livingston, Julie. *Debility and the Moral Imagination in Botswana.* Bloomington: Indiana University Press, 2005.

Lonsdale, John. "Moral and Political Argument in Kenya." In *Ethnicity and Democracy in Africa,* ed. Bruce Berman, Dickson Eyoh, and Will Kymlicka, 73–94. Oxford: James Currey, 2004.

Lonsdale, John. "The Moral Economy of Mau Mau." In Bruce Berman and John Lonsdale, *Violence and Ethnicity,* Book 2 of *Unhappy Valley: Conflict in Kenya and Africa,* 315–504. Athens: Ohio University Press, 1992.

Lonsdale, John. "Moral Ethnicity and Political Tribalism." In *Inventions and Boundaries: Historical and Anthropological Approaches to the Study of Ethnicity and Nationalism,* ed. Preben Kaarsholm and Jan Hultin, 131–50. Roskilde: International Development Studies, Roskilde University, 1994.

Lonsdale, John. "Unhelpful Pasts and a Provisional Present." In *Citizenship, Belonging, and Political Community in Africa: Dialogues between Past and Present*, ed. Emma Hunter, 17–40. Athens: Ohio University Press, 2018.

Lorimer, Norma Octavia. *By the Waters of Africa: British East Africa, Uganda and the Great Lakes*. London: Frederick A. Stokes, 1917.

Low, Donald Anthony. *The Mind of Buganda: Documents of the Modern History of an African Kingdom*. London: Heinemann Educational, 1971.

Low, Donald Anthony, and R. Cranford Pratt. *Buganda and British Overrule: Two Studies*. Nairobi: Oxford University Press, 1970.

Lubalembera, Ipolito W. S. D. "Enyanja yafe Nalubale." *Munno* (June 1922), 87.

Lubogo, Yekoniya K. *A History of Busoga*. Jinja: Cyclostyled, 1960.

Lubogo, Yekoniya K. "Luba of the Nyange Clan." In *Towards a Reconstructed Past: Historical Texts from Busoga, Uganda*, ed. David William Cohen, 115–30. London: Oxford University Press, 1986.

Lunyiigo, Samwiri Lwanga. *Mwanga II: Resistance to Imposition of British Colonial Rule in Buganda, 1884–99*. Kampala: Wavah Books, 2011.

Lunyiigo, Samwiri Lwanga. *The Struggle for Land in Buganda: 1888–2005*. Kampala: Wavah Books, 2007.

Lush, Allan J. "Kiganda Drums." *Uganda Journal* 3, no. 1 (1935), 7–25.

Lyall, Andrew. "Traditional Contracts in German East Africa: The Transition from Pre-Capitalist Forms." *Journal of African Law* 30, no. 2 (1986), 91–129.

MacArthur, Julie. "The Making and Unmaking of African Languages: Oral Communities and Competitive Linguistic Work in Western Kenya." *Journal of African History* 53, no. 2 (2012), 151–72.

MacGaffey, Wyatt. "Kongo Slavery Remembered by Themselves: Texts from 1915." *International Journal of African Historical Studies* 41, no. 1 (2008), 55–76.

Mackay, Alexander M. "Boat Voyage along the Western Shores of Victoria Nyanza." *Proceedings of the Royal Geographical Society and Monthly Record of Geography* 6, no. 5 (1884), 273–83.

Mackay, Alexander M., by His Sister. *A. M. Mackay, Pioneer Missionary of the Church Missionary Society in Uganda*. New York: A. C. Armstrong, 1890.

Maddox, Henry Edward. *An Elementary Lunyoro Grammar*. London: Society for Promoting Christian Knowledge, 1901.

Mair, Lucy. *An African People in the Twentieth Century*. London: Routledge, 1934.

Makoni, Sinfree. "Sociolinguistics, Colonial and Postcolonial: An Integrationist Perspective." *Language Sciences* 33 (2011), 680–88.

Mamdani, Mahmood. *Politics and Class Formation in Uganda*. New York: Monthly Review Press, 1976.

Manicom, Linzi. "Ruling Relations: Rethinking State and Gender in South African History." *Journal of African History* 33, no. 3 (1992), 441–65.

Mann, Kristin, and Richard Roberts (eds.). *Law in Colonial Africa*. Portsmouth, NH: Heinemann, 1991.

Mawanda, J. M. "The Baganda Conception of the Ancestors." *Occasional Research Papers in African Religions and Philosophies* 19, no. 198 (1974), 1–7.

Mazrui, Ali A. "Introduction." In *The Warrior Tradition in Modern Africa*, ed. Ali A. Mazrui, 1–4. Leiden: Brill, 1977.

McCaskie, Thomas C. *State and Society in Pre-Colonial Asante*. Cambridge: Cambridge University Press, 1995.

McClintock, Martha K. "Menstrual Synchrony and Suppression." *Nature* 229 (1971), 244–45.

McClintock, Martha K. "Social Control of the Ovarian Cycle and the Function of Oestrus Synchrony." *American Zoologist* 21 (1981), 243–56.

McFarlane, M. "Some Observations on the Prehistory of the Buvuma Island Group of Lake Victoria." *East African Fisheries Resource Organisation Annual Report, 1967*, 49–54. Nairobi: East African Community Printers, 1968.

Mdee, James S. *Jita-Swahili-English and English-Swahili-Jita Lexicon*. Dar es Salaam: University of Dar es Salaam Press, 2008.

Médard, Claire, and Valérie Golaz, "Entwined Values: Protecting and Subdividing Land in Buganda." *Critical African Studies* 10, no. 1 (2018), 47–66.

Médard, Henri. *Barques et Cimetieres: Une nouvelle histoire lacustre de l'Ouganda (1885–1925)*. Nairobi: Africae, 2021.

Médard, Henri. "Exécutions et esclavage au Royaume de Buganda au XIXe siècle." In *Un demi-siècle d'histoire du Burundi: À Émile Mworoha, un pionnier de l'histoire africaine*, ed. Melchior Mukuri, Jean-Marie Nduwayo, and Nicodème Bugwabari, 303–15. Paris: Karthala, 2017.

Médard, Henri. "La mémoire comme oubli: les transformations Mayanja au Buganda (XVIIIe–XXIe siècles)." *Journal des Africanistes* 86, no. 1 (2016), 130–69.

Médard, Henri. *Le royaume du Buganda au XIXe siècle*. Paris: IFRA-Karthala, 2007.

Meillet, Antoine. "Comment les mots changent de sens." *Année Sociologique* 9 (1906), 1–38.

Meyer, Alois. *Kleines Ruhaya-Deutsches Wörterbuch*. Trier: Mosella Press, 1914.

Meyer, Hans. *Les Barundi*. Ed. Jean-Pierre Chrétien; trans. Françoise Willmann. Paris: Société Française d'Histoire d'Outre-Mer, 1984 [1916].

Monroe, J. Cameron. *The Precolonial State in West Africa: Building Power in Dahomey*. New York: Cambridge University Press, 2014.

Moore, Sally Falk. "Archaic Law and Modern Times on the Zambezi." *International Journal of the Sociology of Law* 7 (1979), 3–30.

Moore, Sally Falk. *Social Facts and Fabrications: "Customary Law" on Kilimanjaro, 1880–1980*. Cambridge: Cambridge University Press, 1986.

Mors, P. Otto. "Notes on Hunting and Fishing in Buhaya." *Anthropological Quarterly* 26, no. 2 (1953), 89–93.

Mougiama-Daouda, Patrick. "Phonological Irregularities, Reconstruction and Cultural Vocabulary: The Names of Fish in the Bantu Languages of the Northwest (Gabon)." *Diachronica* 22, no. 1 (2005), 59–107.

Mukasa, E. W. S. "The Reason for the Creation of the Post of Mugema in Buganda." *Uganda Journal* 10, no. 2 (1946), 150.

Mukasa, Ham. "Ebifa ku Mulembe gwa Kabaka Mutesa." *Uganda Journal* 1, no. 2 (1934), 116–23.

Mukasa, Ham. *Simudda Nyuma*. London: Gambuze Press, 1938.

Mukasa, Ham. *Uganda's Katikkiro in England*. London: Hutchinson, 1904.

Mukasa, Hamu. "The Rule of the Kings of Buganda." *Uganda Journal* 10, no. 2 (1946), 136–43.

M(ukunganya?). "Ekitabo Ekitegereza ekika eky'Emmamba." *Munno* 6, no. 62 (1916), 43.

Mukwaya, Augustine Bikolo. *Land Tenure in Buganda*. Kampala: East African Institute of Social Research, 1953.

Mulira, Eridadi M. K., and E. G. M. Ndawula. *A Luganda-English and English-Luganda Dictionary*. London: Society for Promoting Christian Knowledge, 1952.

Mullins, J. D. *The Wonderful Story of Uganda*. London: Church Missionary Society, 1904.

Musana, T. K. "The Origin of the Bakenye." *Gambuze*, August 11, 1933.

Musimani, Sylvester N. M., and Martin Diprose (eds. and comps.). *Ehyagi hy'ebibono by'Olunyole; Lunyole Dictionary*. Entebbe: SIL International, 2012.

Musisi, Nakanyike B. "The Environment, Gender, and the Development of Unequal Relations in Buganda: A Historical Perspective." *Canadian Woman Studies* 13, no. 3 (1993), 54–59.

Musisi, Nakanyike B. "Gender and the Cultural Construction of 'Bad Women' in the Development of Kampala-Kibuga, 1900–1962." In *"Wicked" Women and the Reconfiguration of Gender in Africa*, ed. Dorothy L. Hodgson and Sheryl A. McCurdy, 171–87. Portsmouth, NH: Heinemann, 2001.

Musisi, Nakanyike B. "Morality as Identity: The Missionary Moral Agenda in Buganda, 1877–1945." *Journal of Religious History* 23, no. 1 (1999), 51–74.

Musisi, Nakanyike B. "Women, 'Elite Polygyny,' and Buganda State Formation." *Signs* 16, no. 4 (1991), 757–86.

Mutaka, Ngessimo M., and Kambale Kavutirwaki. *Kinande/Konzo-English Dictionary, with an English-Kinande Index*. Trenton, NJ: Africa World Press, 2011.

Muzale, Henry R. T. *A Reconstruction of the Proto-Rutara Tense-Aspect System*. Ottawa: National Library of Canada, 1999.

Muzale, Henry R. T. *Ruhaya-English-Kiswahili and English-Ruhaya-Swahili Dictionary*. Dar es Salaam: University of Dar es Salaam Press, 2006.

Mwanja, Wilson W. "The Role of Satellite Water Bodies in the Evolution and Conservation of Lake Victoria Region Fishes." *African Journal of Ecology* 42, Suppl. 1 (August 2004), 14–20.

Mworoha, Emile. "Monarchies, plantes et rituels agraire dans l'Afrique des Grands Lacs est-africains (XVe–XIXe siècles)." In *La diffusion des plantes américaines dans la région des Grands Lacs*, ed. Elizabeth Vignati, special issue of *Les Cahiers d'Afrique de l'Est* 52 (2019), 43–81.

Nakalya, Timoteo Bandasa. "Ebya lubale Wanema." *Munno* 6, no. 69 (1916), 150.

Nakalya, Timoteo, byampebwa Luka Sejamba Semumira. "Bukulu ne Mukazi we Wadda Balubale gye bavwa." *Munno* 5, no. 57 (1915), 145–46.

Nannyonga-Tamusuza, Sylvia. *Baakisimba: Gender in the Music and Dance of the Baganda People of Uganda*. New York: Routledge, 2005.

Nannyonga-Tamusuza, Sylvia. "Female-Men, Male-Women, and Others: Constructing and Negotiating Gender among the Baganda of Uganda." *Journal of Eastern African Studies* 3, no. 2 (2009), 367–80.

Newbury, David. "The Clans of Rwanda: An Historical Hypothesis." *Africa* 50, no. 4 (1980), 389–403.

Nzogi, Richard. and Martin Diprose. *Ekideero ky'oLugwere*. Budaka: Lugwere Bible Translation and Literacy Association, 2012.

N[jovu], Y[osia]. "Ebyafa mu Kyagwe mu Mirembe gy'edda: Okuwangulwa kwa Kyagwe—N'okufa kwa kabaka Kimera." *Munno* 3, no. 31 (1913), 109–12.

Njovutegwamukitimba, Yosia. "Bemba." *Ebifa mu Buganda* (January 1920), 11–12.

Norman, Neil, and Kenneth Kelly. "Landscape Politics: The Serpent Ditch and the Rainbow in West Africa." *American Anthropologist* 104, no. 1 (2006), 98–110.

Nsamba, Yolamu N. *Mystique in Sovereigns' Headgear: A Historical Journey via Bunyoro, Uganda*. Wandsbeck: Reach Publishers, 2016.

Nsimbi, Michael Bazzebulala. *Amannya Amaganda N'Ennono Zaago*. Kampala: Longman's Uganda, 1980 [1956].

Nsimbi, Michael Bazzebulala. "Luganda Names, Clans, and Totems." *Munger Africana Library Notes* 52/53 (1980), 1–102.

Nsimbi, Michael Bazzebulala. "Village Life and Customs in Buganda." *Uganda Journal* 20, no. 1 (1956), 27–36.

Nwokeji, Ugo. *The Slave Trade and Culture in the Bight of Biafra*. Cambridge: Cambridge University Press, 2010.

Nyakatura, John. *Abakama ba Bunyoro Kitara: Abatembuzi, Abacwezi, Ababito*. St. Justin, Quebec: W.-H. Gagne, 1947.

Nyakatura, John. *Aspects of Bunyoro Customs and Traditions*. Trans. Zebiya Kwamya, Kampala: East African Literature Bureau, 1970.

Nyanzi, Stella, Justine Nassimbwa, Vincent Kayizzi, and Strivan Kabanda. "'African Sex Is Dangerous!' Renegotiating 'Ritual Sex' in Contemporary Masaka District." *Africa* 78, no. 4 (2008), 518–39.

Ocyaya-Lakidi, Dent. "Manhood, Warriorhood and Sex in Eastern Africa." In *The Warrior Tradition in Modern Africa*, ed. Ali A. Mazrui, 134–65. Leiden: Brill, 1977.

Ogot, Bethwell Alan. *History of the Southern Luo*, vol. 1. Nairobi: East African Publishing House, 1967.

Oliver, Roland. "The Baganda and the Bakonjo." *Uganda Journal* 18, no. 1 (1954), 31–33.

Oliver, Roland. "The Royal Tombs of Buganda." *Uganda Journal* 23, no. 2 (1959), 124–33.

Opondo, Paul. "Fisheries as Heritage: Indigenous Methods of Fishing and Conservation among the Luo fishers of Lake Victoria, Kenya." In *Conservation of Natural and Cultural Heritage in Kenya*, ed. Anne-Marie Deisser and Njuguna Mugwima, 200–211. London: University College of London Press, 2016.

Oraegbunam, Ikenga K. E. "Crime and Punishment in Igbo Customary Law: The Challenge of Nigerian Jurisprudence." *Ogirisi: A New Journal of African Studies* 7, no. 1 (2010), 1–31.

Ortman, Scott. "Bowls to Gardens: A History of Tewa Community Metaphors." In *Religious Transformation in the Late Pre-Hispanic Pueblo World*, ed. Donna M. Glowacki and Scott Van Keuren, 84–108. Tucson: University of Arizona Press, 2013.

Ortman, Scott. "Conceptual Metaphor in the Archaeological Record: Methods and an Example from the American Southwest." *American Antiquity* 65, no. 4 (2000), 613–45.

Ortman, Scott. *Winds from the North: Tewa Origins and Historical Anthropology*. Salt Lake City: University of Utah Press, 2012.

Osborn, Emily Lynn. *Our New Husbands Are Here: Households, Gender, and Politics in a West African State from the Slave Trade to Colonial Rule*. Athens: Ohio University Press, 2011.

Parkin, David. *Semantic Anthropology*. New York: Academic Press, 1982.

p'Bitek, Okot. *African Religions in Western Scholarship*. Kampala: East African Literature Bureau, 1970.

Peel, John D. Y. *Religious Encounter and the Making of the Yoruba*. Bloomington: Indiana University Press, 2003.

Penningroth, Dylan. "The Claims of Slaves and Ex-Slaves to Family and Property: A Transatlantic Comparison." *American Historical Review* 112, no. 4 (2007), 1039–69.

Peterson, Derek. *Creative Writing: Translation, Bookkeeping, and the Work of Imagination in Colonial Kenya*. Portsmouth, NH: Heinemann, 2004.

Peterson, Derek R. *Ethnic Patriotism and the East African Revival: A History of Dissent, c. 1935–1972*. New York: Cambridge University Press, 2012.

Peterson, Derek R. "Nonconformity in Africa's Cultural History." *Journal of African History* 58, no. 1 (2017), 35–50.

Peterson, Derek R. "The Politics of Transcendance in Colonial Uganda." *Past and Present* 230 (February 2016), 197–225.

Peterson, Derek. "Wordy Women: Gender Trouble and the Oral Politics of the East African Revival in Northern Gikuyuland." *Journal of African History* 42, no. 3 (2001), 469–89.

Peterson, Derek R., and Giacomo Macola. "Introduction: Homespun Historiography and the Academic Profession." In *Recasting the Past*, ed. Derek R. Peterson and Giacomo Macola, 1–28. Athens: Ohio University Press, 2009.

Peterson, Derek R., and Giacomo Macola (eds.). *Recasting the Past: History Writing and Political Work in Modern Africa*. Athens: Ohio University Press, 2009.

Philippe, Antony. *Ouganda au Cœur de l'Afrique: un demi-siècle d'Apostolat au centre Africain, 1878–1928*. Paris: Editions Dillen, 1929.

Pilkington, George. *Luganda-English and English-Luganda Vocabulary*. London: Society for Promoting Christian Knowledge, 1899.

Pirouet, Louise. *Black Evangelists: The Spread of Christianity in Uganda, 1891–1914*. London: Rex Collings, 1978.

Pitman, Charles R. S. "A Guide to the Snakes of Uganda, Part I." *Uganda Journal* 3, no. 1 (1935), 47–78.

Pitman, Charles R. S. "A Guide to the Snakes of Uganda, Part III." *Uganda Journal* 3, no. 3 (1936), 21–29.

Polak-Bynon, Louise. *Lexique Shi-Français suivi d'un index Français-Shi*. Tervuren: Musée royal de l'afrique centrale, 1978.

Poll, M. "Zoogéographie ichthyologique du cours supérieure du Lualaba." *Publications de l'Université d'Elisabethville* 6 (1963), 1–191.

Portal, Gerald. *The British Mission to Uganda in 1893*. London: Edwin Arnold, 1894.

Posnansky, Merrick, Andrew Reid, and Ceri Ashley. "Archaeology on Lolui Island, Uganda 1964–65." *Azania: Archaeological Research in Africa* 40 (2005), 73–100.

Presley, Cora Ann. "Kikuyu Women and the Mau Mau Rebellion." In *In Resistance: Studies in African, Caribbean, and Afro-American History*, ed. Gary Y. Okihiro, 115–37. Amherst: University of Massachusetts Press, 1986.

Quinn, Naomi. "The Cultural Basis of Metaphor." In *Beyond Metaphor*, ed. James Fernandez, 56–93. Stanford, CA: Stanford University Press, 1991.

Ray, Benjamin. *Myth, Ritual, and Kingship in Buganda*. Oxford: Oxford University Press, 1991.

Rehse, Hermann. "Wörtersammlung des Ruziba." *Jahrbuch der Hamburgischen Wissenschaftlichen Anstalten* 31 (1914), 94–140.

Reid, Andrew. "Ntusi and the Development of Social Complexity in Southern Uganda." In *Aspects of African Archaeology*, ed. Gilbert Pwiti and Robert Soper, 621–27. Harare: University of Zimbabwe Press, 1996.

Reid, Andrew. "Recent Research on the Archaeology of Buganda." In *Researching Africa's Past: New Contributions from British Archaeologists*, ed. Peter J. Mitchell, Ann Haour, and John Hobart, 110–17. Oxford: Oxbow, 2003.

Reid, Andrew, and Ceri Z. Ashley. "A Context for the Luzira Head." *Antiquity* 82 (2008), 99–112.

Reid, Andrew, and Ceri Ashley. "Islands of Agriculture on Victoria Nyanza." In *Archaeology of African Plant Use*, ed. Chris J. Stevens, Sam Nixon, Mary Anne Murray, and Dorian Q. Fuller, 179–88. Walnut Creek, CA: Left Coast Press, 2014.

Reid, Richard J. "The Ganda on Lake Victoria." *Journal of African History* 39, no. 3 (1998), 349–63.

Reid, Richard J. *A History of Modern Uganda*. Cambridge: Cambridge University Press, 2017.

Reid, Richard J. *Political Power in Pre-Colonial Buganda*. Oxford: James Currey, 2002.

Reid, Richard J. "The Reign of Kabaka Nakibinge: Myth or Watershed?" *History in Africa* 24 (1997), 287–97.

Reid, Richard J. *Warfare in African History*. Cambridge: Cambridge University Press, 2012.

Reid, Richard J. *War in Pre-Colonial Eastern Africa*. Oxford: James Currey, 2007.

Richards, Audrey Isabel. *The Changing Structure of a Ganda Village: Kisozi, 1892–1952*. Nairobi: East African Publishing House, 1966.

Rigby, Peter. "Prophets, Diviners, and Prophetism: The Recent History of Kiganda Religion." *Journal of Anthropological Research* 31, no. 2 (1975), 116–48.

Rigby, Peter, and Fred D. Lule. "Continuity and Change in Kiganda Religion in Urban and Peri-Urban Kampala." In *Town and Country in Central and East Africa*, ed. David J. Parkin, 213–27. London: Oxford University Press for the International African Institute, 1975.

Roberts, Andrew D. "The Sub-Imperialism of the Baganda." *Journal of African History* 3, no. 3 (1962), 435–50.

Roberts, Simon. "Introduction: Some Notes on 'African Customary Law.'" *Journal of African Law* 28, nos. 1/2 (1984), 1–6.

Robertshaw, Peter T. "Archaeological Survey, Ceramic Analysis, and State Formation in Western Uganda." *African Archaeological Review* 12 (1994), 105–31.

Robertshaw, Peter. "Munsa Earthworks: A Preliminary Report on Recent Excavations." *Azania: Archaeological Research in Africa* 32, no. 1 (1997), 1–20.

Rooijackers, Marinus. *The Beginning of the White Fathers' Mission in Southern Uganda and the Organization of the Catechumenate, 1879–1914.* Rome: Society of Missionaries of Africa, 2008.

Roscoe, John. *The Baganda: An Account of Their Native Customs and Beliefs.* London: Macmillan, 1911.

Roscoe, John. *The Bagesu and Other Tribes of the Uganda Protectorate.* Cambridge: Cambridge University Press, 1924.

Roscoe, John. *The Bakitara or Banyoro.* Cambridge: Cambridge University Press, 1923.

Roscoe, John. *The Banyankole.* Cambridge: Cambridge University Press, 1924.

Roscoe, John. "Further Notes on the Manners and Customs of the Baganda." *Man: Journal of the Royal Anthropological Institute* 32 (1902), 25–80.

Roscoe, John. *The Northern Bantu: An Account of Some Central African Tribes of the Uganda Protectorate.* Cambridge: Cambridge University Press, 1915.

Roscoe, John. "Notes on the Manners and Customs of the Baganda." *Man: Journal of the Royal Anthropological Institute* 31 (1901), 117–30.

Roscoe, John. "Python Worship in Uganda." *Man: Journal of the Royal Anthropological Institute* 9 (1909), 88–90.

Roscoe, John. *The Soul of Central Africa: A General Account of the Mackie Ethnological Expedition.* London: Cassell, 1922.

Roscoe, John. *Twenty-Five Years in East Africa.* Cambridge: Cambridge University Press, 1921.

Roscoe, John. "Worship of the Dead as Practiced by Some African Tribes." *Harvard African Studies* 1 (1917), 33–47.

Rowe, John Allen. "Myth, Memoir, and Moral Admonition: Luganda Historical Writing 1893–1969." *Uganda Journal* 33, no. 2 (1969), 17–40, 218–19.

Rowling, Frank. *A Guide to Luganda Prose Composition.* Kampala: Uganda Bookshop, 1921.

Rubanza, Yunus. *Zinza-English-Swahili and English-Zinza-Swahili Lexicon.* Dar es Salaam: University of Dar es Salaam Press, 2008.

Sacks, Karen Brodkin. *Sisters and Wives: The Past and Future of Sexual Equality.* Boulder, CO: Westview Press, 1979.

Scharping, Nathaniel. "The Banana as We Know It Is Dying . . . Again." *Discover*, December 27, 2017.

Schatzberg, Michael. *Political Legitimacy in Middle Africa: Father, Family, Food.* Bloomington: Indiana University Press, 2001.

Schmidt, Peter R. *Historical Archaeology: A Structural Approach in an African Culture.* Westport, CT: Greenwood Press, 1978.

Schmidt, Peter R. *Iron Technology in East Africa.* Bloomington: Indiana University Press, 1997.

Schoenbrun, David L. "Cattle Herds and Banana Gardens: The Historical Geography of the Western Great Lakes Region, ca. AD 800–1500." *African Archaeological Review* 11 (1993), 39–72.

Schoenbrun, David L. "Conjuring the Modern in Africa: Durability and Rupture in Histories of Public Healing between the Great Lakes of East Africa." *American Historical Review* III, no. 5 (2006), 1403–39.

Schoenbrun, David. "Early African Pasts: Source, Method, and Interpretation." In *Oxford Encyclopedia of African Historiography*, vol. 1, ed. Tom Spear, 7–44. Oxford: Oxford University Press, 2019.

Schoenbrun, David L. "Ethnic Formation with Other-Than-Human Beings: Island Shrine Practice in Uganda's Long Eighteenth Century." *History in Africa* 45 (2018), 397–443.

Schoenbrun, David Lee. *A Green Place, a Good Place: Agrarian Change, Gender, and Social Identity Between the Great Lakes to 1500*. Portsmouth, NH: Heinemann, 1998.

Schoenbrun, David Lee. *The Historical Reconstruction of Great Lakes Bantu Cultural Vocabulary: Etymologies and Distributions*. Köln: Rüdiger Köppe Press, 1997.

Schoenbrun, David. "A Mask of Calm: Emotion and Founding the Kingdom of Bunyoro in the Sixteenth Century." *Comparative Studies in Society and History* 55, no. 3 (2013), 634–64.

Schoenbrun, David. "Mixing, Moving, Making, Meaning: Possible Futures for the Distant Past." *African Archaeological Review* 29, no. 2 (2012), 293–317.

Schoenbrun, David L. "Pythons Worked: Constellating Communities of Practice with Conceptual Metaphor in Northern Lake Victoria, ca. 800–1200 CE." In *Knowledge in Motion: Constellations of Learning Across Time and Space*, ed. Andrew Roddick and Ann Brower Stahl, 216–46. Tucson: University of Arizona Press, 2016.

Schoenbrun, David. "Violence, Marginality, Scorn, and Honour: Language Evidence of Slavery to the Eighteenth Century." In *Slavery in the Great Lakes Region of East Africa*, ed. Henri Médard and Shane Doyle, 38–75. Oxford: James Currey, 2007.

Schweinfurth, Georg August, Friedrich Ratzel, Richard W. Felkin, and Gustav Hartlaub (eds.). *Emin Pasha in Central Africa: Being a Collection of His Letters and Journals*, trans. Mrs. Richard W. Felkin. New York: Dodd, Mead, 1889.

Sekiti, Lawi Wakibi. "Abaganda abe Mbale." *Munno* 6, no. 61 (1916), 6–10.

Shadle, Brett L. *"Girl Cases": Marriage and Colonialism in Gusiland, Kenya, 1890–1970*. Portsmouth, NH: Heinemann, 2006.

Shadle, Brett L. "Patronage, Millennialism and the Serpent God Mumbo in South-West Kenya, 1912–34." *Africa* 72, no. 1 (2002), 29–54.

Shetler, Jan Bender. *Claiming Civic Virtue: Gendered Network Memory in the Mara Region, Tanzania*. Madison: University of Wisconsin Press, 2019.

Shetler, Jan Bender. *Imagining Serengeti: A History of Landscape Memory in Tanzania*. Athens: Ohio University Press, 2007.

Shetler, Jan Bender. "Interpreting Rupture in Oral Memory: The Regional Context for Changes in Western Serengeti Age Organization (1850–1895)." *Journal of African History* 44, no. 3 (2003), 385–412.

Shetler, Jan Bender. *Telling Our Own Stories: Local Histories from South Mara, Tanzania*. Leiden: Brill, 2003.

Snoxall, Ronald A. *Luganda-English Dictionary*. Oxford: Clarendon Press, 1967.

Southwold, Martin. "The History of a History: Royal Succession in Buganda." In *History and Social Anthropology*, ed. Ioan M. Lewis, 127–51. London: Tavistock, 1968.

Southwold, Martin. "Succession to the Throne in Buganda." In *Succession to High Office*, ed. Jack Goody, 82–126. Cambridge: Cambridge University Press, 1966.

Spear, Thomas. "Neo-traditionalism and the Limits of Invention in British Colonial Africa." *Journal of African History* 44, no. 1 (2003), 3–27.

Speke, John Hanning. *Journal of the Discovery of the Source of the Nile*. Edinburgh: William Blackwood, 1863.

Ssenkumba, Abdu-Rahman. *Ebyafaayo By'Ekika ky'Omusu ne Buganda*. Kampala: Lithocraft Investments, 2005.

Stager, J. Curt, Brian F. Cumming, and L. David Meeker. "A 10,000-Year High-Resolution Diatom Record from Pilkington Bay, Lake Victoria, East Africa." *Quaternary Research* 59 (2003), 172–81.

Stager, J. Curt, David Ryves, Brian F. Cumming, L. David Meeker, and Juerg Beer. "Solar Variability and the Levels of Lake Victoria, East Africa, during the Last Millennium." *Journal of Paleolimnology* 33 (2005), 243–51.

Stam, Nicholas. "Religious Conceptions of Some Tribes of Buganda (British Equatorial Africa)." *Anthropos* 3 (1908), 213–18.

Stanley, Henry Morton. *My Dark Companions and Their Strange Stories*. London: Sampson, Low, Marston, 1893.

Stanley, Henry Morton. *Through the Dark Continent*, 2 vols. London: Sampson, Low, Marston, Searle & Rivington, 1878.

Steinmetz, Sebald Rudolf. *Rechtsverhältnisse von eingeborenen Völkern in Afrika und Ozeanien*. Berlin: Springer, 1903.

Stephens, Rhiannon. *A History of African Motherhood: The Case of Uganda, 700–1900*. New York: Cambridge University Press, 2013.

Stroeken, Koen. *Medicinal Rule: A Historical Anthropology of Kingship in East and Central Africa*. New York: Berghahn Books, 2018.

Stuhlmann, Franz. *Die Tagebücher von Dr. Emin Pasha*, 5 vols. Hamburg: G. Westermann, 1916–1927.

Stuhlmann, Franz. *Mit Emin Pasha ins Herz von Afrika*. Berlin: Dietrich Reimer, 1894.

Summers, Carol. "Grandfathers, Grandsons, Morality, and Radical Politics in Late Colonial Buganda." *International Journal of African Historical Studies* 38, no. 3 (2005), 427–47.

Summers, Carol. "Intimate Colonialism: The Imperial Production of Reproduction in Uganda, 1907–1925." *Signs* 16, no. 4 (1991), 787–807.

Summers, Carol. "Young Baganda and Old Boys: Youth, Generational Transition, and Ideas of Leadership in Buganda, 1920–1949." *Africa Today* 51, no. 3 (2005), 109–28.

Sweet, James H. *Domingos Álvarez, African Healing, and the Intellectual History of the Atlantic World*. Chapel Hill: University of North Carolina Press, 2011.

Tamale, Sylvia. "Eroticism, Sensuality and 'Women's Secrets' among the Baganda: A Critical Analysis." *Feminist Africa* 5 (2005), 9–36.

Taylor, Charles V. *A Simplified Runyankore-Rukiga-English and English-Runyankore-Rukiga Dictionary*. Kampala: Eagle Press, 1959.

Taylor, John R., and Thandi Mbense. "Red Dogs and Rotten Mealies: How Zulus Talk about Anger." In *Speaking of Emotions: Conceptualisation and Expression*, ed. Angeliki Athanasiadou and Elzbieta Tabakowska, 191–226. Berlin: Mouton de Gruyter, 1998.

Thibon, Christian. "Croissance démographique, paysage politique et diversification culturale dans la région des Grands Lacs." In *La diffusion des plantes américaines dans la région des Grands Lacs*, ed. Elizabeth Vignati, special issue of *Les Cahiers d'Afrique de l'Est* 52 (2019), 151–240.

Thompson, Gardner. *Governing Uganda: British Colonial Rule and Its Legacy*. Kampala: Fountain Publishers, 2003.

Torelli, Ubaldo. "Notes ethnologiques sur les Banya-Mwenge du Toro (Uganda)." *Annali del Pontificio Museo Missionario Etnologico già Lateranensi* 34–36 (1970–1972), 461–559.

Trowell, Margaret. "Some Royal Craftsmen of Buganda." *Uganda Journal* 8, no. 2 (1941), 47–64.

Trowell, Margaret, with Klaus Wachsmann. *Tribal Crafts of Uganda*. London: Oxford University Press, 1953.

Tuck, Michael. "Women's Experiences of Enslavement and Slavery in Late Nineteenth- and Early Twentieth-Century Uganda." In *Slavery in the Great Lakes Region of East Africa*, ed. Henri Médard and Shane Doyle, 174–88. Oxford: James Currey, 2007.

Tuck, Michael, and John Rowe. "Phoenix from the Ashes: Rediscovery of the Lost Lukiiko Archives." *History in Africa* 32 (2005), 403–14.

Turton, Neville, John Bowes Griffin, and Arthur W. Lewey, *Laws of the Uganda Protectorate*, vol. 6. London: n.p., 1936.

Tushemereirwe, W. K., D. Karamura, H. Ssali, D. Bwamika, I. Kashaija, C. Nankinga, F. Bagamba, A. Kangire, and R. Ssebuliba. "Bananas (*Musa Spp*)." In *Agriculture in Uganda, Volume II, Crops*, ed. J. K. Mukiibi, 281–319. Kampala: Fountain Publishers, 2001.

Twaddle, Michael. "The Bakungu Chiefs of Buganda and British Colonial Rule, 1900–1930." *Journal of African History* 10, no. 3 (1969), 309–22.

Twaddle, Michael. *Kakungulu and the Creation of Uganda, 1868–1928*. Kampala: Fountain Publishers, 1993.

Twaddle, Michael. "Slaves and Peasants in Buganda." In *Slavery and Other Forms of Unfree Labour*, ed. Leonie J. Archer, 118–29. London: Routledge, 1988.

Uzoigwe, Godfrey N. "Precolonial Markets in Bunyoro-Kitara." *Comparative Studies in Society and History* 14, no. 4 (1972), 422–55.

Vansina, Jan. *Antecedents to Modern Rwanda: The Nyiginya Kingdom*. Madison: University of Wisconsin Press, 2004.

Vansina, Jan. *How Societies Are Born: Governance in West Central Africa before 1600*. Charlottesville: University of Virginia Press, 2004.

Vansina, Jan. *Oral Tradition as History*. Madison: University of Wisconsin Press, 1985.

Van Thiel, Paul. "Some Preliminary Notes on the Music of the Cwezi Cult in Ankole." *African Music Society Journal* 5 (1973/1974), 55–64.

Verran, Helen. *Science and an African Logic*. Chicago: University of Chicago Press, 2001.

Von Herrmann, Capitein. "Lusíba, die Sprache der Länder Kisíba, Bugábu, Kjamtwára, Kjánja und Ihángiro, speziell der Dialekt der 'Bayóssa' im Lande Kjamtwára." *Mitteilungen des Seminars für Orientalische Sprachen* 7 (1904), 150–200.

Waliggo, John Mary. *The Catholic Church in the Buddu Province of Buganda, 1879–1925*. Kampala: Angel Agencies, 2010.

Walser, Ferdinand. *Luganda Proverbs.* Berlin: Dietrich Reimer Press, 1982.

Webel, Mari. *The Politics of Disease Control: Sleeping Sickness in Eastern Africa, 1890–1920.* Athens: Ohio University Press, 2019.

Weber, Max. *Economy and Society.* Ed. Guenther Roth and Claus Wittich. Berkeley: University of California Press 2013.

Welbourn, Frederick B. *East African Rebels: A Study of Some Independent Churches.* London: SCM Press, 1961.

Welcomme, Robin L. "A Brief on the Flood Plain Fishery of Africa." *African Journal of Tropical Hydrobiology and Fisheries* 1 (1972), 67–76.

Wenger, Étienne. *Communities of Practice: Learning, Meaning, and Identity.* Cambridge: Cambridge University Press, 1998.

West, Henry W. *The Mailo System in Buganda.* Entebbe: Government Printer, 1965.

White, Luise. *The Comforts of Home: Prostitution in Colonial Nairobi.* Chicago: University of Chicago Press, 1990.

White, Luise. "Matrimony and Rebellion: Masculinity in Mau Mau." In *Men and Masculinities in Modern Africa,* ed. Lisa A. Lindsay and Stephan F. Miescher, 163–87. Portsmouth, NH: Heinemann, 2003.

White, Luise. "Separating the Men from the Boys: Constructions of Sexuality, Gender, and Terrorism in Central Kenya, 1939–1959." *International Journal of African Historical Studies* 23, no. 1 (1990), 1–26.

White, Luise, Stephan Miescher, and David William Cohen (eds.). *African Words, African Voices: Critical Practices in Oral History.* Bloomington: Indiana University Press, 2001.

Whitehead, P. J. P. "The Anadromous Fishes of Lake Victoria." *Revue de zoologie et de botanique africaines* 59 (1959), 329–63.

Williams, F. Lukyn. "Hima Cattle, Part I." *Uganda Journal* 6, no. 1 (1938), 17–24.

Wilson, Charles T. *An Outline Grammar of the Luganda Language.* London: Society for Promoting Christian Knowledge, 1882.

Wilson, H. Clyde. "A Critical Review of Menstrual Synchrony Research." *Psychoneuroendocrinology* 17 (1992), 565–91.

Wiseman, Rob. "Getting beyond Rites of Passage in Archaeology: Conceptual Metaphors of Journeys and Growth." *Current Anthropology* 60, no. 4 (2019), 449–74.

Witte, Frans. "Initial Results of the Ecological Survey of the Haplochromine Cichlid Fishes from the Mwanza Gulf of Lake Victoria (Tanzania)." *Netherlands Journal of Zoology* 31 (1981), 175–202.

Worger, William. "Parsing God: Conversations about the Meaning of Words and Metaphors in Nineteenth-Century Southern Africa." *Journal of African History* 42, no. 3 (2001), 417–47.

Worthington, Edgar Barton. "The Life of Lakes Albert and Kioga." *Geographical Journal* 74, no. 2 (1929), 109–29.

Worthington, Edgar Barton. "Primitive Craft of the Central African Lakes." *Mariner's Mirror: The International Quarterly Journal of the Society for Nautical Research* 19, no. 2 (1933), 146–63.

Wright, Michael. *Buganda in the Heroic Age.* Oxford: Oxford University Press, 1971.

Wrigley, Christopher. "Bananas in Buganda." *Azania: Archaeological Research in Africa* 24 (1989), 64–70.

Wrigley, Christopher. *Kingship and State: The Buganda Dynasty.* Cambridge: Cambridge University Press, 1996.

Yang, Zhengwei, and Jeffrey C. Schank. "Women Do Not Synchronize Their Menstrual Cycles." *Human Nature* (2006), 433–47.

Zawaya, D. W. Z. "Okubola abantu mu Bika." *Ebifa mu Buganda* 169 (January 1921), 47.

Zerêse, Kornelio. "Gundi mugezi nga mubulire." *Munno* 16, no. 5 (1926), 80–81.

Zimbe, Bartolomeyo Musoke. *Buganda ne Kabaka.* Mengo: Gambuze Press 1939.

Zirabamuzale, Kibedi Y. M. "History of Bugweri." In *Towards a Reconstructed Past: Historical Texts from Busoga, Uganda*, ed. David William Cohen, 306–45. London: Oxford University Press, 1986.

Index

Some Luganda spellings differ from current usage because their presence in sources predates the orthographic revisions of the 1950s.

Health in a Fragile State: Science, Sorcery, and Spirit in the Lower Congo
JOHN M. JANZEN

Intermediaries, Interpreters, and Clerks: African Employees in the Making of Colonial Africa
EDITED BY BENJAMIN N. LAWRANCE, EMILY LYNN OSBORN, AND RICHARD L. ROBERTS

Naming Colonialism: History and Collective Memory in the Congo, 1870–1960
OSUMAKA LIKAKA

Early African Entertainments Abroad: From the Hottentot Venus to Africa's First Olympians
BERNTH LINDFORS

Mau Mau's Children: The Making of Kenya's Postcolonial Elite
DAVID P. SANDGREN

The Names of the Python: Belonging in East Africa, 900–1930
DAVID L. SCHOENBRUN

Senegal Abroad: Linguistic Borders, Racial Formations, and Diasporic Imaginaries
MAYA ANGELA SMITH

Whispering Truth to Power: Everyday Resistance to Reconciliation in Postgenocide Rwanda
SUSAN THOMSON

Antecedents to Modern Rwanda: The Nyiginya Kingdom
JAN VANSINA

Being Colonized: The Kuba Experience in Rural Congo, 1880–1960
JAN VANSINA

Kongo in the Age of Empire, 1860–1913: The Breakdown of a Moral Order
JELMER VOS

The Postcolonial State in Africa: Fifty Years of Independence, 1960–2010
CRAWFORD YOUNG